*To my earliest teachers in the classroom and out,
my parents,
Bert and Edith McKeachie*

Teaching Tips

STRATEGIES, RESEARCH, AND THEORY FOR COLLEGE AND UNIVERSITY TEACHERS

Ninth Edition

Wilbert J. McKeachie
University of Michigan

with chapters by

Nancy Chism
Ohio State University

Robert Menges
Northwestern University

Marilla Svinicki
University of Texas at Austin

Claire Ellen Weinstein
University of Texas at Austin

D. C. Heath and Company
Lexington, Massachusetts   Toronto

Address editorial correspondence to:

D. C. Heath and Company
125 Spring Street
Lexington, MA 02173

Acquisitions Editor: Walter Cunningham
Production Editor: Melissa Ray
Designer: Henry Rachlin
Production Coordinator: Chuck Dutton

Published simultaneously in Canada.

Printed in the United States of America.

International Standard Book Number: 0–669–19434–4

Library of Congress Catalog Number: 93–78301

10   9   8   7   6   5

Preface

*T*EACHING *T*IPS was written to answer the questions posed by new college teachers, to place them at ease in their jobs, and to get them started effectively in the classroom.

The organization of the book moves from those issues and techniques most relevant to beginning teachers to methods and issues likely to be of more concern after one has gotten beyond the difficult, immediate problems of the beginning teacher.

I have added several new chapters, some written by friends with special areas of expertise. I am pleased to have persuaded Nancy Chism, Bob Menges, Marilla Svinicki, and Claire Ellen Weinstein to join me in this edition. In order to keep the book pocket-size I had to eliminate the chapters, "Six Roles of Teachers," "Audiovisual Techniques," "PSI, TIPS, Modular Instruction, and Guided Design," and "Faculty Attitudes and Teaching Effectiveness."

Because this book is oriented toward the beginning teacher who faces a number of immediate practical problems, most chapters emphasize "tips," but these are usually accompanied by a discussion of relevant research and theory.

I am pleased that so many copies of previous editions of this guide have been used outside the United States. My increased interaction with colleagues in other countries who are concerned about improving teaching makes me aware of the cultural bias of much of my writing. I trust that *Teaching Tips* will nevertheless have value for everyone concerned about student teaching.

The first edition of this book was prepared in collaboration with Gregory Kimble. His wit and wisdom are still evident at many points in the ninth edition. Edward Bordin, who wrote the section on counseling, also deserves many thanks. I am appreciative of helpful suggestions from Robert Abbott, Marilla Svinicki, Barbara Hofer, Patricia Keith-Spiegle, Yi-Guang Lin, Ronald Simpson, Leo Lambert, George Williams, Larry Greenfield, George Lambrides, and M. Brewster Smith. At D. C. Heath, thanks to Walter Cunningham, Heather Monahan, and Melissa Ray for their help. Maria Huntley, who prepared the manuscript, was once again a great support and an appreciated colleague.

WILBERT J. MCKEACHIE

A Special Preface for Teaching Assistants and Their Supervisors

*T*EACHING *T*IPS was originally written for my own teaching assistants. I am pleased that more experienced teachers have also found it to be helpful, but I still think of my primary audience as being beginning teachers, teaching assistants and new faculty members. I began teaching as a teaching assistant (TA) and have worked with teaching assistants ever since. I try to involve my TAs in course planning both before and during the term. We grade tests in a group the evening after a test is given, bringing in sandwiches and brownies to maintain our energy and good spirits during sessions which may last until midnight. In short, I try to develop the spirit of a collaborative team.

However, I recognize that the TAs are in the difficult position of being in the middle between the students and me. As TAs you want to be liked and respected by your students as well as by your professor; yet there are times when you don't agree with the professor's point of view or even with some of the course policies. You will be tempted to blame the professor or the system when students complain, but overusing this strategy only leads to students' perceiving you as being weak and powerless. On the other hand this doesn't mean that you have to defend everything your professor says. Students, particularly first-year students, need to learn that absolute truth is hard to come by and that it is possible to have well-adjusted differences.

Yet one must be aware of student anxiety when TA and lecturer seem always to be at odds with one another. Support your lecturer when you can, disagree when you must, but recognize that sometimes your students' learning will be best served by your silence. Your role is often that of a coach helping students develop skills in learning and thinking using the knowledge provided by the lecturer and textbook.

Many of you will find it hard to believe that the students accept your authority and expertise and will be ambivalent about whether to dazzle them with your brilliance or to play the role of being just one of the group. Relax! The power of role expectations always amazes me. If you are the teacher, students will accept your authority and expertise without you having to act unnaturally. You may not know everything, but you have enough subject-matter expertise to be helpful. I hope this book will add to your helpfulness.

W. J. M.

Table of Contents

Getting Started

CHAPTER 1

Introduction

THE FIRST FEW MONTHS AND YEARS of teaching are all-important. Experiences during this period can blight a promising teaching career or can start one on a path of continued growth and development.

Most of us go into our first classes as teachers with a good deal of fear and trembling. We don't want to appear to be fools; so we have prepared well, but we dread the embarrassment of not being able to answer students' questions. We want to be liked and respected by our students; yet we know that we have to achieve liking and respect in a new role which carries expectations, such as evaluation, that make our relationship with students edgy and uneasy. We want to get through the first class with éclat, but we don't know how much material we can cover in a class period.

In most cases anxiety passes as one finds that students do respond positively, that one does have some expertise in the subject, and that class periods can be exciting. But for some teachers the first days are not happy experiences. Classes get off on the wrong foot. Sullen hostility sets in. The teacher asserts authority and the students resist. The teacher knows that things are not going well but doesn't know what to do about it.

One likely response of the teacher is retreat—retreat to reading lectures with as little eye contact with students as possible—

retreat to threats of low grades as a motivating device—retreat to research and other aspects of the professional role.

What makes the difference in these first few days?

It's probably not the subject matter. More often than not the key to a good start is not the choice of interesting content (important as that may be) but rather the ability to manage the activities of the class effectively. Teaching techniques get the students involved so that they can get to work and learn. (See Hollingsworth, 1989, for relevant data.)

The new teacher who has techniques for breaking the ice, for encouraging class participation, and for getting the course organized is more likely to get off to a good start. Once you find that teaching can be fun, you enjoy devoting time to it, and if you devote time, you will develop into a competent teacher. Anyone bright enough to complete a graduate degree is bright enough to learn the skills and concepts needed for effective teaching.

What can I do to help you get off to a good start? Simply pass on ideas that have been helpful to me. Some of them won't fit your course or your style, but some may stimulate you to develop your own adaptations.

This is not a textbook in the Educational Psychology of College Teaching. It is merely a compilation of useful (occasionally mechanical) tricks of the trade that I, as a teacher, have found helpful in running classes. What is contained in this discussion will not make you a Great Teacher. It may be that Great Teachers are born and not made, but anyone with ability enough to get a job as a college teacher can be a *good* teacher.

The techniques of teaching that one uses will undoubtedly reflect one's philosophy of teaching. Thus, it might be a good idea for me to state my views here and now. These are some of the considerations that have guided me in making the recommendations in this book:*

1. Education should be guided by a democratic philosophy. This has nothing to do with political-social doctrine, but is

---

* These are based on a list originally developed by Gregory Kimble, who collaborated with me on the first edition of this book.

simply a statement of my belief that education is a cooperative enterprise that works best when the student is allowed to contribute to it—when teachers listen and respond.

2. Students are adults. I feel strongly on this point. One of the severest criticisms that can be leveled against American higher education is that it perpetuates adolescence for another four years. It seems clear that adult behavior is *learned*. If no opportunity to practice adult behavior is allowed, such behavior will not be learned.

3. Instructors can occasionally be wrong. If they are wrong too often, they should not be teaching. If they are never wrong, they belong in heaven, not a college classroom.

4. There are many important goals of college and university teaching. Not the least of these is that of increasing the student's motivation and ability to *continue* learning after leaving college.

5. Most student learning occurs outside the classroom. This is a both humbling and reassuring thought for the beginning teacher. It means that the students' education will neither succeed nor fail simply because of what you do or don't do in the classroom. At the same time it reminds one to direct attention to stimulating and guiding student learning outside class even more than to preparing to give a dazzling classroom performance.

The College or University Culture

A course cannot be divorced from the total college or university culture.

First of all, the university makes certain requirements of instructors. In most colleges you must submit grades for the students' work. You probably must give a final course examination. A classroom is assigned for the class, and the class meets in this assigned place. Smoking in the classroom is ordinarily prohibited. The class meets at certain regularly scheduled periods. It is not implied here that these regulations are harmful, but they do provide boundaries within which instructors have to work.

There are, in addition, areas not covered by the formal rules of the college in which instructors must tread lightly. For example, there may be certain limitations upon the instructor's social relationships with the students. In many college cultures instructors who become intimately involved with their students are overstepping the bounds of propriety. In some colleges it would be deemed improper for instructors to convene classes in bars or off campus. Certain limits upon class discussion of religion, sex, or politics may exist. Instructors must learn not only to operate within the fences of college regulations but also to skirt the pitfalls of the college mores.

But instructors who consider only college mores in plans for their courses are ignoring a far more important limitation upon teaching, for the college or university culture has not only placed limitations upon instructors but has also pretty much hobbled the students. Most important are the students' need for success. To stay in college they must show evidence of achievement. With admission to law, medical, and other graduate and professional schools difficult, they must present evidence of outstanding achievement in college courses to gain admission to these schools.

In many colleges students have had experience in previous classes with instructors who, in a more or less fatherly way, gave information and rewarded those students who could best give it back. Not only has the role of the teacher been similar in these classes, but teaching procedures were probably much the same. Depending upon the college or university, the method used may have been lecture, question and answer, discussion, or something else. The sort of tests, frequency of tests, and methods of grading also have conformed closely to certain norms. As a result instructors who attempt to revolutionize teaching with new methods or techniques may find that they are only frustrating the needs and expectations their students have developed in the culture of the college. Therefore, each reader will need to adapt my suggestions to the college culture of which he or she is a part. When you begin a new teaching position, talk to other faculty members about how they teach and perceive others as teaching. Ask for examples of syllabi, tests, and other course materials.

▰▰▰ *Research vs. Teaching?*

One aspect of the local culture critical for new teachers is the definition of the proper role of a faculty member. In many universities, for example, formal definitions of the criteria for promotion give research and teaching equal weight, but it is not uncommon to find that research is "more equal." This may come about not because of any attempt to hide the truth but because many faculty members serving on promotions committees honestly believe that you cannot be an effective teacher unless you are doing research.

While research on the relationship of research to teaching is difficult to conduct, there is evidence that research and teaching are not necessarily in conflict. Many faculty members are excellent researchers and excellent teachers as well. Some excellent researchers are poor teachers; some excellent teachers do not publish research. The point here is not that you should choose one emphasis at the expense of the other. Rather, find out what the local norms are, and if you feel a conflict, choose the balance that suits your own talents and interests with an informed awareness of the likelihood of support for that self-definition. While time is not infinitely elastic, most faculty members find that a 50 to 60 hour work week is enjoyable because they enjoy both teaching and research. There is never enough time to do everything one would like to do in either teaching or research, but most faculty members find that each provides a useful break from the other. A combination is often more satisfying than single-minded, undeviating focus on either.

Whatever your choice, it is likely that teaching will be a part of your role. Teaching skillfully may be less time-consuming than teaching badly. Teaching well is more fun than teaching poorly. Thus, some investment of time and attention to developing skill in teaching is likely to have substantial pay-off in self-satisfaction and effectiveness in your career.

▰▰▰ *Research in Teaching*

Some of you will disagree with me, at least at certain points. This is your perfect right since my ideas are only partly based on objective evidence. But I believe that my ideas as well as your ideas should be experimentally tested. I hope that this book will not be accepted as infallible, but as the background for research that will give us a better foundation for our teaching practices.

What I have tried to set down here is a set of hints that have seemed to be useful to me. I hope that you can use some of them too and that they add to the enjoyment and learning of your students. If they contribute to your joy in teaching, my purpose will have been fulfilled.

CHAPTER 2

Countdown for Course Preparation

*F*OR TEACHERS, courses do not start on the first day of classes. Rather, a course begins well before they meet their students.

■■■■ *Time: Three Months Before the First Class**

Write Objectives

The first step in preparing for a course is the working out of course objectives, because the choice of text, the selection of the type and order of assignments, the choice of teaching techniques, and all the decisions involved in course planning should derive from your objectives. At this point your list of goals or objectives should be taken only as a rough reminder to be revised as you develop other aspects of the course plan, and to be further revised in interaction with students.

Some of you have heard of behavioral objectives and may wish to phrase your objectives in behavioral terms. If so, do so. But don't omit important objectives simply because you can't think of good ways to convert them to behavioral language. The purpose of phrasing objectives behaviorally is to encourage you to be specific, but usually the behavior specified in a behavioral

---

* I have borrowed the idea of three months, two months, and so on from P. G. Zimbardo and J. W. Newton, *Instructor's Resource Book to Accompany Psychology and Life* (Glenview, IL: Scott, Foresman, 1975).

objective is an indicator of a more general objective you want to achieve. Don't get trapped into thinking that the behavior you list is all you should aim for—and don't become so obsessed with writing objectives that you neglect other parts of planning. The purpose of working out objectives is to facilitate planning, not inhibit it. The clearer you can become about what you're trying to do, the better. Behavioral objectives may help, but there is no evidence that they are better for student learning than other statements of objectives—in fact, there is little evidence that teachers who develop behavioral objectives are more effective than those who don't develop *any* list of objectives.* Nonetheless, behavioral objectives have the great advantage of pointing clearly to what you can look for as evidence that the objective has been achieved. Your students see your methods of assessing or testing achievement of the objectives as the most important operational definition of your goals; hence goals and testing are inseparable teaching tasks.

It seems logical that course planning should start with thinking about goals or objectives. So begin by thinking about your objectives. What should they be? The answer obviously depends upon the course and discipline, but it is important to note that the objectives involve *educating students*; the objective of a course is not to cover a certain set of topics, but rather to facilitate student learning. Ordinarily we are not concerned simply with the learning of a set of facts, but rather with learning that can be applied and used in situations outside the course examinations. In fact, *in most courses we are concerned about helping our students in a lifelong learning process;* that is, *we want to develop interest in further learning* and *provide a base of concepts and skills that will facilitate further learning and thinking.*

Your personal values inevitably enter into your choice of

---

* Duchastel and Merrill (1973) have reviewed empirical studies of the effects of behavioral objectives. Amidst the plethora of nonsignificant results are some studies indicating that sharing behavioral objectives with students may help focus their attention or assist them organizing material. So if you've worked out objectives, let your students know what they are, and if possible give them a chance to help revise them. (This study and others mentioned in the text, as well as supplementary works, are found in the *References* at the back of the book. In addition, some chapters are followed by brief lists of supplementary reading from the *References* that are specifically applicable to those chapters.)

goals. Although many of us were taught to be strictly objective, I have come through the years to believe that this is impossible. Our teaching is always influenced by our values and students have a fairer chance to evaluate our biases or to accept our model if we are explicit about them. Hiding behind the cloak of objectivity simply prevents honest discussion of vital issues.

In thinking about your goals, remember that each course contributes to other general goals of a university education that transcend specific subject matter, such as being willing to explore ideas contrary to one's own beliefs and knowing when information or data are relevant to an issue and how to find relevant information.

In addition to this general perspective you need to keep in mind characteristics of the setting in which you teach. What is the role of this course in your department? Are other instructors depending upon this course to provide specific kinds of background knowledge or skill? What are your students like? What are their current concerns? Self-discovery? Social action? Getting a job?

A committee of college and university examiners developed two books to assist faculty members in thinking about their objectives. The two books entitled *Taxonomy of Educational Objectives, Handbook I: Cognitive Domain* (Bloom, 1956) and *Handbook II: Affective Domain* (Krathwohl et al., 1964) will help point your objective writing in the right direction.*

Having said all this about the importance of starting with clear goals, I would nonetheless not want to make you feel guilty if you started on your syllabus with only vague notions about goals. Many effective teachers never state their goals very explicitly, yet their students achieve the kinds of motivational and cognitive outcomes that we all desire. College teachers are individualists. There are lots of different ways to do a good job.

Draft a Syllabus for the Course

When we think about teaching we usually think about what goes on in the classroom. But since most student learning occurs out-

---

* The *Student Goals Exploration User's Manual* by Stark et al. (1991) also provides guidance for considering student goals.

side the classroom, planning how to help students learn outside classroom meetings is one of the most important tasks of the teacher. A syllabus typically contains such a plan of assigned readings and activities scheduled on dates correlated with lecture topics.

The syllabus will force you to begin thinking about the practicalities of what you must give up in order to fit within the constraints of time, place, students, available resources, and your own limitations.

As you begin to block out activities in relation to the college calendar, you will begin to note when you will want films, guest lecturers, field work, or other things that require scheduling ahead.

Order Textbooks or Other Resources Students May Need

SHOULD YOU USE A TEXT?   The revolution in teaching media has not been the advent of television, teaching machines, or computers, but rather the increased availability of a variety of printed materials. With paperback books, reprint series, and a photocopier* machine in the library, young instructors are immediately beguiled by the thought that they can do a much better job of compiling a set of required readings than any previous author or editor.

There is much to be said for such a procedure. It provides flexibility, a variety of points of view, and an opportunity to maintain maximum interest. Moreover, since no single text covers every topic equally well, the use of a variety of sources enables the teacher to provide more uniformly excellent materials ranging from theoretical papers and research reports to case studies.

The "cons" of not using a textbook are apparent. Without a text the task of integration may be so overwhelming that great pressure is placed on instructors to provide integration. This may limit your freedom to use the class period for problem solving,

---

* Check the copyright laws before making multiple copies.

applications, or other purposes. With a well-chosen textbook, you may rely upon the students to obtain the basic content and structure of the subject matter through reading and thus be freer to vary procedures in the classroom. Moreover, the managerial task of determining appropriate readings and arranging to have them available for students is not to be taken lightly. One is torn between potential student complaints about the cost of buying several sources and complaints from the librarian about the cost of multiple copies along with student complaints about their inability to get a reading assignment in the library.

A final consideration is the extent to which you want to use required vs. free reading, as in my use of a "reading log" (see Chapter 9). I use a text as a base to provide structure and then require students to write a log on readings they choose. To assign diverse required readings and additional free reading seems to me to require too much integration even for well-prepared, bright students.

CHOOSING A TEXT OR READING MATERIALS   In choosing reading materials the most important thing is that they fit your objectives. One of the most annoying and confusing practices to students is instructor disagreement with the textbook. It is doubtful that any book will satisfy you completely, but if you use a text, choose one that is as much in line with your view as possible.

Your library facilities will probably help you decide whether you choose a book that omits materials you would like to cover or a book that contains extra material you consider unimportant. Generally speaking I have found that students prefer to have additional material presented in lecture or by supplementary reading assignments. They dislike reading material the instructor later says isn't important, and, surprisingly enough, they also dislike omitting material in the textbook. (Somehow they feel that they're missing something.) This student need for continuity and closure will influence your outline of assignments. Students prefer going through a book as it was written. If the author also wrote the book in a systematic way, building one concept on another, there may be good pedagogical reasons for following the author's order. Since I know of no text that completely suits many teachers, however, I can only recommend that you keep the skipping around to a minimum.

There is no substitute for detailed review of the competing texts for the course you are teaching. As texts multiply, it becomes increasingly tempting to throw up your hands in frustration over the time required for a conscientious review and to choose the book primarily on the basis of appearance, the personality of the book sales representative, or the inclusion of your name as author of one of the studies cited. Yet research on teaching suggests that the major influence on what students learn is not the teaching method but the textbook. Moreover, some of the superficially most attractive textbooks today are "managed books," written in the offices of the publisher rather than by persons who know the field. Managed books vary a great deal in the degree to which scholars are involved. The most egregious cases of plagiarism and errors in content are now disappearing, but one cannot adopt a textbook on the basis of the sales representative's description any more than physicians should prescribe drugs on the advice of the drug company's detail men.

▬▬ *Time: Two Months Before the First Class*

Work Out a Tentative Set of Assignments for the Students

The next point at which course objectives influence preparation for the course is in terms of the kind, length, and content of assignments. Two instructors who have chosen the same textbooks will probably stress different materials. Since no one but the person teaching from his or her own text is probably well satisfied with the relative weightings of materials in available texts, it will almost always be necessary to assign chapters on some topics which, from your point of view, are incomplete and to assign others that treat a topic more extensively than you would desire. For the former situation, additional readings or lectures may partially solve the problem. For the latter, no completely satisfactory solution is available.

To summarize the argument so far in this chapter, the following schedule suggests the way in which a course may be planned in a preliminary way.

1. Decide what you want the students to gain from the course.
2. Choose one or more texts or other sources that make the point you want made.
3. Plan the course for the whole semester or year in such a way as to allot appropriate amounts of time to various topics.

It is on this third point that elaboration appears to be necessary. In making plans for the term you need to consult (in addition to textbooks and your conscience) the college catalogue or bulletin in order to anticipate some or all of the following circumstances:

1. For a given term you are allowed a certain number of class periods (about 40–45 for a three-hour course in a typical semester). Your wisdom must, therefore, be compressed into a period of somewhat less than two clock days. You will want to decide ahead of time approximately the number of sessions to be allotted to each of the topics you want to cover.
2. My estimate of 40–45 days includes:
    a. one day for orientation (which I recommend).
    b. one day for a final summing up (which the students will probably insist on).
    c. one or more class periods devoted to examinations.

    This, of course, reduces the students' time at your disposal to 35–40 hours.
3. Students (unlike the faculty) get holidays. One must consider them in planning a course in order, insofar as is possible, to avoid:
    a. tests or important class sessions just before or just after holidays or major college events, such as homecoming.
    b. having closely related materials presented partly before and partly after a recess.

Midterm or other preliminary grades may be due at specified times. Such estimates of student achievement should be based upon at least one, and preferably more, examinations or other evidence of achievement.

From what I have said in the preceding paragraphs it is evident by now that the easy accomplishment of course objectives may be frustrated in two ways: by lack of satisfactory text material and by the college schedule.

Decide What Should Be in the Course Outline or Syllabus

Compromising as little as possible with course objectives, if you have followed recommendations to this point you now have a rough course outline completed. You have decided what you want to cover in your course and how to distribute available time. You may even make a schedule of where in the course you expect to be at any given date. My suggestion now is that you make such a schedule and have it copied for distribution to the class. But present it as a basis for discussion and possible revision on the basis of their suggestions. Only after getting their ideas should the final copy be distributed.

How complete, detailed, and precise should your schedule be? My answer is "not very," for three reasons:

1. Like most of us, you are apt to change your mind about the details you will cover before you come to a specific topic. There is little point in committing yourself in print to a course of action you will later regard as ill-advised.

2. Inevitably, circumstances arise that make it advisable to deviate slightly from the schedule.

3. The students themselves are important variables in determining the pace and structure of the course. Some classes gallop along at a fine pace; others are slow to move. Some classes develop great interest in one topic, others in another. Your schedule should be sufficiently flexible to take advantage of the students' own awareness of how they can best learn.

But if an instructor is really student centered, isn't preparation of a course outline a cue that the course is really instructor centered and that student needs are really not going to be considered? Not necessarily so. Research by Richard Mann and his associates at the University of Michigan (1970) suggests that students see the teacher who takes a nondirective, student centered role as not interested in the class.

Your course outline should at least contain the assignments for the semester. One very satisfactory way to prepare such an outline is to provide the students with a topic outline of the course. Under the various topic headings, you can schedule assignments and the dates when they are due. This method has the special advantage of relieving the instructor of the task of making assignments every few days and of repeating the assignment two or three times for the benefit of students who have been absent when the assignment was first announced.

As you lay out your schedule consider alternate ways students might achieve the goals of a particular day or week of class. You will seldom have perfect attendance at every class. Why not build in periodic alternatives to your lecture or class discussion? Students who have options and a sense of personal control are likely to be more highly motivated for learning.

Other items that may be appropriate to include in such an outline are the dates when examinations, quizzes, or laboratory exercises are scheduled; announcements of films to be shown in connection with various topics; and the particular libraries in which collateral reading materials have been placed on reserve if the library facilities in your university are decentralized. Including the call numbers of the books required for library use will save a good deal of student time.

Finally, you may include any special rules of classroom behavior you may want to emphasize, such as a statement to the effect that the assignments for the course are to be completed by the dates indicated in the course outline. In fact it is generally helpful to list the responsibilities of the student and those of the instructor. All of these considerations, of course, help set the stage for the course—they structure the situation, help the students discover at the outset what their responsibilities are going to be, and give them the security of seeing where they are going.

Choose Appropriate Teaching Methods

A third and final point at which your preparation for a course is determined by your objectives is in the type of instruction you will use. For some goals and for some materials, an orthodox lecture presentation is as good as or better than any other. For others, discussion may be preferable. For the accomplishment of still other ends the "buzz session" or "role playing" techniques described later in the book may be useful. Probably most successful teachers vary their methods to suit their objectives. Thus you may wish one day to present some new material in a lecture. You may then follow this with a class discussion on implications of this material or with a laboratory or field exercise. Since your choice in the matter is determined as much by your own personality as by your course objectives, I shall not dwell on it here. From the description of these techniques in later sections of the book, you may be able to decide which techniques are suited to your philosophy of teaching, your abilities, the class you are teaching, and the particular goals you are emphasizing at a particular time.

Generally speaking, it will be wise to find out how the course has been taught in the past and to avoid *major* modifications unless there is some departmental dissatisfaction with the course.

Check Resources Needing Advance Work

Order films and make arrangements for field work, guest lecturers, slides, demonstrations, or other resources needing advance work.

Begin Preparing Lectures (If You Plan to Lecture)

(See Chapter 5.)

▬ *Time: Two Weeks Before the First Class*

Preparation and planning are not done when you've firmed up the syllabus. Now look back over the syllabus to see what resources are required. Presumably your check with a colleague has turned up any gross problems—such as assuming an unlimited budget for films. Visit the classroom you've been assigned. Will the seating be conducive to discussion? Can it be darkened for films? If the room is unsuitable, ask for another. Don't assume that assignments are unchangeable. You probably can't change the time schedule the first time you are assigned it, since a certain time may already be in print with student schedules built around it. But with a term's head start you may be able to shift time of day, length of class period, etc. What are the library policies relevant to putting on reserve any books you may want? Can you assume unlimited photocopying of exams and course materials to give to students? What do you do if you want to show a film? Go on a field trip?

■■■■■ *Time: One Week Before the First Class*

At this point you're ready to prepare for the first class. For ideas about what to do and how to handle this meeting, read the next chapter.

SUPPLEMENTARY READING

A good brief source on how to define objectives is Chapter 3 in S. C. Ericksen, *Motivation for Learning* (Ann Arbor: University of Michigan Press, 1974).

A broader perspective is provided in Kenneth Eble's book *The Aims of College Teaching* (San Francisco: Jossey-Bass, 1983). I particularly like Chapter 2, "Character—The foundation of style."

The relationship between teaching styles and goals is thoughtfully discussed in relation to the limitations of disciplinary perspectives in the book by Paul L. Dressel and Dora Marcus, *On Teaching and Learning in College* (San Francisco: Jossey-Bass, 1982).

Chapter 2 of the book by Barbara Fuhrmann and Anthony Grasha, *A Practical Handbook for College Teachers* (Boston: Little, Brown, 1983), is titled "The Role of Personal Values in Teaching" and is well worth reading.

An excellent aid for preparing your syllabus is M. A. Lowther, J. S. Stark, and G. G. Martens, *Preparing Course Syllabi for Improved Communication* (Ann Arbor, MI: NCRIPTAL, University of Michigan, 1989).

Meeting a Class
for the First Time

*T*HE FIRST CLASS MEETING, like any other situation in which you are meeting a group of strangers who will affect your well being, is at the same time exciting and anxiety producing for both students and teacher. Some teachers handle their anxiety by postponing it, simply handing out the syllabus and leaving. This does not convey the idea that class time is valuable, nor does it capitalize on the fact that first day excitement can be constructive. If you have prepared as suggested in Chapter 2, you're in good shape; the students will be pleased that the instruction is under control, and focusing on meeting the students' concerns can not only help you quell your own anxiety but also make the first class interesting and challenging.

Other things being equal, anxiety is less disruptive in situations where stimulus events are clear and unambiguous. When the students know what to expect they can direct their energy more productively. An important function of the first day's meeting in any class is to provide this structure, that is, to present the classroom situation clearly, so that the students will know from the date of this meeting what you are like and what you expect. They come to the first class wanting to know what the course is all about and what kind of person the teacher is. To this end, the following concrete suggestions are offered.

One point to keep in mind both the first day and throughout the term is that yours is not the students' only class. They come to you from classes in chemistry, music, English, physical education, or rushing from their dormitory beds or from parking lots. The first few minutes need to help this varied group shift their thoughts and feelings to you and your subject.

You can ease them into the course gradually or you can grab their attention by something dramatically different, but in either case you need to think consciously about how you set the stage to facilitate achieving the course objectives. Even before the class period begins you can communicate nonverbally by such things as arranging the seats in a circle and putting your name on the board, or chat with early arrivals about what class they have come from or anything else that would indicate your interest in them. While students are coming in, suggest that they spend the time before class starts by getting acquainted with the students sitting near them.

■■■■ *Breaking the Ice*

You will probably want to use the first period for getting acquainted and establishing goals. You might begin by informally asking first-year students to raise their hands, then sophomores, juniors, seniors, or out-of-staters. This gives you some idea of the composition of the class and gets students started participating.

In my relatively large lecture classes I have then asked the students to take a minute or two to write down words and phrases that describe their feelings on the first day of class. I then ask them, "What have you written?" and list their responses on the blackboard.

Next I ask them, "How do you think your teacher feels on the first day of class?" This takes them aback, but they begin writing, and we now list these responses in a second column and they see some parallels. I comment briefly on my own feelings and then proceed to discussion of our joint responsibilities for learning in the course. (I remember with special affection the senior who came up to me after class and said, "I've been at this university almost four years, and this is the first time it ever occurred to me that professors have feelings.")

In a small class you might then ask all class members (including yourself) to introduce themselves, tell where they're from, mention their field of concentration, and answer any questions the group has. Or you can ask each student to get acquainted with the persons sitting on each side and then go around the class with each student introducing the next or each repeating the names of all those who have been introduced—a good device for promoting development of rapport and for helping you learn the names too. A more demanding, but surprisingly effective device is to have each person introduce everyone who was introduced before, ending with the teacher repeating everyone's names. (Try it! You'll be surprised at how well you do.)

Having established a degree of freedom of communication, the class might discuss the objectives of the course. It seems helpful to list these on the board as class members suggest them or react to your suggestions. After class record them so that the class may periodically refer to them and check progress. Note that these are only a first approximation that can be altered and rephrased as the class becomes aware of new needs during the term, but don't be afraid to let them know your vision for the course.

Problem Posting*

The technique of posting problems is not only a useful first day icebreaker, but one of value whenever it is useful to stimulate interest and assist students in communicating their problems to one another. This may be the case not only at the beginning of the course, but also after a lecture or other classroom method has aroused anxiety or defensiveness. The technique may also be useful to you when you wish to avoid answering questions immediately yourself. This might be because you don't wish to establish an atmosphere in which you dominate, because you wish to lay more groundwork, or because you don't wish to reinforce or to engage in a colloquy with a particular questioner whose concerns are not likely to contribute toward achievement of the goals of the class as a whole.

---

* This technique is one I learned from Norman R. F. Maier, described in his book, *Problem-Solving Discussions and Conferences: Leadership Methods and Skills* (New York: McGraw-Hill, 1963). It is useful in either small or large classes.

Do these potentialities intrigue you? All you need do is to say something like, "Let's see if we can get all the questions out so that we can see what they are and how to handle them."

If it is the first class meeting, you might say, "Let's see what problems you'd like to tackle during the course. What sorts of concerns do you think we might deal with?" or "What kinds of things have you heard about this course?"

The instructor's task then becomes that of understanding and recording briefly on the blackboard the problems contributed by the group. This means that you must be ready to accept all contributions whether or not you yourself feel they are important. To test your understanding of the problem it may be useful to restate the problem in different words. Restatement may also be useful in removing emotional loading or in bringing out implicit feelings. When you feel that a question is ambiguous or too general, it is helpful to ask for an illustration or to ask other group members to help you understand.

As contributions begin to slow down, suggest stopping. But, if possible, the posting should not be ended before there has been a good pause, since some of the most deeply felt problems will not come out until the students have seen that the teacher is really accepting and noncritical. This is a point where sensitivity is particularly important, for one can often see the visible signs of conflict about whether or not to raise an emotion-laden problem. If such a problem does come out and elicits a new batch of problems, forget about the suggested ending and get the problems out.

It is important in problem posting to maintain an accepting, nonevaluative atmosphere. Thus, if other members of the group argue that someone's contribution is not really a problem or that the real problem is different from that stated, the teacher needs to make it clear that even though not everyone agrees about a given problem, anything that is a problem for any member of the group is entitled to be listed. Disagreement should be used to get additional problems out rather than to persuade a group member to withdraw a contribution.

Inevitably some discussion will come out about solutions. While this should not be abruptly censored, if it becomes involved or lengthy the teacher may point out that the task of dealing with the problems comes later.

By the end of the problem posting the class normally has become better acquainted, has become used to active participation, has taken the first step toward developing an attitude of attempting to understand rather than compete with one another, has reduced the attitude that everything must come from the teacher, has learned that the teacher can listen as well as talk (and is not going to reject ideas different from his or her own), and, I hope, has begun to feel some responsibility for solving its own problems rather than waiting for them to be answered by the instructor.

Introducing the Teacher

In presenting the syllabus outline and mechanics you give the students some notion of the kind of person that you are. Although I am not recommending a complete personality change without benefit of at least short-term psychotherapy, three characteristics seem to be especially appreciated by the student: 1) enthusiasm and willingness to work to make the course worthwhile, 2) objectivity (the students will call it "fairness"), and 3) a sympathetic attitude toward the problems of the students. If these characteristics apply to you at all, or if you think they do, let the students know it.

Presenting a syllabus is one demonstration that you have made an investment in the course. Obviously you want to be open to student input, but in my experience students resent an authoritarian teacher much less than the teacher who says, "This is your class," and leaves the organization and structure of the course completely to the student. As we shall see in Chapter 4, student centered discussion is an effective teaching method, but students often interpret a student centered beginning as evidence that the instructor is lazy and uninterested in the course.

Promoting the notion that you are objective or fair can best be handled in connection with marks and the assignment of grades. For this reason, we will postpone direct discussion of the topic until later. But remember that a large part of the students' motivation in the classroom situation is (perhaps unfortunately) directed toward the grades they hope to get from the course. The very least that students can expect of you is that this mark will be arrived at on some impartial basis.

The simplest way to show students that you are objective and fair is to let the students know that you are willing to meet and advise them. Indicate your office hours. In addition to this, students appreciate it if you are willing (and have the time) to spend a few minutes in the classroom after each class answering specific questions. Such queries most often concern questions of fact that can be answered briefly and would hardly warrant a trip to your office at a later time in another building, even if the student could be counted on to remember the question for that long. If time permits, adjournment to a convenient snack bar or lounge may give students with special interests a chance to pursue them and get to know you better.

The first class is not the time to make sure the students understand your inadequacies and limitations. Frankly admitting that you don't know something is fine after the course is under way, but apologies in advance for lack of experience or expertise simply increase student insecurity.

Introducing the Textbook

To continue with the discussion of the first meeting of the class, we turn now to the presentation of the textbook(s). Here the most serious question that arises concerns possible disagreement between the textbook and the materials you intend to present in your lectures. Unfortunately this is a matter that cannot always be solved simply by judicious selection of text materials. In some cases, there is simply no book available that presents certain material as you would like to have it presented. In others, the textbook is decided upon by someone other than yourself, and you have to make the best of it. In the case where disagreement is inevitable, the students have a right to know which version to accept as TRUTH and what they are supposed to do about such discrepancies on examinations. By facing the situation squarely, you can not only escape from the horns of this dilemma but also turn it to your advantage. Explain that rival interpretations stand

or fall on the basis of
reasons for disagreein
accomplish two things
your opinions are base
point out current probl
for the serious student.

Avoid a tirade aga
tional catharsis for the
criticism you raise may
if the student is not co
ize to much of what yc

Questions

Even in a large lectu
descriptions of the co
will be designed as m
the underlying questic

→ "Are you rigid?

→ "Will you really

→ "Are you easily

→ "Are you a per

→ "Can you hand

Ask students to t
their reactions to the
two things: 1) It indic
arts building a lear
for thinking about th
2) It gives you feedba
dents were afraid to v

SUPPLEMENTARY R

Kenneth E. Eble, *The*
1976), Chapter 9.

The First Day of Clas
Aug/Sept 1989, 3

Basic Skills: Leading Discussions, Lecturing, Testing, and Grading

PART II

Basic Skills: Leading Discussions, Lecturing, Testing, and Grading

PART II

involved or lengthy the teacher may point out that the task of dealing with the problems comes later.

By the end of the problem posting the class normally has become better acquainted, has become used to active participation, has taken the first step toward developing an attitude of attempting to understand rather than compete with one another, has reduced the attitude that everything must come from the teacher, has learned that the teacher can listen as well as talk (and is not going to reject ideas different from his or her own), and, I hope, has begun to feel some responsibility for solving its own problems rather than waiting for them to be answered by the instructor.

■■■ *Introducing the Teacher*

In presenting the syllabus outline and mechanics you give the students some notion of the kind of person that you are. Although I am not recommending a complete personality change without benefit of at least short-term psychotherapy, three characteristics seem to be especially appreciated by the student: 1) enthusiasm and willingness to work to make the course worthwhile, 2) objectivity (the students will call it "fairness"), and 3) a sympathetic attitude toward the problems of the students. If these characteristics apply to you at all, or if you think they do, let the students know it.

Presenting a syllabus is one demonstration that you have made an investment in the course. Obviously you want to be open to student input, but in my experience students resent an authoritarian teacher much less than the teacher who says, "This is your class," and leaves the organization and structure of the course completely to the student. As we shall see in Chapter 4, student centered discussion is an effective teaching method, but students often interpret a student centered beginning as evidence that the instructor is lazy and uninterested in the course.

Promoting the notion that you are objective or fair can best be handled in connection with marks and the assignment of grades. For this reason, we will postpone direct discussion of the topic until later. But remember that a large part of the students' motivation in the classroom situation is (perhaps unfortunately) directed toward the grades they hope to get from the course. The very least that students can expect of you is that this mark will be arrived at on some impartial basis.

The simplest way to show students that you are objective and fair is to let the students know that you are willing to meet and advise them. Indicate your office hours. In addition to this, students appreciate it if you are willing (and have the time) to spend a few minutes in the classroom after each class answering specific questions. Such queries most often concern questions of fact that can be answered briefly and would hardly warrant a trip to your office at a later time in another building, even if the student could be counted on to remember the question for that long. If time permits, adjournment to a convenient snack bar or lounge may give students with special interests a chance to pursue them and get to know you better.

The first class is not the time to make sure the students understand your inadequacies and limitations. Frankly admitting that you don't know something is fine after the course is under way, but apologies in advance for lack of experience or expertise simply increase student insecurity.

▅▅▅ *Introducing the Textbook*

To continue with the discussion of the first meeting of the class, we turn now to the presentation of the textbook(s). Here the most serious question that arises concerns possible disagreement between the textbook and the materials you intend to present in your lectures. Unfortunately this is a matter that cannot always be solved simply by judicious selection of text materials. In some cases, there is simply no book available that presents certain material as you would like to have it presented. In others, the textbook is decided upon by someone other than yourself, and you have to make the best of it. In the case where disagreement is inevitable, the students have a right to know which version to accept as TRUTH and what they are supposed to do about such discrepancies on examinations. By facing the situation squarely, you can not only escape from the horns of this dilemma but also turn it to your advantage. Explain that rival interpretations stand or fall on the basis of pertinent evidence and plan to give your reasons for disagreeing with the textbook. This procedure will accomplish two things: 1) it will give the student the notion that your opinions are based upon evidence, and 2) it will frequently point out current problems in theory that often have great appeal for the serious student.

Avoid a tirade against the author. This may serve as an emotional catharsis for the instructor, but for the student, any severe criticism you raise may generalize to the textbook as a whole. Or, if the student is not convinced by your argument, it may generalize to much of what you have to say.

▬▬ *Questions*

Even in a large lecture it seems wise to interrupt these first descriptions of the course for questions. Some of the questions will be designed as much to test you as to get information. Often the underlying questions are such things as:

- → "Are you rigid?"
- → "Will you really try to help students?"
- → "Are you easily rattled?"
- → "Are you a person as well as a teacher?"
- → "Can you handle criticism?"

Ask students to take two minutes at the end of class to write their reactions to the first day (anonymously). This accomplishes two things: 1) It indicates your interest in learning from them and starts building a learning climate in which they are responsible for thinking about their learning and influencing your teaching. 2) It gives you feedback, often revealing doubts or questions students were afraid to verbalize orally.

SUPPLEMENTARY READING

Kenneth E. Eble, *The Craft of Teaching* (San Francisco: Jossey-Bass, 1976), Chapter 9.

The First Day of Class: Advice and Ideas, *The Teaching Professor*, Aug/Sept 1989, 3 (7), 1–2.

CHAPTER 4

Organizing
Effective Discussions

DISCUSSION METHODS are among the most valuable tools in the teacher's repertoire. Often teachers in large classes feel that they must lecture because discussion is impossible. In fact discussion techniques can be used in classes of all sizes. This is not to say that small classes are not desirable—generally they *are* more effective, but large classes should not be allowed to inhibit the teacher's ability to stimulate student thinking and participation.

Discussion is probably not effective for presenting new information the student is already motivated to learn, but discussion techniques seem particularly appropriate when the instructor wants to do the following:

1. Help students learn to think in terms of the subject matter by giving them practice in thinking.

2. Help students learn to evaluate the logic of, and evidence for, their own and others' positions.

3. Give students opportunities to formulate applications of principles.

4. Help students become aware of and formulate problems using information gained from readings or lectures.

5. Use the resources of members of the group.

6. Gain acceptance for information or theories counter to folk-lore or previous beliefs of students.

7. Develop motivation for further learning.

8. Get prompt feedback on how well objectives are being attained.

Why should discussion be the method of choice for achieving such objectives? The first justification is a very simple extrapolation of the old adage, "Practice makes perfect." If instructors expect students to learn how to integrate, apply, and problem solve, it seems reasonable that students should have an opportunity to practice these skills. Most importantly, learning should be facilitated if this practice is accompanied by feedback so that the students can identify their errors and successes.

Further, I would expect learning to be most effective if there is sufficient guidance to ensure some successes. Experiments on learning motor skills reveal that guidance is most helpful in the early stages of learning, suggesting that the instructor should play a more directive role at the beginning of a course than at its end.

▬▬ *A Little Bit of Theory*

Research in cognitive psychology has found that memory is affected by how deeply we process new knowledge (see Chapter 27). Simply listening to or repeating something is likely to store it in such a way that we have difficulty finding it when we want to remember it. If we elaborate our learning by thinking about its relationship to other things we know or by talking about it—explaining, summarizing, or questioning—we are more likely to remember it when we need to use it later.

▬▬ *Problems in Teaching by Discussion*

In discussion groups the instructor is faced with several problems:

1. Getting participation in the discussion.

2. Making progress (or making the student aware of the progress) toward course objectives.

3. Handling emotional reactions of students.

The type of discussion method used will determine the extent to which particular roles are dominant. Student centered discussions tend to be more effective than teacher centered methods, but first I will describe a middle-of-the-road discussion method particularly useful in a problem-solving discussion. For such a discussion to work students must have a sense that a problem exists and that it would be interesting to try to work on that problem.

▰▰▰ *Developmental Discussion*

The term "developmental discussion" was coined by Professor Norman R. F. Maier (1952) to describe a problem-solving discussion technique in which the teacher breaks problems into parts so that all group members are working on the same part of the problem at the same time. One of the reasons discussion often seems ineffective and disorganized is that different members of the group are working on different aspects of the problem and are thus often frustrated by what they perceive as irrelevant comments by other students. In developmental discussion the teacher tries to keep the students aware of the stage of discussion that is the current focus. Typical stages might be:

1. formulating the problem
2. suggesting hypotheses
3. getting relevant data
4. evaluating alternative solutions.

Typically, an early step in developmental discussion is to get information relevant to the problem for discussion. Such information can be supplied by a lecture, by reading, or by group members. In this technique teachers should feel free to give information or raise questions. Often an appropriate problem for developmental discussion is the application or implications of particular principles or findings presented by lectures or reading.

Like other discussion methods, developmental discussion implies active participation of group members. In developmental discussion, participation is directed to a definite goal. However, this does not imply a type of discussion leadership in which the leader manipulates the group to follow the steps and reach a predetermined goal. Rather the leader helps the group progress by dividing the problem up into parts that can be solved in steps. In short, developmental discussion is not nondirective, but neither is it autocratic.

■ *Breaking a Problem into Subproblems*

One of Maier's important contributions to effective group problem solving, as well as to teaching, is to point out that groups are likely to be more effective if they tackle one aspect of a problem at a time rather than skipping from formulation of the problem, to solutions, to evidence, to "what-have-you," as different members of the group toss in their own ideas. In developmental discussion the group tackles one thing at a time.

One of the first tasks is likely to be a *clarification of the problem*. Often groups are ineffective because different participants have different ideas of what the problem is, and group members may feel frustrated at the end of the discussion because "the group never got to the real problem."

A second task is likely to be, "What do we know?" or *"What data are relevant?"*

A third task may be, *"What are the characteristics of an acceptable solution?"*—for example, "What is needed?"

A fourth step could be, *"What are possible solutions?"*, and a fifth step may be to *evaluate these solutions* against the criteria for a solution determined in the previous step.

The developmental discussion technique can be used even in large groups, since there are a limited number of points to be made at each step regardless of the number of participants. Maier and Maier (1957) have shown that developmental discussion techniques improve the quality of decisions as compared with freer, more nondirective discussion methods.

▰▰▰ *Skills in Leading Discussion*

In a developmental discussion the teacher attempts to guide a discussion along a certain line, but not to push it beyond the group's interest and acceptance. Obviously this requires skill in initiating discussion, getting student participation, appraising group progress, asking questions, and overcoming resistance.

Starting Discussion

After a class has been meeting and discussing problems successfully, there is little problem in initiating discussion, for it will develop almost spontaneously from problems encountered in reading, from experiences, or from unresolved problems from the previous meeting. But during the first meetings of new groups, the instructor may need to assume the initiative in beginning the discussion.

STARTING DISCUSSION WITH A COMMON EXPERIENCE   One of the best ways of starting a discussion is to provide a concrete, common experience through presentation of a demonstration, film, role playing, or a short skit. Following such a presentation it's easy to ask, "Why did————?"

Such an opening has a number of advantages. Since everyone in the group has seen it, everyone knows something about the topic under discussion. In addition, by focusing the discussion on the demonstration, the instructor takes some of the pressure off anxious or threatened students who are afraid to reveal their own opinions or feelings.

However, you will not always be able to find the demonstration you need to introduce each discussion, and you may be forced to turn to other techniques of initiating discussion. One such technique is problem posting, which was discussed in Chapter 3.

STARTING DISCUSSION WITH A CONTROVERSY   A second technique of stimulating discussion is through disagreement. Experimental evidence is accumulating to indicate that a certain degree of surprise or uncertainty arouses curiosity, a basic motive for learning (Berlyne, 1960). Some teachers effectively play the role of devil's advocate; others are effective in pointing out differences in point of view.

I have some concerns about the devil's advocate role. I believe that it can be an effective device in getting students to think actively rather than accept passively the instructor's every sentence as "Truth." Yet it has its risks, the most important of which is that it may create lack of trust in the instructor. Of course, instructors want students to challenge their ideas, but few want their students to feel they are untrustworthy, lying about their own beliefs.

A second danger in the "devil's advocate" role is that it will be perceived as manipulative. Students may feel (with justification) that the instructor "is just playing games with us—trying to show how smart he is and how easily he can fool us."

A third danger is that the devil's advocate role will be used as a screen to prevent students from ever successfully challenging the instructor. In this use the instructor, whenever the student wins an argument, simply says, "Well, I just presented that position to see if you could see its weakness."

Not only are all of these possible problems infuriating for the student, but they maintain a superior-subordinate relationship antithetical to the sort of learning environment that this book is plugging for. If the best classroom is one in which both students and teacher are learning, a role that provides armor against the instructor's learning is bad.

Yet the devil's advocate role can be effective. Its success depends a good deal upon the spirit with which it is played. My own compromise solution is to make it clear when I'm taking such a role by saying, "Suppose I take the position that———" or "Let me play the role of devil's advocate for a bit."

In any case the instructor should realize that disagreement is not a sign of failure but may be used constructively. When rigid dogmatism interferes with constructive problem solving following a disagreement, the instructor may ask the disagreeing students to switch sides and argue the opposing point of view. Such a technique seems to be effective in developing awareness of the strengths of other positions.

As Maier has shown in his studies of group leadership, one barrier to effective problem solving is presenting an issue in such a way that participants take sides arguing the apparent solution rather than attempting to solve the problem by considering data and devising alternative solutions. Maier suggests the following principles for group problem solving.*

1. Success in problem solving requires that effort be directed toward overcoming surmountable obstacles.

2. Available facts should be used even when they are inadequate.

3. The starting point of the problem is richest in solution possibilities.

4. Problem-mindedness should be increased while solution-mindedness should be delayed.

5. Whether disagreement leads to hard feelings or to innovation depends on the discussion leadership.

6. The "idea-getting" process should be separated from the "idea-evaluation" process because the latter inhibits the former.

Questioning

The most common discussion opener is the question, and the most common error in questioning is not allowing students time enough to think. You should not expect an immediate response to every question. If your question is intended to stimulate thinking, give the students time to think. A few seconds of silence may seem an eternity, but a pause for thought may result in better discussion than a quick answer generated out of a desire to avoid silence. In some cases you may plan for such a thoughtful silence by asking the students to think about the question a few seconds

---

* N. R. F. Maier, *Problem-Solving Discussions and Conferences* (New York: McGraw-Hill, 1963).

and then write down one element that might help answer the question. Such a technique increases the chance that the shyer or slower students will participate, since they know what they want to say when the discussion begins. In fact you may even draw one in by saying, "You were writing vigorously, Ronnie, what's your suggestion?"

FACTUAL QUESTIONS   There are times when it is appropriate to check student background knowledge with a series of brief factual questions, but more frequently you want to stimulate problem solving. One common error in phrasing questions for this purpose is to ask a question in a form conveying to students the message, "I know something you don't know and you'll look stupid if you don't guess right."

APPLICATION AND INTERPRETATION QUESTIONS   Rather than dealing with factual questions, discussions need to be formulated so as to get at relationships, applications, or analyses of facts and materials. Solomon, Rosenberg, and Bezdek (1964) found that teachers who used interpretation questions produced gains in student comprehension. A question of the type, "How does the idea that———apply to ———?" is much more likely to stimulate discussion than the question, "What is the definition of———?" The secret is not to avoid questions or to lecture in statements, but rather to listen and to reflect upon what is heard. Questions are tools for teaching, but as Dillon (1982) demonstrated they sometimes interfere with as well as facilitate achievement of teaching goals. What happens depends upon the question and its use.

PROBLEM QUESTIONS   A question may arise from a case or it may be a hypothetical problem. It may be a problem whose solution the instructor knows; it may be a problem which the instructor has not solved. In any case it should be a problem that is meaningful to the students, and, for the sake of morale, it should be a problem they can make some progress on. And even if the teacher knows an answer or has a preferred solution, the students should have a chance to come up with new solutions. The teacher's job is not to sell students on a particular solution, but rather to listen and to teach them how to solve problems themselves.

A common error in question phrasing is to frame the question at a level of abstraction inappropriate for the class. Students are most likely to participate in discussion when they feel that they have an experience or idea that will contribute to the discussion. This means that discussion questions need to be phrased as problems that are meaningful to the students as well as to the instructor. Such questions can be devised more easily if you know something of the students' background. An experiment by Sturgis (1959) showed that knowledge of student background makes a significant difference in a teacher's effectiveness as measured by students' learning.

Another error in raising questions is to ask your question before finding out about the students' problems. Often a good question fails to elicit responses because students are hung up on some prior problem.

Suppose you ask a question and no one answers, or the student simply says, "I don't know." Discouraging as this may be, it should not necessarily be the end of the interaction. Usually the student can respond if the question is rephrased. Perhaps you need to give an example of the problem first; perhaps you need to suggest some alternative answer; perhaps you need to reformulate a prior question. More often than not you can help the students discover that they are more competent than they thought.

OTHER TYPES OF QUESTIONS *Connective and causal effect questions* involve attempts to link material or concepts that otherwise might not seem related. One might, for example, cut across disciplines to link literature, music, and historical events or one might ask, "What are the possible causes of this phenomenon?"

Comparative questions, as the name suggests, ask for comparisons between one theory and another, one author and another, one research study and another, etc. Such questions help students determine important dimensions of comparison.

Evaluative questions ask not only for comparisons but for a judgment of the relative value of the points being compared, for example, "Which of two theories better accounts for the data? Which of two essays better contributes to an understanding of the issue?"

Critical questions examine the validity of an author's arguments or discussion. Being so critical that students feel that their reading has been a waste of time is not helpful, but presenting an alternative argument or conclusion may start students analyzing their reading more carefully, and eventually you want students to become critical readers who themselves challenge assumptions and conclusions.

Socratic Discussion

The "classic" (and I do mean *classic*) discussion technique is the Socratic method. In television, novels, and anecdotes about the first year of law school it is usually portrayed as a sadistic, anxiety-producing method of eliciting student stupidity, and even when I place myself in the role of slave boy taught by Socrates in the *Meno* I feel more like a pawn than an active learner.

Perhaps this is why I've never been very good at Socratic teaching; nonetheless I believe that it can be used as an effective method of stimulating student thinking, and it can have the quality of an interesting game rather than that of an inquisition. The leading modern student of Socratic teaching is Allen Collins, who has observed a variety of Socratic dialogues and analyzed the strategies used (Collins, 1977, 1982).

Basically, most Socratic teachers attempt to teach students to reason to general principles from specific cases. Collins (1977) gives twenty-three rules such as the following:

1. Ask about a known case. For example, if I were trying to teach a group of teaching assistants about student cheating, I might say, "Can you describe a situation in which cheating occurred?"

2. Ask for any factors. "Why did the cheating occur?"

3. Ask for intermediate factors. If the student suggests a factor that is not an immediate cause, ask for intermediate steps. For example, if a teaching assistant says, "Students feel a lot of pressure to get good grades," I might say, "Why did the pressure for grades result in cheating in this situation?"

4. Ask for prior factors. If the student gives a factor that has prior factors, ask for the prior factors. For example, "Why do students feel pressure to get good grades?"

5. Form a general rule for an insufficient factor. For example, "Do all students who feel pressure cheat?"

6. Pick a counterexample for an insufficient factor. For example, "Do you think these students cheat on every test?"

7. Form a general rule for an unnecessary factor. For example, if a teaching fellow suggests that cheating occurs when tests are difficult, I might say, "Probably the pressure to cheat is greater when tests are difficult, but does cheating occur only on difficult tests?"

8. Pick a counterexample for an unnecessary factor. For example, "Is cheating likely to occur on college admissions tests, such as the SAT?"

9. Pick a case with an extreme value. For example, "Why is cheating minimized on SAT tests?"

10. Probe for necessary or sufficient factors.

11. Pose two cases and probe for differences. For example, "Why is there more cheating in large classes than in small ones?"

12. Ask for a prediction about an unknown case.

13. Trace the consequences of a general rule. For example, if the teaching assistants conclude that cheating will occur when

tests are difficult and not well proctored, I might say, "Engineering classes are considered difficult, and I understand that there is little cheating even though tests are unproctored." (The school has an honors code.)

In general the rules involve formulating general principles from known cases and then applying the principles to new cases. Even if one does not use the Socratic method to its fullest, the questioning strategies described in Collins's rules may be generally useful in leading discussions.

■■■■ *What Can I Do About Nonparticipants?*

In most classes some students talk too much and others never volunteer a sentence. What can the teacher do?

Unfortunately, most students are used to being passive recipients in class. To help them become participants I try to create an expectation of participation in the discussion section. You can start to do this in the first meeting of the course by defining the functions of various aspects of the course and explaining why discussion is valuable. In addition to this initial structuring, however, you must continually work to increase the students' awareness of the values of participation. Participation is not an end in itself. For many purposes widespread participation may be vital; for others it may be detrimental. But you want to create a climate in which an important contribution is not lost because the person with the necessary idea did not feel free to express it.

What keeps a student from talking? There are a variety of reasons—boredom, lack of knowledge, general habits of passivity—but most compelling is a fear of being embarrassed. When one is surrounded by strangers, when one does not know how critical these strangers may be, when one is not sure how sound one's idea may be, when one is afraid of stammering or forgetting one's point under the stress of speaking—the safest thing to do is keep quiet.

What can reduce this fear? Getting acquainted is one aid. Once students know that they are among friends, they can risk expressing themselves. If they know that at least one classmate supports an idea, the risk is reduced. For both these reasons the technique of subgrouping helps; for example, you can ask students to discuss a question in pairs or small groups before asking for general discussion.

Asking students to take a couple of minutes to write out their initial answers to a question can help. If a student has already written an answer, the step to speaking is much less than answering when asked to respond immediately. Even the shy person will respond when asked, "What did you write?"

Rewarding infrequent contributors at least with a smile helps encourage participation even if the contribution has to be developed or corrected. Calling students by name seems to encourage freer communication. Seating is important too. Rooms with seats in a circle help tremendously.

Getting to know the nonparticipant is also helpful. For example, I have found that it is helpful to ask students to write a brief life history indicating their interests and experiences relevant to the course. These autobiographies help me to gain a better knowledge of each student as an individual, to know what problems or illustrations will be of particular interest to a number of students, and to know whom I can call on for special information. One of the best ways of getting nonparticipants into the discussion is to ask them to contribute in a problem area in which they have special knowledge.

The technique of asking for a student's special knowledge deals directly with one of the major barriers to class discussion—fear of being wrong. No one likes to look foolish, especially in a situation where mistakes may be pounced upon by a teacher or other students. One of the major reasons for the deadliness of a question in which the teacher asks a student to fill in the one right word—such as, "This is an example of what?"—is that it puts the student on the spot. There is an infinity of wrong answers, and obviously the teacher knows the one right answer; so why should the student risk making a mistake when the odds are so much against the student? And even if the answer is obvious, why look like a pawn for the teacher?

One way of putting the student in a more favorable position is to ask general questions that have no wrong answers. For example, you can ask, "How do you feel about this?" or "How does this look to you?" as a first step in analysis of a problem. Students' feelings or perceptions may not be the same as yours, but as reporters of their own feelings, they can't be challenged as being inaccurate. While such an approach by no means eliminates anxiety about participation (for an answer involves revealing oneself as a person), it will more often open up discussion that involves the student than will questions of fact. "Problem Posting," the technique discussed in Chapter 3 as a method for establishing objectives during the first day of class is an example of a discussion technique minimizing risk for students. It can be useful in introducing a new topic at the conclusion of a topic, or for analysis of an experiment or a literary work. An added advantage is that it can be used in large groups as well as small ones.

Another technique for reducing the risk of participation for students is to ask a question a class period before the discussion and ask students to write out answers involving an example from their own experience. Similarly one can ask students to bring one question to class for discussion. This helps participation, helps students learn to formulate questions, and also provides feedback for you.

All of these techniques will still not make every student into an active, verbal participant. Two group techniques can help. One is "buzz groups"; the other is the "inner circle" technique.

Buzz Groups

One of the popular techniques for achieving student participation in groups is the buzz session. In this procedure, classes are split into small subgroups for a brief discussion of a problem. Groups can be asked to come up with one hypothesis that they see as relevant, with one application of a principle, with an example of a concept, or with a solution to a problem. In large classes I march up the aisles saying "Odd," "Even," "Odd," "Even" for each row and ask the "odd" row to turn around to talk to the "even" row behind, forming themselves into groups of four to six. I tell them to first introduce themselves to one another and then to choose a person to report for the group. Next they are to get from each member of the group one idea about the problem or question posed. Finally they are to come up with one idea to report to the total class. I give the group a limited time to work, sometimes five minutes or less, occasionally ten minutes or more, depending on the tasks.

The Inner Circle

In using the inner circle technique I announce that at the next class meeting we are going to have a class within a class, with half the students acting as the discussion group and the other half as observers. If the classroom has moveable chairs, I then arrange the seating in the form of two concentric circles. I may explain that I want to give some of the quieter members of the class a chance to express their ideas. I am impressed that students who are normally silent will talk when they feel the increased sense of responsibility as members of the inner circle.

■■■ *The Discussion Monopolizer*

If you have worked on nonparticipation effectively, the discussion monopolizer is less likely to be a problem, but there will still be classes in which one or two students talk so much that you and the other students become annoyed. As with nonparticipation, one solution is to raise with the class the question of participation in discussion—"Would the class be more effective if participation were more evenly distributed?"

A second technique is to have one or more members of the class act as observers for one or more class periods, reporting back to the class their observations. Perhaps assigning the dominant member to the observer role would help sensitivity.

A third possibility is to audiotape a discussion, and after playing back a portion, ask the class to discuss what might be done to improve the discussion.

A fourth technique is to use buzz groups with one member chosen to be reporter. Often the monopolizer will not be chosen to report.

Finally a direct approach should not be ruled out. Talking to the student individually outside class may be the simplest and most effective solution.

■ *Appraising Progress*

One of the important skills of discussion leaders is the ability to appraise the group's progress and to be aware of barriers or resistances that are blocking learning. This skill depends upon attention to such clues as inattention, hostility, or diversionary questions.

Skill at appraising is of little avail if instructors don't respond to the feedback they receive. In some cases you may need to respond only by interposing a guiding question or by emphasizing a significant contribution. In other cases you may need to summarize progress and restate the current issue or point out the stumbling block or diversion that has stopped progress. In extreme cases, you may have to stop the discussion to begin a discussion of the reasons for lack of progress.

■ *How Can You Have a Discussion if the Students Haven't Read the Assignment?*

It's hard to have a discussion if students haven't studied the material to be discussed. What to do?

One strategy is to give students questions at the end of one class, asking them to get information on the questions before the next class. You might even give different assignments to teams of students.

If there are extenuating circumstances, you (or a student who is prepared) can summarize the needed points. Alternatively you can give students a few minutes to scan the material before beginning the discussion. If used often, however, such strategies may discourage out-of-class preparation.

If the problem persists, present it to the students. What do they suggest? One likely proposal is a short quiz at the beginning of class—which usually works. However, you'd like to have students motivated to study without the threat of a quiz. Usually the quiz can be phased out once students find that discussion really requires preparation and that the assignments are more interesting as they develop competence.

▬ *Barriers to Discussion*

A primary barrier to discussion is the students' feeling that they are not learning. Occasional summaries during the hour not only help students chart their progress but also help smooth out communication problems. A summary need not be a statement of conclusions. In many cases the most effective summary is a restatement of the problem in terms of the issues resolved and those remaining. Keeping a visible record on the blackboard of ideas, questions, data, or points to explore helps maintain focus and give a sense of progress.

Probably one of the most common barriers to good discussion is the instructor's tendency to tell students the answer or to put the solution in abstract or general terms before the students have developed an answer or meaning for themselves. Of course, teachers can sometimes save time by tying things together or stating a generalization that is emerging. But all too often they do this before the class is ready for it.

Another barrier to discussion is agreement. Usually instructors are so eager to reach agreement in groups that they are likely to be happy when the students are agreeing. But agreement is not the objective of most educational discussions. Students come to class with certain common naive attitudes and values. While the attitudes they hold may be "good" ones, they may be so stereotyped that the students fail to develop an understanding of the complex phenomena to which their attitudes apply. The teacher's task is often directed not so much toward attitude change as toward increased sensitivity to other points of view and increased understanding of the phenomena to which the attitude applies. As I suggested earlier, the instructor may sometimes need to assume a role of opposition.

When you oppose a student's opinions, you should be careful not to overwhelm the student with the force of the criticism. Your objective is to start discussion, not smother it. Give students an opportunity to respond to criticisms, examining the point of view that was opposed. Above all, avoid personal criticism of students.

▰▰▰ *Handling Arguments*

In any good discussion conflicts will arise. If such conflicts are left ambiguous and uncertain, they, like repressed conflicts in the individual, may cause continuing trouble. One of the teacher's functions is to help focus these conflicts so that they may contribute to learning.

→ Reference to the text or other authority may be one method of resolution, if the solution depends upon certain facts.

→ Using the conflict as the basis for a library assignment for the class or a delegated group is another solution.

→ If there is an experimentally verified answer, this is a good opportunity to review the method by which the answer could be determined.

→ If the question is one of values, your goal may be to help students become aware of the values involved.

→ In any case it should be clear that conflict may be an aid to learning, and the instructor need not frantically seek to smother it.

→ Sometimes students will dispute your statements or decisions. Such disagreements may sometimes be resolved by a comparison of the evidence for both points of view, but since teachers are human, they are all too likely to become drawn into an argument in which they finally rest upon their own authority. To give yourself time to think as well as to indicate understanding and acceptance of the students' point, I suggest listing the objections on the blackboard. (Incidentally, listing evidence or arguments is also a good technique when the conflict is between two members of the class.) Such listing tends to prevent repetition of the same arguments.

▰▰▰ *The Two-Column Method*

Another of Maier's techniques, the two-column method, is a particularly effective use of the blackboard in a situation where there is a conflict or where a strong bias prevents full consideration of alternative points of view. Experimental studies (Hovland, 1957) suggest that when people hear arguments against their point of view, they become involved in attempting to refute the arguments rather than listening and understanding. Disagreement thus often tends to push the debaters into opposite corners in which every idea is right or wrong, good or bad, black or white. The truth is often more complex and not in either extreme.

The two-column method is designed to permit consideration of complications and alternatives. As in problem posting, leaders using this technique suggest that before the issues are debated before the group, all the arguments on each side be listed on the board. The leader then heads two columns, "Favorable to A" and "Favorable to B" or "For" and "Against," and then asks for the facts or arguments group members wish to present. The instructor's task is to understand and record in brief the arguments presented. If someone wishes to debate an argument presented for the other side, the instructor simply tries to reformulate the point so that it can be listed as a positive point in the debater's own column. But even though an argument is countered or protested it should not be erased, for the rules of the game are that the two columns are to include all ideas that members consider relevant. Evaluation can come later.

When the arguments have been exhausted, discussion can turn to the next step in problem solving. At this point the group can usually identify areas of agreement and disagreement and in many cases it is already clear that the situation is neither black nor white. Now the issue becomes one of *relative* values rather than good vs. bad. When discussion is directed toward agreements, some of the personal animosity is avoided, and some underlying feelings may be brought to light. The next stages of the discussion are thus more likely to be directed toward constructive problem solving.

Challenges and disagreements may be an indication of an alert, involved class. But the instructor should also be aware of the possibility that they may be symptoms of frustration arising because the students are uncertain of what the problem is or how to go about solving it.

■■■ *Teaching Students How to Learn Through Discussion*

I have already implied that classes don't automatically carry on effective discussions. To a large extent students have to learn how to learn from discussions just as they have to learn how to learn from reading. How can this occur?

Some of the attributes are already apparent. For example, one skill is clarification of what it is the group is trying to do. Developmental discussion carries this to the extent of specifying subgoals for each stage of the discussion. One of the skills in learning through discussion is developing sensitivity to confusion about what the group is working on and asking for clarification. For teachers this implies presenting their own goals for the discussion and encouraging students to participate in formulating the group's goals.

A second attribute is the students' development of a willingness to talk about their own ideas openly and to listen and respond to others' ideas. It is important for students to realize that it is easy to deceive themselves about their own insights or understandings and that verbalizing an idea is one way of getting checks upon and extensions of it. Teachers can encourage development of listening skills by asking one group member to repeat or paraphrase what another said before responding to it, and repeatedly pointing out the purpose and values students gain from discussion.

A third skill is planning. Discussions are sometimes frustrating because they are only getting under way when the end of the class period comes. If this results in continuation of the discussion outside the class, so much the better, but often learning is facilitated if students learn to formulate the issues and determine what out-of-class study or follow-up is necessary before the group breaks up.

A fourth skill is building on others' ideas in such a way as to increase their motivation rather than make them feel punished or forgotten. Often students see discussion as a competitive situation in which they win by tearing down other students' ideas. As Haines and McKeachie (1967) have shown, cooperative discussion methods encourage more effective work and better morale than competitive methods.

A fifth attribute is skill in evaluation. If classes are to learn how to discuss issues effectively, they need to review periodically what aspects of their discussion are proving to be worthwhile and what barriers, gaps, or difficulties have arisen. Some classes reserve the last five minutes of the period for a review of the discussion's effectiveness.

A sixth attribute is sensitivity to feelings of other group members. Students need to become aware of the possibility that feelings of rejection, frustration, dependence, and so on, may influence group members' participation in discussion. Sometimes it is more productive to recognize the underlying feeling than to focus on the content of an individual's statement.

Peer learning techniques, such as those discussed in Chapter 13, help in building the sense of community which enables students to confront one another openly and helpfully. Such community does not come overnight, but building a sense of community may be even more important for student learning than covering every chapter in the textbook.

▰▰▰ *Taking Minutes or Notes*

Boris (1983) suggests that a student be assigned each day to keep the "minutes" of the day's discussion and that each class period be initiated with a reading of the minutes. Such a procedure is probably particularly useful for the student taking the minutes, but it also has the value of starting the class with a review of where they have been so that there is a sense of building from one class period to the next.

▰▰▰ *In Conclusion*

The teachers' own needs are more evident in the conduct of discussion than in a lecture, for skillful discussion leading requires a quick awareness of individual and group needs. Instructors must, at least occasionally, relinquish their spots in the limelight and banish the temptation to make the discussion a little lecture.

In general, if an instructor is enthusiastic, friendly, and obviously interested in the subject, students also will be. Let me emphasize again that both lecture and discussion may have advantages at certain points in a course. Skillful teachers will choose the method best adapted to their objectives rather than rigidly sticking to one method only.

SUPPLEMENTARY READING

J. H. Clarke, Designing discussions as group inquiry. *College Teaching*, 1988, 36 (4), 140–146.

A. Collins, Processes in acquiring knowledge. In R. C. Anderson, R. J. Spiro, and W. E. Montague (eds.), *Schooling and the Acquisition of Knowledge* (Hillsdale, NJ: Erlbaum, 1977).

A. Collins, Goals and strategies of inquiry teaching. In R. Glaser (ed.), *Advances in Instructional Psychology* (Hillsdale, NJ: Erlbaum, 1982).

A. Collins, Different goals of inquiry teaching, *Questioning Exchange*, 1988, 2 (1), 39–45.

J. T. Dillon, *Teaching and the Art of Questioning* (Bloomington, IN: Phi Delta Kappa Educational Foundation, 1983).

Barbara Scheider Fuhrmann and Anthony F. Grasha, *A Practical Handbook for College Teachers* (Boston: Little, Brown, 1983), Chapter 6.

S. L. Yelon and C. R. Cooper, Discussion: A naturalistic study of a teaching method, *Instructional Science*, 1984, 13, 213–224.

Lecturing

*T*HE LECTURE is probably the oldest teaching method and still the method most widely used in American colleges and universities. Through the ages a great deal of practical wisdom about techniques of lecturing has accumulated. It is probable that the most effective lecturers utilize this accumulated wisdom plus their own talents in ways that are close to maximally effective. Effective lecturers combine the talents of scholar, writer, producer, comedian, showman, and teacher in ways that contribute to student learning. Nevertheless, it is also true that few college professors combine these talents in optimal ways and that even the best lecturers are not always in top form.

Why have lectures survived since the invention of print? Why have they persisted in the face of the intrusions of radio, television, computers, and other media? Is the lecture an effective method of teaching? If it is, under what conditions is it most effective? These questions will be answered not only in light of research on the lecture as a teaching method but also in terms of analyses of the information-processing techniques used by students in learning from lectures.

▰▰▰▰▰ *Research on the Effectiveness of Lectures*

A large number of studies have compared the effectiveness of lectures with other teaching methods. When measures of knowledge are used, the lecture proves to be as efficient as other methods. Alternatively, in those experiments involving measures of retention of information after the end of a course, measures of transfer of knowledge to new situations, or measures of problem solving, thinking, or attitude change, or motivation for further learning, the results tend to show differences favoring discussion methods over lecture (McKeachie, Pintrich, Lin, Smith, and Sharma, 1990).

■■■■ *What Are Lectures Good For?*

We do not need to lecture when concepts are available in printed form at an appropriate level for our students. In general, print presents information in a form which can be covered more rapidly and in a way more accessible for retrieval than lectures. Students using printed materials can choose their own rate of learning: they can review, they can skip; they can vary the order. The lecturer thus starts with some serious handicaps; however, not all information is available in printed form. For example, most printed sources available to college and university teachers for assignment to students are at least several years out of date by the time they are available for assignments. Lectures are particularly appropriate for helping students get up-to-date information on current research and theories relevant to topics they are studying. Moreover, lecturers may sometimes usefully summarize material scattered over a variety of printed sources, thus providing a more efficient method of conveying information than if students were to be assigned to cover these sources by their own reading. Finally, a lecturer can adapt material to the background and interests of a particular audience—material which in printed form is at a level or in a style not well suited to a particular class.

Lectures also can provide structures to help students read more effectively. In fact the lecture may help students learn to read. Readability of material depends on the expectations brought to material by the reader. Thus, appropriate lectures can build structures and expectations that help students read material in the given subject-matter area more effectively.

Lectures also have indirect values apart from their cognitive content. Many lectures have important motivational functions. By helping students become aware of a problem, of conflicting points of view, or of challenges to ideas they have previously taken for granted, the lecturer can stimulate interest in further learning in an area. Moreover, the lecturer's own attitudes and enthusiasm have an important effect upon student motivation. Research on student ratings of teaching as well as on student learning indicates that the enthusiasm of the lecturer is an important factor in effecting student learning and motivation. Not only is the lecturer a model in terms of motivation and curiosity, the lecturer also models ways of approaching problems, portraying a scholar in action in ways that are difficult for other media or methods of instruction to achieve. In fact there is some evidence suggesting that one of the advantages of live professors is the tendency of people to model themselves after other individuals whom they perceive as living, breathing human beings with characteristics that can be admired and emulated.

Finally, there are values in lecturing for professors themselves. Although there is little direct evidence on the point, there is certainly anecdotal evidence, as well as supporting psychological theory, suggesting that preparing and delivering a lecture is an important factor in the professor's ability to integrate and retrieve the subject matter.

■■■ *A Little Bit of Theory*

The preceding section has included a good bit of theory of learning and motivation, but I want to be more explicit about one aspect of the cognitive theory of learning and memory. As I noted in the preceding chapter, memory depends heavily on the learner's activity—thinking about and elaborating on new knowledge. A key difference between modern theories of memory and earlier theory is that earlier theory thought of knowledge as single associations, in some ways like tucking each bit of knowledge into a pigeonhole. Now we think of knowledge as being stored in structures such as networks with linked concepts, facts, and principles. The lecture thus needs to build a bridge between what is in the students' minds and the structures in the subject matter. Metaphors, examples, and demonstrations are the elements of the bridge. Providing a meaningful organization is thus a key function of the lecture.

■ *How Can Lectures Be Improved?*

The message of this chapter is that one way of improving lectures is to think about how students process lectures. What are students trying to do during a lecture?

As one looks at students at a lecture and observes their behavior, the most impressive thing one notices is the passive role students have in most classrooms. Some students are having difficulty in staying awake; others are attempting to pass the time as easily as possible by reading other materials, counting lecturer mannerisms, or simply doodling and listening in a relatively effortless manner. Many students are taking notes.

Attention

One of the factors determining students' success in information processing is their ability to attend to the lecture. Attention basically involves focusing one's cognitions upon those things which are changing, novel, or motivating. We know that individuals have a limited capacity for attending to the varied features of their environment. The individual's total capacity for attention may vary with the degree of activation or motivation. At any one time part of the capacity is devoted to the task at hand (in this case listening to the lecturer), part is monitoring other aspects of the classroom, and part of the attention capacity may be available for other uses—in other words, it is simply spare capacity.

Hartley and Davies' (1978) review notes that studies of the attention of students during lectures find that, typically, attention increases from the beginning of the lecture to ten minutes into the lecture and decreases after that point. They found that after the lecture students recalled 70 percent of the material covered in the first ten minutes, and only 20 percent of the material covered in the last ten minutes.

One of the characteristics of a passive lecture situation in which a lecturer is using few devices to get students to think actively about the content of the lecture is that attention tends to drift. Probably all of us have had the experience of listening to a speaker and finding with a start that we have not heard the speaker for some time because our attention has drifted on to thoughts that are tangential to the lecturer's theme. Bloom's (1953) studies of students' thinking during lectures and discussion indicated that more of students' thoughts were relevant to the content during lectures than during discussions, but that there was less active thinking in lectures than in discussions.

What Can Be Done to Get Attention?

In determining how to allocate attention, students use various strategies. Any lecturer knows that one way of getting attention is to precede the statement by the phrase, "This will be on the test." In addition, students listen for particular words or phrases that indicate to them that something is worth noting and remembering. Statements that enumerate or list are likely to be on tests and thus are likely to be attended to.

Changes in the environment recruit attention. The ability of changes to capture attention can work to the advantage of the lecturer. Variation in pitch, intensity, and pace of the lecture, and visual cues such as gestures, facial expression, movement to the blackboard, the use of demonstrations or audio-visual aids—all of these recruit and maintain attention to the lecture.

Auditory attention is directed to some extent by visual attention. As the eyes move, auditory attention tends to shift as well. Distracting movements in the classroom are thus likely to cause students to fail to recall what the lecturer has said. On the positive side, there is some evidence that students' comprehension is greater when the students can see the speaker's face and lips. Thus attempts of colleges and universities to conserve energy by reducing the lighting level may also reduce the students' abilities to maintain attention and learn from the lecture.

I indicated above that at most times when students are not highly motivated there is spare capacity of attention available. This spare capacity is very likely to be used for daydreaming or other tasks which may become more engrossing than listening to the lecture. Hence motivation is important in holding student attention. Keeping lectures to student interests, giving examples that are vivid and intriguing, building suspense toward a resolution of a conflict—these are all techniques of gaining and holding attention.

All of these devices will help, but recall the Hartley and Davies finding that students' attention tends to wane after ten minutes. A more radical device for maintaining attention requires breaking up the lecture rather than trying to hold attention for an hour or more. Student activities such as the minute paper,* pairing, or buzz groups can reactivate students' attention.**

Anxiety is a motive with potential negative effects. There is a good deal of evidence that students who are high in anxiety about texts are likely to fail to pay attention to the test while they are taking it because they are distracted by thoughts of failure (Wine, 1971). It seems likely that such anxiety about achievement may also distract a student listening to a lecture. In fact some of the very cues used by the lecturer, such as "this will be on the test," may also cue anxious thoughts about the likelihood of failing the test, about the consequences of failing in college and the resulting disappointment of family. Thus, although heavy emphasis upon tests and grades may cause some students to increase the amount of attention devoted to the lecture, it may also negatively affect others to the degree that their thoughts turn to the consequences of success or failure.

Should Students Take Notes?

Note taking is one of the activities by which students attempt to stay attentive, but note taking is also an aid to memory. "Working memory," or "short term memory," is a term used to describe the fact that one can hold only a given amount of material in mind at one time. When the lecturer presents a succession of new concepts, students' faces begin to show signs of anguish and frustration; some write furiously in their notebooks, while others stop

---

* The minute paper (Wilson, 1986) is described later in this chapter in the section, "How to Get Students Actively Thinking in a Lecture Situation."

** Brown and Atkins (1988, p. 29) list these and other student activities to get attention and students thinking during lectures.

writing in complete discouragement. Note taking thus is dependent upon one's ability, derived from past experience (long term memory), to understand what is being said and to hold it in working memory long enough to write it down. In most cases, when queried about their listening or note-taking habits, students report that they are primarily concerned about getting the gist of the lecture in order to be prepared for an examination. To do this they try to extract significant features from the lecture, to distill some of its meaning.

Hartley and Davies (1978) reviewed the research on note taking and student information processing during lectures. They report that students believe that there are two purposes for taking notes: One is that the process of taking notes will in itself help later recall; the other is that the notes provide external storage of concepts which may be reviewed when needed. The research results indicate some support for both beliefs.

Several studies show that students who take notes remember material better than a control group not taking notes even though the note takers turned in their notes immediately after the lecture. Note taking involves elaboration and transformation of ideas, which increases meaningfulness and retention (Peper and Mayer, 1978; Weiland and Kingbury, 1979). But note taking has costs as well as benefits. Student strategies of note taking differ. Some students take copious notes; others take none. We know that student information processing capacity is limited; that is, people can take in, understand, and store only so much information in any brief period of time. Information will be processed more effectively if the student is actively engaged in analyzing and processing the information rather than passively soaking it up.

Students' ability to process information depends upon the degree to which the information can be integrated or "chunked." No one has great ability at handling large numbers of unrelated items in active memory. Thus when students are in an area of new concepts or when the instructor is using language that is not entirely familiar to the students, students may be processing the lecture word by word or phrase by phrase and lose the sense of a sentence or of a paragraph before the end of the thought is reached. This means that lecturers need to be aware of instances in which new words or concepts are being introduced and to build in greater redundancy as well as pauses during which students can catch up and get appropriate notes.

Snow and Peterson (1980) point out that brighter students benefit more from taking notes than less able students. We believe that this is because the less able students cannot, while they write their notes, keep what they hear in their memories, so that their note taking essentially blocks them from processing parts of the lecture. But this is not simply a matter of intelligence; rather a student's ability to maintain materials in memory while taking notes and even to process and think about relationships between one idea and other ideas depends upon the knowledge or cognitive structures the student has available for organizing and relating the material. Thus the background of the student in the area is probably more important than the student's level of intelligence.

Some faculty members hand out prepared notes or encourage the preparation of notes for students to purchase. Hartley's research, as well as that of Annis (1981) and Kiewra (1989), suggests that a skeletal outline is helpful to students but with detailed notes students relax into passivity. It is better simply to provide an overall framework which they can fill in by selecting important points and interpreting them in their own words. Because student capacity for information processing is limited and because students cannot stop and go over again a confusing part of a lecture, you need to build more redundancy into your lectures than into writing, and you need to build in pauses where students can catch up and think rather than simply struggle to keep up.

■ *How Do Students Process the Content of a Lecture?*

Let us assume that students are allocating attention appropriately to the lecture. This alone, however, does not ensure that the content of the lecture will be understood, remembered, and applied appropriately. Even though students are trying to meet the demands of the situation, they may differ in the ways they go about processing the words that they have heard. Marton and Säljö (1976a,b) and other researchers at the University of Göteborg have used Craik and Lockart's (1972) differentiation of surface versus deep processing to describe differences in the way students go about trying to learn educational materials. Some students process the material as little as possible, simply trying to remember the words the instructor says and doing little beyond this. This would be described by Marton as "surface processing." Other students try to see implications of what the lecturer is saying, try to relate what is currently being said to other information either in the lecture or in their own experience and reading. They elaborate and translate the instructor's words into their own. They may question. This more thoughtful and more active kind of listening is what Marton and Säljö refer to as "deep processing." Experienced students can probably vary their strategies from verbatim memory to memory of concepts, depending upon the demands of the situation. Obviously there are times when exact recall of what the lecturer said is important, but, in general, "deep processing" is more likely to yield long term memory and retrieval of the kind of knowledge needed for solving problems.

Strategies of surface processing or deep processing are probably not fixed, and lecturers may be able to help their students process more material at a deep level, and, in addition, help students to learn from lectures more effectively. Pointing out relationships, asking rhetorical questions, or asking questions to be answered by class members are ways of encouraging active thought. Teachers can also ask for examples of how students apply concepts to their own experiences, thus encouraging all students to realize that it is important to try to think about how concepts relate to oneself. One can train students to write better notes by collecting student notes, evaluating the degree to which they summarize, translate, and show relationships as opposed to simply representing more or less verbatim accounts.

Planning the Lecture Series

A typical lecture strives to present a systematic, concise summary of the knowledge to be covered in the day's assignment. Chang, Crombag, van der Drift, and Moonen (1983, p. 21) call this approach "conclusion oriented." *Don't do it!* The lecturer's task in university teaching is not to be an abstractor of encyclopedias, but to *teach students to learn and think.*

I was a conclusion oriented lecturer for thirty years and I am now trying to move toward a style of lecturing that provides a model of cognitive *activity* rather than cognitive results. I believe that most of our lectures should involve analyzing materials, formulating problems, developing hypotheses, bringing evidence to bear, criticizing and evaluating alternative solutions—revealing methods of learning and thinking.

One of the implications of the theoretical approach we have taken is that what is an ideal approach to lecturing early in a course is likely to be inappropriate later in the course. As we noted earlier, the way students process verbal material depends on the structures that not only enable them to process bigger and bigger chunks of subject matter but also give them tacit knowledge of the methods, procedures, and conventions used in the field and by you as a lecturer. For, intentionally or not, you are teaching students how to become more skilled in learning from your lectures.

Because this is so, one should at the outset of a course go more slowly, pause to allow students with poor short term memory to take notes, and give more "everyday" types of examples early in the term. Pausing to write a phrase or sketch a relationship on the blackboard will not only give students a chance to catch up but also provides visual cues that can serve as points of reference later. Later in the term students should be able to process bigger blocks of material more quickly.

▬▬ *Preparing Your Lecture Notes*

One of the security-inducing features of lectures is that one can prepare a lecture with some sense of control over the content and organization of the class period. In lectures the instructor is usually in control, and this sense of controlled structure helps the anxious teacher avoid pure panic.

But no matter how thoroughly one has prepared the subject matter of the lecture, one must still face the problem of how to retrieve and deliver one's insights during the class period. If one has plenty of time and is compulsive, one is tempted to write out the lecture verbatim. Don't! Or if you must (and writing it out may be useful in clarifying your thoughts), don't take a verbatim version into the classroom. Few lecturers can read a lecture so well that students stay awake and interested.

At the same time few teachers can deliver a lecture with no cues at all. Hence you will ordinarily lecture from notes. Most lecturers use an outline or a sequence of cue words and phrases.

Day (1980) has studied lecture notes used by professors at over seventy-five colleges and universities. She notes that extensive notes take the instructor out of eye contact with students so that students fall into a passive, nonquestioning role. Day suggests the use of graphic representations to increase teaching flexibility and spontaneity. Tree diagrams, computer flow charts, or network models enable a teacher to have at hand a representation of the structure that permits one to answer questions without losing track of the relationship of the question to the lecture organization. Pictorial representations using arrows, faces, Venn diagrams, or drawings that symbolize important concepts may not only provide cues for the instructor but can also be placed on the blackboard to provide additional cues for students. Color coding your notes with procedural directions to yourself also helps. I have a tendency to run overtime, so I put time cues in the margin to remind me to check. I also put in directions to myself such as,

- "Put on blackboard."—(usually a key concept or relationship)
- "Ask students for a show of hands."
- "Put students in pairs to discuss this."

You may not feel at home with all of these possibilities, but some experience with hybrids of graphic and verbal cues will probably facilitate your effectiveness as a lecturer. Whatever your system, indicate *signposts* to tell students what is ahead, *transitions* that tell students when you are finishing one topic and moving to the next, *key points* or *concepts*, and *links* such as "consequently," "therefore," and "because."*

---

* These four types of signposts are discussed in the book by George Brown, *Lecturing and Explaining* (London: Methuen, 1979).

■■■■■ *Organization of Lectures*

In thinking about lecture organization, most teachers think first about the structure of the subject matter, then try to organize the content in some logical fashion, such as building from specifics to generalization or deriving specific implication from general principles. Too often we get so immersed in "covering" the subject that we forget to ask, "What do I really want students to remember from this lecture next week, next year?"

Some common organizing principles used by lecturers are: cause to effect; time sequence (for example, stories); parallel organization such as phenomenon to theory to evidence; problem to solution; pro versus con to resolution; familiar to unfamiliar; and concept to application.

Leith (1977) has suggested that different subjects are basically different in the ways in which progress is made in the field. Some subjects are organized in a linear or hierarchical fashion in which one concept builds upon a preceding one. In such subjects one must follow a particular sequence of ideas in order to reach a sophisticated level. Other subjects are organized more nearly in the manner of a spiral or helix in which the path from one level to the next is not linear but rather depends upon accumulating a number of related ideas before the next level can be achieved; and any of the related ideas at one level need not precede other ideas at that level. Still other subjects are organized in the fashion of networks in which one may start at different points of the network and go in various directions. One may build up a network equally well by starting at any one of a number of places and proceeding through a variety of sequences to arrive at comprehension of the subject matter.

The logical structure of one's subject should be one factor determining the lecture organization, but equally important is the cognitive structure in the students' minds. If we are to teach our students effectively, we need to bridge the gap between the structure in the subject matter and structures in the students' minds. As is indicated in all of the chapters in this book, the learner's mind is not *tabula rasa*. The teacher is not making impressions on a blank slate. Rather our task in teaching is to reorganize existing student cognitive structures or to add new dimensions or new features to existing structures. Thus the organization of the lecture needs to take account of the student's existing knowledge and expectations as well as the structure of the subject matter.

The Introduction

One suggestion for organization is that the *introduction* of the lecture should point to a gap in the student's existing cognitive structure or should challenge or raise a question about something in the student's existing method of organizing material in order to arouse curiosity (Berlyne, 1954a,b). There is a good deal of research on the role of prequestions in directing attention to features of written texts. Prequestions in the introduction of a lecture may help students to discriminate between more and less important features of lectures. For example, before a lecture on cognitive changes in aging, I ask, "Do you get more or less intelligent as you get older?"; "What is a fair test of intelligence for older people?" Such questions may also help to create expectations which will enable the students to allocate their information processing capacity more effectively. If students know what they are expected to learn from a lecture, they learn more of that material (sometimes at the expense of other material; Royer, 1977).

Alternatively you may motivate students by beginning with an example, case, or application that indicates the practical relevance of the topic.

Body of the Lecture

In organizing the *body* of the lecture, the most common error is probably that of trying to include too much. As we have stressed throughout this chapter, students' information processing capacities are limited, and a lecturer who is expert in the field is likely to overestimate the students' ability to grasp large blocks of material and to see relationships. An explanation that would be perfect for advanced students may be incomprehensible to beginning students. Lecturers very often overload the students' information processing capacity so that they become less able to understand the material than if fewer points had been presented. David Katz (1950), a pioneer Gestalt psychologist, called this phenomenon "mental dazzle." He suggested that just as too much light causes our eyes to be dazzled so that we cannot see anything, so too can too many new ideas overload processing capacity so that we cannot understand anything. If the lecture involves a number of abstract concepts, begin to develop them with concrete examples.

It seems likely that students will differ in their ability to benefit from particular kinds of sequences. As Greeno and his colleagues have shown (Larkin, Heller, and Greeno, 1980), some students do better when they are given a sequence of generalizations first and specific drill and practice sequences second, while other students do better when the specifics lead to generalizations.

Use the blackboard or an overhead projector to give the students cues to the organization of the lecture. Placing a skeletal outline (or sequence of questions) on the blackboard before the lecture may help; going to the blackboard to construct an outline, fill in the skeleton, or simply to write key words is useful in three ways.

1. It gives a *visual* representation to supplement your oral presentation.

2. Movement (change) helps retain (or regain) attention.

3. It gives students a chance to catch up with what you've said (perchance to think!).

Whatever the structure one uses, it is clear from research that highlighting the structure and giving students cues to the nature of organization that one is using is helpful to many students, particularly those who are lower in intelligence or more anxious (Snow and Peterson, 1980). Davis's studies of outstanding lectures (1976) indicated that professors known as outstanding lecturers did two things; they used a simple plan and many examples.

Periodic Summaries Within the Lecture

From our knowledge of students' note-taking behavior and from our theory of information processing, it seems likely that students would be better able to learn from lectures if there were periodic summaries of preceding material. These give students a chance to catch up on material covered when they were not tuned in and also give them a check upon possible misperceptions based upon inadequate or misleading expectations. Moreover, such summaries can help make clear to students transitions from one theme to another so that they are aided in organizing the material not only in their notes but in their minds.

Probably one of the greatest barriers to effective lecturing is the feeling that one must cover the material at all costs. Although it may seem irrational to cover material when students are not learning from it, one should not underestimate the compulsion one feels to get through one's lecture notes. A remedy for this compulsion is to put into the lecture notes reminders to oneself to check the students' understanding—both by looking for nonverbal cues of bewilderment or of lack of attention and by raising specific questions that will test the students' understanding.

The Conclusion

In the conclusion of the lecture, one has the opportunity to make up for lapses in the body of the lecture. Encouraging students to formulate questions or asking questions oneself can facilitate understanding and memory. By making the oral headings visible once again, by recapitulating major points, by proposing unanswered questions to be treated in the reading assignments or the future lectures, and by creating an anticipation of the future, the lecturer can help students learn. One good (and humbling) technique is to announce that you will ask a student to summarize the lecture at the end of the period. Another—less threatening—is to have students spend three minutes writing a summary of main points. Either method helps the process of elaboration that is critical for memory. Having suggested all this, I must admit that my own greatest problem as a lecturer is that I never seem to be ready for the conclusion until it is already past time to dismiss the class.

How to Get Students Actively Thinking in a Lecture Situation

As we have seen, a major problem with the lecture is that students assume a passive, non-thinking, information receiving role. Yet, if they are to remember and use the information, they need to be actively engaged in thinking about the content presented. One easy and effective device is the "minute paper." The minute paper is, as its title indicates, a paper literally written in a minute (or it can be a two-minute or three-minute paper). Announce at the beginning of the class period that you will interrupt your lecture midway through the period so that the students may write a one-minute paper on a topic derived from the lecture.

In addition to the large group discussion and subgrouping techniques discussed in Chapters 4 and 13, you can liven up your classes with classroom debates either between faculty members or between student teams.

If you use student debaters, you will need to provide a clear structure, probably through a handout describing the problem, the length of talks, opportunity for rebuttal, and purpose of the debate as a learning device. How are the debaters chosen? One option is to divide the class into six- to eight-person teams who prepare their arguments and evidence and choose one or more representatives to participate in the debate. Another technique is to form smaller teams to prepare together to present either side and to choose the debaters for each side randomly. (I like to allow time for coaching by the team before the rebuttal.)

Whatever the method, you ordinarily will want to end with a discussion of the complexity of the issue, the fact that there are pros and cons for each position, and perhaps that a resolution may be found other than a decision for one position and against the other.

Lecture and Discussion

Lecture has often been compared in effectiveness with discussion. Since discussion offers the opportunity for a good deal of student activity and feedback, it could, according to theory, be more effective than lecture in developing concepts and problem-solving skills. However, because the rate of transmission of information is slow in discussion classes, I would expect lecture classes to be superior in attaining the objective of teaching knowledge.

What this adds up to is the use of lecture for communicating information and modeling problem solving and discussion for practicing problem-solving skills. One way of doing this is to schedule separate lecture and discussion periods. Another is to incorporate both discussion and lecture in the same class period.

◼ *Distribution of Lecture and Discussion Time*

Many universities and large colleges use a method of distributing class meetings between lectures and discussions. This administrative arrangement is supported by a study in the teaching of psychology in which discussion meetings were substituted for one-third of the lectures (Lifson et al., 1956). There were no significant differences in achievement. However, the partial discussion method, as compared with the all lecture method, resulted in more favorable student attitudes that persisted in a follow-up study two years later.

Warren (1954) compared the effectiveness of one lecture and four recitations to two lectures and three demonstrations per week. In one out of five comparisons the four-recitations plan was superior while the other comparisons found nonsignificant differences. Superior students tended to prefer the two-lecture plan while poorer students did not. On the other hand, in Remmers's comparison (1933) of two lectures and one recitation vs. three recitations, the poorer students tended to do better in the lecture-recitation combination. Students preferred the all-recitation classes. In Klapper's study (1958), most NYU students preferred a combination lecture-discussion method to all lectures or all discussions. Iowa students preferred all group discussion or a combination of lecture and discussion to lectures alone (Becker et al., 1958).

In a course in which the instructors must not only give information but also develop concepts, the use of both lectures and discussions would thus seem to be a logical and popular choice.

Sometimes you will be unable to schedule separate small group discussions. Do not despair. Discussion is possible in large groups. As we shall see in Chapter 21 there are many practical methods for achieving the advantages of discussion in large groups.

■■■■ *The Lecturer: A Summary*

What is the role of the lecturer in higher education? The lecture is sometimes an effective way of communicating information, particularly in classes where variations in student background, ability, or interest make feedback to the lecturer important. We have also shown that the organization and presentation of lectures may influence their effectiveness in achieving application of knowledge or in influencing attitudes. Discussion, however, may be more effective than lecturing in achieving some of the higher level cognitive and attitudinal objectives.

Good lecturers probably do intuitively many of the things we have suggested. Becoming conscious of what is going on in the students' heads as we talk, being alert to feedback from students through their facial expressions, nonverbal behavior, or oral comments, adjusting one's strategies in reference to these cues—these will help the lecturer learn and help students to learn from the lecturer more effectively.

SUPPLEMENTARY READING

A very practical guide for lecturers is George Brown's handy paperback, *Lecturing and Explaining* (London: Methuen, 1980).

CHAPTER 6

Tests and Examinations

MOST INSTRUCTORS IN COLLEGES with traditional grading systems deplore the emphasis students place upon getting a good grade. Usually instructors attempt to minimize this aspect of the course by stating that the important thing is what the students learn, not what grade they make. While such words may be accepted intellectually, motivationally the grade remains the most important aspect of the course for most students. Since grades in large courses are determined to a great degree by test scores, tests are among the most frustrating aspects of the course to many students, and arouse a great deal of overt and covert aggression. If teachers attempt to go beyond the usual practice of asking simply for memory of information from the textbook or lectures, they are immediately deluged with the complaint, "These are the most ambiguous tests I have ever taken!"

▅▅▅ Reducing Student Aggression

To most beginning teachers the aggression that students direct against them after a test is very disturbing. It is likely to impair the rapport of the instructor with the class and may actually be a block to learning. Hence, devices for reducing the aggression seem to be worthwhile.

The most obvious solution to the problem is to reduce the frustration involved in taking tests. An aid in this area is to emphasize the contribution the course can make to the long-range goals of the students, so that the need of a good grade is not the only one involved in the situation. Emphasizing the educational and diagnostic value of tests is one application of this principle. Yet, no matter how much the instructor emphasizes long-range goals, the tests are going, in a large measure, to determine the student's goals. Do you want the students to memorize details? Then give the usual memory-of-details test.

The first step in constructing a test is to list your goals for the course. Not all goals can be measured by a test. (New attitudes and interests, for example, are not measured by classroom achievement tests.) Once you have specified objectives you can determine how many test items embody each category of objective. You'll probably be surprised to find out how many of your test items pile up in certain categories.

One way of helping to maintain a balance is to construct a grid, listing objectives along the side of the page and content areas along the top. If you then tally items as you write them, you can monitor the degree to which your test adequately samples the objectives and content desired.

Because some course examinations emphasize recall of facts, many students demand *teaching* that emphasizes memorization of facts. One student wrote on a slip evaluating me, "The instructor is very interesting and worthwhile, but I have rated him low because he doesn't give us enough facts. The sort of job I get will depend on my grades, and I have little chance of beating other students out for an A unless I can get a couple of pages of notes each period."

Students may object at first to tests requiring them to think, but if you emphasize that the tests will measure the students' abilities to use their knowledge, you can greatly influence their goals in the course. This is indicated by a student comment we received: "More of the course should be like the tests. They make us apply what we've learned." Marton and Säljö (1976b) showed that questions demanding understanding rather than memory of detailed facts resulted in differing styles of studying for later tests and better retention. Foos and Fisher (1988) showed that tests requiring inferences enhanced learning more than those requiring memorized knowledge.

Admittedly it is more difficult to devise measures of the more complex, higher-level objectives. Yet the very effort to do so will, I believe, have an influence on student motivation and learning. Moreover, consideration of these objectives may help you break out of the conventional forms of testing. For example, in my classes in introductory psychology, the desired goals include developing greater curiosity about behavior, awareness of dimensions of behavior that might ordinarily be ignored, and increased ability to describe and analyze behavior objectively. To get at this I have sometimes used a film or videotape as a stimulus, with the test questions having to do with the students' reactions to the film; or I have asked students to leave the classroom for fifteen minutes and then return and report on some interesting behavior they have observed. I have brought in collections of journals and asked students to find an article of interest and to write their reactions to it. I have asked for analyses of newspaper items to get at the degree to which students can read critically. Using materials with somewhat greater apparent relevance to course objectives than typical test items is more fun for the students taking the test—and more fun to grade.

■■■■ *When to Test*

Because tests are so important in operationalizing goals and influencing student methods of learning, I give an ungraded quiz during the first week and a graded test after the third or fourth week of a fourteen-week semester. To reduce the stress I weight early tests very little in determining the final grade. But an early test gets students started, in that they don't delay their studying until the conventional midterm examination, and it will help you to identify problems early while they are still remediable. Thus, early tests should demand the style of learning you expect and need to be constructed carefully, even though their purpose is more motivational and diagnostic than evaluative.

I usually also give midterm and final examinations, but the amount and frequency of tests should depend upon the background of your students. In a first-year course in an area new to students, frequent short tests early in the term facilitate learning, as demonstrated in the Personalized System of Instruction

(Keller, 1968). Generally, however, I want to wean students from studying for tests, so that they become lifelong learners who will be able to evaluate their own learning. This implies less frequent testing as learners become more experienced. It probably also implies questions requiring broader integration and more detailed analysis as the learners advance. For this reason my tests are all cumulative; that is, they cover material previously tested as well as material learned since the last test.

■■■■ *Test Construction*

This is not the place to engage in an extended discussion of test-construction theory. However, let me confess that from the students' point of view, tests and marks are frequently the most important part of the instructor's job. Because of this, these topics deserve some consideration.

Choosing the Type of Question

The instructor who is about to give an examination is in a conflict situation. There are two time-consuming procedures involved in the administration of an examination: the first is the construction of the examination; the second is the grading. Unfortunately, it appears to be generally true that the examinations that are easiest to construct are the most difficult to grade and vice versa. Essay examinations that can be made up in a few minutes require hours to grade. Multiple-choice examinations, which can be constructed by an experienced item builder at the rate of three to five items an hour, can be corrected at the rate of about twenty to thirty seconds for a sixty-item test. Short-answer examinations fall somewhere between these two extremes.

Teachers often choose questions solely in terms of class size, using multiple-choice tests for large classes, short-answer questions for medium-sized classes, and essay questions for small classes. Class size is obviously an important factor, but I urge that your educational goals take precedence. This almost always implies use of some essay questions, problems, or other items requiring analysis, integration, or application.

PROBLEMS   In mathematics, science, and some other disciplines a test typically consists of problems. The value of problems depends upon the degree to which they elicit the sort of problem-solving skills that are your goals. Some problems are too trite and stereotypic to have much value as indicators of whether or not students understand the steps they are following. In other cases the answer depends to such a large extent on tedious calculations that only a small sample of problems can be tested. In such cases you might provide calculations leading up to a certain point and ask the student to complete the problem or you might use a multiple-choice question about the proper procedure, for example, "Which of the following problems can be solved by procedure 'x'?"

SHORT-ANSWER TESTS   An example of a short-answer item might be this: "Give one example from your own experience of the concept of elaboration." In responding, a student might describe an experience in explaining a concept to another student or in thinking of the relationship of a fact to a general principle.

Such a question is restricted enough that it is not often difficult to judge whether the expected answer is there. Furthermore, such questions can be presented in a format that allows only a small amount of space for the answer. The student's tendency to employ the "shotgun" approach to the examination is thus inhibited. Short-answer questions permit coverage of assigned materials without asking for petty details. Unfortunately, many short-answer questions test only recall of specific facts.

Short-answer questions can get at other than informational outcomes. If you are trying to develop skill in analysis or diagnosis, for example, you may present case material or description of an experiment and ask the students what questions they would ask. You can then provide additional information that the students can use in an analysis. Or a short-answer question can ask students to solve a problem or propose a hypothesis relevant to information learned earlier. An example is the following question from a course on the psychology of aging:

1. Given the *differences* in ways in which men and women experience middle age, and the fact that depression rises as a psychiatric symptom in middle age, how might the *causes* of the depression differ for men and women at this time in life?

ESSAY TESTS   Although the short-answer examination is very useful in certain situations, I would recommend that, if possible, you include at least one essay question on examinations in most college courses. Experiments indicate that students study more efficiently for essay-type examinations than for objective tests (Monaco, 1977; McClusky, 1934; d'Ydewalle et al., 1983).

Thus in addition to the values of essay tests as evaluation devices, you should also take into consideration their potential educational value. Particularly where the tests can be returned with comments, essay examinations may give students practice in organized, creative thinking about a subject and an opportunity to check their thinking against the standards of someone with more experience and ability in the field. Moreover, they may, as we suggested earlier, orient students to work toward objectives beyond memorization of details. Johnson (1975) demonstrated that when marginal comments on earlier tests emphasized creativity, creativity on the final exam was improved.

Finally, if you read the examinations yourself (or at least some of them), you get some excellent information on what students are learning. While the teacher can also learn from students' responses to objective tests, the impact on the teacher of what students are learning seems to be greater and more vivid in reading essay tests.

TRUE-FALSE TESTS   Although true-false examinations are rather easy to make up, I'm not sure what they measure, and don't ordinarily advocate their use. This is partly a concession to student opinion. Students can usually figure out reasons why any particular item can be either true or false. However, Paul Fields has developed a number of methods of linking true-false items and associations that require more thought and are liked by students (Sax, 1991).

MULTIPLE-CHOICE TESTS   It is improbable that most teachers can adequately measure all their objectives with a test made up entirely of multiple-choice questions. Nonetheless, for some purposes multiple-choice items are useful. They can measure both simple knowledge and precise discrimination. Items need not be entirely verbal. Louis Berman of the University of Illinois, Chicago, has worked out a number of items using cartoons, sketches, graphs, and diagrams, which students feel are more interesting than all-verbal questions. Some students with low verbal ability do better on these questions than on the usual ones.

Good multiple-choice questions are difficult to construct. (As a matter of fact, the greater your experience in their construction, the more you realize how long it takes per item to construct a reasonably fair, accurate, and inclusive question.) Because of this difficulty, the construction of such items is probably not worthwhile unless they will be administered to several hundred students, either in a single year or in successive years. Here are some hints for their construction.

1. Teachers' manuals that are provided for many textbooks contain multiple-choice items—some good, some not so good. You will not be able to rely on a manual as the source of all your questions, because it will not often contain enough good questions.

2. A second source of such items is the **students themselves.** This is not a particularly satisfactory source of test questions because only about 10 percent of the items thus received will be usable. They are typically from obscure passages in reading materials; where they are not, they are apt to be duplicated by many students. However, this technique is a rather successful pedagogical device because it gets the students to read their assignment more analytically. It also gives the instructor a good index of what the students are getting out of the various sections of their reading and gives you a chance to remind them of the goals of the course going beyond memory of details.

3. There are statistical methods for evaluating questions, but I have found that the best suggestions for improvement came from students themselves in their discussion of the test. It seems almost criminal to waste this experience with it, therefore I recommend a permanent file. I have kept it

5" × 8" file cards, one item per card; now a computer provides even more flexible storage.

4. If you have a problem, but no good distractor (incorrect alternative), give the item in short-answer or essay form and use the students' own responses for alternatives for a later use of the item in multiple-choice form.

5. Multiple-choice questions typically have four or five alternatives. Rather than wasting your, and your students', time with extra alternatives that don't test a discrimination that is important, use only as many alternatives as you can construct making meaningful discriminations. Costin (1972) has shown that three-choice items are about as effective as four-choice.

6. For measuring understanding, I like questions that require the student to predict the outcome of a situation rather than those that simply ask the student to label the phenomenon.

7. Multiple-choice items need not stand alone. You can use a sequence of related items to measure more complex thinking.

8. General rules.
   a. The item as a whole should present a problem of significance in the subject-matter field.
   b. The item as a whole should deal with an important aspect of the subject-matter field, not with a minor element that is of significance only to the expert.
   c. The item as a whole should be phrased in language appropriate to the subject-matter field.
   d. Items that attempt to measure understanding should include an element of novelty, but too much novelty is likely to make the problem too hard.

9. Rules for stating the problem.
   a. There must be a single central problem.
   b. The problem should be stated briefly but completely; the problem should not test the student's ability to under-

stand complex sentence structure except when the teacher is deliberately measuring that ability.

c. The problem should be stated in a positive, not a negative, form. Somehow, even intelligent adults often fail to see a "not" in reading a sentence. If you must use "not," underline it.

d. It should be possible to understand the problem without reading the alternatives.

e. Generally speaking, the test is more interesting if the questions are worded in concrete rather than abstract terms. Such items are particularly worthwhile if you wish to measure ability of the student to apply concepts to concrete situations.

10. Rules for developing the suggested solutions.

a. The suggested wrong answers should represent errors commonly made by the students being tested, not popular misconceptions among the public at large.

b. The right answer should be unquestionably right, checked by two or three independent experts.

c. The suggested answers should be as brief as possible.

d. The position of the right answers should be scattered.

e. Numerical answers should be placed in numerical order.

f. Even wrong alternatives should not contain words unfamiliar to students.

g. Use "All of the above" and "None of the above" rarely. Usually they are tossed in when you can't think of another good distractor.

h. The right answer should not be given away by irrelevant clues. A few examples of commonly occurring irrelevant clues are: 1) alternatives that include absolute terms such as "always" and "never" are rarely right answers, 2) alternatives that are longer and more elaborate than the others are frequently right answers, 3) if the lead of the item is an incomplete statement, then alternatives that do not complete it grammatically are obviously wrong.*

Even if you don't pretest the item on students, it is worthwhile to have someone take the test before it is in its final form. If you can persuade a skilled test-taker who doesn't know the subject matter to take the test, you will probably be surprised at how many he or she gets right simply from cues you've provided in the questions.

How Many Questions Should I Use?

Obviously the number of questions depends upon the type and difficulty of each question. I prefer to give tests without a time limit, but the constraints of class scheduling usually require that you clear the classroom so that the next class can begin. Thus, you must plan the length of the exam so that even the slower students have time to finish before the end of the period. As a rule of thumb I allow about a minute per item for multiple-choice or fill-in-the-blank items, two minutes per short-answer question requiring more than a sentence answer, ten or fifteen minutes for a limited essay question, and a half-hour to an hour for a broader question requiring more than a page or two to answer.

▬ *Alternatives to Conventional Tests*

As teachers have become more aware of the importance of testing and evaluation in influencing learning and retention, they have given more thought to the importance of encouraging generalization of learning to out-of-class situations. This leads to consideration of other assessment devices such as simulations (either role-played or on computers); hands-on laboratory or field exercises; projects; "take-home" tests; juried presentations such as those used in music, art, or architecture schools; and paper and pencil or computer devices in nonconventional formats, such as similarity judgments, graphic sorting tasks, representations of concep-

---

* Many of the foregoing rules are derived directly or indirectly from notes taken in the "Test Construction" class of Dr. R. M. W. Travers. For a more detailed exposition, see his book, *How to Make Achievement Tests* (New York: Odyssey Press, 1950), which is still an excellent source.

tual relationships, or sequences of choices to analyze a case, solve a problem, or reach a conclusion when there is no single right answer or algorithm. Since well-learned, automated conceptual structures can be retrieved more rapidly than those less well-learned, one might give students a task producing as large a number of related concepts as they can in a limited time using a word, diagram, example, or picture as a stimulus.

Instructions to the Students

The test instructions should indicate whether or not students are to guess, what the time limit is, and any other directions that define the nature of the expected responses. Emphasizing in the multiple-choice test introduction that the students should choose the *best* answer may help prevent lengthy discussion with the student who can dream up a remote instance in which the correct alternative might be wrong.

In taking a multiple-choice examination, the student has a right to know whether there is a penalty for guessing. For the typical classroom examination, there is no point in a correction for guessing.

Helping Students Become Test-Wise

Particularly in the case of multiple-choice examinations, I have found that a good morale builder is spending fifteen minutes or so the day before the first test telling students how to take a test of this sort.

Some of the points that I make in such a lecture follow.

TAKING MULTIPLE-CHOICE TESTS   Here are some helpful tips.

The student taking a multiple-choice examination is essentially in the same position as a poker player. The object is to get into a position where you are betting on a sure thing. If this is impossible, at least make your bet on the choice where the odds are in your favor. In poker, you are obviously in the strongest position if you know exactly what the opponent has; and in the examination situation, you are also in

the strongest position if you know the material. There is no
substitute for study. At the same time, it is unlikely that you
will be absolutely certain of all the right answers. In these
cases certain techniques may help.

What I recommend (to the student) is this: Go through
the examination a first time and answer all of the items you
know. In addition to getting a certain amount of the examination done without wasting too much time on single, difficult items, it is frequently true that going through the
complete test once in this way will suggest the answers to
questions that might have been difficult had they been
answered in serial order. When you have gone through the
test once in this fashion, go through it again and answer any
questions that are now obvious. There will still usually
remain a few questions that have been left unanswered. It is
in connection with these that certain tricks may be useful.

First of all, if the item is multiple choice, do not simply
guess at this stage of the game. See whether or not it is possible to eliminate some of the choices as incorrect. In a four-
choice, multiple-choice item, the probabilities of getting the
answer right by pure guesswork are one in four; if you can
eliminate two of them, your chances are fifty-fifty. So take
advantage of the mathematics of the situation.

Once some of the answers are eliminated, there are still
better ways of answering the questions than pure guesswork. One of these is to choose the answer that you first
thought was right. A second is to choose one of the middle
alternatives. If you have no notion at all as to the right
answer, and if the "b" or "2" choice is one of the possibilities, use it. There are two reasons for this advice: 1) it gives
you a rule of thumb by which you can answer all highly
doubtful items, thus eliminating anxiety-building, trial-and-
error behavior, and 2) it takes into account instructor behavior in constructing items.

When instructors set out to make up a multiple-choice
item, they usually have 1) a bit of information for which they
want to test, 2) a notion as to what is the right answer, and 3)
one or more "seductive" alternatives. The tendency is, in

listing choices, to make the first choice one of the seductive alternatives, the second choice the right answer, and the remaining choices anything else that they can think of. Most instructors have a feeling that the right answer sticks out if it is first or last. Hence the correct answer on instructor-made tests tends to be in the middle.

Once the examination has been answered completely, it is a good idea to go through the whole thing again to check your choices on the various items to make sure that they are the ones you still regard as correct and to make sure that you have made no clerical errors in recording them on the separate answer sheets. In this connection, it is worthwhile to point out the common misconception that, when you change your answers, you usually change from right answers to wrong ones. As a matter of fact Mueller and Wasser (1977) reviewed eighteen studies demonstrating that most students gain more than they lose on changed answers.

TAKING ESSAY TESTS   My instructions for essay exams are simpler. They include the following:

Outline your answer before writing it. This provides a check against the common error of omitting completely one part of the answer. If a question completely baffles you, start writing on the back of your paper anything you know that could possibly be relevant. This starts your memory functioning and usually you'll soon find that you have some relevant ideas. If you are still at a loss, admit it and write a question you can answer and answer it. Most instructors will give you at least a few points more than if you wrote nothing.

Some will perhaps want to question whether it is wise to give away the secret of examination construction the way I am doing in this discussion. The answer to this question depends upon your purposes in giving the examination. If you want to test for "test-taking" ability, you will not want to give the students these hints. At any rate, this orientation seems to have the effect of giving the students the notion that you are not out to "outsmart" them, but that you are interested in helping them get as high a grade as their learning warrants. In this connection, it is a good idea to point out to the class that the instructor is not out to trick the student through the use of various kinds of sophistry in the examination, and that ordinarily the answer that they think is the right one will be the right one.

I also warn students that their grade will be affected by their writing. Even if I intended not to grade on writing ability, my judgment is negatively influenced when I have to struggle to read poor handwriting or surmount poor grammar and sentence structure. Moreover, since I believe that every course is responsible for teaching writing, writing will enter into grading. It is amazing to me that when I forget to mention writing, the essays are much less readable than when I announce that writing counts. Apparently my students can spell, punctuate, and write clearly if they need to, but don't bother if it isn't expected.

Research by McKeachie, Pollie, and Speisman (1955) and by Smith and Rockett (1958) has demonstrated that on multiple-choice tests the instruction "Feel free to write comments" with blank space by each question for the comments results in higher scores, especially for anxious students.

Another technique I have tried is to permit students to bring a file card to class with as much information as they could cram onto it. This didn't seem to reduce anxiety, but it probably helped their test preparation.

▰▰▰ *Administering the Test*

Handing out a test should be a simple matter. Usually it is, but in large classes, simple administrative matters can become disasters. It is hard to imagine how angry and upset students can become while waiting only ten minutes for the proctors to finish distributing the test forms. And if this doesn't move you, imagine your feelings when you find that you don't have enough tests for all of the students. (It has happened to me twice—deserving a place among my worst moments in teaching!)

How can you avoid such problems?

1. If you are having tests duplicated, ask for at least 10 percent extra—more if the test is administered in several rooms. (Some proctor always walks off with too many.) This gives you insurance against miscounting and against omitted or blank pages on some copies.

2. Unless there is some compelling reason to distribute the tests later, have your proctors pass out the tests as students come in the room. This protects students from mounting waves of panic while they wait for the test to be distributed.

3. Minimize interruptions. Tell students before the exam that you will write announcements, instructions, or corrections on the blackboard. Some exam periods are less a measure of achievement than a test of the students' ability to work despite the instructor's interruptions.

Grading Essay Questions

I recommend that you use essay questions because of their powerful effect upon the way students study, but there is a drawback. Instructors don't grade essay tests very reliably.

One of the problems is that standards vary. First papers are graded differently than later papers; a paper graded immediately after several poor papers is graded differently from one graded after several good papers.

There are seven procedures you can initiate to improve your evaluation of essay examinations—but they entail work.

1. Read all or several of the examinations in a preliminary fashion to establish some notion of the general level of performance.

2. Write (or choose after reading several papers) models of excellent, good, adequate, and poor papers to which you can refer to refresh your memory of the standards by which you are grading. This technique is particularly useful if an assistant is helping to grade or if grading is carried out over a period of time.

3. Establish a set of grading criteria. One of the problems in using essay exams and in assigning term papers is that students feel that the grading represents some mysterious, unfathomable bias. The more that you can write helpful comments on the paper, the more the mystery is dispelled. (I say more about this in Chapter 9, "Writing: Papers, Journals, and Reports.")

   Both for your own guidance and that of the students, develop a set of criteria. Having identified papers of differing levels of excellence, compare them to determine what the distinguishing features were.

4. Give a global grade—not several subgrades which are summed. Your overall impression is likely to be more reliable than the sum of grades on such elements as content, organization, originality, etc. Don't simply give points for each concept or fact mentioned. This simply converts the essay into a recall test rather than measuring higher-level goals of integration and evaluation.

5. Read essay exams without knowledge of the name of the writer.

6. Develop a code for common comments. For example, you might want to use a vertical line alongside paragraphs that are particularly good or "NFD" for "Needs Further Development."

7. Do your grading in teams. My teaching assistants and I gather after administering a test. We bring in draft model answers for each question. We discuss what we expect as answers on each question. We then establish two- to three-person teams for each essay question. Each team then picks eight to twelve test papers, and these are circulated among the team members, with each team member noting privately his or her grade for the question. The team then compares grades and discusses discrepancies until they have reached consensus. A second group of tests is then graded in the same way

with grades compared and discrepancies discussed. This procedure continues until the team is confident that they have arrived at common criteria. From this point on, each member grades independently. When a team member is not sure how to grade a paper, it is passed to another team member for an opinion.

We stay with the grading until all the papers are done, but we make a party of it to alleviate fatigue and boredom. Funny answers are read aloud. Sandwiches are brought in from a delicatessen. Teams help other teams for a change of pace or to balance the workload.

Grading papers is still time-consuming but does not become the sort of aversive task which makes for procrastination and long delays in providing feedback to students.

Helping Students Learn from the Test

The most important function of testing is *not* to provide a basis for grading. Rather tests are an important educational tool. Not only do they direct students' studying, but they can provide important corrective feedback. The comments written on essay tests are far more important than the grade.*

What kind of comments are helpful? First of all rid yourself of the usual teacher's notion that most inadequacies are due to a lack of knowledge so that improvement rests simply on supplying the missing knowledge. Rather we need to look for cues that will help us identify the students' structures of representation of knowledge. Usually the students' problems arise from a lack of ability to see relationships, implications, or applications of material. There is always some discrepancy between the structure of knowledge in the student's mind and that in the instructor's. Students construct their own knowledge based on their individual past experiences and their experiences in the course. Thus comments on essay items are more likely to be helpful if they help students find alternative ways of looking at the problem rather than simply noting that something is wrong.

---

* This holds true except for the final course examination. In my experience few do more than look at the grade on a final examination.

Comments that provide correction and guidance may not achieve their purpose if students become so discouraged that they give up. Thus the motivational as well as the cognitive aspects of comments need to be considered. Misconceptions need to be identified, but not in overwhelming number. Encouragement and guidance for improvement should set the overall tone. Feedback that helps students see their progress helps build self-efficacy and motivation for further learning.

Helping Yourself Learn from the Test

Often we get so wrapped up in the pure mechanics of correcting and grading tests that we overlook the fact that measures of student performance not only can diagnose student weaknesses but also can reveal areas in which our teaching has failed to achieve its purposes. Once you've achieved some ease with the grading process look back at the papers to see what they reveal about problems in student understanding. There may be some things about which the entire class seems a bit shaky; in addition there may be areas of difficulty experienced by certain sub-groups of students—perhaps those with background knowledge or experience different from the rest of the class. In short think about what *you* need to do as well as about what the *students* need to do.

▬ *Grading "on the curve"*: Don't Do It!*

The papers have been corrected, errors noted, comments written, but now you have to worry about grading. I'll have more to say about grading in Chapter 8, but for the moment let's consider grades given on a test when you are expected to convert a number of points into a letter grade such as A, B, C, D, or F.

Grading based upon *relative* achievement in a given group may encourage an undesirably high degree of competition. Despite the absence of absolute standards in any very objective

---

* Grading "on the curve" means to assign grades on the basis of how each student compares with other students who took the test rather than on the basis of the degree to which the student has achieved some standard of performance. For example, in grading on the curve one might give the top 10% of the scores A's, the next 25% B's, the next 35% C's, the next 20% D's, and the bottom 10% F's.

sense, I believe that attempts to avoid competitive grading systems are worthwhile. Grading on the curve stacks the cards against cooperative learning because helping classmates may lower one's own grade.

The problem of grading "on the curve" seems to arouse the most heated discussion around standards for assigning failing grades. Logically, it would seem that an instructor should be able to designate some minimal essentials, mastery of which would be necessary for a passing grade. Keller Plan courses, programmed courses, and contract courses typically specify mastery of certain materials. As I shall show in Chapter 8, so-called mastery grading has some pitfalls, but at least some attempt to get away from strict "grading on the curve" is likely to be helpful for class morale.

I tell my students that I'll grade in terms of percentage of a possible score. Thus if a test has 150 possible points, I say:

> If you make 140 or over (93% +), I'll guarantee an A
> 135 to 139 (90% +) A–
> 131 to 134 (87% +) B+
> 125 to 130 (83% +) B
> 120 to 124 (80% +) B–, etc.
> If everyone gets over 140 points, everyone will get an A, and
> I'll be very pleased if you all do well.

I tell the students that I may grade more generously than the standards I have announced but will promise not to be tougher than announced. As it turns out, my distribution of grades has not turned out to be more generous than that of my colleagues—which may indicate that I'm not teaching as effectively as I'd like.

My "percentage of possible points" system is fairly easy to apply but lacks the educational value of criteria or standards tied more directly to course goals. Royce Sadler (1987) describes the use of exemplars and verbal descriptions of quality to set standards for grading.

▬▬ *Returning Test Papers*

Remember that tests are important tools for learning and discussion of the test is worthwhile use of class time. You don't need to discuss every question, but where there are common errors, try to find out why the error occurred and suggest strategies for avoiding such problems in the future. (See Schultz and Weinstein, 1990.)

Students like to have their examinations back. In the case of multiple-choice examinations developed through a considerable amount of hard work, you may not want to let them have them, because you may want to use the items another year. But you can do this: Return separate answer sheets so that your marking and arithmetic can be checked. Allow the students to have copies of the examination while you go through the test. If you do these things, certain questions arise. Does such a procedure destroy the validity of the item in future tests? Does the student profit from such experience? These are experimental questions to which we have only partial answers, but evidence suggests that validity is not lost and that students do learn from their corrected papers (McClusky, 1934). Although you may not wish to spend class time quibbling over some individual items, you should make known your willingness to discuss the test individually with students who have further questions.

Some instructors return exams with only the total score indicated. They then invite students to retake the exam after consulting reference materials or after discussing the exam with peers (Murray, 1990). The student may then gain partial additional credit for improvement. Such a procedure should enhance learning.

On questions that many students missed, I recommend this sort of procedure:

> When you read a particular question, do not merely read the
> stem of the question or answer the question with the correct
> choice. Instead, read the stem and each of the choices. For
> each of the incorrect choices give your reasons for regarding
> it as incorrect.

This procedure gives you the "jump" on the chronic criticizer. It is more difficult to maintain that a given choice is right under these circumstances than it would be if you had said nothing about the various alternatives and students could argue that the correct alternative was not completely correct. But there will be cases in which a legitimate argument arises. If some ambiguities have gotten through the screening process, and an item is really capable of two equally correct interpretations, admit it and change scores. But remember that you can't escape aggression simply by changing scores, because every time you admit a new right answer, the students who originally had the question right are likely to feel injured.

Accepting students' suggestions for better wording of items reduces their aggressiveness. You can prevent some aggression from being directed against yourself if you have items explained by the students who got them right. However, you should not call upon the same student to explain every difficult question or you may simply be substituting another scapegoat for yourself.

For essay tests I try to describe what we expected in a good answer and the most common inadequacies. I may read an example of a good answer (without identifying the student), and I might construct a synthetic poor answer to contrast with the good one.

One of the techniques for returning tests that seems to reduce much aggression was, I believe, first used in the classes of Dr. N. R. F. Maier. Instructors using this technique break the class into small groups of five to eight students for discussion of the test. Each group discusses the test for part of the class period. When they have finished, unresolved questions are referred to the instructor as the expert. This method seems to permit dissipation of the aggressions aroused and limit arguments to points where there are several aggrieved students.

What about the student who comes to your office in great anger or with a desperate appeal for sympathy but with no educationally valid reason for changing the test grade? First of all, listen. Engaging in a debate will simply prolong the unpleasantness. Ask the student, "Tell me more about how you were thinking as you went about answering the question." Once you have heard the student out, if you have decided not to change the grade, try to convert the discussion from one of stonewall resistance to problem solving. Try to help the student find alternative modes of study that will produce better results. "What can we do to help you do better next time?" Encourage the student to shift from blaming you or the test toward motivation to work more effectively.

But there is a technique that will reduce the number of students coming into your office in a state of high emotion. My colleague Deborah Keller-Cohen asks students coming to see her with complaints about grades to write a paragraph describing their complaint or point-of-view. She declares her willingness to go over the test of anyone who brings in such a paragraph, noting that she may change the grade either positively or negatively. She reports that this technique has a calming effect, resulting in fewer unfounded complaints and more rational discussion with those who do come in.

While these suggestions may save the instructor some bitter moments, they cannot substitute for the time (and it takes lots) devoted to the construction of good tests.

▰▰▰ *What Do You Do About the Student Who Missed the Test?*

In any large class some students are absent from the test. Their excuses vary from very legitimate to very suspicious, but making that discrimination is not always easy. The usual solution is to offer a make-up test.

Make-up tests can involve a good deal of extra work for the instructor. If you devise a new test, you may have trouble assigning a norm with which to grade the make-up comparable to grades on the original test. If you use the same test that the students have missed, you cannot tell how much the student has learned about the test from students who took it at the scheduled time. Hence, I don't usually give make-ups except for the final exam. I simply use marks from the tests the student did take to determine the grade, counting the missed test neither for nor against the student. Most students are happy not to have to make up a test, but I encourage them to take the test for practice.

■ *Retesting*

Covington and Omelich (1984) carried out a well-designed experiment showing that providing an opportunity to take a second test on the same material not only improved performance but also had favorable effects upon motivation. Failing twice is not conducive to heightened motivation, but even students with low self-confidence benefited if they showed improvement on the retest.

SUPPLEMENTARY READING

N. E. Gronlund and R. L. Linn, *Measurement and Evaluation in Teaching* (New York: Macmillan, 1990) has six chapters on constructing classroom tests with good advice on constructing both objective and essay tests.

Terry Crooks wrote an excellent review of research on the effects of questioning, testing, and feedback on student learning and motivation. His recommendations for teachers are sound and helpful. The reference is T. J. Crooks, The impact of classroom evaluation practices on students, *Review of Educational Research*, 1988, *85*(4), 438–481.

What to Do About Cheating

*I*T MAY BE HARD FOR YOU TO BELIEVE that your students would ever cheat—"Maybe other students cheat, but not mine!" Unfortunately studies of cheating behavior invariably find that a significant percentage of students report that they have cheated. I believe that most students would rather not cheat, but the pressures for good grades are so intense that many students feel that they, too, must cheat if they believe that other students are cheating. In my experience the most common excuse given by a student caught cheating is that other students were cheating and that the teacher didn't seem to care, at least not enough to do anything to prevent or stop cheating. Many students thus feel less stress when an examination is well managed and well proctored.

How Do Students Cheat?

1. Students pass information to a neighbor; for example, they may loan a neighbor an eraser with the answer on the eraser.

2. Students use notes written on clothing, skin, or small note cards.

3. Students store answers in calculators or cassette recorders used during the exam.

4. Students peek at a knowledgeable neighbor's exam (sometimes seated in groups around the best student in the fraternity).

5. Students use a tapping or hand code.

6. Students accuse the teacher of losing an exam (which was not turned in).

7. Students pay someone else to take an exam or write a paper for them.

■ *Preventing Cheating*

"O.K., so we want to prevent cheating. What can we do?"

An obvious first answer is to reduce the pressure. While you can't affect the general academic atmosphere that puts heavy emphasis on grades, you can influence the pressure in your own course, for example, by providing a number of opportunities for students to demonstrate achievement of course goals, rather than relying upon a single examination.

A second answer is to make reasonable demands and write a reasonable and interesting test. Some cheating is simply the result of frustration and desperation arising from assignments too long to be covered adequately or tests requiring memorization of trivial details. In some cases cheating is simply a way of getting back at an unreasonable, hostile teacher.

A third answer is to develop group norms supporting honesty. I frequently give my classes a chance to vote on whether or not we will conduct the tests on the honor system. I announce that we will not use the honor system unless the vote is unanimous, since it will not work unless everyone feels committed to it. If the vote is unanimous, I remind the students of it on the day of the exam and ask whether they still wish to have the test under the honor system. While I haven't collected data on the success of this approach, I've never had a complaint about it. Although only a minority of classes vote for the honor system, a discussion of academic dishonesty is itself useful in helping students recognize why cheating is bad.

What else can be done?

One principle is to preserve each student's sense that he or she is an individual with a personal relationship both with the instructor and with other students. Students are not as likely to cheat in situations in which they are known as in situations in which they are anonymous members of a crowd. Thus, if a large course has regular meetings in small discussion or laboratory sections, there is likely to be less cheating if the test is administered in these groups than if the test is administered en masse. Moreover, if it is in their regular classroom they may perform better because of the cues to their original learning (Metzger et al., 1979).

Even in small groups cheating will occur if the instructor seems unconcerned. Graduate student teaching assistants often feel that any show of active proctoring will indicate that they do not trust the students. There is certainly a danger that the teacher will appear to be so poised to spring at a miscreant that the atmosphere becomes tense, but it is possible to convey a sense of alert helpfulness while strolling down the aisles or watching for questions.

The most common form of cheating is copying from another student's paper. To reduce this I usually ask to have a large enough exam room to enable students to sit in alternate seats. I write on the board before students arrive, "Take alternate seats." Some students fail to see the sign, so in large exams you not only need two proctors at each door passing out exams but at least one more to supervise seating.

In the event that you can't get rooms large enough to permit alternate seating, you probably should use two or more alternate forms of the test. Houston (1983) found that scrambling order of items alone did not reduce cheating. Since I prefer to have items on a test follow the same order as the order in which the material has been discussed in the course, I scramble the order of items only within topics and also scramble the order of alternatives. I typically write separate sets of essay questions for the two tests. Since it is difficult to make two tests equally difficult, you probably will want to tabulate separate distributions of scores on each form of the test.

Whether you use one form or two, don't leave copies lying around your office or the typist's office. One of our students was nearly killed by a fall from a third-floor ledge outside the office where he hoped to steal the examination, and janitors have been bribed to turn over the contents of wastebaskets thought to contain discarded drafts of the test.

All this advice will not eliminate cheating. It is a sad commentary on our educational system that it occurs, but recognizing and preventing problems is likely to be less unpleasant than ignoring it.

Handling Cheating

Despite preventive measures, almost every instructor must at some time or other face the problem of what to do about a student who is cheating. For example, as you are administering an examination you note that a student's eyes are on his neighbor's rather than his own paper. Typically you do nothing at this time, for you don't want to embarrass an innocent student. But when the eyes again stray, you are faced with a decision about what to do.

Most colleges have rules about the procedures to be followed in case of cheating. Yet instructors are often reluctant to begin the procedure. The reasons for instructor reluctance vary. Sometimes it is simply uncertainty about whether or not cheating really occurred. Students' eyes do wander without cheating. Answers may be similar simply because two students have studied together. "If the student denies the charge, what evidence do I have to support my accusation?"

Again, unwillingness to invoke the regulations concerning cheating may be based upon distrust of the justice of the eventual disposition of the case. Cheating is common in colleges; few teachers have not been guilty themselves at some stage in their academic careers. Thus, most of us are understandably reluctant to subject the unfortunate one who gets caught to the drastic possible punishments that more skillful cheaters avoid. Such conflicts as these make the problem of handling a cheater one of the most disturbing of those a new teacher faces.

Unfortunately I've never been completely satisfied that I handle the problem adequately; so my "advice" should, like the rest of the advice in this book, be regarded simply as some ideas for your consideration rather than as dicta to be accepted verbatim.

First, let me support the value of following your college's procedures. Even though it may not be long since you were taking examinations yourself, your role as a teacher requires that you represent established authority rather than the schoolboy code that rejects "tattlers." Moreover, your memories of student days may help you recall your own feelings when you saw someone cheating and the instructor took no action.

Further, student or faculty committees dealing with cheating are not as arbitrary and impersonal as you might expect. Typically, they attempt to get at the cause of the cheating and to help students solve their underlying problems. Being apprehended for cheating may, therefore, actually be of real long-term value to the students.

Finally, following college policies protects you in the rare case in which a student initiates legal action against you for an arbitrary punishment.

There still remain cases where the evidence is weak and you're not quite sure whether or not cheating actually occurred. Even here I advise against such individual action as reducing a grade. If you're wrong, the solution is unjust. If you're right, you've failed to give the student feedback which is likely to change his behavior. In such cases I advise calling the chairman of the committee handling cheating cases, the student's counselor, or some other experienced faculty member. It's surprising to find how often your suspicions fit in with other evidence about the student's behavior. Even when they don't, advice from someone who has additional information about the student will frequently be helpful.

Finally, let's return to the case of the straying eyes. Here you haven't time for a phone call to get advice; your decision has to be made now. Rather than arousing the whole class by snatching away the student's paper with a loud denunciation, I simply ask the student unobtrusively to move to a seat where he'll be less crowded. If he says he's not crowded, I simply whisper that I'd prefer that he move. So far no one's refused.

SUPPLEMENTARY READING

S. F. Davis, C. A. Grover, A. H. Becker, and L. N. McGregor, Academic Dishonesty: Prevalence, Determinants, Techniques, and Punishments, *Teaching of Psychology*, 1992, *19*(1), 16–20.

CHAPTER 8

The A B C's of Assigning Grades

G RADING is currently in the news.* Grade inflation, contract grading, mastery grading—all of these stimulate heated discussion and cries of dismay. My own ideas of grading have become somewhat clearer as I have talked to my teaching assistants about grading policies and thought through why some of the new grading systems make me uneasy.

First let us agree that grades are fundamentally a method of communication. Through the grade a professor is presumably trying to communicate something to someone else. The question then becomes, "What does the professor intend to communicate to whom?"

When one puts grading into this context, three things become apparent:

1. Evaluation is a great deal more than giving a grade. In teaching, the major part of evaluation should be in the form of comments on papers, responses to student statements, conversations, and other means of helping students understand where they are and how to do better. A professor giving a grade is communicating to several groups—the student, pro-

---

* The following section is largely derived from my article in the *AAUP Bulletin*, 1976, *62*, 320–322.

fessors teaching advanced courses, graduate or professional school admissions committees, prospective employers, and so on.

2. What professors communicate by a grade depends upon the meaning of the grade to the person reading it—the effect that it has on that person.

3. Professors cannot change the meaning of grades unilaterally. While the grade may have a new meaning for the professor, those reading the grade will interpret it in terms of the meanings they have traditionally assigned to grades, unless the professor specifically interprets for them the new meaning he or she wishes to assign to a grade. The readers' interpretations will be colored by their previous experiences with grades, and they are likely to be disturbed, or to feel that they are being misled, when the professor uses grades in new ways. This explains the strong emotional reaction to "grade inflation," "all A" grading, or other practices deviating from traditional meanings.

What are traditional meanings? What are grades used for? I suggest that the person reading a grade typically wants information with respect to some decision involving a judgment about the student's *future* performance. Mastery systems of grading, pass-fail grading, and other alternative systems are resisted because they may not be efficient conveyors of the information useful in predicting future performance.

▬▬▬ *What Do Students, Professors, and Employers Want from Grades?*

Students want to be able to use grades to assist them in decisions such as the following:

1. Will I do well if I take additional courses in this field?

2. Should I major in this field? Does it represent a potential career in which I'm likely to be successful?

3. Do I have the skills and ability necessary to work independently in this field—learning more, solving problems, able to evaluate my own work?

4. What kind of person am I?

Professors advising the student or determining admissions expect the grade to tell them:

1. Does this student have the motivation, skills, knowledge, and ability needed to do well in advanced courses (insofar as the type of problems dealt with in the earlier course are relevant to the demands of the advanced courses or program)?

2. What kind of person is this? What does the pattern of grades tell us about this student's ability and work habits?

Similarly, prospective *employers* want to use grades to assist in decisions about whether or not the student will do well in the job.

1. How well will the student be able to solve problems on jobs related to the area of his or her coursework?

2. Does the overall pattern of grades indicate that this is the sort of person who will do well in our organization?

From this analysis it seems evident that grades are used not just as a historical record of what has happened but also as information about what the student can do in situations outside the class for which the grade was awarded. For the users the grade is not so much historical as potentially predictive.

■■■ *Do Grades Provide Information Useful for Decision Making?*

One of the arguments against conventional grading is that grades are invalid; that is, they do not provide useful information for the major purposes for which they are usually used.

Most critics would grant that grades are useful for decisions about whether a student is likely to be able to succeed in an advanced course or in a further academic experience such as graduate or professional school, but they do not believe that they provide useful information for students or for potential employers.

Teachers assume that grades have some informational and motivational value for students. Critics argue that punishment and failure are not likely to be conducive to achieving the goal of continued enjoyment of learning, and that the threat of low grades is a crutch used to help inadequate teachers. I think that there is much truth in this argument. Yet uniformly positive feedback is not necessarily the most effective method of motivating all students. In fact there is much evidence that such a pattern of reinforcement sometimes diminishes motivation. Although the research on grading is not conclusive, it does suggest that conventional grading can be conducive to achievement.

What about information for employers? Probably most personnel psychologists would agree that the best predictor of success on a job is successful performance on a similar job. For a young person entering the job market, there is often no record of previous performance on comparable jobs. The employer must then make a decision on the basis of other information such as interviews, letters of recommendation, biographical data, family background, and test scores. Each source is only partially adequate. Insofar as the new job involves at least some expenditure for training, it seems likely that grades, representing the result of skills applied in study, learning, and problem solving, will add some information, albeit incomplete, that will be useful for making the decision.

Since grades are commonly used in combination with other variables, however, one should not expect them to correlate with success for those selected. This is not simply a problem that only the top students were selected; it is a simple mathematical truism that when one uses several selection criteria, each of which has some validity, one should expect low positive, zero, or even negative correlations between any one selection variable and the ultimate criteria of performance. This occurs because one will balance criteria against one another, selecting some people low in other important attributes because they have high grades and vice versa. Thus the common criticism that grades don't predict later performances is largely invalid since most of the studies cited have been carried out in situations where grades have already been used in selection.

Contract Grading

In contract grading students and instructors develop a written contract about what the student will do to achieve given grade levels. Contracts typically specify papers to be written, books to be read, projects to be completed, and so forth. With respect to the contract system of grading, it seems to me that the problem basically is that students often gain points, not for achievement, but rather for carrying out those activities, such as writing papers or reading books, that *should* be conducive to achievement. Thus, rather than measuring learning, you assess whether the student has engaged in activities that are the means to learning. I suspect that this means that in many cases there is a considerable gap between the points the student has earned and the points a similar student would earn if the student's achievement were assessed. If contract grading is used, criteria for quality as well as quantity of achievement are needed.

Assigning grades on the basis of the quantity of work done rather than the degree of competence achieved is not a problem restricted to contract grading. Many instructors subtract points for absences, tardiness, or other things they dislike. In psychology classes, points are sometimes added for participation in research studies, a very dubious practice unless it involves some assessment of what the students learned from research participation.

Competency-Based Grading

In "mastery" or "competency-based" systems, the student is graded on a pass-fail basis for achieving "mastery" or "competence" in terms of carefully specified objectives. The real core of the problem may be in the use of the word "mastery." The mastery concept essentially emphasizes reaching a particular finish line. In fact, however, most educational purposes in higher education have no end point, but are extensive in the breadth and depth of their possibilities. An achievement examination in a course is ordinarily designed to *sample* a domain of problems to solve, or concepts, or generalizations, that the students will be able to generalize to a larger domain. The more limited the definition of those achievements that the students should "master," the less valid a test or grade is in terms of its ability to assess the students with respect to other problems, other concepts, or other generalizations in the total domain.

For example, suppose I give my students a list of five problems at the beginning of the semester and say, "My objectives are that you should be able to solve these five problems." In this situation most students will master the problems but differ substantially in their ability to solve other problems within the same general categories. Five problems that have *not* been specifically studied during the course would be more likely to be a reasonable sample of future problems students might encounter than five problems the students have already memorized, and a larger sample of problems from the domain would be likely to be even better.

Letting students turn in papers or book reports over and over again until they do them correctly is a fine teaching technique. However, the student who writes an acceptable book report after ten trials is probably less able to write a new report acceptably than the student who does it right in the first place. Thus the grade on such a rewritten paper should not be counted as equivalent to that of a paper that has not been rewritten.

Nonetheless, mastery learning has positive features. It forces the teacher to think about goals and it focuses students' learning. Moreover such a focus results in better retention (Glasnapp et al., 1978; Kulik, Kulik, and Bangert-Drowns, 1988).

▬▬ *Grading Group Projects*

With greater use of cooperative learning, the issue of grading group projects is increasingly salient. I have used two approaches:

1. Have each member of the group submit an individual report which is graded, as are other student papers. Students are encouraged to have other members of the group react to their papers, and are told that purely descriptive parts (such as description of the research design or procedures) may be the same on all papers. However, parts involving conceptualization and thinking are to represent the students' own thinking, even though the ideas have been discussed in the group.

2. Assign a group grade for the project. Each member of the group receives the same grade, except that if some members have contributed little to the work their grade is lowered. To implement this, I ask each member of the group to fill out a secret ballot allocating one hundred points among the members of the group in proportion to their contribution. Most ballots allocate the points equally, but occasionally there is consensus that a member did not contribute.

■ *Assigning Grades*

Because grades represent to many students a fearsome, mysterious dragon, anxiety can sometimes be reduced by encouraging the students to participate in planning the methods by which grades will be assigned. Students usually can recognize the need of the instructor to conform to college policy in grade distribution, but the dragon seems less threatening if they have helped determine the system by which they are devoured (or rewarded). At the very least you should be clear about your criteria. Examples of previously graded work or tests may be helpful.

Some instructors have gone so far as to let students determine their own grades or to have groups of students grade one another. I like the idea that students should develop the capacity for self-evaluation, but I recognize that many students resist this procedure, either through modesty or fear that they'll underrate themselves. If you use it, I'd suggest thorough discussion of the plan with students and an agreed-upon, well-defined set of criteria that all students should use. Even if student participation is not possible, anxiety seems to be reduced if you explain the system you use and give your reasons for using this system.

In giving test grades early in a course, two general approaches are sometimes advocated. One of these is to make these grades lower than those one intends to give at the end of the course. This should reduce the number of complaints about final grades. The other approach is to use these grades to motivate students to work harder. This may mean that you use many plus and minus grades. A plus or minus indicates to the students that the grade may be shifted either way and presumably reduces the chance that they'll coast.

You might also ask students to hand in their own estimates of their grades as an aid to knowing how to motivate them, and also in order to develop their abilities for self-evaluation. Atkinson and Litwin's (1960) theory of motivation suggests that the highest motivation to achieve occurs when the probability of success is moderate. This probably explains the finding of Means and Means (1971) that low grade-point-average students achieved more when told that they had done well on an aptitude test, while high grade-point-average students did better when told that they had done poorly. In general motivation is not helped simply by giving high grades; nor is it helped by setting very tough standards. Students are most motivated when they feel that they can achieve success with a reasonable effort (Harter, 1978).

In keeping students informed during the course about where they stand, you probably are also aiding them to control much of the anxiety they feel when the grading system is indefinite and unstructured. Sometimes it may seem easier to fight off grade-conscious students by being very indefinite about grades, but student morale is better when the students know the situation with which they must cope.

Whatever your grading strategy, being more generous in assigning grades to tests and papers than in the final distribution of grades guarantees visits from aggrieved students. One way in which you get yourself into this position is by providing opportunities for students to omit questions on an exam, to throw out the lowest test grade, or to submit extra work for a higher grade. Any of these procedures can have some educational justification, but if you expect to finish the course with grades representative of those for similar courses at your college, you need to devise a system of grading in which the constituents of the total grade will come out at an appropriate level in relation to the standards of grading at your college or university.

Professors sometimes devise systems of grading that allow students to drop out any test scores below A and are then surprised that their grade distribution is not comparable to that of other courses. You will find that your colleagues are not convinced that the students' level of achievement has improved so greatly in your class that they all deserve grades higher than those earned in other classes.

■■■■ *Grading on the Curve: A Mild Reprise*

In Chapter 6 we talked about grading a test on the curve. Now we extend our discussion to final course grades. One of the persisting controversies in college teaching is whether to grade "on the curve" or in terms of an absolute standard. In fact, these two positions are probably not as far apart as the argument would indicate. Even teachers who grade on the curve are influenced in setting their cutoff points between grades in terms of their feelings about whether this was a good or poor class. And similarly, teachers who do not grade on the curve set their standards in terms of what previous experience leads them to regard as reasonable accomplishment in the course. As I indicated earlier, I believe that grading on the curve is educationally dysfunctional. If possible your grades should, both in the students' eyes and in actuality, be more nearly based on absolute standards than on relative standing in this particular class.

The use of an absolute standard is easier if you have formulated your major and minor objectives and tested their achievement. Travers (1950) proposed one set of absolute standards:

→ A: All major and minor goals achieved.

→ B: All major goals achieved; some minor ones not.

→ C: All major goals achieved; many minor ones not.

→ D: A few major goals achieved, but student is not prepared for advanced work.

→ E or F: None of the major goals achieved.

■■■■ *What Do You Do with the Student Who Wants a Grade Changed?*

My basic strategy is the same as that involved in returning tests—go over the criteria used in grading and the student's record during the term.

If students are worried about their grades in connection with their admission to a specialized school or because they are on probation, I may offer to write a letter to their advisor or other authorities describing their work in detail and pointing out any extenuating circumstances that may have influenced the grade. This may serve to cushion the refusal to change the grade.

In addition, of course, you may try to explain to the students the rationale of grades. Usually this doesn't seem to do much good. Both students and faculty sometimes confuse two possible criteria upon which grades may be based. One of these is the relative amount of *progress* the student has made in achieving the goals of the course; the other is achievement of the goals of the course at the end of the term. In most classes, research has demonstrated a relatively low correlation between these two criteria. If you were to mark solely on progress, the students who came into the course with the least background might still be the poorest students in the class at the end of the course and get an A for their progress. Most employers, registrars, and professors interpret a grade in terms of achievement of course goals; hence, professors who grade solely on the students' progress may send the students into advanced courses or jobs for which they lack the requisite skills and knowledge. However, I find it difficult to assign failing grades to students who have made progress in the course, even though they remain the poorest students in the class. My own solution is to give all but failing grades in terms of achievement of course goals. I give failing grades only to those students who not only demonstrate low achievement but have also made little progress.

No matter how you grade, some student will be unhappy. The student who has just missed Phi Beta Kappa may feel just as bad as the student who has been asked to leave school. Be sympathetic, but beware! If you begin changing grades, the jungle drums of the campus will soon spread the word.

Don't finish reading this chapter with your own anxiety aroused by the dangers of grading. It is proper that good teachers should be humble as they see how great is the power they have over the happiness of their students by printing a simple A, B, C, or D. Nevertheless, one of the real satisfactions of teaching is giving a good grade to an ordinarily average student who has come to life in your course.

▬▬ *How to Lose Friends and Alienate Students**

1. Never give students any idea of what their grades are before the final examination. The shock of seeing an F as the final grade will so stun them that they'll be incapable of protest. Or better yet tell them they had A's all the way through the course and got an A on the final, but you have given too many A's, so you're giving them B's.

2. Tell students that you really think they deserved a higher mark, but that you had to conform to department grading policies and hence had to grade them lower.

3. Tell students that their grades on the final exam were higher than their final grades in the course. (Of course they'll understand that the final examination is only one part of the total evaluation.)

4. Even though your school doesn't record pluses, tell a student that his grade was D+, C+, or B+, rather than a straight D, C, or B. He'll gladly accept the fact that the C–, B–, or A– was only three points above him, and will be proud that he did better than anyone else who got a D or C or B.

5. If you make a distribution of total points earned on tests during the term, use large intervals, such as 80 to 90, 90 to 100,

---

* These may look absurd, but they have all happened.

etc. When you show a student her position on the distribution, she'll readily see that the person in the next interval above was really much superior.

6. Tell a student that grades are really very arbitrary, and that you could have split the B's from the C's in many different places, and that grades are so unreliable that you really can't distinguish your top B student from your low A student. He'll appreciate the aesthetic value of your choice of a cutting point.

▰▰▰ *Relevant Research*

Not only do instructors control the pleasantness or unpleasantness of a good many student hours, but because of their power to assign grades they can block or facilitate the achievement of many important goals. The importance of this aspect of the teacher's role is indicated by studies of supervision in industry. In one such study it was discovered that workers were most likely to ask a supervisor for help if the supervisor did not have responsibility for evaluating his subordinates (Ross, 1957). This implies that as long as students are anxious about the grades the instructor will assign, they are likely to avoid exposing their own ignorance.

The students' anxieties about grades are likely to rise if their instructor's procedures make them uncertain about what they must do in order to attain a good grade. For many students, democratic methods seem unorganized and ambiguous. In an ordinary course students know they can pass by reading assignments and studying lecture notes, but in a student-centered class they are in a course where the instructor doesn't lecture, doesn't make assignments, and doesn't even say which student comments are right or wrong. The student simply doesn't know what the instructor is trying to do. Thus, if your teaching or grading procedures differ from those your students are used to, you need to be especially careful to specify the procedures and criteria used in grading.

Some instructors have thought that the grade problem might be licked by using a cooperative system of grading. Deutsch (1949) found no differences in learning between students in groups graded cooperatively and those graded competitively, although the cooperative groups worked together more smoothly. Following up Deutsch's work, Haines and McKeachie (1967) also found no significant achievement advantages for students working cooperatively vs. those working competitively for grades, but did find marked differences in group morale. Haines's work suggests that cooperative grading in the discussion can be successfully combined with individual grading on achievement tests.

Complicating the problem of grading is the probability that low grades produce different effects upon different students. As indicated earlier, Atkinson's theory suggests that low grades should be damaging to the motivation of students with low to moderate expectations, but should increase motivation of those with high expectations. Waterhouse and Child (1953) found that frustration produced deterioration in performance for subjects showing high interference tendencies (or anxiety) as measured by a questionnaire, but produced improved performance for those with low interference tendencies.

Considering the importance of grading for both students and instructors, it is regrettable that there is so little empirical research. How do students learn to evaluate themselves? How do they learn to set goals for themselves? Do differing grading procedures facilitate or block such learning? To these questions we have no answers.

Conclusions

1. Grades are communication devices. Instructors cannot unilaterally change their meaning without distorting the communication process.

2. Grading standards differ from college to college and department to department, but there is some shared sense of the meaning of grades.

SUPPLEMENTARY READING

Although I have pointed to problems with typical mastery or contract grading systems, well-designed programs are worth serious consideration. Even conventional grading systems need to establish criteria. A helpful source is M. F. Shaycoft, *Handbook of Criterion-Referenced Testing* (New York: Garland STPM Press, 1979).

Contracts for contract grading are illustrated in Barbara Fuhrman and Anthony Grasha, *A Practical Handbook for College Teachers* (San Francisco: Jossey-Bass, 1983).

What grades mean to faculty, parents, personnel directors, and students is described in H. R. Pollio, W. L. Humphreys, and O. Milton, Components of Contemporary Grade Meanings, *Contemporary Educational Psychology*, 1989, *14*, 77–91 and in O. Milton, H. R. Pollio, and J. Eison, *Making Sense of College Grades* (San Francisco: Jossey-Bass, 1986).

Teaching Techniques, Tools, and Methods

PART III

CHAPTER 9

Writing: Papers, Journals, and Reports

WHEN I BEGAN TEACHING, most courses in the social sciences and humanities required a term paper. Ordinarily papers were graded for the quality of the content and original thinking, disregarding the quality of writing (if this is possible). All too often students looked at the grade on the term paper returned at the end of the term and paid little attention to helpful comments by the professor. The "writing across the curriculum" revolution taught us that thinking as well as writing is improved by the opportunity to get feedback on a first draft before turning in a paper for a grade. Thus more and more teachers are assigning several shorter papers with multiple drafts evaluated by peers and/or the teacher.

An Essay on Day Two!

Norman Raiford (1991) starts his students writing on the second day of class. Students are asked to write a four-paragraph letter to a friend describing the course as outlined in the syllabus, giving first impressions of the teacher and the students' hopes or concerns for the course.

The Term Paper (or Papers)

When undergraduates are required to write a paper, they seem to face three alternatives:

1. Buy one, or borrow one from a friend or fraternity or sorority file. The student may have this retyped, or, if there are no marks on it, simply retype the title page inserting his or her own name for that of the author.

2. Find a book in the library that covers the needed material. Copy it with varying degrees of paraphrasing and turn it in. Whether or not to list this book in the bibliography is a problem not yet adequately covered by student mores, although it is agreed that if it is listed in the bibliography it should be well hidden between two references with Russian (first choice) or German (second choice) authors.

3. Review relevant resources and, using powers of analysis and integration, develop a paper that reveals understanding and original thinking.

Most teachers prefer that their students adopt the third alternative. Few of us, however, have evolved techniques for eliminating the first two.

I start with the assumption that most students would rather not plagiarize. When they plagiarize it is because they feel trapped with no other way out. Typically in this situation the student feels that it is almost impossible to write a paper that will achieve a satisfactory grade. This may be because of self-perception of lack of ability or background. More often it results from a lack of planning so that the student has arrived at the time the term paper is due with little preparation and no paper. The only way out seems to be to find an already-written paper.

How can one help students avoid such a trap? By pacing the student. I try to break the process of writing a term paper into a series of easy steps such as:

1. Finding a topic
2. Gathering sources, data, or references
3. Developing an outline
4. Writing a first draft
5. Rewriting

I set deadlines for handing in a report at each step. When time permits, I meet with the student to discuss the paper at one of the early steps. In the meeting I not only provide guidance, but I can also offer encouragement and motivation for doing well (and I can sometimes spot and discourage impending signs of plagiarism).

Sandra Powers (1983) uses a technique that neatly breaks up the task of introducing students to a library research paper. Her procedure involves the following tasks:

1. Each student locates a source article and writes a paragraph explaining why this article was chosen.

2. The article and paragraph are discussed in a small peer group.

3. The student writes a one-page summary of a source article.

4. This paper is discussed and evaluated by the peer group and graded by the teacher. The teacher carefully evaluates one paragraph for writing style, grammar, and so on.

5. Students choose a topic and turn in the topic as a question.

6. Each student writes the instructor a one-page letter on "How is my paper going?"

7. The research paper and preceding papers are submitted as a portfolio.

   Other techniques I've used are:

1. Including on a test some question that will require each student to use knowledge gained in preparing his or her term paper.

2. Having students give oral reports on their papers and answer questions from the class.

Using Student Papers as the Basis for Discussion

When my colleague Chris Peterson and I taught a graduate pro-seminar, students were required each week to write a paper on the assigned readings and lecture. The papers were then taped to the wall to be read by other students in their discussion group and to serve as a basis for the day's discussion. Light (1992) describes a similar method in use in undergraduate classes in which a few students are asked to prepare their papers in advance of the due date and to photocopy or post them so that everyone in the class can read them before the class discussion of the topic. One of the advantages of this technique is that students are writing for a real audience—their peers.

■ *Dealing with Plagiarism*

What should you do if you suspect plagiarism? Here you are in a conflict situation. Typically you don't want to reward plagiarism; yet it may be very difficult and time-consuming to locate the original source. Without it you will probably not be able to take formal action. So should you forget it? No.

Ordinarily I recommend a conference with the student. You may use the indirect approach of discussing or questioning the student about the content of the paper to assess the student's knowledge or you may be direct in expressing your suspicions. In many cases the student will admit plagiarism; in some cases you will encounter blustering anger. In any case you will need to arrive at a decision about a) turning the case over to college discipline procedures, b) giving a failing grade, c) permitting the student to write another paper, or d) giving the paper full credit. Often I tell the student that I will consult my department chair or a respected colleague before making a final decision.

■ *Term Papers: A Reprise*

If term papers are frequently so inadequate, why would instructors bother to use them? As I see it, term papers attempt to gain two objectives:

1. To provide an opportunity for students to go beyond conventional course coverage and gain a feeling of expertness in some area. This is an important way in which students learn to value knowledge and learning.

2. To give students an opportunity to explore problems of special significance to them. In this way I hope to capture increased motivation.

▰ *The Student Log or Journal*

For a number of years I have required my students to write logs. Originally the logs dealt only with outside reading, but more recently I have broadened them to encourage students to think about psychology in all settings.

Logs are turned in three times during the term. I don't grade them, but I do write extensive comments pressing for active questioning and thinking rather than descriptive summaries. Students clearly improve; whether or not this carries over beyond the course I don't know, but it seems more likely than for some other types of course activity. In any case there is increasing evidence that writing aids learning and problem solving (Beach and Bridwell, 1984), and students report gains both in thinking and motivation (Hettick, 1990). The best description of what I expect is probably contained in the instructions to students that follow.

Writing Logs on Your Reading, Observing, and Thinking

Your assigned readings are designed to give you a basic knowledge of the terminology and concepts used in psychology. You will also be given the opportunity to read about any topic in psychology that especially interests you. You should keep a log of your reading and thinking as described below. In this course you will have four hours in class, two to four hours of assigned reading, and possibly other activities each week. This means that most weeks you should have two to six hours for your free reading and writing. Logs will not be graded but there will be a question on the final examination assessing the skills you have developed.

WHAT TO READ   You are allowed maximal freedom in selecting readings to enter in your log. Your interest in and profit from what you read is by far the most important criterion of selection. You are encouraged to discard after reading a few pages any material that fails to satisfy either of these criteria.

Chapters of books and journal articles are particularly acceptable for these purposes. At the end of each chapter in the text, there is a list of suggestions for further reading; if you were dissatisfied with your grasp of any particular chapter, or if you just want to learn more about some topic than is available in the text, these "suggestions" are excellent sources. Another method of selection is simply to browse among the books and journals in the library until something catches your interest.

One of the goals of the course is to help you develop skill in reading psychological materials analytically and critically, so that you can learn from reading after you leave college. Thus you are particularly encouraged to use sources that you would be likely to read after college, such as paperback books, *Scientific American*, and articles relevant to psychology in newspapers and popular magazines.

Finally, if your position in the course is for any reason precarious, you are encouraged to improve the situation by reading parts of other elementary texts that might illuminate and strengthen your thinking on material covered during the course so far.

WHERE TO FIND IT   The Undergraduate Library has a basic collection of books and the recent volumes of most journals. You will find a wider selection in the General Library. You might find the *Psychological Abstracts* (the readers' guide to psychological literature) a useful reference to direct you to journal articles concerning the topics of your interest. *The Journal of Experimental Psychology* and the *Journal of Personality and Social Psychology* contain fairly concise reports of research projects and their implications.

WHAT GOES IN THE LOG   The log is to be in no sense a "paper" in any formal sort of way. It should demonstrate that you have thought about what you have read and experienced. This should and must be accomplished without writing a summary of the reading(s). Rather record your comments, criticisms, evaluations, questions, and insights. How did your reading relate to other material of the course? How did it relate to other psychological concepts or theories with which you are familiar? What interested you? Was the evidence convincing? What hypotheses are suggested to you by this reading or experience?

In addition to writing about reading, write about behavior that you observed, discussions in which you participated, or thoughts you had after class. The log is intended to record your thinking about behavior and experience and about psychology in general.

▬▬ *What About Deadlines?*

One of the banes of the teacher's existence is the paper or journal turned in after the due date. Some teachers refuse to accept late papers; more commonly we apply a sliding scale with increasing reduction of the grade the later the paper. Roberts and Semb (1990) let students choose their own deadlines, a method that should help motivation even though it failed to result in fewer late papers. I have sometimes asked the class to discuss the issue of deadlines and late papers, setting a due date that takes account of their schedules and mine. Regardless of the method you use, you need to leave yourself room for exceptions. Grandmothers sometimes really do die, and student illness or other emergencies may need to be recognized.

▬▬ *Correcting Papers, Giving Feedback, and Teaching Writing*

"I'm teaching physics (or psychology or history). It's the job of the English Department to teach writing. It would be unfair to my students to evaluate their writing. Moreover I've never had any training in teaching writing. I'm not even sure when to insert a comma in my own writing."

Such is the outcry of the professoriate when confronting the proposition that writing should be taught in all courses—across the curriculum.

There is some merit in the outcry. Few faculty members have been taught to teach writing—even fewer than have been taught to teach their own disciplines! But lack of training in teaching has not disqualified us from teaching our own disciplines, and all of us have had substantial experience in writing dissertations, reports, papers, books, and incidental letters. Writing is the very essence of academic life. "Publish or perish" is not an idle phrase. We write.

Most of us recognize good or bad writing when we see it. What we often lack are skills of analysis and diagnosis that will help us identify our students' underlying problems as well as skills in providing correction, feedback, and guidance that will enable students to improve.

In addition to concerns about competence, faculty members have concerns about the time required. If one asks students to write more, how can one conscientiously comment on that writing without an impossible increase in time spent grading?

Here are some suggestions:

1. The professor is not the only person who can provide help on writing. Often peers can provide useful suggestions on their classmates' papers. To help students know what to look for you can provide models—both of well-written papers on a given topic as well as of papers with your own comments about some common problems. Form subgroups of four or five students and have each group read and comment on each other's papers. This not only reduces the burden on the teacher but also helps students to learn to evaluate their own work. You can help this learning by evaluating the evaluations periodically. For example, you might say that each group will determine when each paper in the group is ready to be turned in to you. Or you might ask the group to turn in a first and last version together with their suggestions on the earlier drafts.

2. A ten-page paper is not necessarily twice as valuable as a five-page paper. Short papers can be evaluated in less time than long papers, and may provide sufficient stimulus for student thinking and sufficient opportunity for student feedback.

3. More than one draft of a single paper may be more useful for learning than submission of the final version of a paper. (The problem with the final version of papers is that once a grade has been given students sometimes ignore all other feedback.) Having a chance to try out ideas without risk helps free up students to be more thoughtful and creative. Hillocks (1982) found that focused teacher comments facilitate learning, but their effect is twice as great if students have a chance to revise their paper.

4. Up to a point, more comments, and more specific comments, lead to greater learning. There are three kinds of qualifications to this statement:
   a. A student can be overloaded with feedback. There is a limited number of things a student can be expected to learn and remedy at one time.
   b. Motivation for improvement is affected by the balance of encouragement vs. criticism. A heavy dose of criticism may cause a student to feel that there is no use in continuing.
   c. The type of comment makes a difference. Simply noting errors is not helpful if the student doesn't know how to correct the errors. Helpful comments provide guidance about how to improve.

5. Here are some examples of comments that might help:
   "I don't quite follow your organization. Could you give me an outline along with your revision?"
   "You state your position strongly, but you are weak in covering other positions. See if you can find others in class with a different position and listen to their arguments."

What to Do When a Paper Is to Be Graded

As I said in Chapter 6, "Tests and Examinations," a global grade is more reliable than partial grades, but to help students learn to write and think, grades are of little value. Students need more information about criteria. One method is to read several papers and to make specific notes about the criteria which influenced your judgments about the differences between excellent and poorer papers. An alternative procedure is to develop a set of criteria on rational grounds or in discussion with other instructors. A good example of such a statement of criteria is the following outline developed by Gary LaPree of Indiana University (LaPree, 1977).

A. Content

   1. Introduction

      a. Is the topic novel and original?

      b. Does the author state purpose, problem, or question to be considered?

      c. How does the author convince the reader that the paper is worth reading?

      d. Does the author present a preview of how the problem will be handled?

   2. Body

      a. How are the statements made warranted? (Is there evidence that data collected have been analyzed and the literature reviewed? Are the assumptions logical?)

      b. Presentation of evidence

         1. Is contradictory evidence dealt with adequately?

         2. Are multiple sources considered if available?

         3. Is the evidence discussed relevant to the purpose stated?

         4. Is the argument internally consistent, i.e., does one point follow from another?

         5. Is the argument plausible?

         6. Are the methods chosen for testing the argument convincing?

      c. Suitability of paper's focus

         1. Is the problem chosen focused enough to be adequately covered in the space of the paper?

         2. Is the problem chosen too specific for the author's sources of information?

      d. Background information

1. Is enough information given to familiarize the reader with the problem?
2. Is unimportant background material included?
e. Is the presentation easy to follow and well organized?
f. Does the author deal with the problem set up in the introduction?

3. Conclusion
   a. Does the author summarize findings adequately?
   b. Is the conclusion directly related to the questions asked in the introduction?
   c. Does the author suggest areas where further work is needed?

B. Connections to class
   1. Evidence that class materials have been read and understood
   2. Application of lecture materials and assigned readings to paper

C. Form
   1. Spelling
   2. Grammar
   3. Appropriate use of words: Does the writer use words incorrectly, awkwardly, or inappropriately?
   4. Paragraph form: Are ideas presented in coherent order?
   5. Footnotes and bibliography: Are borrowed ideas and statements given credit? Is the form of the footnotes and bibliography understandable and consistent?
   6. Has the paper been proofread?

This list of criteria is not intended to be something one considers only after reading a paper but rather as a guide to the teacher's active thought processes while reading student papers and for suggestions to be made to the student. Just as we teach students to read actively—questioning, relating, synthesizing—so we should be actively questioning the writer's thinking and expression as we read.

SUPPLEMENTARY READING

A nice discussion of the values of student journals is R. L. Roth, Learning about gender through writing: Student journals in the undergraduate classroom, *Teaching Sociology*, *12*(3), 325–338.

Useful analyses of writing processes and implications for teaching may be found in:

L. W. Gregg and E. R. Steinberg (eds.), *Cognitive Processes in Writing* (Hillsdale, NJ: Lawrence Erlbaum, 1980). Note especially the chapter by Hayes and Flower.

E. P. Maimon, G. L. Belcher, G. W. Hearn, B. F. Nodine, and F. W. O'Connor, *Writing in the Arts and Sciences* (Cambridge, MA: Winthrop, 1981).

Alternatives to term papers are discussed in the chapter by Evan I. Farber in Thomas G. Kirk (ed.), Increasing the Teaching Role of Academic Libraries, *New Directions for Teaching and Learning*, *18* (San Francisco: Jossey-Bass, 1984).

Teaching Students How to Learn More from Textbooks and Reading Assignments

WHILE PROFESSORS LIKE TO THINK that students learn from professors, it seems likely that students often learn more efficiently from reading than from listening. The journals (or logs) described in Chapter 9 illustrate one attempt to get students into the library and reading primary sources. Nonetheless textbooks are still a basic tool for teaching most courses.

Textbooks

For decades the demise of the textbook has been eagerly predicted by advocates of each of the new panaceas for the problems of education. First television, then teaching machines, then the computer—each was expected to revolutionize education and free students and teachers from their longtime reliance upon textbooks.

But each of the new media has settled into its niche in the educational arsenal without dislodging the textbook. In fact, the greatest revolution in education has come not from teaching machines or computers but from the greater availability of a wide variety of printed materials.

The introduction of open-stack libraries, paperback books, inexpensive reprint series, and the photocopier has given the college teacher the opportunity to choose from sources varying in style, level, and point of view. Many teachers are substituting paperback books, reprints, and collections of journal articles for the textbook as the sources of the basic information needed by students. The students thus have an opportunity to organize the material in a way meaningful for them. But in most undergraduate courses there is little hope that bits and pieces will be integrated by students into a meaningful whole despite the valiant efforts of instructors to give assistance. They know that learning is facilitated by organization and that, lacking organization, facts and concepts become so many nonsense syllables subject to interference, quickly forgotten and inaccessible. With input from field experience, discussion, paperbacks, reprints, and other sources, the student needs more than ever some frame of reference within which to assimilate the boomin', buzzin' confusion of points of view present in a modern course.

Ideally, the textbook can provide such a structure. That structure need not be dogmatic, but it need not be gutless. It need not be presented as irrevocable truth. Inevitably, certain parts of textbook information become dated. If teachers fail to recognize what is obsolete and insist on its memorization, the students' education is harmed rather than aided. Probably the main drawback of textbooks as teaching tools is their tendency to encourage encyclopedic learning of factual material rather than achievement of the ability to deal with the ideas that have a longer half-life in their application to the transfer-of-learning world. But dogmatic, out-of-date teachers can misuse any source. A good textbook can counter instructor dogmatism by presenting a more open framework. Structures should be presented as tentative, temporary, and incomplete. Textbooks should be up to date and frequently revised. That textbooks in the past have often been little more than a collection of topics is no reason to reject their potential usefulness in meeting important needs for the student learner today.

Modern education is focusing less on imparting facts and theories and more on development of student capacities for judgment, fact-gathering, analysis, and synthesis. Thus the encyclopedic textbook is an anachronism promoting the wrong kind of education. But the modern textbook can and should be aimed at the very goals that are now evolving. None of these desired capacities for critical thinking and usefulness for action can be developed without some grounding in essential facts and concepts. Without the structure provided by a good textbook, students may simply end in confusion and frustration.

Certainly, modern teachers should provide a variety of learning experiences for students. If individual differences are to be attended to in teaching, students need an opportunity to learn in laboratory settings, field experiences, discussion, lectures, or reading from diverse sources. Textbooks are an important part of the teacher's compendium of tools, and the newer teaching methods and aids supplement rather than supplant the textbook. In fact a goodly part of higher education is education in how to read—how to read poems, how to read social science, how to read legal briefs, how to read the literature of our culture and our profession.

▬▬ *Additional Assigned Reading*

Most teachers supplement textbook assignments with assigned readings from other sources. A faculty member in biological sciences gives students two sets of references for optional reading. One set is for students whose background is weak and want to shore up their understanding; the other is for students who want to pursue a topic in greater depth.*

▬▬ *Research on Learning from Reading*

An early study (Greene, 1928) found that students learned as well from reading material as from listening to the same material read aloud. The better students, moreover, profited more from reading than from listening. A number of other studies have compared printed materials with lectures, and the results—at least with difficult materials—favor print (Hartman, 1961). In fact Reder and Anderson (1982) found that students who studied textbook summaries scored better on achievement tests than those who read the entire text. The details in the text were distracting rather than supportive.

---

* Taken from B. G. Davis, L. Wood, and R. C. Wilson, *A B C's of Teaching with Excellence* (Berkeley: University of California, 1983).

Study questions intended to guide the students' reading are often helpful. Marton and Säljö (1976b) found that questions designed to produce more thoughtful, integrative study were more effective than questions of fact. Nevertheless, study questions are not automatically a guarantee of better learning. Students sometimes tended to look only for answers to the questions while disregarding the other content of the chapter (Marton and Säljö, 1976a). Andre (1987) reviewed meta-analyses and other studies of study questions and concluded that questions generally do aid learning and that higher-level questions, rather than low-level factual questions increase the effectiveness of student processing of the reading. Wilhite (1983) found that pre-questions focusing on material at the top of the organizational structure did facilitate learning, especially for the less able students. What instructors need are questions that get students to *think* about the material.

▬ *Teaching Students to Learn More from Reading*

We saw in Chapter 6 that students' study methods and learning were influenced by the sort of test questions they expected. Thus many students can read thoughtfully if tests require deeper understanding and thinking. But other students faithfully read and re-read regardless of the type of assignment, memorizing definitions and facts without thought of the goal of the author and the relationship of this reading assignment to their previous learning. You can help by being explicit about why you chose the textbook and what you expect students to learn from it.

There is now ample evidence that students benefit from specific instruction in selecting main ideas, asking themselves questions, looking for organizational cues, and attempting to summarize or explain what they have read. Particularly in introductory classes you will help learning if you make explicit reference to your goal in assigning a particular chapter and discuss ways in which students can best achieve that goal (Weinstein and Mayer, 1986; McKeachie, Pintrich and Lin, 1985). Encourage students to make marginal notes, to write down questions as they go, and to carry on an active dialogue with the author.

SUPPLEMENTARY READING

Ference Marton, Dai Hounsell, and Noel Entwistle (eds.), *The Experience of Learning* (Edinburgh: Scottish Academic Press, 1984).

T. M. Chang, H. F. Crombag, K. D. J. M. van der Drift, and J. M. Moonen, *Distance Learning* (Boston: Kluwer-Nijhoff Publishing, 1983), Chapter 4.

C. E. Weinstein and R. E. Mayer, The Teaching of Learning Strategies in M. Wittrock (ed.), *Handbook of Research on Teaching* (New York: Macmillan, 1983), pp. 315–327.

CHAPTER 11

Laboratory Teaching*

*T*HE LABORATORY METHOD is now so widely accepted as necessary for scientific education that it may seem heretical to ask whether laboratory experience is an effective way to achieve educational objectives. Fortunately there is evidence that laboratory instruction can be educational. Whether it typically achieves its potential is another question.

Laboratory teaching assumes that first-hand experience in observation and manipulation of the materials of a science is superior to other methods of developing understanding and appreciation of research methods. Laboratory training is also frequently used to develop complex skills necessary for more advanced study or research and to develop familiarity with equipment, measures, and research tools.

From the standpoint of theory, the activity of the student, the sensorimotor nature of the experience, and the individualization of laboratory instruction should contribute positively to learning. However, information cannot usually be obtained by direct experience as rapidly as from abstractions presented orally or by printing. Films, demonstrations, or simulations may also shortcut some of the trial and error of the laboratory. Thus, one would not expect laboratory teaching to have an advantage over other teaching methods in amount of information learned. Rather one might

---

* This chapter deals with traditional "wet" labs. Computer simulation labs are discussed in Chapter 16.

expect the differences to be revealed in retention, in ability to apply learning, or in actual skill in observation or manipulation of materials. Unfortunately, little research has attempted to test out these special types of outcomes. If these outcomes are unmeasured, a finding of no difference in effectiveness between laboratory and other methods of instruction is almost meaningless, since there is little reason to expect laboratory teaching to be effective in simple communication of information.

▬ *Research on Laboratory Teaching*

In an experiment in a course, "Methods of Engineering," White (1945) found that students taught by a group laboratory method achieved more than those taught by a lecture-demonstration method. A study by Balcziak (1954), however, comparing 1) demonstration, 2) individual laboratory, and 3) combined demonstration and laboratory in a college physical science course found no significant differences between them as measured by tests of information, scientific attitude, or laboratory performance.

In experiments in physics and engineering, Kruglak (1952) and White (1945) found that students taught by individual or group laboratory methods achieved more than those taught by lecture-demonstration. In studies by Balcziak (1954), Dearden (1960), Trotter (1960), and Bradley (1963), however, laboratory teaching was compared with 1) lecture-demonstration, 2) combined demonstration and laboratory, 3) workbook, and 4) term paper. The comparisons were in physical science, general biology, and home economics courses. No significant differences were found between methods as measured by tests of information, practical application, scientific attitude, or laboratory performance. Earlier experiments found no significant loss resulting from reduction in laboratory time or from assignment of one cadaver to four students rather than two (Downing, 1913; Hurd, 1929; Jackson, 1929; Noll, 1930).

While reviews of research on laboratory teaching find that laboratory courses are effective in improving skills in handling apparatus or visual-motor skills, laboratories generally are not very effective in teaching scientific method or problem solving

(Shulman and Tamir, 1973; Bligh et al., 1980). Having students design an experiment or analyze data already collected may be a more valuable activity than similar time spent in the laboratory. Doyle (1987) had students design their own demonstrations to present to the class. Computer simulations can also effectively reach many of the objectives of laboratory teaching (Kozma, 1982). Involving students in faculty research projects also can help achieve these objectives (Davis, 1992).

However, don't give up on the lab. Bainter (1955) found that a problem-solving method was superior to traditional laboratory manual methods in teaching students to apply principles of physics in interpreting phenomena. Lahti (1956) also found a problem-solving method to be superior to more conventional procedures in developing students' abilities to design an experiment. All of these studies point to the importance of developing understanding, rather than teaching problem solutions by going through a routine series of steps. Whether the laboratory is superior to the lecture-demonstration in developing understanding and problem-solving skills probably depends upon the extent to which understanding of concepts and general problem-solving procedures are emphasized as opposed to "cookbook" methods.

SUPPLEMENTARY READING

A good, brief review of work on laboratory teaching may be found in Donald Bligh, G. J. Ebrahim, D. Jacques, and D. W. Piper, *Teaching Students* (Devon, England: Exeter University Teaching Services, 1975), pp. 174–175.

CHAPTER 12

Field Work and Experiential Learning

ONE OF THE VALUABLE RESIDUES of the student revolution of the 1960s is the increased use of field experiences as a part of undergraduate education. Not that field education was new. Cooperative education, in which periods of classroom education alternate with on-the-job experiences, had been successfully implemented well before the 1960s by Antioch College and several engineering and other colleges. Disciplines such as marine biology, forestry, archaeology, and geology had routinely required summer field work.

But in the 1960s the educational value of direct experience converged with student idealism and desire for "relevant" meaningful service to produce numerous innovations in experiential education. At my own institution, the University of Michigan, "Project Outreach" became part of the introductory psychology program and the sociology department initiated "Project Community." Students in these courses tutored schoolchildren, conducted recreational programs for patients in a mental hospital, visited and assisted the elderly, and worked with adolescents who were in detention for illegal activities. While neither course enrolls the thousands of students that each had in the 1960s, both are still vital parts of the liberal arts curriculum.

■■■■■ *Experiential Learning*

Experiential learning refers to a broad spectrum of educational experiences, such as community service activities, field work, sensitivity training groups, internships, or cooperative education involving work in business or industry. Clearly such experiences require new learning. But is such learning educational? To my mind the criterion is the degree to which the learning is transferable to other times and places. In deciding whether to develop an experiential "course" or to include experiential elements in an existing course, one must, as in making other educational choices, weigh the expected transferable outcomes derived from experience against the outcomes and costs likely from other educational activities.

■■■■■ *What Are the Goals of Experiential Learning?*

Experiential learning has both cognitive and motivational goals. Educators hope that abstract concepts will become meaningful when students see that they are helpful in describing and understanding "real life" phenomena. Similarly we hope that experiences in the field will stir up questions in students' minds that will lead to active learning. Such questions and students' reports of their experiences in the field should enliven class discussions. Most importantly, field experience links learning, thinking, and doing. Teachers hope that field experiences will not only motivate students to learn current course materials but also increase their intrinsic interest in further learning.

An associated goal, important to me, is to increase students' motivation to be of service to others. I am impressed that even in the materialistic culture of the 1980s, students in my courses found great satisfaction in being helpful to older people, children, their peers, and other human beings. In the 1990s the *Chronicle of Higher Education* and other newspapers report increased student involvement in volunteer work involving service to others.

■■■■■ *Are These Goals Achieved?*

Unfortunately there is relatively little evidence of the effectiveness of field methods in achieving educational goals. Motivation is usually very high; students typically report a high level of interest in their field work. However, this does not always carry over to classroom learning, and linking course concepts to field experiences is also difficult. Students almost invariably report that they learned a great deal from their experience, but the learning may have been local learning relevant to the particular field setting rather than generalizable learning.

■ *How Can We Get Better Outcomes from Field Experiences?*

Supervising experiential learning requires finding a balance between student independence and teacher control. One needs to give the student sufficient freedom to make and learn from mistakes; yet you don't want students to lose so much time and become so frustrated that motivation disintegrates. As in other teaching methods the ideal is to provide sufficient initial support and guidance so that the student can experience some progress, encouraging more independence as the student surmounts initial problems.

How does one ensure that the experience will be educational? Typically the answer is to require a journal or a written or oral report. The rationale for this is a good one. Generally speaking, research suggests that transfer is enhanced by verbalized concepts or principles. However, the key point, as in all education, is to think about the goals of the experience. Are students expected to learn how to apply concepts learned in previous or concomitant education? Are students expected to learn how to distill from real-life complexity generalizations or ideas useful in other situations? Is the experience designed to enhance motivation for learning and to facilitate personality development and altruistic values?

All too often experiential learning is entered as something obviously valuable without enough consideration of the values to be achieved. Consideration of goals or values is necessary if one is to work cooperatively with students to structure and evaluate the experiential learning.

As in the case of laboratories, the educational outcomes depend a great deal upon the way field experiences are integrated with other educational experiences. Students in field experiences need to think about the meaning of the experience just as they need to think about their reading, classroom experiences, writing, and other educational activities. Discussions and lectures explicitly tied to field experiences, written reports and journals, oral presentations, and demonstrations are possible techniques for promoting long-term learning from field experiences. For example, a journal can include both impressions of the field setting and questions or insights about the relevance of related reading or classroom experiences.

SUPPLEMENTARY READING

The classic book on the innovations in education in the 1960s is P. Runkel, R. Harrison, and M. Runkel (eds.), *The Changing College Classroom* (San Francisco: Jossey-Bass, 1972). Chapter 14 by Cytrynbaum and Mann is particularly relevant.

Another classic is Morris Keaton's book (with associates), *Experiential Learning: Rationale, Characteristics, and Assessment* (San Francisco: Jossey-Bass, 1976).

Peer Learning, Collaborative Learning, Cooperative Learning*

ONE OF THE RECURRING CRITICISMS of higher education is that it hasn't increased its productivity at the same rate as industry. By productivity critics typically mean that colleges should turn out more students using fewer teachers—as if colleges were factories producing shoes, automobiles, or soap. I once began to try to help a group of legislators develop a more sophisticated understanding by asking if a legislator's productivity should be measured by the number of bills introduced or if a doctor's productivity should be measured by the number of patients seen, regardless of the number who died. Obviously the product of education is learning, not credit hours.

But aren't professors simply featherbedding when they resist larger classes, television, computers, and other technological aids? "After all, there's no significant difference in effectiveness between these and the traditional classes," says the critic.

I have already shown that the "no significant difference" findings actually turn out quite consistently to favor live, small-class discussions if one is concerned about the longer term goals of higher education such as ability to apply knowledge, solve

---

* We shall use the term "peer learning" to include both "collaborative" and "cooperative" learning. Collaborative and cooperative learning involve peer learning in which there is interdependence of group members in working toward a common goal.

problems, or learn new material. Thus, more "efficient" methods allow professors to teach more students but with a *loss of learning* for the individual students.

The bottleneck in educational efficiency is that learning to think requires thinking and communicating the thinking through talking, writing, or doing, so that others can react to it. Unfortunately a professor can read only one paper at a time, can listen to only one student's comments at a time, and can respond with only one voice.

The problem is not one of communicating knowledge from professors to students more efficiently. Printed materials have done this very well for years, and for most educational purposes are still superior to any of the modern alternatives. The problem is rather one of interaction between the learner and teacher.

▬▬ *Peer Learning and Teaching*

The best answer to the question, "What is the most effective method of teaching?" is that it depends on the goal, the student, the content, and the teacher. But the next best answer is, "Students teaching other students." There is a wealth of evidence that peer learning and teaching is extremely effective for a wide range of goals, content, and students of different levels and personalities (Johnson and Johnson, 1975; Johnson, Maruyama, Johnson, Nelson, and Skon, 1981).

Here are some tips that may be helpful in initiating a variety of types of cooperative learning methods:

1. Explain why working together is important and valuable.

2. Make sure students know what their task is; for example, if it involves out-of-class work, give teams a few minutes before the end of the class period to make plans and to report to you what they plan to do.

3. For in-class group work, move around and listen in to be sure students are not lost and confused.

■■■■ *Student-Led Discussions*

In experiments in educational psychology and general psychology, Gruber and Weitman (1962) found that students taught in small student-led discussion groups without a teacher not only did at least as well on a final examination as students who heard the teacher lecture, but they were also superior in curiosity (as measured by question-asking behavior) and in interest in educational psychology. The discussion students reported a larger number of readings during the term, whereas the lecture students reported more attempts at applying their learning. In an experiment in a physical optics course, the lecture students were superior to student-led discussion students on a test of facts and simple problems but inferior on a test containing complex problems and new material. The superiority of student-led discussions was particularly marked for students below the median in ability. Romig (1972) and Beach (1960, 1968) report similar results in English and psychology classes.

Webb and Grib (1967) reported six studies in which student-led discussions were compared with instructor-led discussions or lectures. Significant differences in achievement tests favored the student-led discussions. Both students and instructors reported that the student-led discussions increased student motivation; and students who had been exposed to student-led discussions tended to favor them over instructor-led discussions as a supplement to lectures.

Webb and Grib also note that students report that the sense of freedom to ask questions and express their own opinions is a major advantage of the student-led discussions. This may explain Gruber and Weitman's (1962) finding that the poorer students benefited most from the student-led discussions. It makes theoretical sense that this opportunity to expose individual conceptions and misconceptions and compare ideas with those of others should contribute to learning if the group contains sufficient resources of knowledge and higher-level thinking to explain things in ways that help the less knowledgeable students restructure their understanding. A student-led group would most likely not be effective in areas in which students simply reinforced each other's biases.

▰▰▰ *Peer Tutoring*

"Pay to be a tutor, not to be tutored" is the message from studies of peer tutoring. For example, Annis (1983) compared learning under five conditions:

1. Students read a textbook passage.
2. Students read the passage and were taught by a peer.
3. Students did not read the passage but were taught by a peer.
4. Students read the passage and prepared to teach it to other students.
5. Students read the passage and taught it to another student.

The results demonstrated that teaching resulted in better learning than being taught. A similar study by Bargh and Schul (1980) also found positive results, with the largest part of the gain in retention being attributable to deeper studying of material when preparing to teach. These results fit well with contemporary theories of learning and memory. Preparing to teach and teaching involve active thought about the material, analysis and selection of main ideas, and processing the concepts into one's own thoughts and words. However, this does not mean that those being tutored fail to learn. Peer tutoring also helps those being tutored (Lidren, Meier, and Brigham, 1991; Cohen, Kulik, and Kulik, 1982).

▰▰▰ *The Learning Cell*

One of the best-developed systems for helping pairs of students learn more effectively is the "Learning Cell" developed by Marcel Goldschmid of the Swiss Federal Institute of Technology in Lausanne (Goldschmid, 1971). The learning cell, or student dyad, refers to a cooperative form of learning in pairs, in which students alternate asking and answering questions on commonly read materials.

1. To prepare for the learning cell, students read an assignment and write questions dealing with the major points raised in the reading or other related materials.

2. At the beginning of each class meeting, students are randomly assigned to pairs and one partner, A, begins by asking the first question.

3. After having answered and perhaps having been corrected or given additional information, the second student, B, puts a question to A, and so on.

4. During this time, the instructor goes from dyad to dyad, giving feedback and asking and answering questions.*

A variation of this procedure has each student read (or prepare) different materials. In this case, A "teaches" B the essentials of his or her readings, then asks B prepared questions, whereupon they switch roles.

The effectiveness of the learning cell method was first explored in a large (250 students) psychology course (Goldschmid, 1970) where four learning options were compared: seminar, discussion, independent study (essay), and learning cell. Students in the learning cell option performed significantly better on an unannounced examination and rated their ongoing learning experience significantly higher. A more extensive field test in a number of other disciplines at the university level (Goldschmid and Shore, 1974) demonstrated the learning cell's effectiveness regardless of the size of the class, its level, or the nature of the subject matter. A third investigation evaluated the learning cell across three age groups (Schirmerhorn, Goldschmid, and Shore, 1975). Fifth- and ninth-grade pupils as well as university students studied probability at their respective intellectual levels for two class periods using the learning cell. All age groups showed significant learning after reading and formulating questions and after the discussions between partners (Goldschmid, 1975). Training students to generate thought-provoking questions enhances learning (King, 1990; Pressley et al., 1992).

---

* Students can also use the learning cell technique outside of class.

■■■■■ *Syndicate-Based Peer Learning*

The term "syndicate" has a faintly evil connotation in the United States, but in Great Britain and other countries "syndicate" is used to describe a team-based system of learning that has proved to be effective. In syndicate-based peer learning, the class is divided into teams (or syndicates) of four to eight students. Each syndicate is given assignments (perhaps three or four questions). References are suggested and members of the syndicate may divide up the readings. The findings may then be discussed by the various syndicates as they meet in small groups during the regular class period. The syndicate may then make a written or oral report to the class as a whole.

Some assignments may be worked on by all the syndicates; others may be covered by two or three syndicates in behalf of the class. Most of the course work is carried out in syndicates working cooperatively (Collier, 1983). Hartman (1989) reports increased student motivation and student perceptions of deeper understanding as a result of the use of this method.

■■■■■ *Student Characteristics and Peer Learning*

Peer learning works better for some students than others. Leith (1974) found that introverts did about as well studying alone as in learning cells; extroverts did better in learning cells if their partners were also extroverts. A learning cell composed of an extrovert paired with an introvert was no more effective than individual learning. In summary, learning cells increase learning for some students and do not hurt the learning of any students.

When dealing with ability differences, however, it may be that heterogeneity is better than homogeneity. Larson, Dansereau, O'Donnell, Hythecker, Lambiotte, and Rocklin (1984) found that cooperative learners with partners with dissimilar vocabulary scores recalled more main ideas after studying a textbook passage not only on the passage studied cooperatively but on a passage studied individually.

Hall et al. (1988), in a review of studies on cooperative learning reported that cognitive differences among students affect learning in cooperative situations. Students strong in induction skill perform substantially better dyadically than individually, while the opposite was true for persons low in induction ability. In the case of field independence/dependence, pairs of heterogeneous abilities perform better than homogeneous pairs.

▰▰▰ *Why Does Peer Learning Work?*

Motivationally the method has the advantages of interaction with a peer—an opportunity for mutual support and stimulation. (One piece of evidence for the motivational value of peer learning [Schomberg, 1986] is that it reduces absenteeism.) Cognitively it provides an opportunity for elaboration—putting material into one's own words—as well as a chance to begin using the language of the discipline. An effective partner can act as a model of useful strategies as well as a teacher. Several of the effective peer learning techniques involve alternating between listening and summarizing or explaining. Structures of peer learning that reduce the chance that one participant is simply a passive recipient seem likely to be better for both motivation and learning.

The task of the successful student in peer learning is to question, explain, express opinions, admit confusion, and reveal misconceptions; but at the same time the student must listen to peers, respond to their questions, question their opinions, and share information or concepts that will clear up their confusion. Accomplishing these tasks requires interpersonal as well as cognitive skills—being able to give feedback in nonthreatening, supportive ways, maintaining a focus on group goals, developing orderly task-oriented procedures, and developing and sustaining mutual tasks. It is little wonder that peer learning sometimes fails; the wonder is that it so frequently works.

Nonetheless, well-planned use of peer learning works. Students are more likely to talk in small groups than large ones; students who are confused are more likely to ask other students questions about their difficulties or failure to understand than to reveal these problems with a faculty member present. Students who are not confused must actively organize and reorganize their own learning in order to explain it. Thus both the confused and unconfused benefit.

SUPPLEMENTARY READING

The Johnson brothers at the University of Minnesota, D. W. Johnson and R. T. Johnson, are outstanding students of cooperative learning. Their book, *Learning Together and Alone: Cooperation, Competition and Individualization* (Englewood Cliffs, NJ: Prentice-Hall, 1975), is a good summary of research at all levels of education.

One of the preeminent scholars of cooperative learning in higher education in Jim Cooper, who in 1991 initiated the newsletter *Cooperative Learning and College Teaching*, an excellent source of ideas for different ways of using cooperative learning. You can subscribe by writing:

> Network for Cooperative Learning in Higher Education
> Dr. Jim Cooper
> HFA–B–316
> CSU Dominquez Hills
> 1000 E. Victoria St.
> Carson, CA 90747

One interesting use of students as observers in panel discussions is reported by Meyer M. Cahn, Teaching Through Student Models. In P. Runkel, R. Harrison, and M. Runkel (eds.), *The Changing College Classroom* (San Francisco: Jossey-Bass, 1972), pp. 36–51.

William Fawcett Hill's book *Learning Through Discussion: A Guide for Leaders and Members of Discussion Groups* (Beverly Hills, CA: Sage Publications, 1977) describes a method of structuring student-led discussions (ETSI—Education Through Student Interaction).

This and other methods are described in Charles A. Goldschmid and Everett K. Wilson, *Passing on Sociology: The Teaching of a Discipline* (Belmont, CA: Wadsworth, 1980).

Team learning and other group methods are discussed in Clark Bouton and Russell Garth, Learning in Groups, *New Directions for Teaching and Learning 14* (San Francisco: Jossey-Bass, 1983).

Tutoring is generally beneficial, but its value can be enhanced by training. A helpful article is H. J. Hartman, Factors affecting the tutoring process, *Journal of Developmental Education*, 1990, *14* (2), 2–6.

CHAPTER 14

Project Methods
and Independent Study

*I*F ONE GOAL OF EDUCATION is to help students develop the ability to continue learning after their formal education is complete, it seems reasonable that they should have supervised experience in learning independently—experience in which the instructor helps students learn how to formulate problems, find answers, and evaluate their progress themselves. One might expect the values of independent study to be greatest for students of high ability with a good deal of background in the area to be covered, since such students should be less likely to be overwhelmed by difficulties encountered. While this expectation contains some truth, motivation and work habits are also important. In this chapter we will consider two forms of independent study: individual projects undertaken as part of a course and small-group independent study. We will also consider team learning in large courses.

Experiential learning (such as field experience and community service) also is aimed at the goal of leading students to view learning as going beyond classroom activities. Projects and independent study often include experiential learning experiences.

■ *The Project Method*

Independent study programs frequently involve the execution of projects in which a student, or group of students, undertakes to gather and integrate data relevant to some more or less important problem.

The results of research on the effectiveness of the project method are not particularly encouraging. One of the first "independent study" experiments was that of Seashore (1928). His course consisted primarily of guided individual study with written reports on eight projects, each of which took about a month to complete. Final examination scores, however, were no different for these students than for students taught by the usual lecture-discussion method (Scheidemann, 1929). Similar results were reported by Barnard (1936) for a "group study" method. In a study in a college botany course, Novak (1958) found that students in conventional classes learned more facts than did those taught by the project method. The project method was particularly ineffective for students in the middle third of the group in intelligence. Similarly, Goldstein (1956) reports that students taught pharmacology by a project method did not learn more than those taught in a standard laboratory.

Unfortunately, criteria such as those used in the studies just noted are probably not sufficient for measuring achievement of the purported objectives of project instruction. Presumably the real superiority of the project method should be revealed in measures of motivation and resourcefulness. One morsel of support comes from Thistlethwaite's (1960) finding that National Merit Scholars checked requirement of a term paper or laboratory project as one characteristic of their most stimulating course.

The student who completes a project often has a sense of mastery going well beyond that of completing a conventional assignment. Students working on a project have to solve real problems and to use their knowledge in new ways—characteristics of learning situations that both motivate and facilitate more lasting learning.

If we grant that projects sometimes fail to work well, what can we do to increase the probability of success? Here are three suggestions:

1. Be sure the student has a clear question, problem, or goal. This doesn't mean that the goal will necessarily be clear initially, but I do advocate monitoring students' progress in arriving at a goal that represents a problem that is meaningful for them.

2. Help students be explicit about the strategies they plan to use, about their time management, and how they will monitor their progress. This is a chance to get students to develop strategic learning.

3. Have students compare notes and get feedback on their progress from fellow students. Producing an independent product can be anxiety producing. Peer support can be helpful both substantively and emotionally.

▬▬ *Research on Independent Study*

With the support of the Fund for Advancement of Education, a number of colleges experimented with large programs of independent study. As with other comparisons of teaching methods, few large differences were found between achievement of students working independently and those taught in conventional classes. The expected gains in independence also often failed to materialize. Students taught by independent study did not always develop greater ability or motivation for learning independently. Nevertheless, a number of encouraging results emerged.

Small Group Independent Study

Favorable results on independent study were obtained in the experiments carried out at the University of Colorado by Gruber and Weitman (1960). In a course in first-year English in which the group met only about 90 percent of the regularly scheduled hours and had little formal training on grammar, the self-directed study group was significantly superior to control groups on a test of grammar. In a course in physical optics, groups of students who attended class without the instructor but were free to consult him learned fewer facts and simple applications, but were superior to students in conventional classes in difficult applications and learning new material. Moreover, the areas of superiority were maintained in a retest three months later when the difference in factual knowledge had disappeared. In educational psychology an experimental class of five or six students without the instructor was equal to a conventional three-lecture-a-week class in mastery of content, and tended to be superior on measures of curiosity.

▰▰▰ *Research on Variations in Amount of Classroom Time*

Independent study experiments have varied greatly in the amount of assistance given students and in the patterning of instructional vs. independent periods. For example, merely excusing students from attending class is one method of stimulating independent study. The results of such a procedure are not uniform but suggest that classroom experience is not essential for learning. However, different kinds of learning may take place out of class than in class.

The experiment reported by McKeachie, Lin, Forrin, and Teevan (1960) involved a fairly high degree of student-instructor contact. In this experiment students normally met with the instructor in small groups weekly or biweekly, but students were free to consult the instructor whenever they wished to. The results of the experiment suggest that the "tutorial" students did not learn as much from the textbook as students taught in conventional lecture periods and discussion sections, but did develop stronger motivation both for course work and for continued learning after the course. This was indicated not only by responses to a questionnaire administered at the end of the course but also by the number of advanced psychology courses later elected.

The results of the studies in a child development course by Parsons (1957) and Parsons, Ketcham, and Beach (1958) were, in a sense, more favorable to independent study. In the latter experiment four teaching methods were compared—lecture, instructor-led discussions, autonomous groups that did not come to class, and individual independent study in which each student was sent home with the syllabus, returning for the final examination. In both experiments, students working independently made the best scores on the final examination, which measured retention of factual material in the textbook. The instructor-led discussion groups were the lowest in performance on the final examination. There were no significant differences between groups on a measure of attitudes toward working with children. The authors explain their results in terms of the independent group's freedom from distraction by interesting examples, possible applications, or opposing points of view from those presented in the text.

Although the Parsons, Ketcham, and Beach results were favorable to independent study, they are not very satisfying to the advocate of this method, for they lead to the conclusion that if students know that they are going to be tested on the factual content of a particular book, it is more advantageous for them to read that book than to participate in other educational activities. But knowledge of specific facts is not the typical major objective of an independent study program. What instructors are hoping for is greater integration, increased purposefulness, and more intense motivation for further study. That independent study can achieve these ends is indicated by the Colorado and Michigan experiments. But the paucity of positive results suggests that we need more research on methods of selecting and training students for independent study, arranging the independent study experience, and measuring outcomes. Note that the Colorado and Penn State results came in courses in which a good deal of contact with the instructor was retained.

Time in Class

The independent study experiments demonstrate that education is not simply a function of time spent in a class with a teacher. Well-planned activities outside teacher-controlled classrooms can be at least as educational as conventional classes. But merely reducing time in class is not independent study. Generally speaking, the more time spent on learning, the greater the learning. Wakely, Marr, Plath, and Wilkins (1960) compared performance in a traditional four-hour-a-week lecture class with that in a class meeting only once a week to clear up questions on the textbook. In this experiment the traditional classes proved to be superior. Similarly, Paul (1932) found fifty-five minute class periods to be superior to thirty-minute periods, as measured by student achievement. Shortening class periods, reducing the number of classes, and cutting the length of the academic term may be advisable as part of a planned educational change, but they should not be undertaken with the blithe assumption that the same educational outcomes will be achieved.

■■■ *Senior Projects*

More and more departments require a project as part of a senior capstone course. The major problem departments encounter is a lack of faculty members and of faculty time to provide adequate guidance and supervision. Even though senior projects usually involve the writing of individual theses, one can still gain some efficiency by grouping students with similar topics and encouraging cooperative work such as that described in Chapter 13, "Peer Learning, Collaborative Learning, Cooperative Learning." Students can cooperate in digging out references for their review of previous research; they can provide frequent feedback to one another; they can support one another when barriers or blocks arise. The tips for term papers included in Chapter 9, "Writing: Papers, Journals, and Reports," as well as our discussion of projects earlier in this chapter are also relevant here.

SUPPLEMENTARY READING

An excellent reference for project learning at all levels of education is:

P. C. Blumenfeld, E. Soloway, R. W. Marx, J. S. Krajcik, M. Guzdial, and A. Palinscar, Motivating project-based learning: Sustaining the doing, supporting the learning, *Educational Psychologist*, 1991, *26*, 369–398. Although this article deals primarily with the project method in pre-college education, the discussion of why projects help, how projects should be developed, and what kinds of difficulties occur is relevant for college teachers.

Teaching with Cases

■■■■ *The Case Method*

The case method is widely used in business and law courses and is frequently incorporated into one or more class sessions in other disciplines. Generally case method discussions produce good student involvement. Case methods, like games and simulations, are intended to develop student ability to solve problems using knowledge, concepts, and skills relevant to a course. The students are also expected to be motivated by the case to learn from readings, lectures, or other resources. Cases provide contextualized learning, as contrasted with learning disassociated from meaningful contexts.

Cases are sometimes actual descriptions of problem situations in the field in which the case is being used; often they are syntheses constructed to represent a particular principle or type of problem. For example, in medicine a case may describe a patient and the patient's symptoms; in psychology the case might describe a group facing a decision; in biology the case might describe an environmental problem. Whatever the case, it typically involves the possibility of several alternative approaches or actions and some evaluation of values and costs of different solutions to the problem posed. Usually cases require that the students not only apply course content but also consult other resources. The major problem in teaching by cases involves going from the students' fascination with the particular case to the general principle or conceptual structure. In choosing a case to discuss, the teacher needs to think, "What is this case a case of?"

The teacher's role in the case method is primarily to facilitate discussion—questioning, listening, challenging, and encouraging analysis and problem solving, and proposing hypothetical situations to test the validity of generalizations.

▰▰▰ *Tips for Teaching with Cases*

A blackboard is useful for recording points established, relevant principles, questions to be answered, information that needs to be researched, possible value considerations, and the evidence for alternative approaches that have been suggested. Usually case discussions are carried out in small groups, but Barrow et al. (1986) report successful case problem solving in large classes. You can increase student involvement (and perhaps learning) by role playing the case, perhaps leading to alternative solutions to the problem posed.

Typically the case method involves a series of cases, but in some case method courses the cases are not well chosen to represent properly sequenced levels of difficulty. Often, in order to make cases realistic, so many details are included that beginning students lose the principles or points the case was intended to demonstrate. As in classic studies in discrimination learning in the laboratory, teachers attempting to help students learn complex discriminations and principles in problem solving need to choose initial cases in which the differences are clear and extreme before moving to more subtle, complex cases. Typically, one of the goals of the case method is to teach students to select important factors from a tangle of less important ones that may, nevertheless, form a context to be considered. One does not learn such skills by being in perpetual confusion, but rather by success in solving more and more difficult problems. For a more detailed exposition see Hunt (1951) and Maier (1971).

▰▰▰ *Research on the Case Method*

Watson (1975) compared classes taught by the case method with a class taught by the lecture method. Students in one of the two case study classes scored better in knowledge and understanding than the lecture class. The other case study class and the lecture class were roughly equal. Both case study classes were superior to the lecture in ability to apply concepts. (In view of the continuing popularity of the case method, it is surprising that so little research has been done on its effectiveness.)

Cases, simulations, and games involve getting, recalling, and using information in order to solve problems. As I shall discuss in Chapter 27, this involves the kind of restructuring that is likely to result in better retention, recall, and use of the information outside the classroom.

SUPPLEMENTARY READING

T. Roman and S. Mahler, A three-dimensional model for using case studies in the academic classroom, *Higher Education*, 1986, *15*, 677–696.

M. McNair (ed.), *The Case Method at the Harvard Business School* (New York: McGraw-Hill, 1954).

C. Argyris, Some limitations of the case method, *Academy of Management Review*, 1980, *5*, 291–298.

M. Berger, In defense of the case method. A reply to Argyris, *Academy of Management Review*, 1983, *8*, 329–333.

C. R. Christensen and A. J. Hansen, *Teaching and the Case Method* (Boston: Harvard Business School, 1987).

A sophisticated description of the use of the case method in medical education as well as two experiments on activating and restructuring prior knowledge in case discussions may be found in H. G. Schmidt, *Activatie Van Voorkennis, Intrinsieke Motivatie en de Verwerking van Tekst* (Apeldoorn, The Netherlands: Van Walraven bv, 1982). (Don't worry. Despite the Dutch title, the text is in English.)

Instructional Games
and Simulations

*F*OR SOME STUDENTS AND SOME TEACHERS, education and games are simply at opposite ends of a continuum—they find it hard to conceive of games as educational. Yet in the past few decades an increasing number of teachers have been finding games to be an important part of their educational resources.

Games and Simulations

An educational game involves students in some sort of competition or achievement in relationship to a goal; it is a game that both teaches and is fun. Many games are simulations; for example, they attempt to model some real-life problem situation. Thus there are business games, international relations games, and many others. Whatever the topic, the planner of the game needs to specify the teaching objectives to be served by the game and then plan the game to highlight features that contribute to those objectives.

The chief advantage of games and simulations is that students are active participants rather than passive observers. Students must make decisions, solve problems, and react to the results of their decisions. Lepper and Malone (1985) have studied the motivational elements in computer games. They found that key features are challenge, self-competence, curiosity, personal control, and fantasy.

Dekkers and Donatti (1981) conducted a meta-analysis of ninety-three studies of simulations and concluded that simulation was not more effective than conventional methods for achieving cognitive objectives but did have a favorable effect upon student attitudes and motivation.

Games typically create a high level of student involvement and thus can be a worthwhile adjunct to many courses. Following is a description of a game used in Russian History.*

Simulation in a Survey Course in Russian History

Game: Parties and Constituencies in Russian Revolution.

Instructor: Bill Rosenberg, Associate Professor of History.

Enrollment: About 100 students.

Game Time: 1 1/2 hours (up to 2 hours).

Preparation: Four or five students volunteered to work out this game as their course project; two or three took a leadership role. The instructor consulted with them in planning; he suggested readings and consultation with an instructor who had worked on gaming and simulation.

The students prepared a twelve-page document on four parties and four constituencies that took part in the Russian Revolution. This program told each group what its orientation was (for example, what their methods tended to be). The program was given to students to read in advance of the day of the simulation.

Purpose of the Game: To look at the electoral processes, in terms of 1) where groups of people stood ideologically, and 2) how they related to each other politically.

Structure of the Game: There were, historically, two elections: in the middle of 1917 and at the end of 1917. One of these elections took place in the game situation after parties and constituencies had been playing their parts for an hour. The game then went on for another half hour or more.

---

* Many of the games used at the University of Michigan were developed in workshops directed by Barbara Steinwachs and the staff of the Gaming Service of the University Extension Service.

Students volunteered for four "party groups" and four "constituency groups." A few were assigned to groups or chose not to participate. Each group consulted the program and met in caucus to decide on its actions. They could do almost anything they wished: attempt to form alliances, appeal to another group for support, influence others, and even lie. Delegates were sent from caucuses to different groups and returned for further strategy discussions.

After an hour, an election was held and tallied on the blackboard. The game continued for about half an hour after the election.

Physical Setting: The game took place in the usual large lecture hall, but smaller groups spilled out into the hallway and beyond the room. The usual lecture time of one hour was extended to two hours that day.

Evaluation: The instructor felt that the simulation was remarkably effective as a recreation of what actually took place in 1917. For example, the Bolsheviks were clear about what they wanted and went directly to the point of gaining power, while the Liberals were meeting in the hall and came in to ask at an advanced stage of the play whether the game had actually begun.

Evaluations of this session were elicited from students, who were uniformly positive. There were some suggestions that the instructions could have been clearer and more time might have been taken to explain in advance.

The educational use of the game might have been strengthened by planning for more student discussion afterwards. About twenty minutes or so were spent in discussion after the game in the lecture room, and there was some discussion in section meetings. However, more planning for postgame discussion might have strengthened this game as a teaching technique.

There are now a number of well-designed games that have been used in enough situations to have the kinks worked out. Some use computers to implement the complex interaction of various decisions. One example is SIMSOC (Gamson, 1966), a sociology game in which students are citizens of a society in which they have economic and social roles; for example, some are members of political parties, and some have police powers. METRO is an urban planning game involving conflicts between politicians, landowners, planners, school personnel, and so on. Games such as this are useful in getting students to consider varied points of view relevant to the issues addressed in the game. Like the case method, an educational game may be either too simple or complex to achieve the kind of generalization of concepts or principles that the teacher desires. The biggest barrier to the use of games is logistic. Often it is hard to find a game that fits the time and facilities limitations of typical classes. Devising one's own game can be fun but also time-consuming. Nonetheless, games are potentially useful tools for effective teaching.

SUPPLEMENTARY READING

H. S. Guetzkow, *Simulation in Social Sciences: Readings* (Englewood Cliffs, NJ: Prentice-Hall, 1962).

CHAPTER 17

Role Playing and Microteaching

■■■ *Role Playing*

Role playing as a teaching device developed from the psychodramatists centered around Moreno and the group dynamicists. Briefly, role playing is the setting up of more or less unstructured situations in which students' behaviors are improvised to fit in with their conceptions of roles to which they have been assigned. Role playing is like a drama in which each participant is assigned a character to portray, but where no lines are learned. The individuals portraying specific roles improvise their responses to the situation.

The purposes of role playing as used in my classes are:

1. To give students practice in using what they've learned.

2. To illustrate principles from the course content.

3. To develop insight into human relations problems.

4. To provide a concrete basis for discussion.

5. To maintain or arouse interest.

6. To provide a channel in which feelings can be expressed under the guise of make-believe.

7. To develop increased awareness of one's own and others' feelings.

Role playing can be utilized in a variety of classes, ranging from complex simulations of political or international situations (as described in Chapter 16) to language classes in which role playing is used for practice of the language. In language classes, for example, role playing can provide useful linguistic information on appropriate speech levels (how to respond to rude questions, how to be politely evasive, persuasive, firm, and so on), use of gestures, and cultural points such as distance between speakers. Students may write and/or act out more than one way of handling a situation. Sometimes teachers take part in the role playing as participants; sometimes they act as "coaches."

In using role playing instructors may begin by bringing to class a problem situation that does not have too direct a relationship to the students' own personal problems. The situation should be one that is familiar enough so that members can understand the roles and their potential responses to the problem. Ordinarily, role playing seems to work best when it arises rather spontaneously from a problem being discussed in class. This does not mean, however, that instructors cannot foresee appropriate uses of role playing. In fact, until they have had some experience with role playing, they will probably role play only those situations they have worked out rather explicitly before class. Nevertheless, instructors should be willing to change plans in accordance with the needs of the group.

Instructors should have in mind some objective for the role playing other than that of showing off a new trick. In introducing the first role-playing situation to the class the instructor should describe the situation quite completely, picturing the roles required and the objective of the role playing before asking for volunteers for the roles.

For example, the instructor in a psychology class might say,

> We've been learning about the differences between Skinnerian and Freudian approaches to treatment. Let's imagine that Freud has come back to life and that he and Skinner have just read an account in the morning paper of a baseball player who punched his manager. Skinner and Freud are having coffee with a student who asks them, "What should be done about this player who punched his manager? This is the third time he has been in trouble for

fighting.'' Who wants to play the role of the student? Who will volunteer to be Skinner? Who will volunteer to be Freud? . . . OK. Here are three chairs; we'll imagine that you're sitting around a table. Let's begin by the student asking her question.

The goal of this role-playing situation would be to get the class actively involved in comparing Skinner's and Freud's viewpoints. The situation can be farfetched or realistic, so long as it is interesting and involving. You might, in fact, even get the class to help you develop the description of the situation to increase their involvement.

Here is another role-playing situation used in language courses:

> Students are shown a picture of an apartment building. Students work in pairs, writing their dialogues first.*
>
> Grammar points: Modal verbs; *too*, *very*.
>
> Instructions: You are the man who lives in the apartment that is too noisy. Call up the mother of the children who are playing football in their apartment. Be polite. *or* You are the man who lives in the apartment that is too noisy. Call up the mother of the children who are playing football in their apartment. Be rude. Be angry.

General considerations in handling role playing are:

→ If you wish to point out different responses or solutions to a given problem, use two or more presentations of the same situation with different participants or have participants switch roles. More natural behavior and more convincing differences are obtained by not permitting participants in the replay of the situation to see the first presentation. This also prevents the feeling of the first group that the second group is trying to show them up.

---

* William Horrell describes the use of dialogues as writing assignments. For example, Horrell assigned students to write a dialogue between Machiavelli and Lao-Tzu that would reveal similarities and differences in their political viewpoints. One might make similar assignments to compare two theorists or major figures in almost any field. (W. Horrell, Using dialogues as writing assignments, *Innovation Abstracts*, 1992, *14* (3).

→ Even if you know the class fairly well, it is usually preferable to get volunteers for the roles rather than to choose
participants, for volunteers are less likely to feel on the
spot.

→ For the usual class situation, it is better to direct discussion away from the reactions of specific participants to the
reactions of people in general in such a situation. As the
group gains a sense of security, more attention can be
paid to feelings of the actual participants, provided you
are aware of the possibility of mobilizing anxiety with
which you may not wish to deal. Situations involving
morals or subjects of high emotional significance, such as
sex taboos, are apt to be disturbing to some students.

→ The situations that are most interesting and reveal the
greatest differences in responses are those involving some
choice or conflict of motives. Often the students themselves will suggest good situations for illustrating certain
principles. In any case, situations that are unrelated to student experience are apt to fall flat. The teacher can to some
extent control the depth of emotions and attitudes
aroused by the context of the situation. For example, the
same situation might be set up as father and son, dean
and student, or boss and employee.

→ To help the nonparticipating members of the class observe
skillfully, assign individuals to watch for specific things.
For example, one observer may be asked to particularly
observe expressive movements of the participants;
another may observe the pattern of interaction between
the participants. The class itself may suggest points to
look for and to discuss.

→ Some role-playing situations may end themselves.
Usually, however, the instructor will have to "cut" the
action. Generally the beginner lets the role playing run too
long. Three to six minutes is usually sufficient to spark
discussion.

→ Players feel less defensive if they are asked to discuss the
situation before the rest of the class begins discussion.

→ After discussing the situation, you may wish to replay the situation reversing the roles, changing one role, altering the situation, or playing a probable following scene.

In general, role playing seems to stimulate much interest and give students the feeling that they are actually making use of what they've learned. As in most other novel teaching techniques, the effectiveness of role playing depends to a large extent upon the confidence of the instructor in the procedure and the students' feeling (gained from the instructor's attitude) that it is going to be a successful and valuable aspect of the course. Like any other technique, it can be used to such an extent that it becomes repetitious, but if used to accomplish definite goals, if you explain the goals, and if students perceive their progress toward those goals, it can be an extremely rewarding technique.

■ *Microteaching*

Microteaching is a technique primarily used in teacher training, but is also potentially useful for training in public speaking, interviewing, leading groups, or other communication or interpersonal skills. Microteaching involves presenting a lesson, speech, and so on in a brief period, for example, five minutes. The microlesson focuses on the use of a particular skill, such as asking questions, establishing rapport, or eliciting student comments. The microlesson may be videotaped to facilitate review and further practice of the skill desired.

By means of microteaching, students can learn specific skills that are elements in large units of performance, such as teaching. Skill development often continues best when learners can progress by achievable steps. Microteaching reduces the complexity and stress that would be associated with a full-scale experience, such as teaching a full class period or delivering a complete oration. Leith (1982) showed that microteaching practice resulted in significantly better teaching than conventional preparation through classroom sessions on classroom management, lesson planning, and so on. But an interesting attribute-treatment interaction emerged. Introverts benefited much more from the microteaching. Two years later the microteaching experience still showed a favorable effect but by this time the extroverts were rated as being superior to the introverts.

Microteaching is a form of role playing, and research results indicate that it is effective in teacher training. But even though you are not in teacher education, you may wish to consider microteaching as a means of enhancing your own skill as a college teacher, or you may find the emphasis upon specific skill and videotape feedback useful in teaching other skills.

SUPPLEMENTARY READING

For further discussion of the use of role playing in teaching, I recommend:

W. Coleman, Role-playing as an instructional aid, *Journal of Educational Psychology*, 1948, *39*, 427–435.

N. R. F. Maier and L. F. Zerfoss, MRP: A technique for training large groups of supervisors and its potential use in social research, *Human Relations*, 1952, *5*, 177–186.

B. S. Fuhrmann and A. F. Grasha, *A Practical Handbook for College Teachers* (Boston: Little, Brown, 1983), pp. 158–160.

CHAPTER 18

One-on-One Teaching and Counseling

*T*HE PRINCIPLES OF TEACHING discussed in earlier chapters are equally valid in the many educational situations in which teacher and student interact one-on-one. Music, art, physical education, dentistry, medicine, social work, and other fields all involve some individualized teaching one-on-one, and every teacher has occasions in which skills in tutoring or one-on-one teaching are needed.

There is relatively little research on one-on-one teaching methods, but several principles mentioned in earlier chapters are relevant:

1. Students are helped by a model of the desired performance. This may be provided by the instructor's demonstration of the technique, by a videotape, or by observation of a skilled performer. Generally speaking, positive examples are more helpful than examples of what not to do. When instructors perform, they should utilize the same techniques they use in presenting other visual aids, particularly in directing the student's attention to crucial aspects of the technique.

2. Students are helped by verbal cues or labels that identify key features of the skill. Students are likely to be distracted by irrelevant details.

3. "Bare bones," simplified simulations or demonstrations, are more useful as starting points than complex real-life situations which may overwhelm the student with too many details.

4. Permit students the maximum freedom to experience successful completion of a task or a part of a task, but give enough guidance so that they will not get bogged down in a rut of errors. This implies that the learning experiences of students go from the simple to the complex, with the steps so ordered that each new problem can be successfully solved.

5. Students need practice with feedback.

6. Feedback from the instructor or from peers may provide more information than the student can assimilate. Don't try to correct everything on the first trial.

7. Feedback can discourage students. Try to provide some encouraging feedback as well as identification of mistakes.

8. Feedback that identifies errors won't help if the learner doesn't know what to do to avoid the errors. Give guidance about what to try next.

9. High-level skills are developed through much practice. Simply reaching the point of successful performance once is not likely to achieve the degree of organization and automatization that is necessary for consistent success.

10. Practice with varied examples is likely to be both more motivating and more likely to transfer to out-of-class performance than is simple drill and repetition.

11. Coaching is not simply one-way telling and criticizing. Asking the learners about their perceptions of what they are doing and helping them evaluate their own performance is also important. In teaching self-evaluation, you may model

the sort of analysis needed. As you evaluate work, verbalize the process you are using and the basis for your evaluation. Like other skills self-evaluation is learned by practice with feedback. Thus students need many opportunities for self-evaluation with feedback *about their evaluation* as well as about the work being evaluated.

12. Peers can help one another. You don't need to monitor everyone all of the time.

■ *Counseling*

Some of your most effective teaching may occur when students come to you with a problem with which they want help. I have already suggested that instructors should establish and keep certain regular office hours for meeting students. In this section I would like to discuss some of the problems that arise in those hours.

I should warn you that a student's ostensible reasons for coming to you may be quite different from the real reasons. Often students ask about a study problem when their real desire is to know the instructor better. They complain of inadequate study habits when underneath there may be difficulties with their home life. I do not mean that you should disregard the problems the students actually present, but if you are aware of possible underlying factors, you may be more understanding and more effective as a counselor.

Counseling need not be restricted to the office. In the classroom the teacher can do much to help individuals by recognizing their potential, by helping them become accepted in the group, and by developing cooperative activities in which they can participate with other class members. Out of the classroom you may be able to get to the real problem more easily over a Coke in the student union than in a more formal office visit.

The most common student problem is worded something like this, "I study harder for this course than for all my other courses, but I just can't seem to pass the tests." In handling this problem I usually encourage the students to express their own ideas about their difficulties. Sometimes their diagnosis and plans for improvement will be much more accurate than any I can give them. Frequently, simple information on budgeting time, on how the students can ask themselves questions about the assignment, or on getting an overview of a chapter before reading it can be of much help.

In general, the key is to get the students away from reading passively or trying to memorize and instead to question, relate, and think more actively about the assignment and lectures.* Sometimes you can help by getting the students to use the student workbook often published as an adjunct to the textbook. Even better may be to encourage peer teaching. In Chapter 13 we found that even poor students can learn by trying to explain something to a peer.

■■■■ *Educational Counseling***

The term educational counseling has been used to refer to three distinctly different types of activity. All of them are inevitable accompaniments of an educational enterprise, but not all of them are equally accepted by faculties as part of their responsibility. The three activities included in educational counseling are 1) program planning, 2) remedial work, and 3) individualized teaching.

Program Planning

The modern university is a complex organization. The student's path through this organization is supposedly mapped by handbooks and catalogues. Unfortunately, most of these documents are, at best, forbiddingly dull and confusingly written. In too many instances they are less than adequate road guides because almost every curriculum has its unwritten requirements. These are preferences for certain sequences of courses or for the choice

---

* For further help you might suggest Linda Annis, *Study Techniques* (Dubuque, IA: Wm. C. Brown, 1983) or Tim Walter and Al Siebert, *Student Success* (New York: Holt, Rinehart & Winston, 5th ed., 1990).

** Much of this section was written by Professor Edward S. Bordin, The University of Michigan.

of one of several alternatives which are so strongly adhered to by the department or college that they become, in effect, requirements for graduation. At the same time, because they are not formal requirements, they exist as part of the folklore rather than as part of the written law.

This state of affairs means that where students are left on their own to select courses, there is great danger of having to extend the normal four-year program because of mistakes in curricular planning. This has given rise to the faculty counselor who is given the responsibility for guiding the students through the intricacies of their chosen curriculum. Often this faculty counselor is expected to double as an amateur professional counselor, one to whom the students can turn for help with any of the other problems that may arise—problems of vocational decision or problems of even more personal import.

The university usually places on this faculty counselor the responsibility for the enforcement of various other regulations governing the students' curricular activities—for example, the number of credits students may elect in a given period, the fulfillment of prerequisites, and the meeting of general requirements for graduation where they exist. The result is that relations between students and faculty are often strained, for the students going to see the faculty members become part of a bureaucratic, impersonal processing that they are impatient to pare down to its irreducible essentials. To the faculty members, these duties loom as demeaning, much-to-be-avoided tasks comparable to KP in military service.

The result of all this is that though many catalogues will carry ambitious statements about faculty counseling, conjuring up an image of the wise, genial, pipe-smoking academician in leisurely discussion with the eager, respectful student who avidly gathers up the words of wisdom that are dropped in the course of this conversation, the stark reality of the relationship is too often that of a meeting between a rebelliously impatient student and a harried and disgruntled faculty member.

Remedial Work

As education has become more individualized in its treatment of the student, educators have become more concerned with special learning problems. Consequently, provision is made for special-ized individualized help in removing blocks to learning and in improving such varied kinds of skills as reading, spelling, arith-metic, and well-articulated speech. In many universities there are specialists to help students overcome deficits in their methods of study or in the basic skills necessary to academic learning. This remedial work is intended to allow for inadequacies in the stu-dents' preparation for college work.

University faculties are not of one mind about the appropri-ateness of providing this kind of educational service. Many of them see these inadequacies as reflections of the failure of pri-mary and secondary schools to perform their functions ade-quately and reject any responsibility for helping to rescue the unfortunate victim. One is tempted to designate this as a Malthusian philosophy because it is sometimes joined with the attitude that too many unqualified students are coming to college anyhow, so that any influences that will decimate the numbers are to be accepted rather than counteracted.

Where remedial counseling is carried on, there may be con-siderable variation in the amount of attention devoted to emo-tional factors in these learning difficulties. There are differences of opinion as to the extent to which emotional and motivational fac-tors are at the roots of learning difficulties or are simply their con-comitants. There seems no real need to choose between these two views of the role of emotion in motivation. One can assume that persons with these learning difficulties will demonstrate symp-toms in varying degrees from the one extreme where the difficul-ties arise primarily from the mechanical sources or cognitive defects, to the other extreme where the difficulty arises because the particular skill has become invested with certain of the emo-tional conflicts of the individual. To the extent that remedial work is aimed at rectifying what must have been defects in the learning sequences by which a skill was acquired, it is a form of educa-tional counseling, and is close to the work of a teacher. To the extent that remedial work deals with the emotional and motiva-tional factors as sources of the difficulty, it becomes a form of psychological counseling.

Psychological Problems

At some point you will recognize that a student needs psycholog-ical counseling. Some of the signs are belligerence, moodiness, excessive worry, suspiciousness, helplessness, emotional out-bursts, or depression. Sometimes you will spot symptoms of drug or alcohol abuse. How do you get the student to the help needed?

The first step may be to get the student to talk to you. Usually this can be handled by asking the student to come in, perhaps to discuss a paper or test. Typically the student will be aware that things aren't going well, and you can talk about what the student might do. One alternative, obviously, is to seek specialized help such as the reading clinic or counseling service. If the student agrees that this might be a good idea, I've found that it helps to pick up the phone and say, "I'll call to see when they can see you." In fact, most such agencies will at least carry out an initial interview with any student who walks in. But the sense of com-mitment involved when a faculty member has called seems to make students more likely to follow through than if they simply agree that they'll go in. Even if the student does not immediately get professional help, your concern and support will be helpful and awareness of the availability of professional help may be valuable later.

Potential Suicides

The increasing concern with suicide risk among college students prompts a few words on the early recognition of the kinds of depressed states that accompany such risks. If you were to notice a sudden falling off of a particular student's faithfulness in attending class, you might want to inquire further, especially if you noted signs of neglect of personal grooming and hygiene, lethargy, and any marked weight changes. Your interest in the student should include concern with any other changes he or she has been experiencing including major separations or losses and mood states. You should listen for talk of death or references to suicide or to getting one's personal and legal affairs in order. Your major concern should not be to reach an accurate assess-ment of suicide risk. A student manifesting any of these characteristics is surely troubled and should be urged to seek whatever professional counseling is available.

Individualized Teaching

The potentially most fruitful and most appropriate interpretation of educational counseling is the one least often defined explicitly and most neglected. When colleges and universities were small communities of a few hundred students and mature scholars, learning and teaching were naturally relatively individualized processes. The size of even the smaller major colleges and universities is such as to make this individualized learning no longer automatic. Even in classes of forty to sixty students, it is difficult for the learning process to include the meeting of a maturing and a mature intellect. Too frequently students must be content to listen to lectures and pursue readings aimed at some abstracted image of a student.

Educational counseling as individualized teaching can represent a method by which this more personalized learning can be preserved even in a large institution. It is particularly necessary for first-year students, to whom new intellectual spheres are being opened, usually at a time when they have taken a big step away from their family and community roots. This is likely to be a time when a great many new assumptions and new ways of dealing with important ideas need to be digested. Educational counselors, because they have no commitment to covering a specific subject matter, can provide students with an opportunity to digest and integrate the intellectual experiences they have been having. Far from being a chore to be assigned to the least successful faculty member, such a demanding responsibility is best undertaken by persons of broad intellectual interests and foundations who, at the same time, have strong pedagogical commitments.

This time, when students are making big strides toward greater independence from family and are trying to search out models who can represent innovations of the adult role to which they aspire, is a time when there should be opportunities for close relationships with faculty members. The very characteristics of the large university throw obstacles in the way of such an experience. Educational counseling is one of the important media for achieving it. It seems probable that the most effective pattern for doing this would be for counselors to plan small group meetings with the students assigned to them for counseling to provide an opportunity for the groups of new students coming from different parts of the state and country to exchange with each other and with a person of fully developed intellectual maturity the impacts of their initial university experiences. A number of colleges and universities group first-year students into interest groups that meet regularly during the first term to help establish both academic and social support systems.

The problems of the older student entering college are in some ways similar despite the obvious differences in life experience. While both younger and older students often feel some anxiety about their ability to carry out academic work successfully, the older students may have even greater concerns than younger students about their ability to adapt to the college environment and to form helpful relationships with peers (most of whom are much younger and experiencing quite different social and recreational lives).

SUPPLEMENTARY READING

In Chickering, *The New American College* (San Francisco: Jossey-Bass, 1988) the chapter by Jane Shipton and Elizabeth Steltenpohl provides a useful perspective on the broad issues faced by academic advisors. The typical schedule of fifteen minutes per advisee is clearly insufficient for planning an academic program in relationship to life-long goals.

ROBERT J. MENGES
Northwestern University

CHAPTER 19

Teaching in the Age of Electronic Information

COMPUTER-BASED TECHNOLOGIES are radically transforming higher education. They expand capabilities for teaching and learning in ways hardly imagined a few years ago. Personal computers readily retrieve and reconfigure vast amounts of electronically stored information, and, through the mass media, we are surrounded with more information than we can comfortably process. In many ways, we are over informed.

In this information environment, teachers do not control access to information as they once did. Instead, it is students who directly receive and interact with data of all kinds. They can transform information from one medium to another, and they create new knowledge as a result of their interactions with teachers and other students.

According to Branson (1991), this is nothing less than a new paradigm for education. The teacher is no longer at the center. The center is occupied by accumulated knowledge and experience, to which students have direct access. Students learn not only by following the teacher; they learn along with the teacher and by interacting with one another. Indeed, students are bound to learn much that the teacher does not know.

▬▬▬ *Electronic Learning Tools*

Computer-based media make possible a rich array of learning tools. Textual, numerical, and graphical sources of great variety are literally at our fingertips.

Examples of Computer-Based Learning Tools

→ Stravinsky's *The Rite of Spring* is the subject of a compact disc/computer disc package. In addition to the stereo performance, there are commentaries that follow the score as it scrolls across the screen and that provide background information about music and dance, a glossary, biographical information, and 200 musical examples featuring single instruments, sections, and the orchestra as a whole.

→ A medical textbook includes bar codes on many pages next to the illustrations. When a wand linked to a videodisc machine scans the code, students see video images (with sound, if appropriate) of the phenomenon discussed in the text.

→ A program called *Perseus* deals with classical and archaic Greece. It includes computer software and a videodisc with narrated scenes and thousands of still and moving pictures. Students navigate through computer and video information covering 800 ancient sites and hundreds of artifacts. Also available on-line are the complete works of Homer, Aeschylus, and Thucydides, an atlas and encyclopedia of Greece, and a Greek-English dictionary, cross-referenced and searchable by key words.

→ All 20 volumes of the *Oxford English Dictionary* are contained on one compact disc. The disc provides instant access to 616,500 words and terms, 137,000 pronunciations, 2.4 million illustrative quotations, 577,000 cross-references, and 249,000 etymologies. (When confronted with a crossword puzzler, just query this disc with whatever letters are known and all compatible words will appear.)

→ *American Memory* includes Library of Congress collections of primary materials from American history. Available on a combination of computer, audio, and video discs, *American Memory* contains 25,500 photographs (dated from 1800 to 1920), mostly by landscape photographer William Henry Jackson; 500 prints and cartoons about Congress; 60 sound recordings (pre-radio) of early 20th-century leaders; 1,610 color photographs taken during World War II; 28 motion pictures of President William McKinley (among the earliest surviving motion pictures); and 350 pamphlets by black authors from Reconstruction to the First World War.

→ The complete library of *Monarch Notes* (112 authors) is on a compact disc. The user can search plot summaries, biographies of authors, critical commentaries, literary analyses, and pictures. Of course, any of the contents can be copied to the user's word processor.

→ Another compact disc holds nationwide economic data covering 3,125 counties, 338 metropolitan areas, and 183 special economic areas during the years 1969 through 1989. Drawing on the Department of Commerce's Regional Economic Information System, it covers personal income, industry earnings, full- and part-time employees, farm income and expenses, and more.

How Students Can Use Electronic Learning Tools for Group Projects

In this information environment, student group projects take on new forms. To begin their work, students might review extensive bibliographies and explore banks of quantitative data, using central computers that are accessed from their desks. They search video and audio archives including cultural artifacts stored in electronic files. Once a specific topic for the project is selected, they assign each other research tasks according to interest and ability; one prefers working with words, another prefers video and animations, and the third likes to work with quantitative information. They discuss their contributions and merge them into a final version. The project takes the form of an electronic document with several audio and video attachments, including some personal photographs scanned into digital form by one of the students.

The completed project is sent to their professional's electronic mailbox. The teacher annotates the document and returns it by electronic mail. After students have read the annotations and made the suggested revisions, they schedule a conference with the teacher. At the conference, revisions are discussed, the quality of the project is assessed, and a grade is assigned.

▬ *Effects on Teaching and Learning*

Under the influence of computer technologies, teaching and learning will change in dramatic ways. These effects have been anticipated by Collins (1991) in terms of eight "shifts" that he believes computers will bring to pre-college education. In essence, these shifts put greater emphasis "on the activity of the student than on that of the teacher" (p. 29). I believe that we should begin to anticipate how the shifts he describes are likely to challenge colleges and universities.

1. A shift from lecture and recitation to coaching. When subject matter is available via interactive technologies, there is less burden on the teacher to present information and more opportunity to diagnose learning problems and help learners find solutions. Research shows that when students work with computers, teachers reduce the time they spend directing students; they spend more of their time facilitating student learning.

2. A shift from whole-class instruction to small group instruction. When students work with computers, they progress at different rates. Therefore, it makes less sense to teach the class as a whole, expecting students to move in lockstep. Teachers interact more with individual students and small groups, becoming better informed about individual students' understandings and misunderstandings.

3. A shift from working with better students to working with weaker students. The need to choose a single level of difficulty for class instruction disappears when the teacher can work with individuals and small groups. The teacher is then able to aim instruction at one specific target group and to devote time to those who most need help.

4. A shift from all students learning the same things to different students learning different things. It has always been naive to expect that all students will learn the same things, that is, that they will learn what the teacher intends to teach them. Students learn what they need and want to learn, and, while there are some common attainments, there is also much individuality. When resources for learning are available through electronic technologies, it becomes possible to recognize, accept, and even reward the attainments of individuals.

5. A shift toward more engaged students. In most college classrooms the great majority of students are passive most of the time. Classes proceed whether or not everyone is engaged and whether or not everyone understands. With interactive technology, attention is ensured. Instruction comes to a halt when there are no responses from learners. Well-designed computer-mediated instruction is more likely to engage individuals than are the words of a professor in front of a room filled with students.

6. A shift from assessment based on test performance to assessment based on products and progress. Rather than repeating or paraphrasing information from lectures and textbooks, students devote their energies to more creative projects. The best projects include realistic tasks that generalize what is being learned and show how it applies to new areas.

7. A shift from a competitive to a cooperative goal structure. Collaboration is encouraged when students have access to extensive data bases and share their own developing work through networked communications. Under these circumstances, products are truly collaborative, and teachers must learn how to assess work in light of the collaborative nature of student projects.

8. A shift from the primacy of verbal thinking to the integration of visual and verbal thinking. Students have more extensive experience with video than with print, yet instruction is based primarily on print. Visual literacy is poorly understood and poorly utilized in the service of instruction. We need to consider what capacities for visual knowledge and skills educated citizens should possess, and determine how we can ensure progress toward developing those capacities.

These shifts suggested by Collins also imply a shift in the teacher's role—liberation from the role of content provider to a more flexible, helping role.

New Roles for Professors

In the age of electronic information, effective and efficient learning is potentially possible at any time and any place, on any topic, in any sequence, and at any age. Bringing large groups of students together for content-centered presentations by professors can no longer be justified as the dominant method of instruction.

College teachers will spend much of their time in other ways. Time will be spent in collegial teams preparing and evaluating instructional materials and organizing data into accessible form. Time will be spent coaching students, helping them learn to navigate these vast seas of information. Group presentations—when they occur—will be left to the faculty who are most talented and interested in teaching in that setting. Presentations will not be used to provide new information for students to record in their notebooks. Instead, presentations will be carefully constructed to model how the discipline uses information to answer existing questions and solve current problems. They will also demonstrate the potential for using information to formulate new questions and to construct problems for the future of the discipline.

As I consider likely changes in roles for professors, the following six shifts seem most urgent and challenging.

1. A shift from covering material to assisting students in sampling material. When there is too much to cover, teachers have to decide what is essential and what is optional. What is

essential can be assigned and the rest must be sampled. The content sampled should span a variety of media to ensure that students become adept at using electronic sources and that they experience the effects of diverse media.

2. A shift from unilaterally declaring what is worth knowing to negotiating criteria that identify what is important. Instead of providing neat packages of content, the teacher plunges into primary sources with students. Together they develop ways to discriminate the more important from the less important. Course exercises can help develop criteria about what information is relevant for what purposes, and the class can discuss these criteria. Criteria for valid information must be discipline-specific. They must also be specific to each medium, since the characteristics of print and nonprint information differ so significantly. When students deal with electronically stored items—literary works, anthropological artifacts, historical photographs—important contextual cues are lost. One cannot touch the artifact, heft the original manuscript while searching for a passage, or easily detect an image's cultural and social context. One comes to appreciate how decontextualized most electronic information is.

3. A shift from ranking students relative to one another to negotiating standards specific to individuals. Electronic technologies make it possible for each student to travel a unique route. Of course, some students will progress more slowly than others. When a student pursues distinctive objectives, the teacher can no longer use uniform standards of achievement and uniform rates of learning to evaluate student work. Instead it is necessary to negotiate learning objectives and rates of progress that reflect individual interests, abilities, and needs. For what reasons should students who need more time be given that time? Because they learn more slowly? Because they are especially ambitious? Because the computer memory failed? Should proficiency in the use of media be directly recognized and rewarded? How can standards be maintained and fairness be ensured while recognizing the unique objectives of individual students?

4. A shift from grading according to individual attainments to grading according to collaborative contributions. Judging and rewarding group efforts is difficult because roles and responsibilities of group members vary. Electronic technology permits almost infinite variability in the tasks that group members pursue. Should people be rewarded in proportion to their proficiency in the skills of collaboration? Should individual work—which especially in an electronic environment is likely to be less thorough and less varied than group work—receive lower grades than group work does? What role should students have in assessing one another's collaborative contributions?

5. A shift from merely verifying student sources to deriving standards for fair use and credit. Some professors expend considerable energy checking sources cited by students in order to ensure that work is the student's own. This role of plagiarism detector is impractical when sources are so numerous and when information can be so easily altered. At issue is not only the accountability of students but also the rights of original authors, artists, and performers, and these are issues that copyright laws have not yet resolved. One solution is to permit inclusion of only what is in the public domain, but that would seriously limit the quality and comprehensiveness of student work.

6. A shift from requiring students to reproduce knowledge to rewarding them for demonstrating originality. A student should be held accountable for producing knowledge and understanding which, for that student, is new. In many fields students can master more than the basic information and concepts that conventionally have been memorized, graded, and (soon) forgotten. They should be able to apply core concepts to new examples and to generalize principles to situations significantly different from situations through which those principles were originally taught. How are novelty and originality defined when the project is largely a reconfiguration from existing media sources? Projects in electronic form are

ephemeral. They have no existence in space and, because they are so easily altered, they may exist only briefly in time. Whose property are they? Who gets credit for them? How do concepts of authorship and ownership apply?

Preparing for the Revolution

This new paradigm and the shifts that it will bring signal nothing less than a revolution in the way faculty and students relate to one another and to the subjects they study. How rapidly these changes will occur depends significantly on the information infrastructure at a college or university and on the intensity of resistance from faculty and administrators. The ease with which faculty adapt to changes depends on their openness to change and on the support that is available from colleagues, administrators, and technical specialists.

To prepare for this revolution, I suggest gradual encounters with the technologies that are limited in scope. Here are ways that some teachers are anticipating what higher education will be like in the age of electronic information. They are

→ requiring students to use electronic data bases in their bibliographic searches.

→ encouraging students to use electronic mail to ask questions of the teacher and for submitting assignments.

→ becoming familiar with the advantages and disadvantages of videotape and videodisc and exploring the capabilities of compact disc read-only memory (CD ROM).

→ surveying students about their familiarity with these electronic media and asking if they will share their knowledge and skills with the class.

→ using a word processor to develop class notes and editing a version to use as student handouts and a version for overhead transparencies.

→ using computer programs for keeping records in large classes—enrollment lists, grades, test items, and so on;

having students review and update their own records from time to time.

→ encouraging students to include visual elements as parts of their projects—charts and tables, graphical models, still and moving pictures.

→ introducing raw data—numbers, artifacts, texts, images—and helping students organize and interpret the information. Developing criteria for the importance and validity of such data, criteria that are consistent with the discipline being studied.

→ spending time at a multimedia work station planning a teaching presentation; assembling projection graphics, video clips, animation, sound, and other materials; trying to match particular materials with specific learning objectives; and integrating the materials into a unified presentation.

■ *A Gradual Beginning*

These technologies and the new teaching roles they require can prompt a good deal of anxiety. They should be experienced gradually, or small frustrations may prompt resistance to the larger changes they portend. Chapter 28 discusses in more detail how to make gradual, yet significant, changes in one's teaching.

Using technology for teaching and learning is an adventure with unpredictable outcomes. What we can predict with certainty, however, is the fascination that technology holds and the fact that its mastery will be indispensable for productive and fulfilling lives in the twenty-first century.

SUPPLEMENTARY READING

M. J. Albright and D. L. Graf (eds.), Teaching in the Information Age: The Role of Electronic Technology, *New Directions for Teaching and Learning, no. 51* (San Francisco: Jossey-Bass, 1992).

I. de Sola Pool, *Technology Without Boundaries* (Cambridge, MA: Harvard University Press, 1990).

D. W. Farmer and T. F. Mech (eds.), Information Literacy: Developing Students as Independent Learners, *New Directions for Higher Education, no. 78* (San Francisco: Jossey-Bass, 1992).

S. W. Gilbert and P. Lyman, Intellectual property in the information age, *Change*, 1989, *21*, 23–28.

J. Johnston, *Electronic Learning: From Audiotape to Videodisc* (Hillsdale, NJ: Erlbaum, 1987).

L. L. Jones and S. G. Smith, Can multimedia instruction meet our expectations? *EDUCOM Bulletin*, 1992, *27*(1), 39–43.

R. B. Kozma, Learning with media, *Review of Educational Research*, 1991, *61*, 179–211.

R. J. Spinrad, The electronic university, *EDUCOM Bulletin*, 1983, *18*(5), 4–8.

Teaching Large Classes
(and Small Ones, Too)

PART

Why Classes Should Be Small, but How to Help Your Students Be Active Learners Even in Large Classes

*A*S BUDGETS DROP, more and more college teachers have to deal with large numbers of students enrolled in a single course. Typically, budget cuts result in gradual shrinkage in the number of courses available and the number of sections or frequency of offerings of remaining courses. Class sizes creep upward.

In writing this book, I originally began with the topic, "Class Size." I concluded that section by stating that more meaningful research on class size must take into account the methods of teaching classes of differing sizes. I thought this was a pretty insightful statement, but now I think that it was naive, for size and method are almost inextricably intertwined. Thus the research on class size and that on lecture vs. discussion overlap. Large classes are most likely to use lecture methods and less likely to use discussion than small classes. Since discussion tends to be more effective than lecture for achieving changes in thinking and problem solving, we might expect large classes to be less effective than small classes.

■ *Research on Class Size*

The question of class size was probably the first problem of college teaching approached by research. Are small classes really more effective for teaching than large classes? The professor's answer has generally been "yes." But the refreshing empiricism of the 1920s looked hard at many "self-evident truths" about human behavior; among them was the assumption that class size had something to do with educational effectiveness.

Among the first investigators were Edmondson and Mulder (1924), who compared the performance of students enrolled in a 109-student class with students enrolled in a 43-student class of the same course in education. Achievement of the two groups was approximately equal, with a slight edge for the small class on an essay and the mid-semester tests, and for the large class on quizzes and the final examination. Students reported a preference for small classes. A number of experiments over the next six to seven decades generally supported these findings.

The Macomber and Siegel experiments at Miami University (1957a,b,1960) are particularly important because their measures included, in addition to conventional achievement tests, measures of critical thinking and problem solving, scales measuring stereotypic attitudes, and tests of student attitudes toward instruction. Statistically significant differences favored the smaller classes (particularly for high ability students). When retention of knowledge was measured one to two years after completion of the courses, small differences favored the smaller classes in eight of the nine courses compared (Siegel, Adams, and Macomber, 1960). Meta-analyses of research on class size in classes ranging in level from elementary schools to universities also tend to support small classes (Kulik and Kulik, 1989).

Few instructors are satisfied with the achievement of knowledge if it is not remembered, if the students are unable to use it in solving problems where the knowledge is relevant, or if the students fail to relate the knowledge to relevant attitudes. If one takes these more basic outcomes of retention, problem solving, and attitude differentiation as criteria of learning, the weight of the evidence favors small classes.

▬ *Class Size: Theory*

How can we account for these results?

Let us briefly return to theory. Insofar as information communication is a one-way process, size of group should be limited only by the audibility of the lecturer's voice. In fact, as Hudelson suggests, a large class may have sufficient motivational value for instructors to cause them to spend more time in preparation of their lectures, resulting, I would hope, in better teaching and in greater student achievement.

But usually we have goals going beyond communication of knowledge. If educators are to make wise decisions about when and where small classes are most important, we need to analyze more carefully the changes in educationally relevant variables associated with changes in size. One lead comes from social psychologists Thomas and Fink (1963), who have reviewed research on face-to-face groups—not only classroom groups, but laboratory, business, and other groups also. They suggest that two types of input increase with increasing group size—*resource input* (skills, knowledge, and so on) and *demand input* (needs). It is clear that the larger the number of group members, the greater is the likelihood that some members will have resources of knowledge, intelligence, or other skills needed for the education purposes of the group. It seems likely, however, that there is a limited amount of relevant knowledge and skills, so that beyond some point additional students contribute little that is not already part of the group's resources. A group's utilization of resources is constrained by the simple facts that 1) in a large group a smaller proportion of group members can participate orally, and 2) the larger the group, the less likely it is that a given person will feel free to volunteer a contribution. Because active thinking is so important to learning and retention of learning, constraints upon oral participation are likely not only to induce passivity but also to be educationally harmful. This chapter suggests strategies to use to achieve better learning. Clearly large classes can be effective. The problem is that most faculty members lack the skills to compensate for large size. They use less discussion, require less writing, are less likely to use essay exams—in short, the way we teach large classes is different (and usually less effective) than the way we teach small classes.

▬▬▬ *Determining When Small Classes Are Needed*

In order to apply these general propositions to teaching, educators need to ask the following questions:

In What Teaching Situations Is the Amount of Information in the Group Important?

One might, for example, hypothesize that in most courses in which knowledge is the primary goal, the relevant information is contained in books and the instructor's mind, and the amount added by students is likely to be inconsequential; thus class size should be unimportant for this goal. On the other hand, if application is an important goal, varied knowledge of application situations contributed by students may well be significant; thus, if Thomas and Fink's principles are valid, there may be groups too small, as well as too large, to be maximally effective for this goal.

What Kinds of Students Benefit Most from Small Sections?

Both Ward (1956) and Macomber and Siegel report results suggesting that the ablest students are most favorably affected by being taught in small classes. Siegel and Siegel (1964) report that personal contact with the instructor was particularly important for acquisition of concepts by three types of students: 1) those with low motivation, 2) those who are unsophisticated in the subject-matter area, and 3) those who are predisposed to learn facts rather than to apply or synthesize. However, Wulff, Nyquist, and Abbott (1987) found that many students liked the lack of pressure, the independence, and freedom to skip meetings in large classes.

Don't be surprised to find that many students prefer large classes. Many students feel more comfortable being anonymous where there is no threat of exposure—no discussion, no writing—just taking notes and answering objective test questions. But these may be the very students who need most to find that others respect their ideas, that they can carry through a project, or can write a paper successfully.

Class Size: Conclusions

It is commonplace to suggest that the effect of class size depends upon the method used, and it is probably true that the size of the group is less critical for success of lecture, for example, than for that of discussion (Attiyeh and Lumsden, 1972). Moreover, class size interacts with student characteristics; that is, small classes are educationally more important for some students than for others. But most important, analysis of research suggests that the importance of size depends upon educational goals. In general, large classes are simply not as effective as small classes for retention of knowledge, critical thinking, and attitude change. Note, however, that large-group discussion methods can be used effectively, and pairing, buzz groups, and other peer learning techniques increase the effectiveness of learning in large classes. (See Chapters 4 and 13.)

■ *Multi-Section Courses*

Unfortunately, there are seldom enough funds to teach all courses in small groups. As a compromise solution, I have scheduled large courses for two hours of lecture (in large sections) and two hours of discussion (in small sections). The assumption here is that lectures are valuable for certain purposes, such as communicating information, and that the effectiveness of the lecture method is not greatly affected by class size. Furthermore, large-group class meetings are economical for test administration, guest lecturers, and some films or videotapes. By teaching the students in large sections part of the time, it becomes economically feasible to keep the discussion sections small enough to permit wide student participation. Thus, rather than offering 5 sections of 45 students each, you might consider the possible advantages of a 225-student lecture section and 9 discussion sections of 20 to 30 students.

In universities these sections are usually taught by graduate student teaching assistants; if faculty or graduate students aren't available, don't be afraid to use undergraduate students. As we saw in earlier chapters both the student discussion leaders and the students being taught benefit from this arrangement. At the University of Michigan we give undergraduate teaching assistants course credit for teaching (and if advanced undergraduates aren't available, peer-led groups can be effective, as we saw in Chapter 13).

Coordinating Multi-Section Courses

In any multi-section course taught by several different instructors the problem of coordination inevitably arises. In some courses this problem is resolved by enforced uniformity of course content, sequence of topics, testing, grading, and even anecdotes. Such a procedure has the advantage that students who later elect more advanced courses can be presumed to have a certain uniform amount of background experience. It also is efficient in that only one final examination must be constructed, only one course outline devised, and students can transfer from section to section with no difficulty in catching up.

The disadvantage of this approach is that such uniformity often makes for dull, uninteresting teaching. If the teaching assistants are unenthusiastic about the course outline, they are likely to communicate this attitude to the students. If the course can be jointly planned, this may make for greater acceptance, but may also take a great deal of time.

A second approach to this problem is to set up completely autonomous sections, with all the instructors organizing and conducting their sections as they wish. While this means that Psychology 1 with Professor Smith may be quite different from Psychology 1 with Professor Jones, proponents of this solution point out that transfer students who are accepted for advanced work are likely to differ even more from local students than local students differ from section to section under this plan, and that the difference in student learning between instructors is relatively small when compared with the total range of differences between students at the end of a course.

In the general psychology course at the University of Michigan we developed a plan that is in many ways a compromise between these two positions. We worked out together a set of objectives we all strove to accomplish. Half of the final examination was based on these objectives and given to all sections. In addition we agreed that the average grade given by each instructor would fall within a limited range. Grading comparability is not a minor matter, for one of the most common sources of friction in multi-section courses is the complaint from students that they got "C's" in Mr. Jones' section, but if they'd been in Mr. Smith's they would have made "A's" for the same work.

Whether or not variation between sections is permitted, a frequent sore spot in multi-section courses is the tendency for students to leave or avoid sections taught by certain instructors and to crowd into others. Some instructors intentionally depict their sections as being more difficult in order to drive away less motivated students. If this produces large disparities in the numbers of students taught by "popular" and "unpopular" instructors, the cohesiveness of the instructional staff is likely to be threatened. On the other hand, from the standpoints of both student learning and instructor satisfaction, it would seem wise to give students some opportunity to select the section they feel will be most valuable (or pleasant) for them.

Conflict may be minimized and education enhanced if certain sections are specifically labeled as being for a particular purpose. For example, certain sections may be labeled Honors sections or for graduate students; certain sections may be labeled as placing greater emphasis upon theory; certain other sections may be taught entirely by discussion and so labeled. One of the advantages of a multi-section course is the opportunity it provides for establishing groupings with similar interests or backgrounds.

▄▄▄ *Training and Supervising Teaching Assistants*

Most large universities use graduate or undergraduate student assistants to teach discussion or laboratory sessions in large courses. As the course coordinator, you are responsible for the quality of education your students receive, and to a large extent this depends upon the motivation and skill of the teaching assistants.

Your responsibility begins well before the first class meetings, for your teaching assistants need to know what you expect in terms of attendance at lectures, participation in weekly planning and training sessions, testing and grading, office hours, and such. But even more important than the formal requirements are the aspects of preparing the teaching assistants for meeting their first classes, establishing a good working relationship with their students, and developing the skills needed for leading discussions, answering questions, or carrying out other teaching responsibilities.

Once the term is under way, a weekly meeting provides an opportunity for solving teaching problems and providing tips about what to expect. In addition, you will want to help monitor progress by observing the teaching assistants' classes or obtaining student reactions early in the term. To get student feedback you can use simple open-ended questions, such as:

"What have you liked about the class so far?"
"What suggestions do you have for improvement?"

Whether you observe or collect ratings, consultation with the teaching assistant is a vital opportunity to identify problems, suggest alternative approaches, and provide encouragement. (See Chapter 23 for more detail.)

■ *Some Tips for Teaching Large Classes*

Often one assumes that a large class simply requires skills in lecturing and writing objective tests. These are important, but one can do more. Large classes need not constrain you as much as you might expect. You don't need to lecture or at least you don't need to lecture all the time.

Getting Student Participation in Large Classes

While sectioning is preferable to the large class without sections, most teachers will at some time be faced with the necessity of teaching an unsectioned large class. In this situation my first advice is to try "learning cells" or student-led discussions. If this is impractical, you can still get the advantages of student participation if you plan for it. Some techniques such as buzz groups, problem posting, and the two-column method of large-group discussions were described earlier. The technique of role playing, discussed in Chapter 17, can be used for multiple role playing, with all students involved as role players. Maier (1971) gives examples of the use of such techniques.

Lumsden (1976) gives each student in his section a large square card with the letters A, B, C, and D printed so that one of the letters is visible at the top when each edge of the card is held up. For example, if A is first on the top side, B will be visible at the top when the card is rotated 90 degrees. Lumsden interjects multiple-choice questions into his lecture either orally, on the blackboard, or by use of a transparency, and then asks students to answer all at once by raising their cards. This enables him to get student participation and feedback on whether his points are understood.

Encouraging Student Writing in Large Classes

One of the most important drawbacks of large classes is the lack of student writing. Because grading essays is so time-consuming, most faculty members reduce, or eliminate, writing assignments in a large class. Take heart! You can get some of the educational advantages of writing, and at the same time improve attention to the lecture, without being submerged by papers to grade.

The "minute paper," described earlier, is one valuable tool. At an appropriate point in the lecture, announce the paper and the topic or question you want students to address; for example, you might ask the students to summarize the major point or points made so far. Or you might give the students a choice of topics, such as a summary, a question, an application, or an example. When the minute is up, you may either collect the papers or break the class into pairs or subgroups to review and discuss one another's papers.

If you wish, you can evaluate and comment on the papers as you would any other student papers. If the class is exceptionally large, you may announce that you'll read and return only a sample of the papers. Students can be motivated to think and write without the threat of grades, and this technique not only gets students thinking actively during the lecture but gives you feedback about what students are learning from the lecture.

Similar to the "minute paper" is the "half-sheet response" (Weaver and Cotrell, 1985). In this technique students tear out a half-sheet of notebook paper to respond to a question or instruction such as:

"What do you think about this concept?"
"Give an example of this concept or principle."
"Explain this concept in your own words."
"How does this idea relate to your own experience?"
"What are some of your feelings as you listen to these ideas?"
"How could you use this idea in your own life?"

Once the half-sheet responses have been written, you can ask students to tell what they have written as a lead-in to large group discussions. The papers need not always be collected if you explain that your purpose in using the technique is to stimulate active thinking. Normally, however, you will want the feedback provided by the responses. Referring to your interpretation of the responses the next class day will also provide feedback to the students.

Large-Group Discussion Methods

Techniques such as "problem posting" (Chapter 3), "the two-column method," and "developmental discussion" (Chapter 4) can be used in large classes as well as small. Short written responses, such as the "minute paper" or the "half-sheet response" can help in initiating large-group discussions.

Other Ways to Maintain Student Involvement

There are a variety of techniques that can help break the deadly routine of lectures day after day. For example, you can have each discussion section prepare participants for a debate, perhaps having one representative on each side. In a non-sectioned course you might have buzz groups prepare representatives or have buzz groups of four to six students divide their group so that there are equal numbers of advocates on each side, prepare for the debate outside of class, and carry out many simultaneous debates in buzz groups. To aid students in seeing the complexity of the problem being debated you might then have students reverse their roles and repeat the debate with each person now speaking for the side he or she formerly opposed.

Another break in lectures can be provided by an interview—perhaps of a colleague with special expertise, someone from outside the university, or one of the students with special experience. A variant might be a dialogue on a topic in which you and a colleague have somewhat different views.

Student Anonymity

The major problem of teaching a large class is that students not only feel anonymous, they usually *are* anonymous. And as social psychological research has shown, people who are anonymous feel less personal responsibility—a consequence not only damaging to morale and order but also unlikely to facilitate learning. Moreover, the sense of distance from the instructor, the loss of interpersonal bonds with the instructor and with other students—these diminish motivation for learning.

What can we do? The fact that with increasing class size it becomes less and less possible to know students as individuals is likely to make us feel that it is not worth trying to do anything. I think this is a mistake. In my experience the students appreciate whatever efforts you make even if they do not take advantage of them. Here are some things I've tried:

1. Announce that you'll meet any students who are free for coffee after class. (You won't be swamped.)

2. Pass out invitations to several students to join you for coffee and to get acquainted after class.

3. Pass out brief student observation forms to several students at the beginning of class and ask them to meet you to discuss their observations.

4. Circulate among early arriving students to get acquainted before class starts.

5. Circulate among lab or discussion sections.

6. Use a seating chart so that you can call students by name when they participate.

7. Move out into the aisles during your lecture to solicit comments.

8. Teach one discussion or lab section yourself.

9. If you can't use regularly scheduled discussion sections, set up an occasional afternoon or evening session for more informal discussion of an interesting question or for review before an examination.

10. Have students fill out an autobiographical sketch with name, hometown, year in college, and what they hope to get out of the course (Benjamin, 1991).

Giving Tests in Large Classes

In classes of 200 or more, unwary instructors are likely to run into problems they would never dream of in teaching classes with an enrollment of 20 to 30. Most of these problems are administrative. For example, course planning almost inevitably becomes more rigid in a large class because almost anything involving the participation of the students requires more preparation time.

Perhaps you're used to making up your tests the day before you administer them. With a large class this is almost impossible. Essay and short-answer tests that take relatively little time to construct take a long time to score for 200 students; so you may spend long hours trying to devise thought-provoking objective questions for a part of the test. But once you've made up the questions your troubles are not over, for secretaries require a good deal of time to make several hundred copies of a test. Thus, spur-of-the-moment tests are almost an impossibility, and by virtue of the necessity of planning ahead for tests, other aspects of the course also become more rigid.

As I indicated in Chapter 6, essay examinations are superior to typical objective examinations in their effect on student study and learning. Thus you are likely to regret the loss of the opportunity to give essay tests in a large group. But this loss is not inevitable. To some extent it can be compensated for by greater care in the construction of objective test items. But it is also possible to use essay items without increasing your load beyond reason. In a 500-student lecture course I regularly included an essay item on the final examination with the stipulation that I would read it only if it would affect the student's letter grade for the course. Since the majority of the students were fairly clearly established as A, B, C, or D students on the basis of other work and the objective part of the final examination, the number of essays I needed to read was not excessive. My subjective impression was that knowledge of the inclusion of an essay item did affect the students' preparation for the exam.

Outside Reading

The testing problem is just one of several factors structuring the conduct of large classes. Another is the assignment of readings in the library. With a small group you can assign library work with little difficulty, only making sure that the materials needed are available and, if necessary, reserved for the class. With a class of several hundred students a library assignment without previous planning can be disastrous. The library's single copy of a book or journal is obviously inadequate, and will probably be stolen within a few hours by some student who wants to ensure time enough to study the assignment thoroughly. The librarians are then faced by hordes of desperate students begging for the book. Thus a library assignment must be conceived far enough in advance (usually several months) that enough copies of the book can be obtained, and the librarian can prepare for the fray.

▬ *Teaching Large Classes: Conclusion*

Large classes are probably generally less effective than small ones for higher-level goals. Nonetheless, they are not likely to disappear, and they can be very effective when taught by methods that stimulate students to active, mindful thinking rather than passive absorption. In any case, it is clear that large classes pose problems for teachers. I have touched on only a few of the most salient ones. If you become involved in a large course, you'll also bump into such problems as whether or not to encourage individual contacts between yourself and students, how to use assistants effectively, and how to amplify your voice, gestures, facial expressions, and writing in order to communicate to the back rows. This is a challenge, but teaching stays interesting because of challenges!

SUPPLEMENTARY READING

Kenneth E. Eble, *The Craft of Teaching* (San Francisco: Jossey-Bass, 1976), Chapter 13.

M. G. Weimer (ed.), *Teaching Large Classes Well* (San Francisco: Jossey-Bass, 1987).

Ludy Benjamin's article, Personalization and Active Learning in the Large Introductory Psychology Class, *Teaching of Psychology*, 1991, *18*(2), 68–74, has a number of good suggestions whose usefulness is not restricted to psychology courses.

The "Minute Paper" is described in R. C. Wilson, Improving Faculty Teaching: Effective Use of Student Evaluations and Consultants, *Journal of Higher Education*, 1986, *57*(2), 196–211.

CHAPTER 21

Large Classes: Morale, Discipline, and Order

*T*HE THINGS UNDER CONSIDERATION HERE are mainly practical problems of the social psychology of the classroom.* No single set of recommendations will work for any particular instructor or for any particular classroom situation. What is considered good discipline will vary from instructor to instructor and from one situation to another. What I recommend is based on the philosophy stated in the introduction of this book—basically respect for students.

▰▰ Order in the Classroom

I now turn to some specific considerations. The first of these concerns order in the classroom. A certain degree of quiet and attention seems to be almost essential to the effective running of the educational enterprise. How can this end be achieved? There seem to be two ways to go about it. The first is to insist upon strict attention, set up stringent rules on the point, and enforce them. This is not, however, a method I recommend in spite of its rather common adoption. One difficulty with such a method is that order, when it is achieved in this fashion, is dictated to the

---

* Much of this chapter is derived from Gregory Kimble's advice to young faculty
  members.

students. It has a way of putting the instructor into perpetual conflict with the students. The general upshot appears to be that, in such a classroom, the students try, in the numerous ways at their disposal, to beat the game. Whether or not this involves basic needs for revolt against authority, it seems that any interest that they may have initially had in cooperating with the instructor in an attempt to accomplish certain purposes is at least partly supplanted by a feeling of revolt. Furthermore, this policing technique contradicts two basic considerations. As I have already indicated, education, pursued in this manner, is a noncooperative enterprise. Students get to play a much less active part in the classroom than they might. Their enthusiasm is dampened; their tendency to ask questions is reduced; even if they are cooperative, their behavior seems to be directed less toward a real understanding of materials than toward an effort to parrot the wisdom of the instructor. Their learning thus becomes learning by rote, which minimizes understanding and thus defeats part of the purpose of being in the class in the first place. This rather common disciplinary procedure is also one of the major contributors to the perpetuated adolescence of college students. Instructors who use this method set themselves up as parent figures. By doing this, they may elicit the submissive, unthinking obedience that is rarely characteristic of children's behavior toward their parents.

Having to some extent discredited the austere schoolmaster method of handling a class, I turn now to the positive side of my argument. I want to suggest a method that will give you almost as good order in the classroom without sacrificing education itself. To accomplish this, three procedures that parallel the basic considerations just discussed seem to be useful:

1. Give the students the notion that the accomplishment of course objectives is partly their problem.

2. Give the students the notion that they have certain responsibilities and, at the same time, certain rights. (More of this later.)

3. Give the students the notion that you are willing to entertain reasonable suggestions, objections, and questions in connection with course materials.

Unfortunately these ideas are new to many students and cannot be accomplished in a single day. They are ideas that mean the students will have to learn what may be a new adjustment to the classroom situation. If you use these ideas, you will have to be willing to put up with a certain amount of disorder in the class for a short time. They mean that you sometimes suppress your own needs for aggression and prestige and maintain a constant awareness of student needs.

I try to use this method consistently in classes where enrollment may run as high as 500. The class is permitted to operate on an informal basis. Questions and comments from the floor are allowed. (In a class this size, questions from the floor should be repeated for the benefit of the class as a whole before they are answered. Avoid the entirely informal discussion with a single student.) The result of this informality may be an initial unruliness in the class. It does not, however, interfere to any important extent with a well-planned lecture, and it disappears after five or six lectures. The students placed in an informally run class of this sort seem to be in a situation analogous to that of the boys in the Lewin, Lippitt, and White investigation (1939) who shifted from the autocratic to the democratic group atmosphere, and their behavior is much the same. There is the initial outburst of horseplay (and occasionally aggression) and finally the settling down to a more cooperative, objective, and efficient level of performance.

Whether I am correct in recommending the democratic as opposed to the authoritarian group atmosphere in a *particular* class is a question of fact; it can be decided by experimentation.

I want to consider now some typical problems of discipline and order and attempt a few concrete suggestions of methods of handling these problems.

Questions and Answers in a Large Class

The lecture section sometimes is not regarded as the place for questions and discussions from the floor. Instructors often try to have the questions handled by an assistant in a quiz or discussion section. Potentially this solution is a good one; actually, it often leaves much to be desired for two reasons:

1. Handling a discussion section is sometimes more difficult than giving a lecture. The difficulties in discussion sections are apt to be that the assistants are not well enough acquainted with the materials the lecturers have covered. This can be surmounted if the assistants attend the lectures, participate in lecture planning, and receive help and supervision in planning the discussion, but the discussion-leader role should be one of developing skills in application and problem solving rather than interpreting the lecture. Thus, to the extent feasible, questions of fact and interpretation are best answered in the lecture itself.

2. Whatever its potential usefulness, the discussion section does not provide for the prompt answering of questions that arise in connection with specific lecture materials.

In most classes (even large ones) I believe that it is possible to answer such questions. If you also believe this and want to try to handle such questions, keep some of the following relevant considerations in mind.

The students must know that such questions are permitted. This is usually not difficult because certain students try to ask questions in almost any class. If you find yourself with a particularly inhibited group, questions written out and passed to the front of the room may handle the situation, or you may ask students to write out questions and then ask for them orally. In any event it is important to repeat the question before answering it.

One of the problems in large-group question answering and discussion is that a student's question may, in a group where several hands are raised, refer to something that was covered several questions back. By writing all questions on the board before beginning to answer them, you may save time and confusion since some groupings and relationships are apparent. Also, grouping questions enables you to better apportion your time to those that are most significant or troublesome.

Experience in teaching a particular class will give you an understanding of the sort of questions that are apt to be asked on particular topics. Thus, you can be ready for the typical questions.

Occasionally, however, you will be asked an atypical question; and it can happen that, for some of them, you will not know the answer. In this event, about the only course open to you is to admit that you do not know, promise to look up the answer, and report on it at a later class meeting. If you use this method, *try to find the answer*. I do not recommend the technique of telling students to look up the answer for themselves. The students usually will not take the trouble, and they are apt to discover that this is simply a way of hiding your own ignorance. So far as finding the answers is concerned, remember that your colleagues are a good source, probably more useful than text materials.

Irrelevant questions may sometimes prevent important points from coming out. One way of handling such questions is to write the question on the board to answer later. By writing it down you indicate that you've heard the question and remove the necessity for the student to keep thinking about it. Frequently the question will have been answered by the end of the hour.

A somewhat different situation arises in the case of the student who flatly disagrees with you. Such disagreements are apt to be presented with at least the suggestion that anyone's opinion is as good as anyone else's. In such cases, factual evidence for your point of view would appear to be in order. In cases where the question is a controversial one, you may have to admit the possibility that the student is right. If this is necessary, you can turn the situation to your advantage by showing the kind of experimental test of the question that is implied. My own discipline, psychology, is vulnerable in this connection. Students come to the psychology class (and sometimes leave it) with the notion that everyone is a psychologist. A part of the purpose of the elementary course is to demonstrate that this is the case, but that there are still characteristics of rational scientific thought that make some hypotheses more tenable than others. But the task is not an easy one. The reason for this seems to be that since everyone has experiences and observes behavior, they demand of the psychologist something they demand of no other scientist—namely, that the psychological account of emotion, perception, or whatnot corresponds to their own naive experience of them. This is to be contrasted with the position of the physicist. Physics also presents the students with an account of the nature of a part of the world. The tables and chairs of the physicist are not solid objects, but are actually made up of minute whirling particles. It is a tribute to the maturity of physics that this nonsense view of the world can be made reasonable. And it will presumably sometime come about that psychology will be able to describe its subject matter in this way. For some students, it may be useful to point out this sort of thing. For many it will not. While psychology is particularly vulnerable on this point, I have the notion that instructors in other disciplines face some of the same problems. Certainly in the arts and literature there is something of the "I know what I like" syndrome.

If I were asked how to summarize my ideas about handling questions, disagreement, and discussion in the classroom, I might put my argument this way: There are two stock formulas that seem to go a long way toward handling these problems. One is, "This is the evidence." The other is, "You may be right."

In summary, my general advice is to encourage rather than discourage questioning. For more detailed consideration of large group discussion techniques, see Chapter 4.

Interference with the Course Routine by Other "Interests"

Here I refer to the students who knit, sleep, read comic books, draw pictures, gossip, or do any of the other things that students are apt to do instead of taking notes. As a general rule, the desirable way to eliminate these practices is by making it important to the students to listen to your lectures. This can be accomplished in one of two ways. Probably the most satisfactory from your point of view would be to discover ways of making your presentation interesting enough to command the attention of the student.

If you are convinced that you are already doing everything that you can in this connection, it may be worthwhile to look at your examination procedures. If you do not include lecture materials on your examinations, some students will feel that there is very little to be gained in listening to you or in making notes on anything you say. This can be true of the most interesting lecturer. Since a large part of the students' motivation is directed toward passing examinations, you can make use of this in getting a class to pay attention and at the same time probably improve your teaching. There is nothing wrong, as I see it, in telling the students that material from the lectures will probably be tested on examinations.

Use of active learning techniques such as those discussed in Chapter 20 may help in getting the non-attentive students involved in learning.

You are not the only one affected by these evidences of student inattention. Other students are distracted and disturbed. Sometimes peer pressure will be more effective than that of the teacher. To mobilize it you may need to say, "I seem to be having trouble holding everyone's attention. Do you have any suggestions of what might help?"

▬▬ *Preparing for a Class Period*

Disciplinary problems sometimes are a reflection of student dissatisfaction with your teaching. The time college teachers spend in specific preparation for their classes varies from none at all to many hours. Those who are low on the scale usually rationalize that the most effective illustrations and problems are those that arise spontaneously from the class. This may be true, but instructors who make effective use of them are usually those who have thought through their goals and procedures so well that they no longer have to worry about whether or not the class is going to fall apart.

Thus, I do advocate preparation for each class and suggest that the following steps be included:

1. Consideration of specific goals for the day in the light of overall course goals.

2. Review of previous work and especially of the previous day's discussion.

3. Review of the day's assignment.

4. Reading background materials related to the day's lesson.

5. Looking at work ahead and future assignments. As in most matters, students like to know where they stand in relation to assignments. They appreciate a schedule of future assignments passed out early in the semester. In courses without laboratories, students are conventionally expected to do two hours work outside class for each hour in class. In an introductory or sophomore course, the average students seem to be able to master up to a hundred pages a week for a three-hour course. This figure, of course, will vary depending upon the difficulty of the reading, the accessibility of the books, and the amount of written work required.

6. Choosing the teaching methods or techniques to be used in terms of the goals to be attained and remembering that it pays to "throw a change of pace" now and then.

7. Working out an estimated budget of time for each activity in the class period, remembering that it is to be a guide, not a straitjacket, and allowing time for a summary and lead-in to the next day's work.

■■■■ *What to Do When You're Not Prepared*

Unless you are exceptional, there will be some classes where you arrive without preparation, despite your dedication to good teaching. This can provide an exciting learning experience for you, but it can also be educational for the class. Here are some techniques to use when your car has broken down, you were called before the President for an unexpected honor, or you simply overslept.

1. Use the technique of problem posting described in Chapter 3.

2. Ask students to spend the first five minutes reviewing the assignment and previous lecture notes before writing down the one question each would most like to have you discuss. Collect the questions. Answer one or more yourself, then throw one out to the class, and while a student is answering, do a quick sort of the questions to group them more logically.

3. Split the class into buzz groups (see Chapter 4) and ask each buzz group to come up with one question to be discussed. Ask the first group for its question, discuss it, and ask if any other group had a question related to the first. Answer that and go on in a similar fashion.

4. Ask the class to spend the first ten minutes reviewing a particular part of the assignment so that they have it clearly in mind. While they are reviewing it, think of a discussion problem involving the material they are reviewing. Then break the class into buzz groups to discuss the problem. Use the remainder of the time to get reports from the discussion groups or start a second cycle by asking each group to discuss the advantages or disadvantages of two of the groups' solutions to the problem.

5. Admit that you're unprepared and ask the class how the time can best be spent. (Don't spend so much time discussing what to do that there's no time left to do it.)

▬▬ *What to Do When You Have to Miss Class*

Visiting Lecturers

There are inevitably times when you will be over committed—too busy to prepare a decent lecture and too rushed to think of an alternative. The preceding section deals with last minute situations. But sometimes pressures can be anticipated. Scheduling a film, videotape, a guest lecturer, or giving students a class day off to work on projects are techniques for prevention of being overwhelmed. If they are used frequently, students may question your commitment to their education. Properly planned they can provide a welcome change of pace and can enhance learning.

How do you find an appropriate visiting lecturer? Oftentimes students themselves will know someone with special expertise and experience in an area being discussed. A first person account has impact much beyond that of pages of print. Letting a student, or group of students, host the guest, helping prepare the guest for the class, and the class for the guest, encourages a sense of responsibility for learning that is important for effective education.

For maximum success the students need to be prepared for the visitor and some effort should be made to get the class to formulate the questions the expert will attempt to answer. If the visitor is to lecture, he or she should be warned to allow some of the class period for questions so that students can follow up with the questions formulated before and during the visit. Then part of the following class period should be allotted to discussion of the visitor's contributions. Often it is more fun both for the visitor and the class if class members are selected to form a panel to interview the visitor rather than for the visitor simply to lecture.

When possible, I encourage students to join the guest and me for coffee after class. This gives the most interested students a chance for personal contact and the guest a chance to relax.

A guest need not spend an entire class period. Ten or fifteen minutes may be sufficient to achieve your objectives.

Jane Halonen of Alverno College has developed a "Non-Shirker's Guide to Active Learning during Teacher Absence" (1990). She makes the following points:

1. Don't cancel class.

2. Plan your course calendar around known dates of unavoidable absences.

3. Tell students where you will be and why.

4. Hold students accountable for learning. This means planning a class activity that requires active learning; e.g., a reaction paper following the guest lecturer, videotape, or student-led discussion.

5. Have Plan B ready in case something goes wrong; e.g., the film or visiting lecturer doesn't arrive.

6. Recruit an advanced undergraduate or graduate student to convene and assist the class.

7. Vary activities if you must miss more than one class.

SUPPLEMENTARY READING

R. D. Mann et al., *The College Classroom* (New York: Wiley, 1970).

Jane Halonen, *Active Learning During Teacher Absence* (Milwaukee: Alverno College, 1990).

Nancy Chism
The Ohio State University

CHAPTER 22

Taking Student Diversity into Account

TRADITIONAL DISCUSSIONS of student differences have focused on variations in cognitive style, cognitive development, motivation, speed, and preferred physiological modality. Recently, discussion of difference has centered on social diversity as well. As the demographic makeup of the traditional college-going population has changed, students who have previously been underrepresented, given the total population, are attending college (Levine et al., 1989). More students who are older than the traditional 17–22-year-old range are now reentering the education system; women now constitute half or more of the total population at many institutions; students of diverse racial and ethnic backgrounds are a greater presence on campus (following a decline in participation during the 1980s); students with physical or learning disabilities are attending and self-identifying in higher numbers; and gay, lesbian, and bisexual students (who have heretofore been a largely "invisible" population) are becoming increasingly articulate about their participation.

Although these groups are different from one another and even different within each group (for example, as Nieves-Squires [1991] notes, the label "Hispanic" is used to refer to people from more than five major social groups, each of which is further differentiated internally by gender, socioeconomic, and other differences), the groups are united by a past and current experience of both blatant and subtle forms of exclusion in higher education and in society more generally. Within each group, there is a sense of patterns of values, ways of thinking and acting, and a spirit of community that are distinct enough to be considered "cultural" characteristics.

A persistent theme connected with social diversity in higher education has been disappointing retention rates and discouragement on the part of many traditionally underrepresented students. Although research on the issue is in its infancy, it is clear that students from diverse groups identify the quality of relationships they have with faculty as a critical factor influencing their learning and comfort level with the institution. Although financial aid, residential life, and a host of other factors are important, students have reported in several studies that positive in- and out-of-class relationships with their teachers can enable them to overcome constraints and achieve academic success (Sedlacek, 1983; Ferguson, 1989; Astin, 1975).

Some faculty members are unconvinced that there are any teaching issues surrounding social diversity. Others, who are in the process of evaluating their role in responding to student social diversity, often wonder whether attention to difference will fragment and irritate social relations and prevent, rather than encourage, student success. Many worry about "canon" issues, fearing a watering down of the curriculum. They may fear that the purposes of social diversity will call upon them to treat students preferentially—a practice that they have always been careful to avoid. They may also feel that they are walking on eggshells or that whatever action they take will be misinterpreted. But it is clear that the problems need to be addressed openly. The payoff is not only for the students themselves but for the colleges and universities who profit from truly embracing the opportunity to let previously unheard or unheeded voices enrich and broaden ways of thinking and knowing.

The main teaching issues connected with social diversity fall into two broad categories: curriculum and instructional strategies issues. The first, curriculum issues, is the most frequently debated. Socially diverse groups have claimed that the content of most courses is very narrowly focused on the Western intellectual tradition, specifically the experience of the mainstream European-descended male. The effect is that they feel marginal to the academic experience. They see no role models and feel that their experience is not valued. Secondly, students from diverse groups often feel that the way in which instruction takes place inhibits their academic success. They argue that classroom interactions, academic discourse, cognitive style, and other aspects of teaching and learning are also based on a male European cultural style that does not permit their full participation and excludes insights from other cultures. Majority as well as minority students, then, experience an education that is far too narrow given the possibilities.

The literature on the needs expressed by students from previously underrepresented groups (Green, 1988; Pemberton, 1988; Hall and Sandler, 1982; Steele, 1992) bears several messages for faculty to consider: 1) These students need to feel welcome; 2) they need to feel that they are being treated as individuals; 3) they need to feel that they can participate fully; and 4) they need to be treated fairly.

▰▰▰ *Feeling Welcome*

Students from socially diverse groups frequently report experiencing alienation on college campuses. They recount instances of overt hostility, ignorance, and insensitivity, as well as more subtle messages they receive that their cultural heritage is not valued. In student-teacher interactions, overt problems can result from comments that are openly racist, such as "Black people never contributed anything of worth to society," or homophobic, such as "Gay men are immoral and don't belong on campus," or sexist, such as "The women in this class will probably have trouble with this concept." Although students report that most faculty do not voice such overt hostility, they pick up on more subtle cues, often entangled in instructors' attempts to be humorous, such as jokes about sexual orientation, physical disabilities, or women. The message received is that there is an underlying resentment about the presence of students who "don't fit." Many times, well-meaning but ignorant statements are the cause for discomfort. A faculty member who was in the habit of following his slips into profanity with "My apologies to the ladies" was seen as patronizing by his women students; one teacher who addressed a student with a learning disability with exaggerated enunciation made the student feel that it was assumed he was dull-witted.

Language is a cue to the instructor's stance for many students. When instructors refer to groups in terms that the groups do not prefer, such as "homosexual" for gay and lesbian students, or "Oriental" for Asian-American students, or "gals" for women, they give off a signal that they are not in tune with new developments in language preference, which is often interpreted by students as an uncaring or insensitive attitude. Students expect instructors to be aware of the dialogue around them and to demonstrate appropriate social skills. The emphasis is not so much on policing language or "political correctness" as it is on being considerate in addressing people as they wish to be addressed.

Welcoming not only involves being personally sensitive as the instructor but also helping all students to display welcoming behavior in the classroom. Most students from diverse groups say they more frequently hear insensitive comments from fellow classmates than from faculty. They emphasize that faculty must monitor classroom behavior and address problems when they occur as part of the learning experience. Rather than hurriedly passing over the comment of a student who refers to "niggers on welfare," it is important for instructors to openly discuss issues surrounding the negative image and language choice of the response, even if embarrassment is a possibility. Teaching for diversity not only involves being more welcoming to diverse groups but also means increasing the sensitivity of majority students to cultural differences.

For students from diverse groups to feel valued, instructors must go beyond neutrality. Frequently, the students experience alienation because their presence is not acknowledged at all. They are upset that instructors do not call them by name. Students expecting, according to their cultural background, to engage in formal greetings or "small talk" before an interpersonal exchange begins often interpret the impersonal, businesslike behavior of many instructors as instances of personal rejection. They frequently use the term "invisible" to describe how they feel. Although majority students sometimes describe the same feeling, it is experienced more deeply by students who are from a group that has traditionally experienced exclusion, since they are more likely to take it personally. Teachers who acknowledge diversity at the beginning of a course by indicating that they welcome different perspectives and want to accommodate different needs set the tone for students to feel respected and free to communicate with the teacher.

One of the biggest problems with helping underrepresented students feel welcome is large class size. They can feel lost and may also feel that the peer environment is more likely to get out-of-hand since classroom management is more of a challenge to the teacher. Students from non-dominant racial and ethnic groups, for example, often say that they are very hesitant to speak out on issues about people from their groups in large group settings because they fear physical violence and slurs that the instructor will not witness. Attempts by instructors to manage large class environments well and to increase personal contact with students by engaging in informal conversation before class, scheduling out-of-class visits with students, or working closely with small groups of students on a rotating basis are especially important gestures that can be made to students experiencing the "outsider" syndrome.

Messages in the Curriculum

Similarly, students from non-mainstream groups fail to find their culture or perspective acknowledged in the curriculum. For example, works by or about people of color or gay, lesbian, or bisexual people are noticeable by their absence. References are often minimized or negative. One gay student reported looking forward to the day when his American history instructor would lecture on a section of the text that dealt with the gay pride movement, only to hear the instructor say that he would not deal with the "so-called Stonewall Riots." Another reported that a human sexuality instructor said that the class would skip the chapter on homosexuality because the course was only about "normal" sexuality. In an ethics class, another student reported, the treatment of homosexuality was one of three sections in the text that the instructor chose to omit because of time constraints. The students report that examples used in classes and assignments consistently presume a heterosexual orientation. When these things happen, students report feeling that their point of view, their culture, their heritage is not welcome. They look for role models of scholars, practitioners, and artists in their field of study and find few examples that would encourage them to persist in school. Simple attempts at inclusion can be of enormous importance to students seeking validation. They can also increase the breadth of exposure of majority students.

As many scholars have noted (Banks, 1988; Butler, 1989; Sleeter, 1991; Toombs and Tierney, 1992), rethinking the curriculum often begins with including references to or about scholars or issues connected with socially diverse groups, but ultimately involves a transformative approach whereby the entire assumptions and content of a given field are reconsidered from the perspectives of diverse people. Transformation in sociology, for example, could begin with attention to eliminating stereotyped references that occur or including mention of the work of some current sociologists of color, but would move on to rethink some basic ways of doing or thinking about sociology in light of feminist epistemology or other paradigms. Often the scholarship necessary to revise courses is underdeveloped or hard to access. It takes both personal and institutional commitment and much original scholarship to do this work.

■■■ *Being Treated as an Individual*

Stereotyping

While students from diverse groups are very eager that their social group be welcomed on campus, they also want to be treated as individuals. One barrier that prevents this is stereotyping. Images of the African-American student as a "dumb jock" or "special admissions" student, of the female sorority student as a "fluffhead," or of the lesbian student as an "argumentative dyke" influence teacher expectations, often in unconscious ways. Stereotypes that are ostensibly positive, such as the "math whiz" Asian American or the "wise" older student, are also problematic since they may place unrealistically high expectations on some students. Teachers do not have to voice these stereotypes for students—they often get the message indirectly. For example, a faculty member may lavish excessive praise on a Native-American student, causing the student to feel that the expectations for him are low because of his ethnicity. An instructor might consistently ask female students, rather than males, to take notes for students who are ill, or ask males, rather than females, to lead lab groups.

Tokenism

Students from diverse cultural groups also feel that their individuality is not acknowledged when they are called upon as representatives of their group. When teachers say, "John, how do disabled people feel about this issue?" they potentially put the student in an uncomfortable position. John may not have an opinion; he may feel that there is likely to be a range of opinions on the topic among students with disabilities; and he might feel put on the spot. While it is understandable that faculty might want to include the student in the treatment of a topic and hear the voice of the "local expert," most students want to be respected as individuals and to contribute on their own volition when these issues are addressed. Likewise, many underrepresented students who are invited to serve on committees or panels are very wary of being the "token" member and want to participate based on their personal qualities rather than social group membership.

Mentoring

Individual nurturing through mentoring relationships is also important, yet women and students of color report much lower instances of being mentored than male European Americans (Hall and Sandler, 1982; Blackwell, 1990). In commenting on the reasons for the lack of mentoring and graduate associateships reported by minority graduate students, Blackwell concludes that faculty do not choose students who are different from them-

selves, since there is a "tendency for faculty members to consciously or subconsciously attempt to reproduce themselves
through persons chosen as their protegees" (p. 8). Keeping an
open mind about having work go in a new direction or appreciat-
ing stylistic differences as potentially complementary or liberat-
ing are often involved in mentoring previously underrepresented
students.

■■■ *Full Participation*

The Dominant Classroom

Valuing people who think and act in ways that are consistent
with the traditional culture of the institution often leads to inad-
vertent or deliberate exclusion of those who are different. Usually
faculty are unaware that they are operating within a cultural perspective, since the dominant culture is taken for granted. As
Adams (1992) describes, this culture is uncomfortable for many
students from socially diverse groups because in its most extreme
form it is "narrow in that it rules out nonverbal, empathic, visual,
symbolic, or nuanced communication; it neglects the social
processes by which interpersonal communication, influence, consensus, and commitment are included in problem solving; it over-
looks the social environment as a source of information . . . ; it
ignores the values and emotions that nonacademics attach to reasons and facts" (p. 6).

The disjuncture between the dominant classroom culture and
the culture of many students can be extreme. Collett and Serrano
(1992) point out that for students who have not had a great deal
of mainstream culture experience and whose native language is
not English, the differences are enormous. Many scholars have
pointed out differences between particular cultures and academic
culture. Hofstede (1986), for example, talks about differences in
whether the individual or group is valued, whether there are
large or small power distances between people, whether the culture seeks certainty or tolerates ambiguity, and whether the culture stresses the "masculine" characteristics of material success
and assertiveness or the "feminine" characteristics of quality of
life and interpersonal relationships. She describes the classroom

culture as very different from the cultural expectations of many groups. Much has been written about the differences between an Afro-centric versus Eurocentric worldview (Asante, 1987 and 1988; Branch-Simpson, 1988), the Afro-centric stressing harmony, egalitarian social relations, a fluid notion of time and space, the social world, nonverbal communication, holistic thinking, intuitive reasoning, and approximation; and the Eurocentric stressing competition, power, numerical precision, abstract thinking, verbal communication, analytical thinking, logic, and quantitative accuracy. This literature portrays American classrooms as valuing the Eurocentric worldview.

Cognitive Styles

There is not a clear consensus on whether one can draw implications on learning styles from cultural styles or whether particular learning styles are associated with particular groups. In the case of some of the populations being discussed, such as gay, lesbian, and bisexual students, there is no present evidence to indicate that there are clear patterns. For some other groups, such as students with learning disabilities, there are clear differences (by definition) connected with the disability. The literature on nontraditional-age students (from the adult education literature), women, and students of color does discuss patterns. These descriptions must be viewed with caution, however, since talking about broad patterns across groups of people who have many intragroup differences can lead to stereotyping and overgeneralization. On the other hand, if descriptions of styles are considered as tools to illustrate differences rather than as applicable to every individual in the categories described, they can be helpful.

When scholars talk about major differences in cognitive and social-interactional styles across various cultures, they often use the work of learning style theorists and apply their constructs, which are usually polar opposites, such as abstract vs. concrete thinking, to a particular cultural group. Anderson and Adams (1992), for example, use Anderson's categories of relational and analytical and Witkin and Moore's (1975) categories of field independence and field dependence (also termed "field sensitivity") to illustrate differences in style. They argue that women from the European-American culture and men and women from Native-American, Hispanic, and African-American cultures often exhibit a style that is relational and field dependent. They suggest that many people from these groups are more improvisational and intuitive than sequential and structured; more interested in material with social or concrete content than abstract material; more holistic than analytic; and more cooperative than competitive. Most European-American males (most faculty members) and Asian-American males would tend to fall into the opposite categories. They have been socialized through their culture and the academic tradition to value analytic, structured, abstract approaches. The danger that this research warns against is that faculty might view differences from the traditional norm as deficits, devaluing the work of some students and preventing them from learning well.

Gender Differences

Similarly, there is a body of literature on cognitive development in women that discusses patterns in the way women take in and process information. Belenky et al. (1986) and Baxter Magolda (1992) have looked closely at epistemological development. Their findings are often compared with a model posed by Perry (1970), whose research was conducted with a sample of students that was mostly male. (See page 248 of the 8th edition of *Teaching Tips* for a description of his work.) Although the recent studies resist the strict association of one pattern with male students and one with females, they do discuss contrasting styles that are gender-related. Both Belenky et al. and Baxter Magolda find that development in the women they studied culminates in levels of thinking that are as complex as those described by Perry but are qualitatively different at each stage in gender-related ways. Baxter Magolda, for example, describes four levels of epistemological reflection: absolute, transitional, independent, and contextual knowing. There are rough parallels to these within the schemes of both Perry and Belenky et al. Within each of the first three levels described by Baxter Magolda, however, students demonstrate contrasting approaches, generally termed "relational" and "abstract." For example, transitional knowers, the most prevalent type of knowers among traditional-age college students, demonstrate two patterns: the interpersonal pattern, found more frequently in women, and the impersonal, found more frequently in men. Although both genders are transitional knowers in that they view knowledge as uncertain (at least in some areas) and understanding as more important than acquiring and remembering information, they demonstrate different gender-related patterns (see Table 22–1). The patterns described by Belenky et al. are compatible with these findings.

One area of research that documents how different ways of knowing affect classroom learning is the literature on classroom participation. Several researchers, such as Sadkar and Sadkar (1992), Allen and Niss (1990), and Trujillo (1986), have found in empirical studies that in classroom discussion white males speak more frequently and for longer periods than white females and males and females of color and that the latter are treated deferentially by teachers. Clearly, the style associated with European-American males is dominant in many American college classrooms, making it difficult for others to participate.

Working with Different Styles

What can faculty do about styles? First, teachers can be aware that different styles exist. They can reflect on their own style and

TABLE 22–1 Gender-Related Patterns of Thinking in Traditional-Age College Students

Interpersonal	Impersonal
Want to exchange ideas with others	Want to debate ideas
Seek rapport with the instructor	Want to be challenged by the instructor
Want evaluation to take individual differences into account	Want fair and practical evaluation
Resolve uncertainty by personal judgment	Resolve uncertainty by logic and research

on the extent to which their preference for a style leads to teaching practices that exclude others. They can be alert to stylistic differences among their students, drawing upon the literature on gender and cultural differences, being careful to note individual characteristics of a particular student before assuming that he or she will demonstrate characteristics associated with her or his group.

Secondly, teachers can use varied instructional approaches. Moving between lecture, discussion, small group work, experiential learning, simulations, and other strategies allows more possibilities for students to find learning opportunities and for all to expand their own stylistic repertoires. Similarly, using redundancy in teaching modalities, such as visual aids accompanying verbal descriptions, helps students with different stylistic preferences or physical abilities to learn. Providing for options in assignments, such as a choice of an individual term paper or a collaborative project, or options in assessment, such as the choice of an essay or oral exam, is another helpful approach.

Third, teachers can evaluate work from multiple perspectives. For example, rather than viewing a personal narrative by a non-traditional-age student as "subjective, emotional, and unscholarly" it can be seen as an alternative kind of contribution to the traditional footnoted and impersonal paper, each valuable in a different way. Welcoming comments that seek synthesis and understanding rather than argumentation and analysis can promote more balanced discussion. Rewarding collaboration as well as individual effort can affirm those students whose strengths and values are in social interaction.

▰▰▰ *Being Treated Fairly*

Egalitarian treatment of students is a very valued norm in American higher education. Grading anonymously, giving all students the same amount of time to complete a test or assignment, and requiring the same number and type of assignments by each student are common practices. Teachers often say, "I treat all students the same." Yet a closer look reveals that they do not treat all students the same, nor should they. Students with disabilities are often allowed more time for exams, the help of a reader, or a special setting for taking the test. Non-native speakers may be allowed to use dictionaries during test-taking and their work may be graded more for content than expression of ideas. Equal treatment involves not necessarily *same* treatment, then, but treatment that respects the individual needs of particular learners.

While teachers may readily accept different treatment for students who are disabled, non-native speakers, or even those older students who have hearing impairments or work slowly, they find it much more difficult to justify different treatment based on gender or cultural characteristics. Once again, however, beginning with the individual student is important. It is important to have expectations that are appropriate to the student. Some disjuncture between the student's point of entry and the dominant culture may occur and balance should be sought. For example, students coming from cultures where time is viewed fluidly may have difficulty understanding that due dates will be interpreted literally or that class begins promptly on the hour. Most students have learned to be bicultural and to operate under different sets of assumptions based on the cultural context. Others, however, may need help. It may be necessary to have individual conversations with such students emphasizing the expectations or giving reminders about due dates. It may be important to tolerate a few mistakes before penalizing students or to rethink the cultural-embedment of the rule. A conversation at the start of the course on expectations and standards, coupled with a clear syllabus, can help communications immeasurably.

Teachers can also consider cultural or gender-related issues that may impact class discussion. Many female students or male and female students from Native-American or Asian-American backgrounds have been socialized to value listening more than speaking. For them, a class participation grading scheme based on number of contributions in class may be problematic. Fair treatment might be based on quality of comment rather than quantity or on performance in dyad or small group, rather than whole class, conversation. Students who are from more reflective than spontaneous cultures can be helped by giving the class time for silent thought before responses are solicited. They may need to learn the culture. Conversely, students from the dominant culture may learn from them, incorporating the strengths of silent reflection into class routines. Myra and David Sadkar (1992) recommend that teachers ask an observer to record participation levels in their classes to give them a sense of the patterns that are occurring so that they may avoid the pitfall of unequal discussion.

Inherent in all discussion about fairness is mutuality. The need for order and routine must be balanced by appreciation for variation and richness of perspective. Strongly forcing students from nontraditional backgrounds to acculturate to the institution in order to succeed prevents the institution from learning and expanding its potential. Pervading considerations of social diversity are issues involved in the ongoing revitalization of colleges as places of learning.

SUPPLEMENTARY READING

L. Border and N. Chism (eds.), Teaching for Diversity, *New Directions in Teaching and Learning, 49* (San Francisco: Jossey-Bass, 1992). This collection of essays treats the following topics: the culture of the classroom, learning styles of diverse learners, gender equity in the classroom, feminist pedagogy, and developing programs to promote inclusive teaching. Descriptions of successful programs and a resource guide are included.

J. H. Cones, J. F. Noonan, and J. Jahna (eds.), Teaching Minority Students, *New Directions in Teaching and Learning, 16* (San Francisco: Jossey-Bass, 1983). This sourcebook contains many insightful chapters on how majority faculty and others can explore their own racial assumptions in order to work more effectively with underrepresented students.

M. F. Green (ed.), *Minorities on Campus: A Handbook for Enhancing Diversity* (Washington, D.C.: American Council on Education, 1988). Chapter 8 of this overview volume deals directly with teaching, learning, and curriculum issues. Many program examples are given.

G. Pemberton, *On Teaching the Minority Student: Problems and Strategies* (Brunswick, ME: Bowdoin College, 1988). This guide discusses problems and specific strategies for interactions both in and outside the classroom.

The Teaching Assistantship: A Preparation for Multiple Roles

▰▰▰ *To the TA*

A part of graduate training of an ever-increasing number of students is the teaching assistantship. For some it is viewed as simply a way to get financial support; for others it is just a job, one which takes them away from their "real" studies; for others it is the first try at what might be their future careers. Whatever your personal feelings at this time, let me try to convince you that this is an opportunity to learn some really important lessons, no matter what your ultimate professional goals may be. The skills involved in teaching are generalizable to just about every other position of responsibility to which you might aspire.

Teaching requires that you be able to communicate technical material to specialists and nonspecialists alike in both oral and written form, an important component of both business and research. Teaching requires that you be able to guide the learning of others and to establish and maintain good interpersonal relationships with those "below" and "above" you in the hierarchy, which is essentially what management positions require. Teaching requires you to evaluate the performance of others, one of the most critical and difficult skills for anyone in a management position. Teaching requires you to be able to listen to someone else struggling with a problem and help them solve it, the basis of consultation in most fields.

Of course, what you learn as a TA will be directly relevant to any academic position you assume. Not only will you learn about teaching, but teaching is one of the best ways to learn what you know and don't know about the content. There is no better review for comprehensive exams than serving as a teaching assistant in lower division courses. Being a TA also gives you a glimpse of things from the other side of the desk. Up until now you saw only the end result of the planning and problems that are an integral part of teaching. As the TA you'll see all the other aspects of running a course that students are never allowed to know. It is hoped that it will give you a better appreciation for your own classes. One thing is guaranteed: You'll never look at your own classes the same way again.

So instead of looking at the teaching assistantship as just a job or something that takes you away from your real vocation, you'll get a lot more out of the time you spend if you approach the opportunity in the same spirit of learning you approach your own courses. What follows later in this section are some suggestions for ways to learn as much as you can from the experience.

■ *To the TA Supervisor*

Some individuals reading this volume have moved beyond being a TA and are now in faculty positions where they supervise the work of TAs. This chapter is equally for you. As someone older and wiser, you have the potential for making the TA experience of those who work for you a real professional development opportunity, which in turn will make them more enthusiastic participants in the success of your course. Or you could end up souring them on teaching altogether. It is worth your while to spend some time thinking about and planning the work you assign your TAs and the ways you can guide them as they develop as teachers. This chapter can give you some useful ideas about the kinds of activities that might be helpful.

Different Responsibilities and Skills Needed of TAs

Just what do TAs do? There is no one answer to that question. The range of activities that are possible is enormous. Here are some examples.

Graders

Some TAs are only given the task of grading papers, homework, exams and such. This is not as easy a task as it might appear. Graders need a good grasp of the content, not in just a general sense, but in the way the content is presented and analyzed in the course for which they are grading. They need to be able to follow a student's thinking in order to interpret answers that might not be complete. They need to be able to set and maintain consistent standards as laid out by the instructor so that grading will be fair and reliable. In some cases they need to be able to communicate with students about the grading procedures, answering questions and even tutoring those whose performance is not up to par.

Laboratory Assistants

In science classes the TAs serve as laboratory assistants, something that on the surface might seem fairly straightforward but on closer inspection requires quite a bit of teaching. Most laboratory assistants have to be familiar with the equipment so they can set up demonstrations and student stations. But beyond that they also usually need to be able to fix things on the spur of the moment when a student complains about malfunctioning equipment. They often have to demonstrate the lab procedures clearly enough so the students will be able to repeat what they have observed; this requires great skill at explaining and breaking down procedures into simple enough steps to be understood by a novice. Lab assistants have to circulate and provide assistance to students as they work on their tasks. This requires sensitivity about when and how to help and when to let the student work it out alone. Some lab assistants also grade lab performance and lab reports, a task requiring good observation and evaluation skills.

Tutors

Occasionally TAs are assigned primarily as tutors or helpers for individual student problems. Their primary responsibility is to hold office hours for students who need help. This is an especially challenging assignment because you are working with one student on his or her most pressing need. The difficulty is that you are working with students who are having problems understanding, and the TA must be able to listen carefully to what is troubling the student and then help the student find the way out of his or her difficulty. It is very tempting in this situation to solve the problem yourself and send them on their merry way, possibly more confused and frustrated than before. The good tutor doesn't answer the question directly, but rather helps the student find the answer. That way the student will know where or how to look the next time a similar problem arises.

Discussion or Review Section Leaders

Another group of TAs is responsible for heading up class sessions to allow the students to discuss what they have heard in lecture or read in the text or tried on the homework. In my opinion this is one of the most demanding tasks in teaching, far more difficult than giving a lecture. In a lecture the instructor has planned out what is going to be said when and how with very little fear of interruption or deviation from the script. In the discussion or review section the whole idea is to allow the students to participate; there is no way to predict where that participation will lead or what form it will take. The section leader has to be ready for anything. In addition to that you are usually working mostly on those things that the students didn't understand in the first place, and now you are trying to explain the most difficult concepts to them. So the TAs who serve as discussion or review section leaders have a particularly difficult assignment.

■■■ *What Are TAs Most Worried About?*

Being a TA is not always an easy assignment. You're halfway between being a student and a teacher yourself and halfway between the students and the teacher of your course. It's normal to feel a bit confused and apprehensive, so here are some of the common concerns that TAs voice.

Do I Know Enough?

First, you know a lot more than most of the students in your class so you've got a good head start on them. Second, you're not expected to know everything all the time. It's perfectly acceptable to say, "I don't know," as long as you try to figure it out or find the answer eventually. Third, you can go a long way toward avoiding problems in this area by being well prepared for class. Know the assignment, the equipment, what was said in lectures, how the grading was done, whatever you will be expected to respond to in class. It just doesn't pay to try to slide by.

Will They Respect Me and Accept My Authority?

A lot of this will depend on how you view yourself. The students will see you as part of the teaching staff, and that alone will give you authority. But it's how you use that authority that is important. The best way to handle problems is to avoid them in the first place by being very clear about your expectations. The next component to authority is to think of yourself as responsible for the class not in a dictatorial way but in a senior scholar way. You're there as a coach to help them. If you expect them to listen to you, they will, without you having to be very forceful about it.

Will I Be Able to Balance My Teaching Responsibilities with My Own Work?

This is a key worry, and one you should be attentive to. It will be important early on in the semester to establish your time ground rules, both with the students and with the supervising professor. Be sure to have a conference with your supervisor about what is expected of you and what support you can expect. A little prevention can go a long way. Later, if you see yourself starting to get into trouble, talk to your supervisor before it gets too bad. Maybe there's a way of working things out or shifting them around. Just don't suffer in silence.

▬▬▬ *How to Get the Most Out of Being a TA*

Think About How Your TA Assignment Is Related to Your Future Work

Earlier in this chapter I described how the tasks which are associated with teaching have correlates in other professional activities. The examples given at that point were just a hint of the possibilities. Some careful thinking about what is involved in the future you see for yourself and the responsibilities of your TA assignment could result in a whole array of similar tasks. When you identify these similarities, concentrate a little more closely on what you are doing and how you are doing it. Adopt the view that your teaching assistantship is more than just a job; it is a chance to practice some of those future responsibilities in a fairly non-threatening environment.

Be Observant About the Practices of Those for Whom You Work

Another way to benefit from the time you spend as a TA is to become an observer of those who are already teaching, both good and bad models. Think of this as an apprenticeship, an opportunity to watch someone else engage in the tasks of teaching and to learn from them. Take an active interest in the how and why of the teaching that is occurring. Ask friendly questions. Why was this particular teaching method chosen? What is the thinking behind the objectives of this course? How does the instructor deal with the various in-class situations that could be a problem, such as student questions, challenges to authority, or lack of understanding? If you have the chance to assist more than one instructor in your tenure as a TA, you have an even better array of examples from which to learn. Make comparisons between the various instructors as they handle similar situations. Ask questions about their choices and practices. How do they prepare for class? What do they look for in a student's work? Most instructors will welcome the opportunity to talk about their classes, provided the questions are offered in the spirit of learning rather than as a challenge.

Take Advantage of Opportunities for Increasing Responsibilities

Related to the advice above is the idea that you should welcome the opportunity to take part in as many aspects of the course for which you are the TA as possible. Not only is this a good way to be sure that you know all you need to know to fulfill your responsibilities to that particular course, but it gives you a chance to observe firsthand much of the day to day decision-making and fine-tuning that is involved in teaching. For example, offer to assist the instructor in gathering information for lectures or in preparing exams. You'll probably already be involved in the grading of exams, but it is a good experience to see how the exam was developed from the beginning. Why were certain concepts included and others excluded? How are questions generated and revised? How is the grading scheme developed?

If you are given the opportunity to occasionally lead the class or give a short lecture, take it, especially if the instructor will be present. The feedback you can get from this experience will help you build your confidence and skills as a presenter. It may seem like extra work or a frightening situation, but the learning that can result is worth the extra discomfort.

Be Reflective About Your Practice

One of the current movements in professional development these days is the concept of the reflective practitioner. It means that a professional's actions and decisions are not made at random, but reflect an underlying set of theories and assumptions. To improve, the professional constantly reflects on those theories and assumptions and how they relate to behavior. Therefore, to be professional as a teacher means getting in the habit of examining what you do and why you do it. One useful aid in this is keeping a journal on your teaching experiences. When things go well, note what was good about it. When things go wrong, try to think about what happened and why. Just the act of noting the successes and problems will increase your awareness of what it is that guides you as a teacher and that awareness will serve as the first step toward improvement.

Learn from Reading as Well as Practice

I know that it feels like there is already too much work to do in graduate school without adding more, but getting in the habit of reading about all aspects of your profession is a good tradition to develop early on. The fact that you are reading this book is a good start. There are many books on teaching by philosophers and practitioners alike. In addition, most disciplines have journals that are devoted to the teaching of the discipline. Alternatively, there may be special issues of the disciplinary research journals that once a year focus on teaching. There are other more general periodicals that discuss teaching in general or issues in higher education. These would be of special interest to those planning a career in teaching.

If you don't have time for that kind of reading, you might try a different tack. Read your regular reading from a different perspective; look at your own textbooks and reading assignments from the perspective of a teacher. If you were the instructor of the class using this material, what would you do to make the material comprehensible to students? How do the different textbooks you encounter handle that task? What is the difference between reading textbooks and primary sources? And what is the significance of that difference for teaching? By developing a "second eye" when reading the printed matter of your discipline you can accomplish two tasks at once: You can digest the content of the reading, and you think about ways to teach using that particular type of material.

Documentation of Activities with the Teaching Portfolio

Another way to learn and profit from being a teaching assistant is to be on the lookout for things that will make you more marketable when you enter the job market. If you can document these activities to show potential employers the degree of sophistication about teaching (or even other activities) you have developed during your graduate years, you could make yourself stand out among a large field of candidates, all of whom have very similar credentials. The name given this documentation is the "teaching portfolio."

What might you include in such a portfolio? As you work with various typical undergraduate courses, particularly those that are taught in nearly every institution, create sample course descriptions for the courses as you might teach them under various conditions. What textbooks or types of textbooks would you use? What objectives and activities would you include? Have you had experience with those activities? What is your analysis of their effectiveness? Can you give examples of the work of students with whom you have worked and how you evaluated their efforts?

As you begin to develop a philosophy of teaching and learning, creating a series of descriptions of that philosophy and what has shaped it could tell potential employers whether or not you would fit with their departments. Just as employing departments will expect you to have a coherent research program focusing on a few relevant themes or contributions, you can provide them with a similar coherent description of the contributions you would make to their educational mission as well.

Create descriptions of the different types of activities you were required to perform in your various TA positions. Not every TA position has the same responsibilities or means the same thing to every person. You need to illustrate what you have learned and what your strengths are. Just as you strive to document your research experiences through papers and presentations, you should document your teaching experience.

▆ *Additional Suggestions for Supervisors*

If you are the supervisor of a TA rather than a graduate student yourself, you can still take the above suggestions and pass them along to those you are working with. More important, however, you can create the opportunities for them to try out some of the suggestions. Here are some examples.

Team Teach

Try thinking about your TA as an apprentice who will learn a lot from the experiences you make available. Include him or her in the important design decisions of the course, if not as an active participant, at least as an observer. Give your TA opportunities to teach the class as a whole, preferably not just when you have to be out of town, but also when you are there to provide moral support and feedback. When such opportunities arise, talk them over both before and after, highlighting what was good, what needs work, and how to improve. You will find that helping a graduate student learn to teach will eventually benefit your own teaching.

Observe

If your TA does conduct sessions of the class regularly, make it a point to stop by occasionally to observe how things are going. Don't make it a big deal, but just an opportunity for you to understand what is going on in those sessions because it will help both of you. Don't wait until there is a problem to come to the class. If you make it a regular occurrence, it will lose some of its threatening nature and be seen more as encouragement and support.

Beginning of the Semester Conference on Responsibilities

Just as different faculty have different ideas about what a TA's responsibilities should be, graduate students are just as likely to be confused about what they're supposed to be doing. You can save a lot of time and trouble by clarifying your expectations and those of your TA right at the beginning of the semester. Beforehand make a checklist of the kinds of tasks that the course will require of both of you and include some general items about time commitments, class attendance, office hours, appropriate relationships with students, and so on. Then sit down with your TA and go over your respective responsibilities to the course, to the students and to each other. By doing this early in the semester, you'll be opening lines of communication that will stand you in good stead later.

The teaching assistant is a wonderful bridge between student and instructor in two different ways. The individual serving as the TA serves as a bridge between the students in a class and the faculty member who is the instructor—sometimes an awkward position. In another way the teaching assistantship itself is the activity that brings the individual graduate student from the student role to the instructor role—sometimes an awkward transition. Whichever way you want to think about it, the bridge should be built thoughtfully and reflectively if it is to stand up to the stresses it is bound to experience.

SUPPLEMENTARY READING

J. D. Nyquist, R. D. Abbott, D. H. Wulff, and J. Sprague (eds.), *Preparing the Professoriate of Tomorrow to Teach* (Dubuque, IA: Kendall/Hunt, 1991).

J. D. Nyquist, R. D. Abbott, and D. H. Wulff (eds.), Teaching Assistant Training in the 1990s, *New Directions for Teaching and Learning, 39* (San Francisco: Jossey-Bass, 1989).

J. Janes and D. Hauer, *Now What?* Readings on surviving (and even enjoying) your first experience at college teaching, 2nd ed. (Acton, MA: Copley, 1988).

CHAPTER 24

Problem Situations and Problem Students (There's Almost Always at Least One!)

*P*ERIODICALLY DURING MY WEEKLY MEETINGS with teaching assistants, I suggest that we discuss problem students or situations in their classes as an agenda item for the next week. I have never found that the next week's discussion ended early for lack of examples. My advice may not be helpful, but often it is at least reassuring to know that one is not alone in having a particular problem and that it is probably not due solely to one's inadequacy as a teacher. This chapter will discuss some of the common problems that have been raised by my teaching assistants and will suggest some strategies to try. But first a word of general advice:

It is human nature for us to perceive the problem as the student; but before focusing on changing the students' behavior, take a few moments to look at what you are doing that might be related to the student's behavior. Interpersonal problems involve at least two people, and in many cases the difficulties are not one-sided.

■■■■ The Angry, Aggressive Student

Every once in a while a class will include one or more students who seem to have a chip on their shoulder—who convey both verbally and non-verbally hostility toward you and the whole enterprise. What can you do?

Probably the most common strategy we use is to try to ignore them. This strategy often succeeds in avoiding a public confrontation and disruption of the class. However, it may not result in better motivation and learning for the student. Thus I try to become better acquainted with the student. If I have had students turn in "minute papers" or longer classroom assignments, I read the angry student's paper more carefully to try to understand what is the problem. I try to make encouraging comments; I may ask the student to come in to see me and discuss the paper, leading to questions about how the student feels about the course, what things he enjoys, what topics might be interesting to him. (I use the male pronoun because these students are most likely to be males, but I have also encountered hostile female students.) Sometimes you will feel in such a conversation that you have to drag each word from the student; yet the student will accept your invitation to come in for another discussion. Sometimes you may need to invite a small group of students to meet with you (including the hostile student) in order to make the situation less threatening for the hostile student who hides fear with aggressiveness.

Whatever your strategy, it seems to me important to let the student know that you recognize him as an individual, that you are committed to his learning, and that you are willing to listen and respond as constructively as possible.

What about overt hostility—the student who attacks your point of view during a lecture or class discussion, or the student who feels that your poor teaching or unfair grading caused students' poor performance on a test.

First of all, listen carefully and respectfully. Nothing is more frustrating than to be interrupted before your argument or complaint has been heard. Next, acknowledge that there is a possibility that the student may be right or at least that there is some logic or evidence on his or her side. Then you have at least two or three alternatives:

1. State your position as calmly and rationally as you can recognizing that not everyone will agree. If the issue is one of substance, ask the class what evidence might be obtained to resolve or clarify the issue. If the issue is one of judgment about grading, state your reason for asking the question,

what sort of thinking you were hoping to assess, and how students who did well went about answering the question. Note that your judgment may not be perfect, but you have the responsibility to make the best judgment you can and you have done so.

2. Present the issue to the class. "How do the rest of you feel about this?" This has the obvious danger that either you or the aggressor may find no support and feel alienated from the class, but more often than not it will bring the issues and arguments for both sides into the open and be a useful experience in thinking for everyone. This might be a place to use the two-column method described in Chapter 4, listing on the blackboard without comments the arguments on both sides.

3. Admit that you may have been wrong and say that you will take time to reconsider and report back at the next class session. If the student really does have a good point, this will gain you respect and a reputation for fairness. If the student's argument was groundless, you may gain the reputation of being easy to influence, and have an increasing crowd of students asking for changes in their grades.

What about the student who comes into your office all charged up to attack your grading of what was clearly a very good exam paper?

Again, the first step is to listen. As suggested in Chapter 6, you may gain some time to think if you have announced that students who have questions or complaints about grading of their tests should bring a written explanation to your office of their point of view and the rationale for their request for a higher grade.

But, once again, don't be so defensive about your grading that you fail to make an adjustment if the student has a valid point.

If you don't feel that the student has a valid point and your explanation is not convincing, you may simply have to say that while the student may be right, you have to assign the grades in terms of what seems to you the appropriate criteria. While instructors, like umpires and referees, are fallible, the college pays them to make the best judgments they can.

◼ *Attention Seekers and Students Who Dominate Discussions*

In their book, *The College Classroom*, Dick Mann (1970) and his graduate students describe eight clusters or types of students:

1. Compliant Students
2. Anxious Dependent Students
3. Discouraged Workers
4. Independents
5. Heroes
6. Snipers
7. Silent Students
8. Attention Seekers

Attention seekers talk whether or not they have anything to say; they joke, show off, compliment the teacher or other students—they continually try to be noticed (Mann et al., 1970).

At the beginning of the term when I am trying to get discussions started I am grateful for the attention seekers. They help keep the discussion going while others sit back waiting to see if it is safe to talk. But as the class develops both the other students and I tend to be disturbed by the students who talk too much and interfere with other students' chances to talk. What do I do then?

Usually I start by suggesting that I want to get everyone's ideas—that each student has a unique perspective and that it is important that we bring as many perspectives and ideas as possible to bear on the subject under discussion. If hands are raised to participate, I call first on those who haven't talked recently.

If the problem persists, I may suggest to the class that some people seem to participate much more than others and ask them for suggestions about what might be done to give all students a chance to participate.

Alternatively, I might ask two or three students to act as

"process observers" for a day to report at the end of the class or at the beginning of the next class on their observations of how the discussion went, what problems they noticed, and what suggestions they have. (I might even ask the attention seeker to be a process observer one day.) Or you might audiotape or videotape a class and play back one or more portions at the next class period for student reactions.

If all else fails, I ask the student to see me outside class and mention that I'm concerned about the class discussions. Much as I appreciate his involvement it would be helpful if he would hold back some of his comments until everyone else has been heard.

In the preceding comments I may have assumed that the attention seeker was not making good, helpful comments. There are also dominant students who are knowledgeable, fluent, and eager to contribute relevant information, contribute real insights, and solve problems. We prize such students; yet there is still the potential danger that other students will withdraw, feeling that there is no need to participate since the dominant student is so brilliant or articulate that their own ideas and questions will seem weak and inadequate. Here subgrouping may help, with the stipulation that each student must present his or her question, idea, or reaction to the task of the group before beginning a general discussion.

In his newsletter, *The University Teacher* (Vol. 13, No. 1) Harry Stanton (1992), consultant on higher education at the University of Tasmania, suggests that each student be given three matches or markers at the beginning of the class. Each time they speak they must put down one of their markers and when their markers are gone, their contributions are over for the day. Perhaps subgroups could pool their markers or one could borrow or bargain for an extra marker for a really good idea that needs to be presented at this time.

■ *The Silent Students*

What to do about the students who never participate in class discussions? If we believe that it is important for students to practice thinking and get reactions to their ideas, students who fail to participate are perhaps more of a problem than the attention seekers.

You may argue that students have the right to remain silent, and I have some sympathy for that position; yet it seems to me that we do not suggest that students have a right to omit tests or to opt out of writing papers or other assignments that we believe contribute to learning. Students have a right to expect that we tell them why we expect active participation or why other assigned activities will contribute to learning, but this does not mean that they should be able to omit anything that they wish to.

We have already discussed some techniques of getting participation such as minute papers, pairing, buzz groups, and problem posting in earlier chapters. These techniques, useful for all students, are also helpful for students who would otherwise be silent. But there may still be students who, despite having written a minute paper and participated in a buzz group, remain silent in general class discussions. What can we do?

One aid involves getting to know the students' interests or special experiences well enough that you can call upon them for some item on which they have special expertise. We have discussed such techniques as papers or file cards filled out the first week of class with information about relevant student experiences. A silent student's research paper may give the student expertise or information useful at some point in a class discussion. A student panel in which students prepare presentations on different aspects or sides of some theoretical or applied issue may provide an opportunity to involve one or more silent students. (If you use such a panel, it is probably wise to meet with them to give support and guidance both in preparation of the content and in planning how to make the presentation interesting and informative.) And, as in dealing with the aggressive and attention-seeking students, getting to know the student outside of class is likely to help you generate strategies for facilitating learning.

Both nonparticipants and discussion monopolizers have been discussed in Chapter 4, which presents some of these and other strategies for dealing with such students.

■■■ *Inattentive Students*

Periodically I have a class in which two or three students in the back of the classroom carry on their own conversation during my lecture. This is annoying not only to me but to students sitting near them. What to do?

Think back to my first word of advice. Is the lecture material too difficult? Too easy? Is the topic of discussion one that arouses anxiety? Assuming that the answer to these questions is "No," and the behavior persists despite changes in topic or level of difficulty, what next?

My first attempt is typically to break the class into buzz groups assigned to work on some problem or to come up with an hypothesis, and to move around the class to see how the groups are progressing, making sure that I get to the group including the disruptive students to see that they are working on the group task. Usually this works, and sometimes this gets the students reengaged in the class for the rest of the class period.

But suppose that in the next class period the same problem recurs? This time I might have the class write "minute papers" and call upon one of the inattentive students to report what he or she has written, or alternatively call upon someone seated near the inattentive group centering activity toward that part of the classroom.

Another possibility is to announce that because research evidence indicates that students who sit in front get better grades (and you can explain why seeing an instructor's face and mouth improves attention and understanding), you have a policy of rotating seats periodically so that next week you will expect those sitting in the back row to move to the front row and all other rows to move back one row.

If all else fails, I might have a general class feedback discussion on what factors facilitated and what factors might have interfered with learning in the class thus far in the term. Alternatively I might ask one or more of the students to see me outside of class to ask about their feelings about the class and to express my concern about not being able to teach in a way that would capture their attention.

The Unprepared Students

There are often good reasons why students come to class unprepared, but there are also students who are chronically unprepared for no apparent reason. What can we do?

In my introductory course I try to communicate from the beginning that I expect students to read the assignments before class by announcing that I will give a brief quiz the second day of class based on the first lecture or discussion and the assignment for the next class. I give the quiz and then ask students to correct their own papers, indicating that this quiz had two purposes: to start the habit of reading the assignment before class, and to give them an idea of whether or not they were getting the main points of the assignment. Thus there was no need to turn it in for a grade. I give a second quiz a week later and a longer one three weeks later. By this point I hope that my students have established a routine for keeping up with their assignments.

Such a procedure assumes that students know what is expected of them. One of the most common causes of underpreparation is that students don't really know what is expected. Often instructors say something like, "You might want to look at the next chapter of the book before the next class," or they state that the next lecture will be on Topic X without indicating that this is also the topic of the next reading. One of the advantages of a well-written syllabus is that it communicates your expectations and typically lists the assignments for each class period or week.

▬ *The Flatterer, Disciple, Con Man (or Woman)*

If one is new or somewhat insecure, it is tempting to respond positively to anyone who tells you that you are the best teacher he or she has ever had, or who is impressed with the depth of your knowledge and wants to learn more about your special research interests. In fact one does not need to be new or insecure; we all relish compliments and interest in our work. More often than not such interest is genuine and can be genuinely enriching both for you and the student; but there are students for whom such an approach is a conscious strategy for winning better grades or getting exceptions from deadlines for papers or other requirements.

The real danger presented by such students is that you will begin to mistrust all students and lose compassion for students who really need an extension of time or some other indication of flexibility. I would rather be conned a couple of times then to turn off a student in real need by cold rigidity. Thus my advice is to start with an assumption of honesty; nonetheless, in general, don't change the rules of the game unless you are willing to change them for everyone or unless you are convinced that there are reasonable grounds for a special exception.

▰▰▰ *The Discouraged, Ready-to-Give-up Students*

Often after the first few weeks you will spot some students missing who seem depressed and discouraged. Sometimes they come to class late or miss class; often their papers are constricted and lack any sense of enthusiasm or creativity. In my introductory classes, students begin with great enthusiasm and energy and a few weeks later seem to have lost their energy; interestingly, we spot the same phenomenon in our proseminar for the beginning Ph.D. students.

In both cases the transition to a new level of education brings demands greater than those students have experienced in the past. Often their familiar supports from family and friends are no longer available; they begin to doubt their own ability to achieve their goals.

There is a magic elixir for this problem that research has demonstrated to be surprisingly effective. This is to bring in students from the previous year who describe their experiences of frustration and self-doubt during their first year and report that they surmounted them and survived. The theory explaining why this works basically states that the task is to convince the discouraged students that their problems need not be attributed to a lack of ability that cannot be changed but rather is a temporary problem. By developing more effective strategies, investing more effort, or simply becoming less worried, better results are likely to follow (Wilson and Linville, 1982, 1985; Van Overwalle, Segebarth, and Goldchstein, 1989).

▰▰▰ *Students with Excuses*

As indicated earlier, I believe that it is better to be taken in by a fraudulent excuse than to be seen as unfair in response to a legitimate excuse. Nonetheless, one doesn't want to be seen as so gullible that students come to rely upon excuses rather than doing their assignments. Caron, Whitbourne, and Halgin (1992) studied excuse-making and in their sample found that about two-thirds of their students admitted having made at least one false excuse while in college. From these students' reports it appears that fraudulent excuses were about as frequent as legitimate ones. In most cases the excuse was used to gain more time for an assignment.

The Caron et al. data do not give many clues about what one can do to prevent or detect false excuses. If the problem is one of time, one might build in checks on the progress of a paper or other assignment to reduce the tendency to put off work until the last minute—you could, for example, have students turn in an outline or bibliography some time before a paper is due.

Sometimes we have announced in the syllabus that there would be a graded series of penalties depending upon how late a paper was, indicating that this was to make up for the advantage the late students had in having extra time to look up more sources, get comments and feedback from other students, etc. An alternative that I have not used, but might be more advantageous psychologically, would be to offer a bonus for papers turned in early.

It might also be wise to put in your syllabus that you want to be flexible on deadlines and recognize that unforeseen events may prevent students from being able to meet a deadline. But in making exceptions you will require evidence supporting the request for an extension.

▪▪▪ *The Student Who Wants the TRUTH*

You have just given a superb lecture comparing two competing theories. A student comes up after class and says, "That was a great lecture, but which theory is right?"

All too many students feel that the teacher's task is to tell students the facts and larger truths and the student's task is to listen to the truth, learn it, and be able to give it back on exams. This conception seemed to William Perry, of Harvard University, to be particularly common among first-year students.

Perry (1981) suggested that individual differences in student responses to teaching may be conceptualized in terms of student stages of cognitive development. In any class students at differing stages are present, but those at the lower stages are more common in introductory courses and those at the higher stages are more common in senior courses.

Students at the lower stages are characterized by a dualistic view of knowledge. Things are either true or false, right or wrong. The teacher knows the truth; the student's job is to learn the truth. Students in the middle stages have learned that authorities differ. There seems to be no settled truth; everyone has a right to his or her own opinions. This stage is succeeded by the recognition that some opinions and generalizations are better supported than others. The student's task is to learn the criteria needed for evaluating the validity of assertions in different subject-matter fields. The final stages involve student commitment to values, beliefs, and goals with the recognition that despite the lack of complete certainty one must make decisions and act on one's values.

Perry suggests that the effective teacher must find a way to provide support and stretching for those at the lower levels while avoiding boredom for students at the higher levels. One practical suggestion is that a term paper may be challenging to the advanced students and at the same time stretch the less advanced students by letting them see that not all sources agree.

SUPPLEMENTARY READING

An excellent review of the attributional retraining research dealing with motivation of discouraged students is R. P. Perry, F. J. Hechter, V. H. Menec, and L. Weinberg, *A Review of Attributional Motivation and Performance in College Students from an Attributional Retraining Perspective.* Occasional Papers in Higher Education, Centre for Higher Education Research and Development, The University of Manitoba, Winnipeg, Manitoba, Canada R3T 2N2.

A Potpourri of Practical and Theoretical Topics

PART

How to Win Friends and Influence Custodians

*T*HE BEGINNING INSTRUCTOR'S TEACHING may be greatly facilitated or hampered by relationships with other personnel of the college or university.

Secretaries

In most colleges and universities the secretaries are the most important aids or barriers to getting things done. Establishing a good relationship with the secretary who handles your work is one of the most important keys to happiness and success in your academic life. You will not achieve such a relationship if you turn in work at the last minute. In planning your syllabi, tests, or other tasks requiring secretarial help, give enough lead time to allow the secretary an opportunity to plan how to schedule your task and meet other demands. The secretary is an important colleague and often has tacit knowledge of how to cope with the university bureaucracy that can be invaluable to you.

Librarians

You will occasionally wish to recommend or assign readings in library references. Sometimes instructors make such assignments without informing the librarian. The frustrated librarians are then deluged with students demanding a book that has already been taken out for two weeks or that is not even listed in the catalogue. After a few such experiences, the librarian may not greet requests for special favors with much enthusiasm. Thus, one of the essentials of pre-course planning is giving the library a list of books that will be required reading, perhaps with a description of the nature and time of use, making sure that students are given the correct authors and titles.

Often, too, instructors ask the library to order many copies of books they plan to use. The next year they decide to use different sources, and the library is left with twenty copies of a book when only one or two copies have ever been used. Usually librarians are happy to advise an instructor how many copies of a supplementary book should be ordered in terms of the number of students and the extent of the readings required.

Audio-Visual Centers

Similar problems may arise in scheduling videotapes and audio-visual aids. It should be obvious that instructors cannot expect videotapes or films and projectionists to be available the day they decide to use them without advance notice. Effective use of visual aids requires planning. Moreover, if you have scheduled a movie, it is not conducive to good relations with projectionists to tell the operator when he or she appears loaded with projector and screen that you have decided not to use the film.

Custodians

Relationships with custodians are also important. Instructors sometimes complain of lack of chalk, messy rooms, or broken seats but fail to recognize their own responsibilities in building maintenance. You can hardly blame custodians for getting discouraged when they enter a classroom to find the floor littered with bits of paper, chalk, or food, the blackboard smeared with scrawling, and the room in general disorder.

Administrators, Colleagues, and Students

In beginning work in a different college, you may find that the rules, traditions, and usual channels to go through for a particular service are not the same as you are accustomed to. If you ask for information with humility rather than attempt to order conformity to your expectations, you will have a much easier time in learning the ropes.

Important problems also arise in relationships with administrators, colleagues, and the student body. For example, the records and deadlines required by the registrar's office and other administrative offices often seem unimportant to instructors, and they are apt to feel that a slight delay is of no consequence. However, an office that processes hundreds or thousands of records must have scheduling as rigorous as that of a factory production line. Laxness on the part of a few instructors may ruin a beautiful schedule.

Instructors also sometimes fail to remember that their courses may have relevance for the courses of their colleagues. If the faculty members who teach courses following yours know what you are doing, they can shape their own courses accordingly. Because they have an interest in the course, they are usually pleased if they are consulted when any drastic changes are to be made. Certainly the department chair should be kept informed.

It should be evident that students, too, have an interest in your teaching. One of your first obligations is to make sure that the course description in the college catalogue is adequate. The academic counselors should have a more detailed description of the course if they are to counsel students wisely.

Periodic student evaluation of teaching and courses is helpful to most instructors. I have found that it is helpful simply to have students write "Things I like," "Criticisms," and "Suggestions." Often it is helpful to get evaluations not only from students taking the course but also from students who took the course at an earlier date.

Most college instructors are asked at some time to sponsor a student group, to give an informal talk at a student meeting, or to meet with a student committee. My only words of advice here are, "Act naturally." Don't try to knock yourself out trying to prove that you're a human being, and don't fear that the proper barriers between students and faculty will be breached.

There is one exception to my advice to act naturally—when college regulations prohibit certain activities that are condoned in our own circle of society. The most common issue is that of student drinking or use of drugs. Whether you approve or disapprove of the college's regulations, I see no great gain in achieving popularity as a faculty member who winks at violations.

SUPPLEMENTARY READING

Kenneth E. Eble, *The Craft of Teaching* (San Francisco: Jossey-Bass, 1976), Chapter 6, pp. 163–172.

MARILLA SVINICKI
University of Texas at Austin

CHAPTER  26

Ethics in College Teaching

*I*MAGINE YOU'RE TEACHING A COURSE at the introductory level, one that is required of all students who want to proceed on to major in your department. And let's suppose that you are approached by a student after the first exam, someone whose performance was much below standard. And that person offers you a considerable sum of money if you'll change a grade on the exam so the student can pass. What is the ethical thing to do in this situation?

Now suppose that it's the same situation, but instead of offering you money, the student pleads for an opportunity to retake the exam because of extenuating circumstances during the first test administration. Now what is the ethical choice?

Now it's the same situation, but this time you are the one who notices that a student who's been working hard in your class and whom you expected to do very well has instead failed the exam miserably. How does this situation compare with those above from an ethical standpoint?

The first of these scenarios seems fairly straightforward, a definite violation of ethics if you were to accept the money to change the grade. The second example is not as straightforward; to what extent should the student be allowed an opportunity that is not available to all the other students? Does providing that opportunity constitute unethical behavior? Or is it just unfair? Or is there a difference? And in the third instance, to what extent should your assessment of a student's abilities counter actual performance? Where do you draw the line in helping students?

The most difficult questions that teachers face often have nothing to do with the content of a course or the way it is presented. They focus instead on the ethical issues of teaching, how we relate to our students, our institution, our discipline, and society at large. What are our responsibilities to each constituency and what do we do when they conflict? Unfortunately there are no easy answers to these questions. I raise them here as food for thought because you *will* face them sometime in your teaching career.

■■■■ *What Does It Mean?*

This chapter addresses the issue of ethics in teaching. It is something that is seldom overtly taught, even in matters of scholarship. It is either assumed that "everyone knows what that means" or it is learned in the process of apprenticeship to a more advanced scholar as in the research laboratory or research assistantship. As evidenced by some recent scandals in the conduct of research, it is not always learned very well. It is even more likely that the ethical decisions in teaching are difficult to learn because they are not generally in the public view. The students in an individual's class are usually not aware of the ethical standards that shape an instructor's course policies and teaching practices; they see only the outcomes of those standards. Teaching assistants frequently have to face questions of conflict with students or questions of an ethical nature. Just as frequently they do so with very little guidance.

What is an ethical question in teaching? There are many interpretations of that issue, but in general, ethical standards are intended to guide us in carrying out the responsibilities we have to the different groups with whom we interact. Ethics violations can occur when we are tempted to act contrary to those standards. Ethical dilemmas occur when multiple responsibilities conflict. It is often surprising to consider all the different things that can cause ethical problems for instructors. They range from the obvious bribe attempt described above, to failure to present all legitimate sides of an issue adequately, to accepting remuneration for extra tutoring for a class with which one is connected.

In a 1991 research study of psychologists teaching at academic institutions, Tabachnick, Keith-Spiegel, and Pope reported reactions to various ethical questions involved in teaching at the college level. Respondents were asked to report if and how frequently they engaged in a wide range of various activities and rate the extent to which they felt those activities were ethical or unethical. The activities included things as drastic as sexual harassment to more mundane activities such as teaching material that the instructor had not yet fully mastered. The authors then assessed which items most respondents reported engaging in at some time, which were the most controversial in terms of ethical judgments, and which were extremely rare.

The behavior most often engaged in was teaching when not adequately prepared, although it was not a consistent pattern for most people. The authors attribute this more to busy workloads and rapid advances in the field than to the shirking of responsibilities. Respondents also reported that they tried to teach ethics or values, a practice that could be seen as either positive or negative depending on precisely what is being taught and how.

The rarest behaviors were those related to sexual harassment. Whether this is an accurate reflection of behavior or a reluctance to report such behavior is impossible to tell. Also rare were actual sexual encounters with students. Less drastic but still questionable practices that rarely occur were such things as conflicts of interest with book publishers.

Perhaps the most interesting sources of ethical conflicts for this group were a result of the conflicting roles of mentor/sponsor and evaluator. The respondents had great difficulties in sorting out their loyalties. For example, over two-thirds believed allowing a student's likeability to influence a grade was unethical, but over two-thirds reported doing it at some point anyway. The same sort of dilemma is seen when instructors interact socially with students. On the one hand, the interaction with faculty is reported as vital to student growth by Pascarella and Terenzini (1991), while on the other it raises the possibility of conflict.

How can an instructor decide what is best? The American Association for University Professors has provided a statement of professional ethics dealing with the responsibilities of faculty members that highlights what they consider to be the special responsibilities of one in an academic position (AAUP, 1987). Perhaps using these standards as a guide can help highlight what a faculty member should consider in making personal choices.

■ *Responsibilities to the Students*

To Encourage the Free Pursuit of Learning, to Demonstrate Respect for Students, and to Respect Confidentiality

The primary purpose of teaching is to encourage learning; therefore the first ethical responsibility an instructor has is to that goal. What do we do to meet that responsibility? All that we do to prepare and conduct well-designed instruction is part of that effort. The ethical instructor knows the content to be learned, the students who will do the learning, and the methods that could be used to foster that learning. A second part is to protect and encourage the autonomy of our students so that eventually the students no longer need our constant guidance. Ethical instructors also respect the "otherness of students" (Churchill, 1982); that is, the individual and independent nature of the students and the fact that students are at different stages of their lives than are the instructors. That respect implies that the students have a right to privacy in their dealings with us.

There are many ways an instructor might violate these standards. Here are some examples:

- → The most obvious is to fail in our duties in class preparation. One can't always be in top form, but just as we expect students to come to class prepared, we must make the same effort.

- → Another violation would be an insistence that students adopt the same values and philosophies that we hold in areas where there is room for disagreement. We have a responsibility to help students learn how to evaluate a position, but to force a position on them is indoctrination, not instruction.

↪ A violation of omission rather than commission would be to allow the students to become too dependent on us as instructors. We have a responsibility to help them grow into independent learners.

↪ When we ridicule a student's ideas or dismiss their questions as trivial, we violate the principle of respect. Any good teacher knows that a question asked by one student probably echoes the questions of at least a dozen others. Failure to respond to genuine attempts at understanding discourages learning.

↪ Discussion of a student's problems with anyone who does not have a genuine part in that student's education is another violation. Just as there is a confidential relationship between doctor and patient, lawyer and client, there is one between teacher and student. It must be based on trust and that trust should not be taken lightly.

To Model the Best Scholarly and Ethical Standards

A teacher, whether by accident or design is more to students than a content expert. The teacher is a model of all that it means to be a scholar. The teacher is also a model of what it means to be a thinking person. We teach not only what we know but what we are. Part of the ethics of teaching is to realize this responsibility and to become the best models we can be, which requires some serious self-reflection on our personal standards of scholarship and living. For example, the way in which you discuss points of view that differ from your own speaks volumes to the students about reasoned discourse. This does not imply that you must always take a dispassionate stance; but even, or perhaps especially, when one feels strongly about an issue, it is necessary to demonstrate by your actions that intelligent people can disagree and still remain rational.

To Foster Honest Academic Conduct and to Ensure Fair Evaluation

Perhaps the most obvious ethical problems arise in the area of evaluation of student learning. Instructors are the arbiters of entrance into the profession and are therefore responsible for seeing to it that standards are upheld. However, we are also responsible for guaranteeing that all are given a fair chance at demonstrating their abilities. When we allow academic dishonesty to go unheeded, we violate the rights of all the other students who are abiding by the rules. If we fail to establish an evaluation system that accurately assesses the students' progress, we are abdicating our responsibilities to both the students and the profession.

The conflicts most often occur when this standard is pitted against the first one, that of respecting the individual and fostering independence. The examples that opened this chapter speak to this issue. How important is it that all students be evaluated in the same way? Are we being fairer if we maintain standards and vary conditions of evaluation or if we use individual standards according the special situation of each student? Which factors are legitimate considerations? There is no agreement on these issues. The best we can do is to continue to discuss and deliberate, alone and in groups, because the conditions under which we operate today will not be the same as those in the future. The decisions we make today might be made obsolete by changing circumstances, as has happened in the past.

To Avoid Exploitation, Harassment, or Discrimination

One of the guidelines that should be at the forefront of our thinking about the ethics of teaching is the fact that there is a great power discrepancy between the teacher and the students. Whether we like it or not, whether we seek it or not, by virtue of our position alone, we are invested with a great deal of power over the lives of our students. To make matters worse, many students invest us with even more power than we are entitled to.

It is the abuse of this power imbalance that is at the base of many of the ethical traps that lie strewn across our paths as teachers. The most blatant examples of unethical behavior, those most frequently mentioned in written codes of ethics, deal with the abuse of power, especially in the form of exploitation or harassment of various types: sexual, racial, religious, even intellectual. For example, requiring students to engage in class activities that are unrelated to the educational purposes of the course but that serve our personal ends is an abuse of power. Making derogatory comments about population subgroups is an obvious example of harassment. A less obvious example is ignoring the special needs of a subgroup completely, either consciously or unconsciously. An even less obvious example is engaging in intellectual snobbery by setting course standards at levels far beyond the capabilities of the students in the class ("No one earns an A in my class!"). Perhaps the best way to avoid violations of this standard is to keep the first standard in mind: Respect the students as individuals and keep the purpose of learning primary in all course-related decisions.

Another area of ethical problems involves receiving special considerations or benefits as a result of being in a position of authority, especially when those considerations come from those over whom you exercise that authority. For example, many instructors receive complimentary copies of textbooks in hopes that those books will be adopted for a course. Is it a violation of ethics to adopt a less-than-adequate book simply because of incentive made available by the publisher or to turn around and sell those copies to someone else? Is it a violation to even accept them in the first place? How legitimate is it to accept an invitation to a party or other event as the guest of a student in your class? Does it matter if that student is no longer in your class? Does it matter if the event is somehow connected with the student's academic program, for example, a dinner honoring that student's work? What constitutes "a bribe"? Or "special consideration"? I don't know the answers to these questions, but we must be aware that by our position alone we will sometimes be put in a compromised situation in all innocence on our part or the student's part.

■ *Responsibilities to Colleagues, the Institution, and the Discipline*

The AAUP guidelines go beyond those just focused on our role as teacher; they deal with all aspects of faculty life, including relations with colleagues, responsibilities to the institution for which we work and to the discipline we represent. Taken as a whole, however, the same ideas apply. The standards cluster around the issues of promoting and defending free and honest inquiry, showing respect for others, meeting institutional and professional responsibilities, and continuing to grow as scholars throughout professional life.

Ethical failures in this area include examples such as falsification of research results, failure to give due credit to the work of colleagues or students, unwillingness to participate in institutional governance, and unfair or unfounded evaluation of colleagues. More difficult choices might be things like continuing to teach in a situation that does not meet the needs of the students, such as overcrowded or understaffed classes, ignoring the inadequate teaching of colleagues, taking on so much outside work that work with the students suffers, or refusing to teach a sufficient number of "service" courses to help students graduate in a timely manner.

■ *Making Ethical Choices*

The array of possibilities for problems seems endless. How then can we avoid stumbling somewhere along the line? While there are no easy answers, there may be some ways of thinking about our actions as professionals that will maximize the possibility of acting ethically. I draw the following principles for evaluating one's actions from two sources, the first five from Brown and Krager (1985) and the last from Schon (1983).

1. Autonomy—Am I acting in ways that respect freedom and treat others as autonomous?

2. Non-maleficence—Am I causing harm through either commission or omission?

3. Beneficence—Do my actions benefit the other person rather than myself?
4. Justice—Do I treat those for whom I am responsible equitably?
5. Fidelity—Do I uphold my part of any relationship?
6. Act consciously—What are the assumptions on which I base my actions and are they valid?

It is a great privilege to be a teacher. But all great privileges carry great responsibilities as well. Many of those responsibilities are subtle, thrust on us by the expectations of others rather than sought by us. Keeping these six principles in mind won't solve all the ethical dilemmas you face as a teacher, but they might give you a way to reflect on them alone and with other teachers. That reflection should never stop, because conscious reflection on values is perhaps the cornerstone of the ethics of teaching.

SUPPLEMENTARY READING

American Association of University Professors, Statement on professional ethics, *Academe*, 1987, *73*(4), 49.

R. D. Brown and L. Krager, Ethical issues in graduate education: Faculty and student responsibilities, *Journal of Higher Education*, 1985, *56*, 403–418.

S. M. Cahn, *Saints and Scamps: Ethics in Academia* (Totowa, NJ: Rowman & Littlefield, 1982).

L. R. Churchill, The teaching of ethics and moral values in teaching, *Journal of Higher Education*, 1982, *53*(3), 296–306.

D. D. Dill, Professional ethics, *Journal of Higher Education*, 1982, *53*(3), 255–267.

E. Pascarella and P. Terenzini, *How College Affects Students* (San Francisco: Jossey-Bass, 1991).

D. Schon, *The Reflective Practitioner* (San Francisco: Jossey-Bass, 1983).

B. Tabachnick, P. Keith-Spiegel, and K. Pope, Ethics of teaching: Beliefs and behaviors of psychologists as educators, *American Psychologist*, 1991, *46*(5), 506–515.

CHAPTER 27

Learning and Cognition in the College Classroom

A TEACHER'S JOB isn't done when he or she interests the class, for the amount students learn depends upon the amount taught, and this is not so simple as it may at first appear. It may well be that the more instructors teach the *less* their students learn! Several years ago some of our teaching assistants were arguing furiously over how to teach about the nervous system. One group argued that since students wouldn't remember all of the details, they should omit details and teach only the basic essentials that we want everyone to learn. Another group argued that students would forget much of what they learned. "But," they said, "if they're going to forget a large percentage, we need to teach much more than we expect them to remember. Otherwise they'll forget even the important things."

To a psychologist such an argument is simply an invitation to an experiment, and consequently the combatants agreed that they'd try out their ideas in their own classes and compare the results on the final exam questions covering the nervous system. The outcome was clear. The students whose instructor had omitted details were clearly superior to those whose instructor had given them the whole story. This result would not have been surprising to David Katz (1950), the German-Swedish psychologist who devised a number of unique experiments demonstrating that, beyond a certain point, adding to the elements in an intellectual task causes confusion and inefficiency. Katz called this phenomenon "mental dazzle."

■■■■ *Organization*

Fortunately, teaching is an area where you can have your cake and eat it too, for it is possible to teach more and have it remembered better. The magic formula is *organization*. As Katona (1940) demonstrated in a series of experiments on organization and memory, people can learn and remember much more when their learning fits into an organization. If I give you a series of numbers chosen at random, like 73810547, and ask you what the fourth number was, you probably have difficulty remembering, but if I give the numbers 12345678, you can remember immediately what the fourth number was. Cognitive theorists sometimes differentiate "working memory" from "long-term memory." *Working memory*, the part of the memory that is active as you read this, has limited capacity. If I were to write this sentence in a series of new words, you would have trouble because you would have to keep each word of the sentence in mind. With familiar English words you can store whole sentences and paragraphs in your memory. *Long-term memory* has virtually unlimited capacity, but we are likely to have difficulty retrieving isolated facts when we need them. Teaching that helps students find a framework within which to fit new facts is likely to be more effective than teaching that simply communicates masses of material in which the student can see no organization.

The successful teacher is one whose students see meaningful problems. The ideal class would begin with a problem so meaningful that the students are always just a step ahead of the teacher in approaching a solution. If students can develop their own ways of structuring the material, it is likely to be recalled and used better than if the structure is provided by the teacher. My own research suggests that students often dislike and do not necessarily learn well from teachers who are highly organized—you can have too much organization as well as too little. The important thing is that students find some way of structuring the material. Students with more background and ability can do this even in relatively unstructured situations, but in courses where the material is new to the students it is probably important that the teacher provide ways of organizing the material. There is an old maxim, "Tell them what you're going to tell them. Tell them. Tell them what you've told them." Like many old maxims, this one is not true—or at least is oversimplified. Giving a summary in advance sometimes helps, but it is detrimental for some students (for example, extroverts; Leith, 1974a), and its effectiveness depends not only upon the type of organization provided but also upon the succeeding content and the previous background of the students. Questions are likely to be better than statements, and questions requiring thinking are generally better than those simply calling attention to main points.

■■■■ *Variability and Verbalization*

How can instructors help students develop principles and concepts they can apply much more broadly than answering a problem requiring only a memorized answer? I suppose all instructors have been disheartened by having a student answer a routine problem perfectly and then fail to use the same knowledge in solving another problem where it is relevant. There have been a number of educational attempts to solve this problem. One of the early slogans was "learning by doing," a theory that if people learned something in the situation where the learning was to be used they wouldn't have the added step of learning when to apply it. This is perfectly reasonable and makes sense psychologically. The only problem is that the number of situations in which one must use knowledge is infinite. If each human being had to learn everything by doing it, civilization would still be in the Stone Age.

Our whole civilization is based on the fact that people can use words to shortcut the long process of learning by trial and error, but direct experience may be useful at certain stages of learning. If we are to learn to apply a principle in new situations, we need to develop it from experiencing specific instances in varying contexts. A number of experiments have demonstrated that repetitive drill is much less effective than varying problems which help to develop principles that can be applied to new situations (for example, Wolfle, 1935). Verbalization can help us identify the common elements in these situations and shorten the learning process. In fact research suggests that even such a complex skill as learning to solo an airplane can be learned in much shorter air time if the learner practices the skill mentally and verbally.

Among the most interesting research programs were the studies of learning by monkeys carried out by Harlow and his colleagues at the University of Wisconsin (Harlow et al., 1949). Harlow was studying discrimination learning in monkeys. The monkey was rewarded with food whenever he chose the correct one of two objects, such as a cube or sphere. Harlow's monkeys displayed the usual pattern of beginning with virtually chance responses and gradually becoming more consistently accurate. Harlow, however, did not stop with one problem as most learning experimenters have done. Rather, his monkeys were kept at work learning one problem after another, and the monkeys' learning curve gradually changed. With more and more experience the monkeys learned the problems more and more quickly until eventually they needed only one trial to learn which was the correct object. Harlow's monkeys had learned how to learn. They might have learned how to learn even more rapidly had Harlow been able to talk to them about the critical dimensions of their problem solving.

If these experiments are relevant to college teaching (and I think they are), instructors may be able to teach students how to solve problems in their fields by giving them a series of related problems to solve, so that they learn the critical dimensions and most likely approaches.

■■■ *Feedback, Contiguity, and Active Learning*

If instructors expect students to learn skills, the students have to practice, but practice doesn't make perfect. Practice works if learners *see the results* of their practice and gain information from the results about what to do.

A number of experiments suggest that active learning is usually more efficient than passive learning. One reason for this may be the improved opportunities for feedback in active learning. Discussion techniques may help develop critical thinking because students do the thinking, and there is an opportunity to check their thinking against each other. But one of the dangers of "student-centered" or "nondirective" discussions is that the results are not apparent. Students may make comments, express opinions, and participate actively, but this doesn't guarantee that their opinions are any more informed at the end of a semester than they were at the beginning. Of course not all feedback has to come from the instructor—students can learn much from other students or from books—but in order to learn, students need to test out their ideas in a situation in which they can get the results of the test and see examples of better thinking.

Nevertheless, instructors need to go a step beyond the principle that students learn what they practice with knowledge of results. It's not always easy to get students to practice critical thinking in the classroom. After all, why stick your neck out? The student who remains quiet in class avoids the risks of disagreement, criticism, and embarrassment. To develop critical thinking, students must learn to want to think.

This brings us back to motivation. Curiosity and competence are powerful motives, but a smile, a nod of encouragement, an excited, "Good. Let's follow that idea through"—these are also tools that teachers can use, not only to provide knowledge of results, but also to develop the motivation to continue intellectual activity.

To maintain motivation instructors need to pose problems that are within the range of their students' abilities. Studies of the development of achievement motivation in children indicate that parents develop this motivation by encouraging the child to do well and by setting standards that the child can achieve. Other parents who orient their children toward achievement fail because they set unreasonable goals. Both for the purposes of motivating students for critical thinking and for developing the ability to think critically, experience in solving problems within the students' ken is essential. This by no means implies that students should not experience failure or criticism, but it does not mean that they should be faced with problems that will, as often as not, be soluble.

Active learning works not only because it helps motivation and feedback but also because active learners are more likely to be attentive and to be thinking about the topic, relating new knowledge to previous learning, and elaborating the implications of what they have learned.

▄▄▄▄▄ *Cognition*

Psychology has been undergoing a revolution in theory during the past three decades. The older associationist-behaviorist approaches have been superseded by and incorporated into newer information-processing approaches, derived in part from computer analogies and in part from a long tradition of cognitive theories. These approaches, called cognitive psychology, seek to explain behavior in terms of mental processes. Methodological and theoretical advances have enabled psychologists to make precise tests of theories about the processes human beings use in learning, memory, problem solving, and decision making.

As compared with earliest research on human and animal learning, cognitive approaches place more emphasis upon meaningful human learning. They thus have more potential applicability to problems of education than earlier theories had.

Learning, Semantic Memory, and Retrieval

Until the past few years the basic construct of learning theory was "reinforcement." For many years psychologists believed that stimulus-response associations were stamped in by rewards or "reinforcements." Memory was the reactivation of these connections.

Present-day theorists go beyond simple associations. Some think of memory as consisting of different types of storage. The fundamental units of storage are meaningful propositions, concepts, or images. Instead of a telephone switchboard metaphor of the mind, theorists now think of semantic learning as more like the building up of structures, networks, or maps. When we learn, we may add more details to the maps, or we may add more connections between points on the map, or we may even construct alternative maps that are more compact and useful for certain purposes, much as a map of the Interstate Highway system omits details, but is useful in planning long auto trips. But even these metaphors are inadequate; they imply a static storage. The current view is rather that memory refers to some properties of an information-processing system—a system involving nerve cells in activity—activities having to do with learning and retrieving meaningful relationships. Learning and remembering are active processes.

Students differ not only in how they fit what instructors teach into their existing structures but also in how readily they develop appropriate new structures. The task of the teacher differs depending upon which kind of learning is involved. *Accretion* of knowledge may be achieved simply by referral to a previously learned principle or use of a familiar example; *restructuring* may require challenges to old structures and much activity on the part of the student in trying out new understanding.

Instead of thinking of learning and memory in terms of tighter and stronger associations between stimuli and responses, with the associations strengthened by reward, psychologists now think of storage as being influenced by attending to things and interacting with them in such a way that they are related to existing memory structure. We store memories in terms of their potential uses—their meanings. What we store is not just what was said, read, or observed at a particular time; rather what is stored depends also upon previous experience.

Collins and Quillian (1972), who have proposed one model of memory, give as an example the sentence: "The police officer held up his hand and the cars stopped." We accept this statement matter-of-factly and probably remember it as a police officer standing in an intersection directing traffic. Had an earthquake started parked cars rolling down a hill, the sentence becomes surprising.

In any case, the point here is that we store the sentence about the police officer not just in terms of the dictionary meanings of the words in the sentence but also in terms of other things we know, such as that police officers often direct traffic, and that moving cars normally have drivers. We process and store meanings without thinking about the process consciously until something does not fit with our previous experience.

Because understanding and learning involve adding previously learned relationships of meanings, students differ in what and how they learn in a particular lecture or assignment. Often teachers have an inadequate comprehension of what students have learned and what is blocking understanding. If you can link what you teach to what students already know, they are more likely to understand and remember it.

Analysis of Cognitive Processes

Since students' previous knowledge determines how they will learn what we teach, an important part of effective teaching is to analyze students' existing structures of knowledge as well as the learning tasks we are asking them to perform. Effective teaching is as much diagnosis as presentation.

The kind of education involved in higher learning is more general-purpose than that involved in simple rote learning. Higher learning needs to be more modifiable and more transferable to situations remote from the training situation. Thus the problem of task analysis is complex.

If education is general, it should be possible to define general kinds of tasks cutting across situations. If educational psychologists can define intellectual factors in terms of the cognitive processes demanded, they probably have a good start at defining generalizable task characteristics. They can then analyze learning tasks such as studying a textbook or listening to a lecture, both with respect to the cognitive processes involved and the structure of the content.

Even a relatively simple analysis of an educational task may be useful. For example, one might ask, "Why does a student fail an essay question on an exam?"

1. The student does not understand the question.

2. The student has not learned the material.

3. The student lacks specific cues for retrieval.

4. The student lacks an appropriate strategy for retrieving the material.

5. The student lacks words needed for an answer.

6. The student lacks a conception of the required solution; for example, when asked to "explain," she lacks an adequate conception of what is involved in an adequate explanation.

7. The student cannot hold the required material in active memory while writing the answer.

The thought that one could forget part of an answer while beginning to write it may seem preposterous. Yet when long-term memory is unorganized, a heavy load is placed on working memory during the task of writing an appropriate answer. For example, Cole et al. (1971) found that nonliterate African children seemed deficient on free-recall tests, but when they were led by special techniques to respond in meaningful *categories*, recall was similar to that of American children. Some college students may have similar difficulties in organizing course material into meaningful categories.

The point of such an analysis of an essay test is that rather than simply telling a student to study a particular chapter more thoroughly, instructors can look for common threads of difficulties exemplified in several questions; they can even design tests laying bare different possible sources of difficulty, so that remedial action can be taken.

▬▬ *Teaching Students to Be Better Learners*

I teach an introductory course in cognitive psychology called "Learning to Learn." In this course I try to teach students more effective strategies for learning. I not only try to help students learn these strategies or methods of getting meaning from their reading and classes, but I also try to help them understand the theoretical reasons why these strategies work. By giving them an awareness of the processes they use in learning I hope to enable them to develop more personal control over their education.

Most of you who read this book will not be teaching such a course, but you still can have great impact upon your students' later learning. All too often we make assignments, lecture, discuss, and give tests on the blissful assumption that it is obvious why what we are doing facilitates learning. Cognitive psychology reminds us that as students learn a subject matter they also learn something about the skills involved in learning that subject matter. I would suggest that we help students become more effective at learning if we are explicit about the reasons we engage them in discussion, require a term paper, or carry out other activities.

In lectures we all too often present the products of our thinking without revealing the process by which we arrive at our conclusions. If our goal is to help students develop as learners and thinkers, more of our lectures should model the processes we use in arriving at conclusions, and we should identify the directions we have followed in order that students can understand the model we represent.

Not all teachers need to be cognitive psychologists, but all teachers have some implicit or explicit theories about how one learns and thinks in one's own discipline. Helping students become aware of these theories is an important aspect of teaching. Claire Ellen Weinstein is one of the pioneers in teaching learning strategies, and Chapter 32, which she co-wrote, is a detailed guide to teaching students how to learn.

■ Can Teachers Be Helped by Cognitive Psychology?

Teachers should not expect to make big improvements in education. Norman (1977) suggested that good lecturers and good textbook writers today are probably close to the best that is achievable; similarly, good students probably learn about as efficiently as they can. But many teachers and learners are probably not very efficient. When preparing a course, teachers may simply update a set of lecture notes; when told to learn something, students may simply repeat and rehearse materials—using methods not very effective for learning, remembering, and using meanings. Analyses of the processes students use in reading an assignment, in answering a question, or in other aspects of education may be useful in locating difficulties and suggesting more effective learning and teaching strategies.

Granted that teachers lack much of the research needed to apply cognitive theory to higher education today, are there any suggestions that might be helpful to them right now?

I do not think psychologists can any longer simply say, "Reward correct responses." But I think some general statements may be helpful as you analyze the problems of teaching:

1. Human beings are learning organisms—seeking, organizing, coding, storing, and retrieving information all their lives; building on cognitive structures to continue learning throughout life (certainly not losing capacity to learn); continually seeking meaning.

2. Human beings can remember images; they can remember transcriptions of the exact words that were used in a lecture or textbook; or they can remember *meanings*, depending upon the demands of the situation. Meanings tend to be recalled more easily than exact words. The meaning a student gets depends not only upon the student's past experience and expectations but also upon the student's learning strategies.

Marton and Säljö (1976b) differentiate among students in terms of depth of processing, a concept current in cognitive psychology (for example, Craik and Lockhart, 1972).

Probably the easiest way to communicate Marton and Säljö's distinction is to quote an actual example from their study. Their students read chapters from Coombs, *The World Educational Crisis: A Systems Analysis* (1971, Swedish edition). They were then asked, "What is meant by the output of an educational system?" Answers going from surface to deep processing were the following:

→ Level 1: (Surface) What Comes Out of the Education System.

"Something to do with . . . well . . . you know, the result of." "The product . . . I think."

→ Level 2: Those Who Leave the Education System with a Completed Education.

"It's the trained work-force that the educational system produces. It's, well, for example . . . well, simply the trained work-force."

→ Level 3: (Deep) The Effects of Education on Society and on Individuals Produced by Knowledge and Attitudes Acquired Through Schooling.

> "Mm, it's the knowledge that . . . and values . . . yes, the knowledge and values that students have acquired. That is, whatever it is that influences them and makes them read this or that and do this or that."

Surface-level processors tend to study as if learning were something that happens to the learner; deep-level processors act much more as if learning is something the learner *does* (Dahlgren and Marton, 1976).

3.   Instructors teach students not only the *knowledge* of history, biology, or psychology but also structures, modes of thought, and strategies for learning (Olson, 1976). The important thing taught is form, not content. Different means may produce the same knowledge but not the same broader understanding for different learners or different uses. Comparisons of college teaching methods typically find no significant differences in tests of knowledge. There are, however, differences between teaching methods in retention, application, transfer, and other outcomes (McKeachie and Kulik, 1975).

Greeno (1976) suggests that general cognitive structures not only are taught along with content but are also prerequisites to understanding content. Students who have no general structures for understanding science may be as lost in a biological science course as an American attempting to use our conventional narrative structures to understand an Indian folk-tale using a different kind of narrative structure. Thus, teachers have to consider structures not only as results of instruction but also as prerequisites for instruction. In addition, teachers must find ways of getting from the structures in students' minds to the desired structures. It may be that sometimes inadequate, and even incorrect, simple concepts or analogies are the quickest way to bridge the gap. Summaries and reviews also help (Leith, 1971).

At the very least, the cognitive approach indicates that teachers need to be aware of several kinds of outcomes—not just *how much* was learned but also *what kinds of learning* took place.

4. Intellectual ability—skills in learning, problem solving, and decision making are strongly influenced by prior knowledge. This means that persons who are excellent problem solvers in a familiar domain may seem completely unintelligent when asked to solve problems in domains in which they lack experience.

5. Learning something in the classroom may have different consequences than learning it from peers, from books, or learning it from one's own experience.

This does not mean that all learning should be experiential. Written language is very powerful.

6. In addition to the differentiated effectiveness of different methods for different outcomes, methods are differentially effective for different learners.

Egan and Greeno (1973) found that some learners learned most readily by the formula, or algorithmic, method, while others learned more effectively by the meaning method. The optimal method of training involved a combination of methods. For learners who did well with algorithms, additional training on the meaning of the variables (after the normal training) resulted in good performance on both criterion measures, while for the meaning group, additional drill on problem solving brought their performance on routine problems up to that of the other group. Thus, adaptation of instruction to individual differences in cognitive abilities or styles can result in greater effectiveness.

7. Because of interactions among student characteristics, teacher characteristics, goals, subject matter, and methods (Cronbach and Snow, 1977), flexibility and variability of approaches are more likely to be effective than a single method. Any given method is likely to be effective for some students and ineffective for others.

Perhaps one of the problems is that many students are unable to identify their own most effective style. Pask and Scott (1973) taught elementary concepts of probability theory by a system in which the computer carried on a tutorial conversation with the student in order to learn the student's idiosyncratic method of problem solving. Adaptive teaching systems are designed to present material at increasing levels of difficulty as students become more proficient. Pask and Scott argue that such systems will not be effective if students use different problem-solving strategies.

Pask and Scott studied two strategy classes—serialist and holist. Students using a serialist strategy break problems into subproblems, taking one step at a time. They assimilate data from specific relations of low order. Students using a holist strategy solve problems *in toto*; they assimilate data widely from high-order relations without certainty about particulars. Holist students tended to come from philosophy, history, and the social sciences; serialists were more likely to come from natural science and mathematics.

Pask and Scott developed a test to identify serialist vs. holist disposition of students and developed teaching heuristics to match the serialist and holist strategies. When students were matched with the appropriate teaching treatment, they learned and retained material well; those who were mismatched learned very little. Unfortunately, students given their choice of treatments did not consistently choose the optimal method for their own strategy.

8. In addition to teaching students to identify their own most effective learning strategies, can instructors teach students to be able to use a larger repertoire of strategies? If this were achieved, instead of adapting teaching methods to students, students could adopt the learning strategy most effective for whatever teaching method they encountered.

9. Testing practices influence students' learning strategies. The classic study in this area antedates cognitive approaches by three decades (McCluskey, 1934). It was concerned with the practical problem of the relative advantages of essay vs. objective tests. One group of students expected to be tested by an objective test; another group expected to be tested by an essay test. Each group was tested with both objective and essay questions. The groups made equivalent scores on the objective test, but the students preparing for an essay test did better than the objective test group on the essay questions. The results suggest that the strategy used by students preparing for an essay test is superior to that used when studying for an objective test.

In a more recent study Marton and Säljö (1976b) showed that students' depth of processing of a given chapter was influenced by the type of questions asked following the reading of an earlier chapter. Rote memory questions such as, "According to the author the shortage of teachers depends on three factors. Which three?" produced surface-level processing, while deep-level processing was induced by questions such as, "Explain the meaning of the following quotation—'Too many poor teachers will drive good ones out of the market.'"

Does a course using essay tests have different effects on students' later approaches to similar subject matter than a similar course using objective tests? Does the type of questions used produce an effect lasting beyond the particular course? My guess is that the breadth of effect of essay testing may well depend upon the sort of comments or questions written by the instructor on the test. Comments may help students learn new strategies or skills for learning and using a particular subject matter—and perhaps several types of courses taught in this way may produce effects generalizing across subject matters.

How do you teach such general skills or strategies? As far as I know there are no systematic rules; yet I suspect that good teachers do it intuitively. Probably helpful comments not only indicate errors and inadequacies but also ask questions or make suggestions steering students to a more sophisticated, or deeper, approach. Johnson (1975) has shown that creativity of answers is influenced by marginal comments. Probably most teachers have some implicit models of how they can influence student learning and such models probably contain much truth. If psychologists can help teachers become more explicit, there should be a better chance for the model to improve with experience.

10.   The cognitive structure of each student is different from that of the teacher. Thus, the paradox arises that the teacher must learn from students the students' structures if the teacher is to be effective in helping students learn from the teacher.

11.   Talking, writing, doing, interacting, and teaching others are important means for learners to restructure their learning.

If teachers are to make bridges between a) structures in the subject matter, curriculum, or course design, b) structures in the teacher, and c) structures in learners, they need to carry on discussions in which students have an opportunity to externalize their problems and progress. Since each interaction becomes increasingly difficult as class size increases, teachers need to provide at least some opportunities for small-group discussion, dialogue, writing, explaining, or doing something to which the teacher, other students, and the learner, herself, can respond (for example, Leith, 1974b).

12.   Several kinds of learning are going on in the classroom. The first, *subject matter content*, is figural. Other kinds of learning, which seldom become the focus of attention, may be even more important. These kinds of learning may be incidental, but they are almost inseparable from subject-matter learning. Specific attention to them can make a big difference in the long-term educational value of a course. Here are some examples:

   a. *Cognitive or conceptual structures.* The ease of further learning depends greatly upon the development of organized conceptual relationships.
   b. *Skills and strategies for learning and thinking.*
   c. *Motives for learning:* interest, curiosity, a sense of progress.
   d. *Self-efficacy.* Feeling competent to use current learning and to learn more.
   e. *Interpersonal or group skills,* such as leadership, cooperation, giving and receiving help.

Psychologists know little about how to integrate these levels in such ways as to optimize education, but it is clearly a dynamic, ongoing process involving much adaptation on the part of both teacher and students.

13.   Increases in effectiveness of education may come as much, or more, from helping students understand their own learning processes as from varying your teaching (Norman, 1977).

SUPPLEMENTARY READING

W. J. McKeachie (ed.), *Learning, Cognition, and College Teaching* (San Francisco: Jossey-Bass, 1980).

John D. Bransford and Barry S. Stein, *The Ideal Problem Solver* (New York: W. H. Freeman, 1984).

One of the more readable recent textbooks on cognition is S. K. Reed, *Cognition*, 3rd ed. (Pacific Grove, CA: Brooks-Cole, 1992).

F. Martin, D. Hounsell, and N. Entwistle (eds.), *The Experience of Learning* (Edinburgh: Scottish Academic Press, 1984).

W. J. McKeachie, P. R. Pintrich, Y-G. Lin, D. A. F. Smith, and R. Sharma, *Teaching and Learning in the College Classroom: A Review of the Research Literature*, 2nd ed. (Ann Arbor, MI: NCRIPTAL, University of Michigan, 1990).

Our research group has developed measures to assess how students have related course content. We use these measures both for instruction and for assessment:

M. Naveh-Benjamin and Y-G. Lin, *Assessing Students' Organization of Concepts: A Manual for Measuring Course-Specific Knowledge Structures* (Ann Arbor, MI: NCRIPTAL, University of Michigan, 1991).

In addition, we have developed a self-report questionnaire to assess students' motivation and learning strategies. It is described in P. R. Pintrich, D. A. F. Smith, T. Garcia, and W. J. McKeachie, *A Manual for the Use of the Motivated Strategies for Learning Questionnaire (MSLQ)* (Ann Arbor, MI: NCRIPTAL, University of Michigan, 1991).

ROBERT J. MENGES
Northwestern University

CHAPTER  28

Improving Your Teaching

IMPROVEMENTS IN TEACHING may arise from any number of sources, including experiences in the classroom, reading about teaching, attending workshops and seminars, and conversations with colleagues and students. This chapter discusses both incidental and deliberate attempts to improve teaching and offers a four-step procedure for implementing planned changes. The difficulties of making changes are also discussed with reference to innovations that, despite evidence of effectiveness, have not persisted.

◼◼◼ *The Inclination Toward Change*

Change is the constant companion of professors. In graduate school, academics learn how scholarly fields change over time, and graduate study culminates with a dissertation intended as yet one more contribution to the discipline. Academics devise multi-year plans that chart intended changes in scholarly and creative activities. These habits of continuous improvement carry naturally into teaching.

The inclination toward change is in part intellectual. Exceptional curiosity and creativity contributed to professors' success as students and these intellectual qualities sustain subsequent work in academia. Rather than being put off by problems, professors seek them out, and after solving one problem proceed to deconstruct another.

Teaching offers no end of problems that challenge the intellect—how to engage students at different levels of maturity with the fundamental concepts of a field, how to link those concepts with the world of experience that students bring to class, how to connect the content of one course with content of other courses, and how to bring coherence to the immense amount of fragmentary information potentially relevant to a curriculum.

Second, change has a motivational component. Like other professionals, college teachers are motivated to seek feedback. As teachers we want to know how well we are doing, and we change what we do on the basis of information about our performance. Higher education is information-rich, but that information is rarely fed back to teachers in a constructive and systematic way. Many teaching objectives are vague, and teachers get little information about how well objectives have been met. Important consequences of teaching may be long delayed, perhaps never becoming visible to the teacher. The paucity of pertinent feedback about teaching creates considerable stress for academics (Gmelch, Lovrich, and Wilke, 1984). It is often left to the teacher's initiative to clarify expectations about teaching performance, to solicit more frequent and specific performance feedback, and to make use of campus resources such as a teaching center. When feedback is available, it enhances motivation by increasing feelings of control and efficacy.

Third, the inclination toward change has a social component. Academics as a group are no less likely than other professionals to want to be highly regarded. Professors are alert for clues about what is expected by colleagues and students. How we present ourselves to others depends in part on what we think they expect and on the value we place on meeting their expectations.

The institutional culture for teaching is critical for change. In departments and schools where the teaching culture is strong, newcomers quickly discern social norms that promote inquiry and innovation. Where high priority is given to student learning and involvement, student-centered teaching is more likely. Where teaching consultants and other teaching support services are easily available to faculty, instructional experimentation is more frequent. Of course, not all norms are supportive of teaching. Norms carried from graduate training may emphasize research at the expense of teaching. Thus, graduate school socialization into the discipline may be dissonant with the institution's socialization into the workplace.

Teaching improvement can be facilitated by each of these professorial characteristics: the desire to solve intellectual problems, the motivation to seek feedback, and sensitivity to social norms.

■■■■ *Identifying Improvements through Reading, Workshops, and Conversations*

Reading about Teaching

One might assume from the abundance of books, periodicals, and newsletters on college teaching that professors voraciously consume writings about pedagogy. Our surveys, however, find that reading about teaching and learning lags far behind reading about one's field of specialization. Faculty, at least those at research universities, report that they spend about an hour a week on average doing professional reading about teaching, with full professors doing considerably less than junior faculty (Quinn, 1993).

Nevertheless, the variety of available reading materials is impressive. Books like *Teaching Tips* are used in courses on college teaching and at orientation programs for new faculty and teaching assistants. Most disciplines and professional fields have journals devoted to college teaching. Cross-disciplinary periodicals, such as *College Teaching, The National Teaching and Learning Forum,* and *New Directions for Teaching and Learning,* are available through college libraries and teaching centers. *The Teaching Professor* and other newsletters are distributed nationally, and many individual campuses circulate their own teaching-oriented publications. (A selective list of books on college teaching appears at the end of this chapter. For a more comprehensive guide to books and a list of several dozen periodicals on college teaching, see Menges and Mathis, 1988.)

As a way to acquire ideas about improving teaching, reading is uniquely convenient and efficient. Weimer (1988) notes that reading can be inspirational as well as instructive, that it may lead to exploration of related topics, and that it often stimulates discussions about teaching with colleagues. Further, reading is discreet, "a quiet and private way to improve instruction" (Weimer, 1988, p. 48), and, because it is self-directed, reading is fully under one's own control.

Whether reading about teaching leads to actual improvements in teaching is difficult to say. I am not aware of studies on that precise topic, but there is some interesting research from the related field of psychotherapy. Authors of therapeutic self-help books claim that their texts help one understand problems and change behavior. Treating problems of living by prescribing a book, as some therapists do, is known as "bibliotherapy," and research on its effectiveness has produced mixed results. There is some evidence that books oriented toward specific behavior changes are effective, but less support exists for books of fiction, poetry, or inspirational reading (Riordan and Wilson, 1989) despite claims by their authors and publishers.

If we generalize this research to teaching, it implies that change is more likely if readings include detailed discussions and concrete examples at the level of specific behavior. Further, I believe that details and examples are most effective if they are placed in the context of a conceptual framework that makes apparent the rationale underlying their use. According to Weimer (1988), the most effective personal reading programs are regular and systematic, readings are approached with some detachment and objectivity, and the reader is consciously committed not only to reflection but also to action.

Workshops and Seminars

Workshops and seminars are common activities at most campus teaching centers. Their topics range from theories of learning to skills of teaching to techniques for managing time and writing grants. When workshops and seminars are carefully planned in response to needs expressed by faculty and when they are skillfully conducted by informed leaders, they can be highly rewarding. At the very least, they occasion interactions among colleagues on topics related to teaching, interactions that might not otherwise occur.

ON CHOOSING WORKSHOPS Here are some consumer tips for identifying workshops that are likely to be worthwhile.

- → Clear objectives. Know in advance what the session claims to accomplish so you can judge whether your own work will benefit.

- → Qualified leadership. The leader should be expert about the topic of the meeting, and the presentation should model relevant skills of teaching and learning.

- → Interactive format. Passive listening is insufficient. One might as well read independently about the topic. Further, sessions that center on the presenter fail to draw out the considerable expertise present in a group. Be sure the format is interactive.

- → Opportunity to practice and demonstrate. For skill objectives in particular, learning cannot be assumed unless there are opportunities to practice skills and to receive feedback. Check that practice is part of the workshop design.

- → Explicit behavioral intentions. If a workshop is to make a difference in subsequent weeks and months, specific goals of behavioral change should be explicated by each participant before the session ends. The workshop should devote time to develop goals. Persons who do not want to commit themselves to specific changes should avoid the workshop.

- → Obligatory follow-up. The greatest weakness of workshops is the lack of follow-up. A savvy leader works out a contract with each participant and subsequently checks about progress toward individual goals. How has teaching changed? Which goals have been realized and which have not? What additional support is needed?

Conversations about Teaching

Faculty tell us that new ideas about teaching come more frequently from colleagues than from readings or workshops. I suspect this is because conversations with departmental colleagues are likely to cover content as well as method. Conversations with students can be highly informative if they are kept to areas where student reactions are credible and thoughtful. Students cannot accurately judge the quality or currency of course content, but they are reliable reporters about such matters as attentiveness during class, the teacher's clarity, and the value of various components of the course including readings, examinations, and projects.

Conversations about teaching that have some structure are likely to be most productive. At a brown-bag discussion, for example, a skillful convener can play devil's advocate, ask for evidence to support speculative comments, and insist that participants pursue implications of their suggestions. Elsewhere I outlined a four-step discussion process for such meetings: 1) articulate a belief about teaching; 2) identify a situation that is problematic with regard to that belief; 3) describe a behavior intended to resolve the problem; and 4) articulate a rationale that links the belief with the behavior (Menges, 1990).

Here is an example of how that discussion process might work. Suppose the belief in question is stated as "Students never come to class prepared." A likely problematic situation is the classroom silence that follows questions posed by the teacher. Suppose that the teacher suggests daily quizzes as a way of dealing with this problem. Her colleagues will challenge her to find a rationale that links the behavior (giving quizzes) and the belief. They will offer their own advice, and the group will discuss various actions that the teacher might take. The convener ensures that all relevant views are aired, introduces information from research that may illuminate the discussion, and ultimately helps the teacher develop a feasible and defensible plan to try. Results can be reported at the next meeting.

Conversations with students also benefit from structure. Structure protects against undue attention to an opinionated student whose views are unrepresentative. Structure can also rule out comments that are disparaging and unconstructive. Structured conversations might be held with small groups of students and focus less on what the teacher does and more on how students learn. Students might be asked under what circumstances they learn best, are most attentive, are most inclined to contribute to discussion, and so on.

Teaching improvements derived from readings, workshops, and conversations are not implemented automatically, of course. In the following section, steps in a deliberate implementation process are described.

■ *Implementing Change*

Here is my four-step plan for improving teaching. It carries no guarantees, but proceeding in this way has served many teachers well.

Step One: Get Ready—Look for Ideas

This step was anticipated in the earlier discussion about finding new ideas in reading, workshops, and conversations. Here I discuss how those ideas affect the teacher in ways that create conditions favorable for change.

NEW KNOWLEDGE AND CONCEPTS MODIFY COGNITIVE STRUCTURES   Reading about attribution theory, for example, provides a wealth of knowledge and concepts. Attribution theory deals with how we explain the causes of events. When students think about a test on which they did not do as well as expected, they may attribute their performance to circumstances that are outside their control, thereby escaping responsibility for improving performance next time. A teacher who wants to encourage students to attribute exam performance to controllable causes should avoid sympathizing about the difficult material or the inconvenient test schedule. Instead, emphasis should be on things that are under the control of students such as "effort, note-taking skill, diligence, preparation . . ." (McMillan and Forsyth, 1991, p. 59). A teacher who becomes well versed in attribution theory has acquired a new cognitive structure through which to view instruction.

NEW SKILLS MODIFY SCHEMAS   A likely topic at a workshop on the skills of questioning is "wait time," the skill of pausing for an appropriate interval after posing a question. Wait time in college classes tends to be shorter than students require, especially if the question is one that calls for a complex response. Once the teacher's "question-posing schema" has been altered by practicing the skill, it is more likely that longer pauses will be used during class discussion. (For more about schemas, see previous chapters.)

NEW BELIEFS MODIFY PERSONAL THEORIES   Conversations as sources of new ideas are likely to influence the teacher's beliefs. Students often say that they are disappointed to be in so many classes where faculty merely expect them to memorize information and then to regurgitate it for tests. Faculty, on the other hand, complain about students' lack of motivation saying that students simply *want* to memorize and regurgitate information for tests. (These mirrored views by faculty and students were documented in a report of focus group discussions held at eighteen colleges in New Jersey. More than 400 faculty and students discussed the "major challenges" in facilitating student learning. Faculty focused on students and commented that they are academically unprepared, distracted by outside commitments, and generally unmotivated. Students focused on faculty whom they saw as unreasonable in their expectations, unavailable due to outside commitments, and uninterested in motivating students (New Jersey Institute for Collegiate Teaching and Learning, 1990).

Teachers' beliefs are put to the test by such student views. Articulating beliefs about students and how they learn makes explicit one's previously implicit theory of teaching. If information from students fails to fit the theory, dissonance occurs and that dissonance creates pressure for change.

Step Two: Get Set—Keep a Clear Goal in Sight

It seems obvious that success is more likely when the end is clearly identified and the means are well defined. Yet many plans to improve teaching founder for lack of clear goals or because progress toward success cannot be measured.

CHOOSE CLEAR AND MEASURABLE GOALS   Here are some goals that teachers have expressed.

1. I want to motivate my students.
2. I want to explain things more clearly in my lectures.
3. I want more students to participate in the discussion.
4. I want to pause longer after asking a question in class.
5. I want students to come to class prepared for discussion.
6. I want to raise student achievement in my course.
7. I want to create a new interdisciplinary course.

These goals vary in numerous ways. Some refer to what the teacher does, some refer to what students do, and at least one (creating an interdisciplinary course) refers to what happens in committees and departments. For some goals it is fairly clear what should happen, but others (motivating students, raising achievement) imply little about what the teacher should do differently. Criteria of success can be specified for some of these goals (the length of a pause, the number of students participating), but vague goals (such as wanting to motivate students) typically elude measurement.

IDENTIFY PARTICULAR CHANGES AND CREATE CONDITIONS THAT ENCOURAGE THOSE CHANGES   Ask if the goal is related to the person or to the environment. Longer pauses, for example, are probably well within the teacher's capacity, but environmental conditions may make it difficult to monitor that behavior. Explaining things more clearly in lectures may require the teacher to develop a new capacity, perhaps the skill of creating appropriate analogies and metaphors. Students may not prepare because they cannot understand course material or because they feel anxious about speaking in class (characteristics of the person). Or students may think that they have no incentive to prepare. They may reason that participating in discussion will not help their performance in the course because test questions are drawn only from lecture material (a characteristic of the incentive structure of the course).

Once changes are clearly envisioned, the new conditions should be planned in detail and new behaviors should be rehearsed. Rehearsing new skills is most productive in a safe setting, perhaps using a mirror or video camera or working with a colleague or teaching consultant. The new behaviors should feel natural and comfortable. Persistent discomfort probably means that something is wrong with either the goal or the plan.

Step Three: Go—Take the Plunge

Expectations should be significant but modest. A few long pauses will demonstrate to the teacher that the new behavior is possible and will convey to students that the teacher has different expectations. A small increase in student participation may be reward enough to continue the new behavior. The general principle is to start with manageable changes that can be further increased or elaborated as appropriate.

Monitor progress regularly. What information is necessary to decide how well the change is going? Who can supply that information? Consider using a short survey at the end of class. It might include one or two questions about content and one or two questions about teaching method. Collect representative student notes. Make an audiotape for later review, or invite a colleague to visit the class or to interview students. Since end-of-course evaluations and final examinations are too general and too long delayed to be very useful as sources of information, consider ways of gathering early feedback from students (see suggestions in Lenze and Rando, 1993).

Note that new goals may emerge as the change proceeds. Longer wait time, for example, may come to be seen as a means to a more important goal, perhaps the goal of raising the quality of student contributions during discussion.

Step Four: Persist

Successful change is often slow and sometimes comes only after considerable effort. Improving teaching is hard work, and it may require uncomfortable adjustments.

COSTS AND BENEFITS   Especially at the beginning, when success is not certain, regressing to the comfortable patterns of the past can be appealing. Do not ignore the costs of change, but also acknowledge and anticipate the benefits.

Significant change goals may challenge typical classroom roles where the teacher is the active presenter and students are relatively passive. A teacher experimenting with new, unpracticed roles naturally feels vulnerable. Students, uncertain of what is expected of them, may become resentful or withdrawn. It is only fair to explain to students what is expected and to invite their endorsement of a new classroom compact.

These reactions are natural emotional correlates of change. No one wants to fail and everyone wants to appear to be in control. Enlisting colleagues as allies in the improvement plan helps to maintain a sense of control. They will understand your intention and are likely to support and admire your attempt to change. If the attempt fails, remember that even failure can be instructive, particularly if the experience is reviewed and analyzed with students and other interested parties.

With each success, even a small success, there are great benefits—increased confidence, a sense of learning, and a feeling of growth—all of which help to renew professional vitality.

ANTICIPATE RELAPSE   Maintaining new behaviors is difficult, and it is important to have procedures in place that reduce the risk of relapsing into old patterns (Walton, 1989). Effective strategies for anticipating and preventing relapse include how to deal with slips and how to enlist support from others.

Impending relapse may be signaled by a slip. For a dieter, a slip is a small, but clear, violation of the eating plan. For a teacher trying to increase class discussion, a slip would be lapsing into a lecture when confronted with unprepared students. A slip should be dealt with immediately according to procedures developed in advance. Perhaps a discussion should be held with the class about what happened and why it happened. In any case, the slip should be regarded as nothing more than a mistake that need not be repeated rather than as a failure of the entire improvement project. If circumstances that led to the slip are carefully analyzed, the experience becomes one of learning rather than of failure.

Enlisting support from others is a second relapse prevention strategy, one that is social in nature. A trusted colleague or someone from the campus teaching center might be asked to provide regular feedback by directly observing the target behaviors or by phoning the teacher at regular intervals for a progress report. Or the teacher's log of events, reactions, and feelings about the improvement is shared on a regular schedule with a friend or consultant. These procedures themselves influence improvement, since one naturally wishes to avoid failure in the eyes of friend and since close monitoring of behavior may itself enhance change.

■ *Why Proven Innovations Sometimes Fail*

Instructional improvements sometimes fail for expected reasons, that is, they fail because they do not reach their goals or because the costs of success exceed the benefits. Many early attempts to introduce computer-assisted instruction failed for cost reasons. Developing adequate software was sometimes too costly for the budget, or software that was developed within budget constraints was not effective with students.

Other instructional innovations do reach their goals but nevertheless fail to endure. Reasons for failure may be related more to characteristics of the people involved or of the organizational environment than to the innovation itself. An instructive example is the Personalized System of Instruction (PSI) developed by Fred Keller in 1964 for teaching large university classes (Keller, 1968).

The Case of the Personalized System of Instruction

Like other approaches to individualized instruction, PSI involves carefully sequenced units of material, frequent readiness testing, and individual pacing. Instructor-prepared written materials supplement textbooks, and tutors provide individual assistance and evaluation of students. There are few lectures, and they are intended primarily to stimulate and motivate students.

Course work is divided into topics or units. At the start of a PSI course, students receive a printed study guide to direct their work on the first unit. A typical study guide introduces the unit, states objectives, suggests study procedures, and lists study questions. Before moving to the second unit in the sequence, students must demonstrate mastery of the first unit by perfect or near-perfect performances on a short examination. They report for the test only when they feel adequately prepared, and they are not penalized for failure to pass a first, a second, or a later examination on the unit. When students demonstrate mastery of the first unit, they are given a study guide for the next unit, and thus move through the course at their own pace. Some students meet all course requirements before the term is half over and others may require more than a term to complete the course.

Staff for a PSI course includes the instructor and undergraduate tutors. The instructor selects and organizes material used in the course, constructs examinations, and provides a few lectures and demonstrations (perhaps six during a semester). Lectures are not compulsory, and examinations are not based on them. The tutors evaluate readiness tests as satisfactory or unsatisfactory and prescribe remedial steps for students who encounter difficulties with course material. Tutors also offer support and encouragement for beginning students.

Research shows that learning and satisfaction are significantly higher with PSI than under conventional instruction. The mastery requirement seems to be an especially significant component. Small units and frequent quizzes with immediate feedback also appear to be important for learning, while self-pacing is related more to student morale than to achievement. Results of comparisons between PSI and conventional instruction are clear; PSI is "so consistently found superior that it must rank as the method with the greatest research support in the history of research on teaching" (Dunkin, 1986, p. 759).

Why Hasn't PSI Persisted?

It is not difficult to find reasons why PSI did not persist despite evidence of its effectiveness. First, startup is expensive. Considerably more time is required to plan a PSI course than to plan a traditional course. When repeated, a PSI course is economical, but the initial investment of time may discourage teachers from implementing the model. Second, PSI demands a new role for the teacher. Ordinarily teachers present information and answer questions from students. "In PSI it is the teachers who ask the questions, the students give the answers, and the teachers say 'you are getting warm, you are getting warmer, you are getting colder'" (Sherman, 1992, p. 62). PSI teachers are more like coaches and tutors than like information providers. Third, organizational logistics and institutional policies may be barriers to PSI. Is there space for these nontraditional activities? How does an institution accommodate a course that is completed by some students much more quickly than by others? Will colleagues tolerate a course in which a high proportion of students achieve A-level work? Can students and administrators accept nontraditional teacher roles? (On the latter point, one unsympathetic department chair effectively eliminated PSI courses by decreeing that about "50% of class time must be devoted to lecturing . . . since it is the clash of intellects in the classroom that informs the student" [Sherman, 1992, p. 63]. In making that decision the chair paid no attention to data on student achievement.)

All of these individual and organizational circumstances contributed to the decline of PSI. Parallel circumstances can be identified that work against the persistence of other innovations.

■ *Predicting Whether Improvements Will Succeed*

Whether the change is as organizationally complex as PSI or as behaviorally specific as pausing longer after questions, it pays to reflect on possible impediments to success. A particular improvement is less likely to succeed if it seriously clashes with the teacher's personal theories of teaching and learning. Or the improvement may be something that the teacher feels little control over. Or its consequences, though generally positive, may be viewed as unlikely or unimportant. Or social and institutional structures may be unsupportive.

Here are some questions worth asking before deciding whether or not to pursue an improvement project. (These are derived from the theory of reasoned action [Ajzen and Madden, 1986].) Each of these questions should be asked with reference to a particular goal. As an example, I have chosen the goal of "increasing student discussion in class."

First, ask about your *beliefs*. How do you regard increased student discussion? To what extent is it useful, good, wise, important? Answers that are not strongly positive probably reveal dissonance between the goal and your personal theories.

Second, ask about the *control* you have in the situation. To what extent are *you* able to bring about increased student discussion? What aspects of this change can you control? What aspects are outside of your control?

Third, consider the *consequences*. Possible consequences of increased discussion include more animated students, noisier classrooms, less content coverage, better critical thinking, and so on. How positive do you find each of these consequences? How likely is it that each consequence will occur?

Finally, ask about the *views others hold* about the change. People whose views you regard as important might include colleagues, students, dean, research collaborators, spouse, and so on. How positive is each of them regarding this change? How important to you is each one's view and how much do you wish to conform to it?

Depending on how these questions are answered prior to the start of a planned improvement, you may modify the plan and make success more likely. The time and effort needed to answer questions like these pay good dividends, enhancing both the intellectual and the emotional satisfactions that accompany successful improvements in teaching.

SUPPLEMENTARY READING

The following books treat a broad range of topics related to college teaching. Each takes a multidisciplinary perspective and offers advice in light of the best available research.

G. Brown and M. Atkins, *Effective Teaching in Higher Education* (New York: Methuen, 1988).

K. E. Eble, *The Craft of Teaching: A Guide to Mastering the Professor's Art*, 2nd ed. (San Francisco: Jossey-Bass, 1988).

S. C. Ericksen, *The Essence of Good Teaching* (San Francisco: Jossey-Bass, 1984).

M. M. Gullette (ed.), *The Art and Craft of Teaching* (Cambridge, MA: Harvard University, Harvard-Danforth Center for Teaching and Learning, 1982).

J. Katz and M. Henry, *Turning Professors into Teachers* (New York: Macmillan, 1988).

J. Lowman, *Mastering the Techniques of Teaching* (San Francisco: Jossey-Bass, 1984).

R. J. Menges and M. D. Svinicki (eds.), College Teaching: From Theory to Practice, *New Directions for Teaching and Learning, no. 45* (San Francisco: Jossey-Bass, 1991).

R. J. Menges and M. G. Weimer (eds.), *Better Teaching and Learning in College: Using Scholarship to Improve Practice*, A publication of the National Center on Postsecondary Teaching, Learning and Assessment (San Francisco: Jossey-Bass).

CHAPTER 29

Appraising Teaching

*I*MPROVEMENT IN TEACHING is facilitated by feedback. We need ways to find out how we are doing. Data about teaching effectiveness may also be used by our departments in decisions about salary and promotions.

This chapter discusses some of the methods used to appraise teaching, particularly student ratings, which are almost universally used in the United States and are becoming more common in other countries.

■ *Student Learning*

The ultimate criterion for evaluating teaching is student learning. John Dewey said, "Teaching is like selling; you can't have a sale unless someone buys. You haven't taught unless someone has learned." Not that student learning is simply a function of the teacher. You may face classes in which students lack the necessary prerequisites; you may be assigned to a classroom in the deepest cell in a dungeon; you may encounter a group of anxious, hostile, students; or you may have a class full of eager, highly motivated, well-prepared students who would learn well regardless of the teacher.

Nonetheless, we teachers all too often evaluate student papers, examinations, clinical work, or other performance thinking only of grading the student without looking at the implications of common student difficulties for our own teaching. After you have graded an examination look back to see what errors were common and think about how you can do a better job of teaching those topics next time.

But using student learning as a method of appraising teaching has limitations. While it may point to areas where there are problems, it offers no guidance about what to do to improve. And if the purpose of appraising teaching is to provide evidence for promotion or salary decisions, it is difficult to judge whether the learning evidenced is greater or less than might be expected. Thus we need to consider other possible sources of evidence. Among these are student ratings, peer visitation of classes, group interviews, peer evaluation of syllabi, examinations and student products, and development of a portfolio of various kinds of data.

▮▮▮▮ *Student Ratings of Instruction*

In 1969 I was commissioned by the AAUP Committee C on College and University Teaching, Research, and Publication to write an article on student ratings of faculty for the *AAUP Bulletin*. I updated the article in *Academe* in 1979, and believe the two articles still provide a sound basis for the non-specialist concerned about student ratings of faculty. In this chapter I will bring the reader up-to-date on the evidence with respect to the issues discussed earlier, as well as on additional issues that have come to the fore more recently. For a more extensive review I recommend Marsh (1987).

▮▮▮▮ *Validity: Do Student Ratings Measure Teaching Effectiveness?*

There is now a good deal of evidence that student ratings provide useful evidence of teaching effectiveness, but it has also become evident that the question is overly simple. With respect to the general validity question, the cumulating evidence continues to support the conclusion that highly rated teachers tend to be those whose students achieve well. Such a statement is, however, better understood in the context of two more analytic questions:

1. How are different aspects of teaching effectiveness related to student ratings? Or put in other words, "What educational outcomes are related to student ratings of effectiveness?" Ratings may be differentially valid for different educational goals. There is ample evidence that we achieve some goals at the expense of others. Teachers effective in teaching a good deal of knowledge are not necessarily effective in teaching critical thinking. So one needs to make value judgments about the importance of differing goals of education.

2. What is the intended use of student ratings of teaching? For personnel decisions? For improving teaching? For facilitating student choice of courses and teachers? Ratings may be differentially valid for different uses.

For decisions about promotion or salary we want student ratings to be valid measures of overall teaching effectiveness. For improving teaching we want student ratings to be valid in terms of accurate diagnosis of problems and, perhaps, for prescription of solutions. Let us consider these purposes in turn.

What Do We Mean by Teaching Effectiveness?

Obviously if we are to answer the question "Are student ratings valid measures of teaching effectiveness?" we need to define "teaching effectiveness." Simply put, we take teaching effectiveness to be the degree to which one has facilitated student achievement of educational goals. But assessing teaching effectiveness is not simple. Much of student achievement is determined by factors other than teaching, for example, student ability or previous experience. Moreover, student achievement in different courses is not comparable since there is no way of estimating how many units of mathematics achievement equal a given number of units of achievement in English.

One might expect that one could simply judge effectiveness in terms of how well students achieve course goals. But such "criterion referenced" measurement ultimately rests upon a judgment about what sort of achievement it is reasonable to expect, and what is reasonable to expect depends upon knowledge of what other teachers have done with similar classes. Thus, to validate a measure of teaching effectiveness, such as student ratings, we must have a number of teachers teaching the same course to comparable groups of students. Only in such a situation can we determine whether those teachers whose students learn the most are rated highest by their students. Let us now examine the evidence from such situations with respect to teaching effectiveness for different educational goals.

Validity of Student Ratings as a Measure of Teaching Effectiveness on Achieving Cognitive Goals

Most college professors who have thought about their goals describe both cognitive and motivational goals for their courses. We want students to make gains toward such cognitive goals as knowledge, skill in solving problems, and ability to evaluate. Typically we also want to achieve affective goals, such as increasing students' interest in the area studied, so that they will be motivated to continue learning after they leave college.

When we speak of student learning as the ultimate criterion of teaching effectiveness, we usually think of the cognitive outcomes. Usually we assume that these outcomes are measured by the final examination for the course. In fact, however, final examinations typically weigh knowledge much more heavily than application, problem solving, or other cognitive objectives. Moreover, since students are strongly motivated for grades, they will do the best they can to pass the examination regardless of the quality of teaching they have had. If the teacher has been confusing or unhelpful, students often will make up for deficiencies by extra studying. Thus performance of students on a final examination is not an ideal measure of teaching effectiveness. Nevertheless, this is the best measure we have in most of our validity studies.

In my 1969 article, the most persuasive evidence cited for the validity of student ratings of instruction was the research by

Elliott (1949) who demonstrated that student ratings of instruction were related to teaching effectiveness in terms of student achievement in multi-section courses in chemistry.

A substantial amount of research on validity has been carried out since 1969. The results are mixed, but taken as a whole they confirm our earlier conclusion that teachers rated as effective by students are generally those teachers whose students achieve most.

The studies by Sullivan and Skanes (1974) and Centra (1977) are the only studies in which students were randomly assigned to instructors. Such random assignment is an important feature in designing validity studies since differences in mean student achievement between teachers may otherwise be the result of differences between the students rather than differences in teaching. Thus, the substantial positive relationships (.4 to .6) between mean student ratings and mean student achievement found in these two studies are particularly significant.

Of especial interest in the Centra study is the finding that global ratings of value of the course to the student tended to have higher validities than items assessing specific aspects of teaching. Ratings of the difficulty of the course, for example, had no significant relationship to student achievement. The Sullivan and Skanes study is also interesting in that greater validity was found for student ratings of regular faculty than for rating of teaching assistants. It may well be that when students feel that they have learned a good deal in a course they are more likely to attribute their success to their own efforts if their teacher was a teaching assistant and more likely to give the teacher some credit if the teacher is a professor.

Cohen (1981) carried out a meta-analysis of forty-one validity studies of student ratings. The overall correlation between course rating and mean student achievement was .47, a higher correlation than expected in view of numerous factors other than teaching that affect student learning.

One important educational goal is that of helping students develop the ability to evaluate their own learning. If we are at all successful, we would expect greater validity for student ratings in advanced courses than in elementary courses. Unfortunately, validity studies require multi-section courses in order to compare the effectiveness of several teachers on common measures of student achievement. Such multi-section courses are most commonly found at the elementary level so that we cannot compare the validities of student ratings in elementary courses with those in advanced courses.

The studies of the validity of student ratings are thus reasonably encouraging with respect to the goal of achievement on course examinations measuring cognitive goals. What of other educational outcomes?

Validity of Student Ratings as a Measure of Teaching Effectiveness in Achieving Attitudinal and Motivational Goals

One important goal of higher education is that of motivating students for continued learning—lifelong learning. In most courses one would not be happy if students mastered the content of the course but wanted never to learn anything more about that sort of material. The ultimate measure of achievement of this goal is later learning behavior, such as buying books or magazines related to the discipline, later reading habits, attendance at lectures, workshops, or other opportunities for learning, election of further courses, and so on. For end-of-the-course evidence it is hard to conceive of a measure with more face validity than answers to such items as "This course is increasing my interest in learning more about this area."

With respect to the goal of motivating further student learning, a small study by McKeachie and Solomon (1958) found that students of highly rated introductory psychology teachers tended to elect more advanced courses in psychology. Sullivan and Skanes reported that students of highly rated psychology teachers were more likely to major in psychology: teachers who were effective in terms of student achievement also influenced course elections positively, even when the instructors did not receive high ratings.

In the attitudinal domain, Mann (1968) found that students in classes of highly rated teachers developed more sophisticated attitudes about economics than students of less highly rated instructors.

Other Data Relevant to Questions of Validity of Student Ratings as Measures of Teaching Effectiveness

One common criticism of student ratings is the plaint, "You can't really appreciate good teachers until you have been out of college a while. We hated 'Old So-and-So' when we were students, but now we know he really was a great teacher."

The evidence is that such cases are the exception rather than the rule. Drucker and Remmers (1951) and Centra (1974) found that alumni ratings of faculty correlate highly with those of current students. Aleamoni (1981) and Marsh (1984) report similar results in comparing current ratings with those by graduating seniors. Additional evidence supporting the validity of student ratings comes ironically from a series of studies widely believed to attack their validity. The Dr. Fox studies (Naftulin, Ware, and Donnelly, 1973) demonstrated that even professors, professionals, and administrators are unable to tell when a single lecture not directly in their field of expertise is not authentic.

The series of studies following this finding indicate that students, too, are not always good judges of whether teachers presented more or less material than normal. This is not a surprising finding since the students haven't been through the course before. However, when content is equivalent, students tend to rate higher the teachers from whom they learn most.

Perry, Abrami, and Leventhal (1979) carried out a well-controlled study replicating the Dr. Fox research. Their results, however, did not replicate those reported in the original Dr. Fox studies. In only one of four situations were the results similar. In general, students both learned more and rated instructors higher in sections with more content and in sections in which the instructor was more expressive. However, ratings were influenced more by the instructor's expressiveness than by achievement. This finding was confirmed by Meier and Feldhusen (1979) and fits with Frey et al.'s finding (1975) that student ratings of instructor skill are more highly related to student learning criteria than are student ratings on the "rapport" dimension. This does not mean that student ratings are invalid measures of "rapport"; it simply means that "rapport" is not highly related to student achievement. In fact, the Dr. Fox studies provide further evidence that students rate teacher *behavior* validly, since the item showing the largest difference between their high-expressive and low-expressive conditions was "The lecturer was enthusiastic about the subject."

To sum up, students know when they are learning, but they do not know whether what they are learning is current, biased, or appropriate for course goals. They do rate lower an instructor who provides less content, but their ratings of effectiveness are probably less affected by amount of content than by other characteristics of teaching. These findings suggest that when student ratings are used as evidence of teaching in promotion decisions, peers should check term papers, examinations, syllabi, etc., to determine that the content is appropriate. (Although we do not know how reliable and valid such peer judgments are, one hopes that peers can provide useful data.)

Faculty critics of student ratings sometimes complain that students cannot evaluate academic competence. Such criticism seems oddly misdirected. Surely students should not be expected to be better judges of subject-matter competence than the department chairperson, who assigned the instructor to the course. One does not need to be an internationally famous researcher to teach an undergraduate course effectively; students should have the right to assume that an instructor assigned to a course will have adequate subject-matter competence. If faculty members have doubts about an instructor's competence in the subject matter, it seems illogical for them to turn to students for such judgments. On the other hand, when there are questions about what instructors do in the classroom or how they affect students, the students themselves seem a plausible source of information.

Can Student Ratings Help Teachers Improve?

The ultimate test of the usefulness of student ratings as a measure for improving teaching is whether teaching becomes more effective as a result of the use of student ratings. Although some studies have reported no improvement, most have reported positive results. The most impressive results are those reported by Overall and Marsh (1979). As compared with a control group, students of instructors receiving feedback from student ratings not only gave their instructors more favorable ratings at the end of the year but also scored higher on an achievement test and on a measure of motivation for further learning and application of the material learned.

Failure of improvement after feedback from student ratings may be due to any of three factors:

1. The ratings may not provide new information.

2. Low ratings and critical comments may create anxiety, discouragement, and lack of enthusiasm for teaching—lowering rather than improving motivation for teaching.

3. Even when faculty members want to improve they may not know what to do.

Centra (1973) and Pambookian (1972) demonstrated that new information was important. Their research revealed that teachers whose self-ratings were higher than their students' ratings improved after receiving the student rating; teachers who were accurate or who underestimated the student ratings did not improve. Braunstein, Klein, and Pachla (1973) obtained similar results. Pambookian found that instructors in the middle range of ratings tended to benefit from feedback while the top and bottom teachers did not, suggesting that teachers receiving low ratings may become discouraged.

In a study at the University of Michigan (McKeachie et al., 1980), we attempted to meet the conditions governing improvement following feedback of ratings by giving counseling to provide encouragement and suggesting alternative teaching strategies. This proved to be superior to a printed report of the results. Marsh and Roche (1992) reviewed previous research showing the positive effects of consultation and carried out a carefully controlled study demonstrating significant improvement in teaching after feedback with consultation.

General Thoughts About Validity

Even though the data are now strongly supportive of the validity of student ratings for certain goals, this does not mean that they are impervious to influences by other factors. Validity studies are carried out within a given course in which a group of teachers with comparable students and comparable teaching conditions is working toward common goals. In such circumstances, student ratings provide good evidence of teaching effectiveness. But promotions committees and administrators want to use student ratings to make judgments comparing individuals in different courses and in different departments. Obviously, comparing the effectiveness of a mathematics teacher with that of a teacher of history is comparing apples and oranges. Even though one may be able to evaluate apples or oranges validly, one cannot as easily evaluate the relative worth of an apple versus an orange.

In everyday life we do, nevertheless, make such judgments regularly, deciding whether a new television set should be purchased rather than a new hi-fi, whether the iceberg lettuce is better than the romaine, and so forth. And in academia, comparisons of two professors' research are made without concern that the research may deal with different problems in different fields. If I am deciding whether to hire one professor rather than another, I make a judgment of relative merit. In our own grading of students we may worry and vacillate, but we still are able to assign grades to students who differ in terms of how well they do on objective tests, how well they have written their term papers, or how well they have participated in class discussion. So we *are* able to make judgments about relative excellence even though the excellence may be achieved along different dimensions.

Student ratings can provide information that may help us make such judgments, but we should remember that ratings by different groups of students about different teachers do not necessarily provide valid comparisons between two teachers, even though the ratings result in numbers that appear to be comparable. The evaluative judgments need to be made by peers or administrators using *evidence* from student ratings but not by mechanically assigning certain values to certain numbers.

Moreover, when using student ratings to evaluate teaching, we should remember that students cannot judge all aspects of teaching effectiveness equally well. Student ratings are highly valid as indices of achievement of attitudinal and motivational goals of education. They are reasonably valid as indices of achievement of conventional cognitive goals. Judgments of the appropriateness of content, goals, and level of achievement are probably more competently made by peers.

■■■■ *What Factors Influence Student Ratings of Teaching?*

We have now seen that student ratings can provide valid evidence with respect to important aspects of teaching effectiveness, but, if we are to make good use of them, we need to know what factors may influence student ratings. Some of these factors may be valid in the sense that students may learn more and rate teachers higher in certain situations; other variables may contribute to misinterpretation. In general, the results to be reported are encouraging in that most of the factors which might be expected to invalidate ratings have relatively small effects and those factors which affect ratings also affect learning. We shall examine the evidence with respect to characteristics of students, of courses, of teachers, and of the scales themselves.

Student Characteristics

A common misconception is that only more mature, more experienced students can be expected to rate instructors validly. As indicated in my 1969 article, and in more recent reviews, relatively few student characteristics have significant effects on student ratings. Age, sex, and level of student are among the variables that have been shown to have little effect upon student ratings of teaching.

Probably the single most important student variable affecting satisfaction is student expectations. Students who expect a course or teacher to be good generally find it to be so. As Leventhal, Abrami, Perry, and Breen (1975) have shown, students may choose certain classes or sections of classes because of the reputation of the instructor. Thus a professor's current student rating may well be a function, in part, of the reactions of former students. Students who expect a teacher to be good may be more attentive, more highly motivated, and more likely to learn than those with poor expectations.

Some writers appear to believe that students should all evaluate teachers the same way, that is, that a teacher is equally effective with all students. When they find that some kinds of students rate a teacher higher than others do, they assume that student ratings are invalid. However, since there is evidence that teachers may be differentially effective for different students, within-class correlations between student characteristics and ratings are not necessarily indications of invalidity of ratings. Within-class correlations between student needs and course ratings may arise because teachers who met the relevant needs were indeed more effective for those students.

For example, some studies have found that particular types of students respond differently to different teaching styles. Domino (1971), for example, found that students scoring high on the Achievement via Conformance scale of the California Psychological Inventory achieved more and rated the teaching higher in psychology sections taught in a conforming manner; students high in Achievement via Independence did relatively better and rated the teaching as more effective in sections taught in a manner emphasizing independence.

Course and Class Characteristics

The size of a class, whether or not it is required, and the subject matter are all characteristics that may affect ratings. While some studies have shown these variables to make a difference, others have shown no effect, so that the amount of effect seems to be smaller than might be expected. Nevertheless, it seems wise not to lay heavy weight on comparisons of ratings in courses differing greatly in such characteristics. Centra (1979) reports that classes of fifteen or less are more effective in producing student learning and are also rated higher by students. Required courses tend to be rated lower than electives.

Many teachers recognize that some classes go well and others more poorly simply because of key individuals in a class or particular combinations of individuals. One student continually raising anxious questions about tests and grades can demoralize a whole class. Such characteristics of classes have not been assessed, but the possibility of such effects suggests that when student ratings are used in personnel decisions, ratings should be obtained from several classes.

Teacher Characteristics

What characteristics of instructors are related to student ratings of teaching effectiveness? For example, are certain personality characteristics related to effective teaching or to inflated student ratings? Do instructors who are easy graders get higher ratings?

Research shows relatively small effects of instructor characteristics. For example, sex of instructor makes little difference in the student ratings; conflicting results have been found with respect to faculty rank; and personality characteristics do not show consistent relationships to ratings of effectiveness. In one of our studies of student ratings at the University of Michigan, we did find that teaching assistants rated highly by their peers in general cultural attainment were rated as more effective by students.

Some other personality characteristics may be related to student ratings. For example, Hart and Driver (1978) found that teachers scoring high in extraversion, intuitiveness, and "feeling" on the Myers-Briggs Type Indicator tended to receive higher student ratings. Similarity of teacher and student personality and instructor personality did not affect ratings. Murray (1980) found that peer ratings of instructor extraversion, lack of anxiety, leadership, and objectivity correlated positively with mean student ratings of teaching effectiveness. Sherman and Blackburn (1975) found that highly rated teachers were perceived to be dynamic, amicable, and highly intellectual.

The research on grading practices has produced mixed results. A number of studies have found no overall effect of grading practices, although an instructor who is a hard grader is more likely to be rated low on the item "Fairness in grading." Some studies have found a tendency for teachers giving higher grades to get higher ratings. However, one might argue that in courses in which students learn more the grades should be higher and the ratings should be higher so that a correlation between average grades and ratings is not necessarily a sign of invalidity. Palmer, Carliner, and Romer (1978) controlled for student achievement and found no effect of severity of grading on student ratings. My own conclusion is that one need not worry much about grading standards within the range of normal variability. If, however, grading standards seem unusually lenient, one might want to look more closely at the standards of achievement and the bases for grading in the course.

In general, it seems unwise to assume that certain characteristics denote good teaching and to use student judgments about these characteristics to evaluate teaching. There is ample research evidence that good teachers come in many styles. Most presumed essentials of good teaching, such as organization, warmth, or research ability, are not highly valid.

Other Factors

One would expect that the validity of ratings would be affected by the time when they are collected. This seems not to be a critical variable. Frey, Leonard, and Beatty (1975) found that ratings collected the last week of classes were not significantly different from those collected the first week of the following term.

It may make a difference, however, whether the ratings are to be used for improving the course or for evaluating the instructor for promotion. Ratings collected after the first few weeks of a course or at mid-term seem to be particularly useful for improvement of teaching. On ratings at the end of the term students may be more generous to a reasonably good teacher if they believe that the ratings will affect promotion.

■■■■ *Choosing Scales or Items for Scales*

Establishing the Purpose of Collecting Student Opinion

Whether one plans to use one of the ready-make scales or construct one's own, a necessary prerequisite is to examine one's goals in gathering student impressions, for different goals imply different items. If the goal is to assist in personnel decisions, two to five general items may be sufficient; if the purpose is to improve instruction, a more detailed, behaviorally oriented set of items relevant to particular kinds of courses is probably more appropriate.

I shall discuss particular items useful for each of these purposes. But as an alternative to developing your own scales, you might wish to consider the use of a scale developed elsewhere, such as those developed at the Educational Testing Service, Northwestern, Kansas State, or other universities included in the book by Genova, Madoff, Chin, and Thomas (1976).

In choosing items appropriate for different goals you may be helped by differentiating five types of items.

1. items in which students report classroom events or teacher behaviors

2. items reporting the student's perception of his or her achievement of course goals

3. items reporting the student's own evaluation of the effectiveness of different aspects of the course

4. items reporting the student's own behavior or thinking in the course

5. items reporting student satisfaction

Different kinds of items are useful for each major purpose for which student ratings scales are used. Moreover, differing items are appropriate for differing types of instruction, such as lectures, seminars, laboratory, or tutorial instruction.

Choosing Student Rating Items for Improving Instruction

As we saw earlier, the use of student ratings is likely to result in improvement when a) the ratings provide new information; b) the teacher is motivated to improve; or c) the teacher can use alternative methods of teaching effectively.

This has implications for choice of items. Items chosen by the instructor because he or she wants the information are more likely to be informative than items on scales written for more general purposes. Aside from an item or two to indicate general feelings of satisfaction, more specific items reporting perceptions or evaluations of teacher behaviors or specific aspects of the course are likely to be more helpful than very general items.

Moreover one would guess that items worded in an evaluative fashion would elicit more defensiveness then those that are worded descriptively. Thus one might prefer such an item as:

"The instructor writes key points on the blackboard,"

to an item such as:

"Lectures are well organized."

Factor analyses reveal the major dimensions students and faculty members use in thinking about teaching. In constructing a scale it seems reasonable to include one or two items from each of the major factors. Among the factors commonly identified are:

Skill—Enthusiasm
"The teacher was enthusiastic."

Structure
"The teacher defined the objectives of the class."

Rapport
"The teacher was friendly."

Work load—Difficulty
"The work load was heavy."

Group interaction
"The teacher encouraged class discussion."

Mazzuca and Feldhusen (1977) found in a survey of students that the first two factors above were particularly important to students.

To facilitate adaptation of student ratings to the needs of individual instructors, Purdue University developed the Purdue Cafeteria System. This system permits instructors to choose items from a catalogue of items that have been previously used. Other universities have now adopted or adapted the Cafeteria System to provide flexibility in obtaining student ratings likely to give the instructor useful information.

Choosing Student Rating Items for Personnel Decisions

The current press for teacher accountability is one of the factors leading to attempts to mandate the use of standard, uniform student rating scales for assessing teaching effectiveness. As we have already seen, student ratings of teaching are related to teacher effectiveness as measured by the achievement of the teacher's students. Nevertheless this does not mean that student ratings are sufficient evidence of teaching effectiveness. Ideally one would gather evidence from a number of sources, giving most weight to those sources most expert with respect to different aspects of teaching. For example, it is hard to conceive of anyone more expert than students themselves with respect to the degree to which the teacher has stimulated intellectual curiosity and interest in the subject-matter field—an important educational goal; on the other hand, one would expect peers to be most competent in judging the scholarly content of a course, assuming that they have examined syllabi, examination papers, instructor and student lecture notes, or other sources of evidence. Thus personnel decisions inevitably involve value judgments using data from several sources with respect to a teacher's effectiveness in achieving a number of different goals.

As suggested earlier, a uniform standard scale is not likely to be very helpful for improving teaching—nor is a lengthy standard scale likely to be helpful for personnel decisions since it is unlikely to be equally well suited for different disciplines or different courses within a discipline. Since comparisons between instructors in different courses can at best be only very general, one should probably not attempt much more than to determine whether students rate an instructor as excellent, adequate, or poor. An item or two of the degree to which a course stimulated interest or curiosity, and perhaps another item or two on general effectiveness, should be sufficient for most personnel purposes. In addition, it may be helpful to have marker items on some of the factors usually found to differentiate teachers. Some instructors achieve excellence through skillful presentations; others achieve excellence through stimulating high student involvement. It is all too easy for faculty committees to develop stereotypes of faculty teaching on the basis of hearsay, and having scores on somewhat differentiated dimensions of teaching should help break down the simple good-bad classification that we all too often fall into.

Certain items have proved to relate to teacher effectiveness as measured by mean student performance on an examination. Unfortunately such studies must be done in a multi-section course, and it is often difficult to know how much the results can be generalized to other courses. Frey, Leonard, and Beatty's (1975) validity studies included both calculus and psychology courses so that Frey's items are particularly worthy of consideration. Three likely candidates are:

"Each class period was carefully planned in advance."
"The instructor presented the material clearly."
"This course has increased my knowledge and competence."

Other validated items include:

"Does the professor make students feel free to ask questions, disagree, express their ideas, etc.?"
"Does the professor use examples from his/her own research or experience?"

I like to use items that ask students about themselves rather than focusing on evaluation of the teacher. Examples of such items are:

"I learned a great deal in this course."
"I became more interested in this subject matter."
"I tried to relate material in the course to my own experience."
"I developed an overall framework for learning and understanding this topic."

Items Designed to Be Educational for Students

One of the potential unfortunate outcomes of the use of student ratings is that students are influenced to focus upon the instructor as the person chiefly responsible for student learning. In fact, however, learning should be a joint responsibility of students and instructor. Before blaming the instructor for failure to achieve educational goals, students should consider whether they have done all they could to make the course a valuable experience.

On my own student rating form I include a section on student responsibility for learning. My purpose is to increase students' sense of responsibility for their own learning and to encourage them to think about their own educational goals. I include such items as:

→ I attend class regularly.

→ I have created learning experiences for myself in connection with the course.

→ I have helped classmates learn.

General Comments About Procedures for Student Ratings of Teaching

1. Allow space for comments. Faculty members uniformly report that these are helpful. Students need the chance to express feelings that do not quite fit the prestructured questionnaire format. Frequently comments give examples or incidents that clarify the meaning of ratings or indicate what changes need to be made.

2. Indicate in the instructions who will read the comments. Students will be more focused if they understand to whom they are writing.

3. I prefer items worded in terms of the individual student's perception or evaluation to more general statements. I think a faculty member is likely to resent global evaluations more

than those worded in terms of the impression made on a particular student, and I think a student is generally better able to report how he or she felt than to make global judgments.

4. Faculty members should have the right to participate in the selection of items or forms to be used in evaluating teaching in order that the form may be appropriate for the goals of the particular classes in which the data are to be collected.

5. If ratings are to be used in personnel decisions, some control should be exercised over conditions of administration. Rumors circulate about instructors who roam up and down the aisles, lose poor evaluations, or introduce the ratings by announcing that the students will be determining not only the instructor's fate but that of spouse and children.

6. I believe teachers are likely to be more effective and are more likely to improve if they enjoy teaching. This implies that reports of student ratings should be in a format that encourages good feelings rather than discouragement. Thus a report emphasizing percentile ranks in relation to norms may be less helpful than a report emphasizing the distribution of student responses (since typical classes like their instructor). It probably is not very helpful to tell teachers rated as "good" by their students that this is only "average."

7. If teaching ratings are to be published in a booklet for students and made available to colleagues, experience indicates that faculty motivation is enhanced if the booklet reports teacher strengths rather than weaknesses.

8. Effective teaching is a skill that can be learned and that develops over time. Teaching ratings can help development. Basing career decisions on ratings in a single course early in a teaching career is not wise or fair. Basing decisions on a single visit by a peer or superior is even more unwise.

9. If student ratings are used in personnel decisions, the instructor should have an opportunity to present his or her interpretation of the data as well as whatever additional evidence seems relevant.

10. Student ratings tend to focus on classroom teaching. Evidence with respect to out-of-class educational functions such as course planning, advising, etc., also is needed.

11. When student ratings are used in personnel decisions, they should be evaluated by peers who are familiar with the courses in which the ratings were gathered, know the teaching methods used, and can take into account the circumstances under which the course was taught.

▰▰▰ *Summary of Student Ratings*

Student ratings of teaching can be useful for several purposes, such as:

1. improving teaching
2. providing data relevant to judgment about teaching effectiveness
3. aiding student choice of course and instructor
4. stimulating students to think about their education

Student ratings are not automatically valid and useful for any of these purposes. Thus we need to understand what student ratings can and cannot do before embarking upon large-scale institutional programs of student ratings.

We use ratings to improve the quality of education. No matter how technically sophisticated our questionnaire and our evaluation system, they are worthless if their use generates such conflict, anxiety, or confusion that education is affected adversely.

Student ratings should not be used as the single measure of teaching. Rather we should think of them as data valuable for problem solving. Their impact upon the climate for teaching is more important than the technical excellence of the form to be used.

If students are to provide careful ratings and if faculty members are to make good use of the information, both need to have confidence in the methods used. Thus even a good form may need to be reexamined and revised frequently by student-faculty committees if new generations are to have a sense that the system is theirs rather than one imposed upon them.

In the Appendix I have suggested a form for collecting student opinion. Feel free to use any items from it which would be useful in your situation.

▬▬▬ *Peer or Consultant Visitation*

One of the most frequently used methods of appraising teaching is classroom visitation by administrators or fellow teachers. Such visits can be helpful for improving teaching; however, their value as evidence for promotion decisions is probably over-estimated.

To take this last point first—the problem is reliability. Centra (1975) showed that peer ratings based on classroom visitation failed to discriminate between teachers consistently. The problem is that it is difficult to get a good estimate of teachers' abilities from a few visits, especially when the teachers are under the special pressure of knowing that their performance on these days may affect their salary or future. Thus using peer visitation as a primary source of data for personnel decisions is probably not cost-effective.

Peer visitation to assist in improving teaching is quite another matter. As we saw in the previous section on student ratings, consultation adds greatly to the value of feedback. So talking to colleagues about teaching is an important strategy for improvement, and talking to a colleague who has visited your class is especially useful. You can increase the value of such a visitation if you brief your colleague before class about what you are hoping to accomplish and your plan for accomplishment. If there are particular things that you would like observed, mention them.

In training university teachers I have frequently asked them to form pairs for mutual observation. One learns both by observing how one's partner handles problems as well as by getting advice on the basis of one's partner's observations.

While peers have the advantage of knowing the particularities of teaching your discipline, consultants from a faculty development center can also be useful in having a broader knowledge of a range of teaching strategies and the ability to look at teaching characteristics independently of subject-matter issues. We sometimes videotape classes and refer to the videotapes to allow the teacher to see particular incidents illustrating points that need attention.

Consultants from a faculty development center also have the advantage of not being involved in personnel decisions—an important consideration. Robert Wilson at the University of California at Berkeley handled the problem of the conflict between the two purposes of helping and personnel evaluating by arranging for retired professors to act as mentors for new faculty members.

Group Interviews

The University of Illinois (Braskamp et al., 1984) and other institutions have used group interviews to appraise teaching. In this approach a consultant visits a class and asks groups of students to comment on the strengths and to recommend changes. Using this technique the consultant can probe more deeply into sources of difficulty, uncovering critical incidents or examples that clarify problems. This method also has the advantage of demonstrating to students that the complaints of some students are not shared by their classmates. Abbott et al. (1990) compared eight methods of collecting student opinions of instruction. It was found that students preferred interviews at mid-term. Satisfaction was greatly increased if the instructor talked about the consultants' summary of student opinion and discussed what changes could be made as well as what could not be changed.

Measuring Gains in Motivation and Learning Strategies

The group interview is particularly useful for getting information about students' reactions to what the teacher does. It is thus primarily used as a source of information for teaching improvement. But, it is also useful to know how well students are progressing in achieving educational goals. Thus student rating forms typically include items such as:

"I learned a great deal in this course."
"I am learning to think more clearly about the area of this course."
"I became more interested in the subject matter of this course."

In courses I am studying or teaching, I also like to get more detailed information on the students' gains, or losses, in motivation and learning strategies using a measure such as the LASSI (Learning and Study Strategies Inventory) (Weinstein, 1987) or the MSLQ (Motivated Strategies for Learning Questionnaire) (Pintrich et al., 1991).

■■■■ *The Teaching Portfolio*

The "Teaching Portfolio" is an increasingly popular method of evaluating teaching both for personnel decisions and for teaching improvement. Essentially your portfolio can include any material you feel might help document your teaching effectiveness. Thus your portfolio might include summaries of student ratings of teaching, syllabi, samples of student papers, exams or other indicators of learning, reports of peer visitation to classes, a self-evaluation, a journal of reflections on your experiences in teaching, descriptions of things you have done to develop new teaching methods or course materials, examples of research on teaching, and/or plans or goals for the future.

■■■■ *What Do You Do with Feedback?*

So you've given out a student rating form and now you have them back. Naturally you'll use this feedback to improve—maybe! As we saw earlier, feedback from student ratings generally results in improvement, but not much. What can you do to use the information effectively?

1. Don't become obsessed with the criticisms and negative ratings of a few students. The biggest barrier to improvement is discouragement. No matter how well I'm rated, the negative comments still feel like stabs. Everybody gets some low ratings; no matter how good you are, some students will be critical. Focus on the positive comments, and keep them in sight while you look at the criticisms. Then see if there are some things you could do to reduce the number of criticisms without losing your supporters.

2. Ask a colleague or consultant to go over the ratings with you to help interpret them and make suggestions of alternative strategies you might try.

3. Summarize your impressions and plans for change or continuity and discuss them with the class to get their reactions. Regardless of the effectiveness of your planned changes, your students will give you credit for listening and trying.

SUPPLEMENTARY READING

Good guides to evaluating teaching include L. A. Braskamp, D. C. Brandenburg, and J. C. Ory, *Evaluating Teaching Effectiveness: A Practical Guide* (Beverly Hills, CA: Sage, 1984); J. A. Centra, Colleagues as Raters of Classroom Instruction, *Journal of Higher Education*, 1975, *46*, 327–337; and Kenneth O. Doyle, *Student Evaluation of Instruction* (Lexington, MA: D. C. Heath, 1975). Also, his *Evaluating Teaching*, from the same publisher, 1983.

H. W. Marsh, *Students' Evaluations of University Teaching. Research Findings, Methodological Issues, and Directions for Further Research* (Elmsford, NY: Pergamon Press, 1984).

Herbert W. Marsh, Students' evaluations of university teaching: Dimensionality, reliability, validity, potential biases, and utility, *Journal of Educational Psychology*, 1984, *76*, 707–754.

What should you do if your ratings on some items are lower than you'd like? Consult the manual by Barbara Gross Davis, Lynn Wood, and Robert C. Wilson, *ABCs of Teaching with Excellence* (Berkeley, CA: University of California, Berkeley, 1983). This book is a compendium of brief suggestions made by excellent teachers at the University of California, Berkeley. Many of these are directly related to items commonly included on student rating forms.

One of the best published student rating forms is the IDEA, developed at Kansas State University. For a sample copy write to the following:

Dr. William Cashen
Center for Faculty Evaluation and Development
1615 Anderson Ave.
Manhattan, KS 66502-1604

One of the most studied and validated instruments is SEEQ. H. W. Marsh, SEEQ: A reliable, valid, and useful instrument for collecting students' evaluations of university teaching, *British Journal of Educational Psychology*, 1982, *52*, 77–95.

Probably the first detailed description of the teaching portfolio (or dossier) is found in a report by a committee of the Canadian Association of Teachers: B. M. Shore, S. F. Foster, C. K. Knapper, G. G. Nadeau, N. Neill, and V. W. Sim, *The Teaching Dossier: A Guide to Its Preparation and Use* (Montreal: Canadian Association of University Teachers, 1986). Thorough descriptions with examples may be found in P. Seldin, *The Teaching Portfolio* (Bolton, MA: Anker, 1991) and in R. Edgerton, P. Hutchings, and K. Quinlan, *The Teaching Portfolio: Capturing the Scholarship in Teaching* (Washington, DC: American Association for Higher Education, 1991).

Classroom Research

*A*S YOU BECOME MORE INTERESTED IN TEACHING you are likely to want to test your ideas in ways going beyond your own subjective impressions. Much of the progress made in understanding the practical aspects of teaching and learning has come from individual faculty members who have carried out studies in their own and colleagues' classes to get empirical evidence with respect to some issue, such as the effectiveness of some teaching innovation or the student characteristics affecting responses to some aspect of teaching or testing. Planning such a study is one of the best ways of clarifying your thinking, and in my experience teachers who get involved in such studies become better teachers, not so much from the results per se as from the insights gained in doing and interpreting the research.

Tom Angelo and Pat Cross (1993) have prepared a compendium of techniques for getting feedback from students and evaluating the effectiveness of aspects of teaching and learning. You will find helpful ideas even if you don't carry out a systematic study.

I hope, however, that you will do such studies, and the following section contains some general advice about classroom research which may be helpful as you plan your own study or read reports of other studies. Determining which of two teaching methods is more effective looks like a simple matter. Presumably all that is necessary is to teach something by both methods and then compare the results. This is essentially the research design of many of the studies that are widely quoted to show the effectiveness of PSI, television, discussion, independent study, or other methods. Unfortunately, there are some hidden traps that enthusiasts for one method or another are likely to overlook.

■■■■ *The Methodological Problems*

Suppose, for example, that a group of students is given an opportunity to take a class taught by a method quite unusual in their college. The very fact that the method is different gives it excitement. Sometimes the reaction may be one of enthusiasm; in other cases it may be one of outraged hostility. The latter reaction seems to be particularly likely when students taught by a new method know that they are competing on examinations with students taught by the tried and true traditional methods. In any case it is difficult to know how much of student improvement (or loss) in learning may be accounted for by the emotional reaction to a new and different method and how much can be expected when the new method is routine. This "Hawthorne effect" influences not only students but also professors. How many new curricula, courses, or teaching methods have flowered briefly and then faded as the innovators' enthusiasm waned or as new staff members replaced the originators? Unfortunately, relatively few studies have made comparisons over a period longer than one semester. Students who have experienced a semester of instruction by a new method (except television) are generally more likely to choose a section taught by this method than are students without previous experience. This difference in motivation, as well as added skill in the requisites of "studentship" in a new method, might result in greater advantages for a new method after two or more semesters of trial than after a single semester.

A second methodological problem is establishing a suitable control group. In some experiments a single instructor uses both teaching methods. Here the obvious problem is that it is difficult to determine how much the instructor's own personality and skills have influenced the outcome. It is impossible to know whether or not other teachers would obtain similar results. The obvious remedy for this defect is to persuade several professors to use both methods. Leaving aside the salesmanship necessary to institute such a research design, the effort involved in trying to teach by two methods, keeping strictly to each, is tremendous. As a result, either the methods tend to coalesce or, in an overzealous attempt to avoid this, the experimenter institutes artificial and additional constraints to accentuate the differences.

Another problem in establishing controls is that the conditions of the experiment may introduce special factors that interfere with normal results. For example, the experiment may require extensive testing, the presence of observers in the class, or other interferences with normal classroom routine. A class in which a "live" professor is talking to television cameras is probably not a suitable comparison group for classes watching the lesson on television receivers.

A fourth problem is biased sampling. According to newspaper reports, studies of educational television have demonstrated that students taking the course at home learn as much as those on campus. The obvious problem is that people who sign up for a television course and come to campus to take the exam are probably somewhat different in motivation and background from typical college students. As Greenhill points out (1959), efforts to equate such groups are never successful.

A fifth problem arises in the statistical methods used to analyze the results of teaching-methods experiments. Ordinarily experimenters are concerned about avoiding the type of error involved in concluding that one method is more effective than another when in reality they do not differ significantly. However, they are less likely to be sensitive to another type of error that may be just as damaging—the error of concluding that there is no difference in effectiveness when two methods are not found to differ significantly. In addition to the logical fallacy involved in accepting failure to disprove the null hypothesis as proof of no difference, there is the problem of choice of methods of analysis. The chance of obtaining such results depends upon the type of statistical analysis used. With "weak" statistics, a difference is less likely to be detected than with "strong" statistics. The true effect of a variable may be clouded if no effort is made to remove other sources of variance. As I suggest later, the application of multivariate statistics, might, by taking out other sources of variance, reveal more clearly the true effects of varying methods. Further, when several tests of the same hypothesis are made with different groups, experimenters might well use combined tests of significance. For example, if ten groups come out in the same direction, it is extremely unlikely that the methods are not differentially effective even though no one difference would be statistically significant.

A sixth problem is the interaction among teaching methods, student characteristics, teacher characteristics, or other variables. What is effective for some students may not be for others.

But even with better statistical methods, large, consistent effects are not likely. Education is a tremendously complex effort affected by many variables. No one thing, or group of variables, is likely to stand out clearly amidst the presence of the other variables not under study.

Qualitative Methods

Qualitative methods of collecting data often provide insights that go beyond those of statistical tests. In our own research we use interviews of instructors and students; we videotape classes or cooperative learning groups; we use "stimulated recall" (playing audiotapes or videotapes of classes and asking the students involved what they were thinking at certain points of the episode); we have students think aloud while studying or solving problems. All of these have given us useful information.

■ *The Criterion Problem*

The major problem in experimental comparisons of teaching methods is the criterion problem. Stuit and Wilson's (1946) prediction studies in naval training showed that as the criterion was increasingly well defined, prediction of success improved. Undoubtedly one of the reasons for the many nonsignificant differences in studies of teaching is poor criterion measures.

The criterion problem is illustrated by the experiment of Parsons, Ketcham, and Beach (1958). In order to determine the effectiveness of various methods, they took the brave step of setting up some groups in which students didn't come to class at all. The groups who didn't come to class did *best of all* on the final examination. The catch is that the examination was based entirely upon the textbook. As Parsons and Ketcham point out, their results with the other groups suggest that as more and more new ideas and points of view are introduced, students become less likely to remember what the textbook says. This points to the problem of evaluation of effectiveness. If the instructor's goal is that students remember the textbook, a test on the textbook material is appropriate; but one cannot conclude that a particular method is superior in achieving all goals if only one outcome has been measured. Frequently comparisons of two teaching methods only assess learning of content common to both methods.

All too often, studies of teaching effectiveness have confused different goals of evaluation. Course examinations are typically intended to aid teachers in determining student grades. For this use fairness requires that the examination give each student an equal opportunity to obtain a good score. Thus the content of the examination is ordinarily that studied by all students. But when comparing two methods of teaching, you want to know what each group learned that the other did not. Thus a comparison of the lecture method with a discussion method based on a common final examination from a textbook does not really compare what the two groups of students learned in their different classes, but rather what they learned from reading the text. Many of the early experiments on PSI tested material covered in the PSI course and actually used on the criterion test items that students in PSI had answered on previous quizzes. The point here is that the criterion measure should sample progress on all goals, not just a small sample chosen for a particular method. If separate scores for different goals can be assigned, the researcher and the audience are then free to assign their own values to those goals well achieved vs. those poorly achieved.

The difficulty in arriving at an overall index of teaching effectiveness is complicated by the probability that a teacher effective in achieving one course objective is not necessarily effective in achieving others. Bendig (1955), for example, found a significant interaction between instructors and tests in an introductory psychology course. Some instructors' students did particularly well on certain tests during the course, but not well on other tests. Cross (1958) and McKeachie (1959a) found that instructors whose students did well on an objective test in psychology were ineffective when their students' achievement was measured on an essay test designed to gauge understanding and integration of the materials. In studies of teaching it is thus important to specify objectives and to use measures of each objective. Measures of retention after the end of a course can often add to your confidence in reported differences.

Few professors complain that students are too highly motivated. Yet for purposes of research, the degree of student motivation for good grades may actually make it very difficult to evaluate the effectiveness of two teaching procedures. Because passing or excellent grades are so important to students, they may compensate for ineffective teaching by additional study in order to pass the course examination at the level to which they aspire. Thus, the results of ineffective procedures may be masked or even misinterpreted when course examinations are used as criterion measures. Nachman and Opochinsky (1958) provided a neat demonstration of this when they found differences between a small and large class on surprise quizzes, but no difference on a final examination. When significant differences in achievement are found in an experiment, the difference may simply reflect the degree to which students in differing classes were able to find out what the examination was to be and the degree to which it would determine their course grade.

Because achievement measures have been so insensitive to differences in teaching methods, most experimenters stress the favorable student reactions to the new method they have introduced. Although the relationship between student satisfaction and learning is moderate, it can certainly be argued that, assuming equal learning between two methods, teachers would prefer to have students leave their classes with warm feelings about their experiences. Moreover, teachers would expect these feelings to be related to interest in learning more, and there is some evidence to support this (McKeachie and Solomon, 1958). However, when researchers use student satisfaction as a criterion, they should be aware of the fact that it is highly influenced by the role expectations students have of college teachers. Marked deviations from these expectations almost inevitably will be rated lower than more conventional teaching behavior. Laboratory studies of problem-solving groups reveal that authoritarian leaders are rated by group members as being more efficient than democratic leaders (Haythorn et al., 1956). This makes sense both in terms of members' expectations for leaders and also because a leader who plays an active role is almost inevitably going to make a more vivid impression on a group than a leader whose behavior is more subtle. In evaluating student reactions, therefore, researchers need to be conscious of these role expectancies and determine what is a proper baseline against which to evaluate the reactions.

As an aside here, let me also point out that new methods are not usually tested except by a teacher who is enthusiastic about them. Consequently the comparison may be between student reactions to a new method and an enthusiastic teacher vs. an old method taught unenthusiastically.

The prospective researcher also needs to be warned that even a careful definition of desirable outcomes does not end the criterion problem. In many cases, laudable attempts to measure attitudinal or affective outcomes have led to the conclusion that neither of two teaching methods was superior to the other in achieving this or that goal, when there is no evidence that *any* teaching could affect the goal as measured by the tests used. At the very least, the experimenter needs to report some evidence that the measure is at least sufficiently sensitive to reveal significant changes from the beginning to the end of the semester. If there is no change on a variable over a semester, it is unlikely that two teaching methods will differ in the amount of the change they cause.

Finally, evaluation need not end with tests given to the students who are enrolled in the experimental classes. In a large university it is easy to assume that an experimental course is assimilated into the whirlpool of activity without even a ripple.

Seldom, however, has this assumption been tested, and in smaller colleges or for large-scale innovations it is not a safe assumption. Researchers might gain much useful knowledge by looking outside their experimental classrooms to other effects of the experiment. Do students taught by one method rather than another make more use of their knowledge and skills in other courses they are electing? Is superior achievement in the experimental course won at the expense of achievement in other courses? What is the impact of the use of a particular teaching method upon other faculty members? How does the use of a new method change faculty perceptions of teaching and its value; how does it affect faculty-administration relationships? In short, what effects does a new method have upon the total culture of the college?

SUPPLEMENTARY READING

Lee Cronbach and Richard Snow, *Aptitudes and Instructional Methods* (New York: Irvington, 1977).

Carolyn L. Ellner and Carol P. Barnes, *Studies of College Teaching* (Lexington, MA: D. C. Heath, 1983).

T. A. Angelo and K. P. Cross, *Classroom Assessment Techniques: A Handbook for College Faculty*, 2nd ed. (San Francisco: Jossey-Bass, 1993).

Teaching for Lifetime Outcomes

PART VI

Motivating Students for Your Course and for Lifelong Learning

*I*F I WERE FOLLOWING a purely logical approach to the organization of this book, chapters on motivation and learning would certainly come early, for decisions about teaching techniques should be based upon the principles of learning. However, I have found that most beginning teachers have so many immediate problems that they don't worry very much about general questions of educational theory. It is only after you have mastered some of the day-to-day problems that you are able to sit back and wonder why some things work and others don't. The next four chapters deal with psychological material relevant to the broader concerns of lifetime educational goals.

▬▬▬ Motivation Theory

Instructors know that student learning and memory are closely tied to *motivation*. Students will learn what they want to learn and will have great difficulty learning material that does not interest them. Students are not poor learners; nor are they unmotivated. They are learning all the time—new dance steps, the status hierarchy on campus, football strategy, and other more or less complex things—but the sort of learning for which students are motivated is not always that which contributes to attaining the goals of our courses. Too often teachers think of learning only in terms of formal instruction. It might be more realistic for teachers to think of themselves as individuals who facilitate the kinds of learning that are called "education." They can neither learn for their students nor stop them from learning.

A primary problem, then, is motivating students toward course goals. Basically one can affect motivation for learning in two ways: by increasing the *value* of learning or by affecting the students' *expectancy* that investment in course activities will lead to success in achieving their *goals* (values).

One way to increase the value of learning is to link the course to the motives students bring to class—motives that have developed through years of socialization at home and in school. Teachers know, for example, that many of their students are taught by their parents to want to do well in school. Thus we can count on motivation for *achievement* as important for many students. There are other motives that are also important.

■■■■ *Intrinsic Motivation: Curiosity*

Psychology has a good deal more to contribute on the subject of motivation for learning than it did a few years ago. A few decades ago psychologists would have talked about reward and punishment and would have asked you to look at the rewards for learning in the classroom. This is still worth considering. Rewards and punishments often influence learning. But the revolution in research and theory lies in evidence that people are naturally curious. They seek new experiences; they enjoy learning new things; they find satisfaction in solving puzzles, perfecting skills, and developing competence.

Thus, one of the major tasks in teaching is not how to scare students into doing their homework, but rather how to nurture their curiosity and to use curiosity as a motive for learning.

Fortunately, I can do more than point to curiosity as an important motive for learning. A good deal of research suggests that people seek and enjoy stimuli that are different from those they are used to—but that these stimuli must not be too different. When stimuli are totally incongruous or very strange, students develop anxiety instead of curiosity.

How does this generalization apply to learning in college? It is tempting to answer this question in vague phrases like "varied teaching methods," "posing new, but soluble problems," or "setting realistic standards of achievement." But it is possible to go beyond this. One hint comes from studies by Berlyne (1954a and b). He found that asking students questions, rather than presenting statements of fact, not only improved learning but also increased interest in learning more about the topic. Questions were particularly effective in arousing curiosity about things that were already familiar. The most successful questions were those that were most unexpected. This agrees with the finding that National Merit Scholars describe the classes that influenced their choice of field as ones where they didn't know what to expect next (Thistlethwaite, 1960). The interplay between familiar and novel may be very significant in the development of curiosity.

How do instructors bring students into contact with novelty? Meaningful field or laboratory experience may be on answer. For example, outstanding scientists report that their motivation for science resulted from early participation in research. This has implications for other disciplines. Perhaps instructors offer too few opportunities for students to experience the thrill of discovery.

Complexity can also arouse curiosity. Chapter 10 reviewed evidence that study questions requiring thought produce greater learning from reading. This is not only because of greater meaningfulness but also because questions requiring "deep processing" make studying more interesting (Svensson, 1976).

One of the reasons curiosity is important is that it is a motive intrinsic to learning, and thus continued learning is not dependent upon a teacher to reward learning.

▆▆▆ *Competence*

Another intrinsic motive for learning is competence or self-efficacy. Human beings receive pleasure from doing things well. To the degree that teachers can help students develop a sense of standards that will enable them to see that they are developing increasing skill, teachers can also contribute to the goal of continued learning after the class has been completed.

Bandura (1977) has developed in some depth a theory of self-efficacy. This theory suggests that while teachers are important sources of information about self-efficacy, students will interpret the same information in differing ways depending upon the context of the information and their previous experience. Thus, seeing the teacher or other students perform a task will encourage students who see themselves as similar to the successful students, but will not help students who see themselves as so different that another's success bears no relationship to their own chances of success. Even their own success may be misinterpreted as luck. For such students teachers need to link success with the perception that the success was due to the student's own ability and effort. Success alone is not enough. For students who lack a sense of efficacy teachers must not only provide situations where success occurs but also give students opportunities to undertake challenging tasks on their own to prove to themselves that they can achieve (McKeachie, 1990).

■■■■ *Conflicting Motives: Affiliation and Achievement*

Most students want to be liked. In general warm, friendly teachers are more effective than cold, distant ones, but this motive may work against instructors as well as for them. In some colleges, students who want acceptance by their classmates may avoid any conspicuous display of academic achievement. Many students suffer from conflict between the need to get good grades and the need to be well liked. One of the symptoms of this conflict is the ostentatious neglect of study by some bright students and their apparent surprise when they get good grades.

Another common conflict is between independence and dependence. This means that students are likely to resent the teacher who directs their activities too closely, but they also are likely to be anxious when given independence; so the teachers have the neat trick of finding ways of simultaneously satisfying both needs. As a result of this conflict some students disagree with their teachers not on rational grounds but simply as a way of expressing emotions. Similarly, student apathy in a required course may be irrational expression of resentment about being required to do anything.

Achievement Motivation and Expectancy

Atkinson's theory of achievement motivation suggested that students with high achievement motivation would be more highly motivated in situations where they perceived their chances of success as about fifty-fifty or higher. From Berlyne we have the suggestion that motivation is highest in situations of moderate novelty. Both of these findings point to the value of pacing learning so that each step offers some newness and only a moderate risk of failure—a motivational principle also found by Lepper and Malone (1985) in their analysis of motivational elements in computer games.

One of the first steps in teaching may be to stimulate doubt about what has previously been taken for granted. Playing the "devil's advocate" may be a way to stimulate motivation for students who feel they already know all the answers.

To sum up this section: When students are confident that they have the answers and can achieve their goals without effort, you need to provide challenges; for students who lack confidence you need to provide support and opportunities to show progress and achieve success.

Grades as Incentives

Let us consider the case of the most important motivational device—grades. Whatever students' motivations for being in college, grades are important to them. If students are really interested in learning, grades represent an expert's appraisal of their success; if they're interested in getting into professional school, good grades are the key that unlock graduate school doors; if they want to play basketball, grades are necessary for maintaining eligibility. Most students are motivated to get at least passing grades, and much as instructors resent record keeping, the grades they are responsible for are a powerful motivational tool. Unfortunately, grades motivate studying to get a good grade rather than studying for learning that will be retained and used.

Many teachers regard grades as one of the necessary evils of teaching. They try to discount grades in discussion of the organization of the course and try to arrive at grades in such a way that they can avoid trouble with disappointed students. And they frequently fail to use grades to bring about the sort of learning they desire.

Because grades are important to them, many students will learn whatever is necessary to get the grades they desire. If instructors base grades on memorization of details, students will memorize the text. If they believe grades are based upon their ability to integrate and apply principles, they'll attempt to do this.

Grades can be used to induce students to get through some of the drudgery of initial learning to the point where the student feels a sense of mastery and can enjoy learning. A good deal of evidence has accumulated to suggest that negative (fear) and positive (hope) motives affect behavior differently. When students are motivated by the threat of low grades, they may work hard, but only if this is the only way to avoid undesirable consequences. If there are other ways out of the situation, they'll take them. The result frequently is that students do the least they can get away with or spend their time devising elaborate methods of cheating.

Negative motives are not as effective outside the learning situation as are positive motives, because fear is a more effective motivational device if the threatened danger is close than if it is distant. Students who are afraid are likely to want to avoid being reminded of the possibility of failure. Hence they may avoid study until the pressures are so great that they simply have no alternative. Thus, teachers who motivate their students by fear of bad grades need to use frequent tests if their threats are to be effective.

The striking difference in behavior between students motivated by fear and students motivated by hope is illustrated in their behavior during examinations. A study by Atkinson and Litwin (1960) showed that male students who were high in anxiety about tests were among the first to leave the examination room and tended to do more poorly on the examination than in their work during the course. Students with positive motivation to succeed tended to stay in the examination room longer. (Note that this illustrates the tendency of the fearful person to avoid the situation that arouses anxiety.)

■ *Attributions*

Such students can be helped. Heckhausen (1974) showed that students who fear failure improved in performance when they were helped to attribute failure to lack of effort rather than to lack of ability and to set reasonable standards for themselves. But many students work hard and still do poorly. Is there hope for them? Yes! I currently teach a course, "Learning to Learn," that has both cognitive and motivational goals. Motivationally I aim at teaching students that they can achieve better success by practicing skills for effective learning, such as peer learning, and by using these skills strategically. A study by Anderson and Jennings (1980) showed that attributing failure to ineffective strategies improved motivation for success.

To sum up my argument thus far, motivation is important in learning. Curiosity and competence motivation are important motives for learning. We can use student motivation for success, approval, and so on to produce learning. Grades are important incentives for many kinds of motivation. Thus it's important to make sure that grades are not separate from the kind of learning desired. Using grades chiefly as a threat may produce avoidance rather than interest.

■ *The Teacher as Model*

One of the major sources of stimulation of motivation is the teacher. Your own enthusiasm and values have much to do with your students' interest in the subject matter. Probably nonverbal as well as verbal methods communicate such attitudes; facial expression, animation, and vocal intensity may be as important as the words you use.

■■■■ *Competition vs. Cooperation*

Teachers sometimes attempt to stimulate motivation by engendering competition. In American society competition is valued, and if carried out in game-like situations competition can be a stimulating motivational device. For example, my teaching assistants frequently hold a "quiz bowl" as a review session before a major test or examination. Students and teachers prepare questions in advance for the quiz bowl. (The teacher may screen out inappropriate questions.) The class is divided into two or more groups. The teacher draws the first question for the first team; the teams are given one minute to consult (more for some questions) and then the first team presents its answer which is then given 0 to 2 points by the teacher. If the question is not answered adequately, other groups may gain the remaining points by giving a better answer. Another question is then drawn and given to the second group and the game continues in this fashion.

In an atmosphere of fun and group support such competition can be a useful motivational device, but intense individual competition often is detrimental to learning for most students. When there are few winners and many losers, it may be easier to protect one's sense of self-worth by not trying, than to try and still not succeed.

■■■■ *What Can You Do to Help Students Improve Their Motivational Strategies?*

We have seen that motivation is a function of one's goals and expectations about what will lead to those goals (self-efficacy). Can we help students develop strategies that will not only increase their motivation for learning in our course but also be useful for motivating other learning? The answer is "Yes." In fact these are strategies that we can use for ourselves as well.

1. Establish specific, challenging goals. Having students write specific goals for learning in your course should increase their motivation.

   If your course is one in which student motivation is particularly low, as may be the case in some required courses, you may need to start on a less direct level. For example, you might suggest that they begin by answering questions such as:

a. "What do I want out of my life?"
b. "What do I hope to get out of college?"
c. "Why did anyone think this course should be required? What did they expect students to learn from it?"
d. "What would I like to get out of this course?" (other than a decent grade!)

2. Have students record progress toward their goals. For example, you might have them write goals for this month, this week, today, and tomorrow and check off those they achieve. Writing short-term and intermediate goals does two things. First, it brings long-term goals into focus, increasing the sense that the goals are achievable. Second, it provides a way of monitoring progress. If most short-term goals are achieved, the students' self-efficacy is likely to be enhanced.

SUPPLEMENTARY READING

T. W. Malone and M. R. Lepper, Making learning fun: A taxonomy of intrinsic motivations for learning. In R. E. Snow and M. J. Farr (eds.), *Aptitude, Learning, and Instruction: III. Conative and Affective Process Analysis* (Hillsdale, NJ: Erlbaum, 1987), pp. 223–253. Malone and Lepper carried out an elegant study of what makes computer games so motivating, and here they provide a list of ways teachers can design educational experiences that are intrinsically motivating.

Claire Weinstein and her graduate students at the University of Texas have integrated goal setting and learning strategies. They describe goal setting in C. E. Weinstein, P. A. Schultz, D. S. Ridley, and R. S. Glanz, Goal setting and goal-using: Developing personal meaning to enhance the use of learning strategies, *Innovation Abstracts*, 1989, *11*(11) 1–2.

My colleagues and I developed a questionnaire to assess student motivation and learning strategies. We used it in our own courses and for research but it is now used by many teachers, not only in the United States but also in Europe, Asia, Africa, and New Zealand: P. R. Pintrich, D. A. F. Smith, T. Garcia, and W. J. McKeachie, *A Manual for the Use of the Motivated Strategies for Learning Questionnaire (MSLQ)* (Ann Arbor, MI: National Center for Research to Improve Postsecondary Learning and Teaching, School of Education, University of Michigan, 1991).

A group of experts in training college teachers developed a manual for faculty members to use in improving student motivation and learning: G. R. Johnson, J. A. Eison, R. Abbott, G. T. Meiss, K. Moran, J. A. Morgan, T. L. Pasternack, and E. Zaremba, *Teaching Tips for Users of the Motivated Strategies for Learning Questionnaire* (Ann Arbor, MI: National Center for Research to Improve Postsecondary Learning and Teaching, School of Education, University of Michigan, 1991).

CLAIRE E. WEINSTEIN
DEBRA K. MEYER
GRETCHEN VAN MATER STONE
University of Texas

CTER 32

Teaching Students How to Learn

FOR MANY YEARS, the study of student learning was divorced from the study of teaching. Good teaching practices were assumed to be universals that did not depend on individual differences among students or on teaching students to think and learn. We now know that it is the interaction of good instructional practices with students' strategic learning strategies and skills that results in learning outcomes. However, many college students do not know what to do to learn the content in the different courses they study in college. Therefore, it is important that college instructors use effective instructional practices for presenting content information as well as effective instructional practices for fostering the development and elaboration of both general and content-specific learning strategies. Information must be processed effectively to become knowledge, and knowledge must be organized and accessible to be used. You can help your student learn more effectively not only in your course but in other courses, and in later life.

How can you do this? First of all, we know that strategic learners need to be able to set and use meaningful goals to help them learn and to help them generate and maintain their motivation for studying (Schunk, 1989). As discussed in Chapter 31, we can help students think clearer about their goals by encouraging them to set useful goals for our classes. Unfortunately, many students are not clear about their educational goals, in general, or their goals for specific courses. Not every course will hold the same interest value for every student, but usually there are at least some aspects of the course that can be perceived as useful for each person. Helping students to identify how the material presented in our courses might be useful to them as they strive to reach their own education, personal, social, or occupational goals can enhance motivation and cognitive effort. Even a brief discussion about upcoming topics and how these topics might relate to present or future interests of the students can help. Asking students to write a brief paragraph or two about a topic and why it might be relevant to them now or in the future is another way to establish perceived relevance. It is important to remember that we cannot give students goals—they must *own* their goals.

Increasing Students' Self-Awareness

Students who are aware of their learning goals tend to reflect on what is involved in learning. Thinking about thinking, or knowing about knowing, has come to be referred to as metacognition (Flavell, 1979). Metacognition includes knowledge about ourselves as learners, knowledge about academic tasks, and knowledge about strategies to use in order to accomplish academic tasks. Awareness about themselves as learners helps students to allocate their personal resources or the resources that are available in their academic institution, such as group study sessions, tutoring programs, or learning centers. If students do not anticipate needing help with a potentially difficult course, it is unlikely that they will take advantage of available resources. It also will be difficult for them to judge the personal resources they will need, such as extra study time or more opportunities for review and consolidation of the material before a test (Entwistle, 1992).

Teaching Strategies for Accomplishing Specific Academic Tasks

Helping students understand the nature and requirements of academic tasks is an area of strategic learning in which college faculty can have a particularly strong impact on their students. Each of us will be involved in or assign a number of different academic tasks throughout a course. It is important that we clearly define and explain how each task is expected to contribute to learning so that students can approach the tasks strategically. It is also useful to model the ways you want students to interact with and learn from these tasks. For example, early in the course, when you first introduce a textbook or other written source, point out the characteristics of the material and your expectations for what students should learn from it. If it is an introductory course and you are not sure if students are familiar with the reading skills needed for your content area, you might also go over a few paragraphs and identify what you would do to help focus on the important ideas and information in the textbook. If you deliver lectures in your course, you might bring in an overhead projector for a couple of classes and take notes on your own presentations, explaining why you have recorded some things and not others. When making assignments, have one or two students paraphrase what you have said to see if they understood it. If possible, provide previous samples of students' work and compare good and poor answers. This is particularly important for unusual assignments or tasks that are unfamiliar to many students in your class.

▆▆▆ *Using Existing Knowledge to Help Learn New Things*

College professors have long known that teaching an introductory course is often more difficult than teaching an advanced course in the same area. While many explanations for this finding have been offered, most of them involve the students' lack of prior knowledge. It is all but impossible to think or solve problems in an area without relevant knowledge. In addition, thinking about relevant knowledge also can strengthen new learning by generating meaningful relations to new information. For example, thinking about the economic causes of World War I can help a student understand the economic causes of the Second World War. Strategic learners understand the role of relevant prior knowledge and can use this knowledge to help learn new things

(Alexander and Judy, 1988). We tend to use prior knowledge in one of two ways: to create direct relations, and to create analogical relations. When we create direct relations, we directly relate our prior knowledge to what we are trying to learn. For example, comparing and contrasting the causes of the two world wars involves direct relations. However, there are times when we do not have directly applicable prior knowledge, but we do have knowledge in an area that is somehow similar and may help us to understand the new information, ideas, or skills we are trying to learn. For example, we use analogies to help us relate familiar and new things that share some key characteristics but are very different in other ways. Using a post office to explain aspects of computer storage, referring to social disagreements to explain conflicts in organizations, and using the structure of a bird to explain design elements of an airplane are all ways we use analogies to help students build meaning for new concepts that may, at first, seem totally unfamiliar.

▬ *Using Cognitive Learning Strategies*

We have said that strategic learners can take much of the responsibility for helping themselves study effectively and reach their learning goals. For these students, a core component of strategic learning is their repertoire of cognitive learning strategies (Weinstein and Meyer, 1986). These strategies are used to help build meaning in such a way that new information becomes part of an organized knowledge base that can be accessed in the future for recall, application, or problem solving. Research has shown that one of the hallmarks of expertise in an area is an organized knowledge base and a set of strategies for acquiring and integrating new knowledge (Chi, Glaser, and Farr, 1988).

The simplest forms of learning strategies involve repetition or review, such as reading over a difficult section of text or repeating an equation or rule. A bit more complexity is added when we try to paraphrase or summarize in our own words the material we are studying. Other strategies focus on organizing the information we are trying to learn by creating some type of scheme for the material. For example, creating an outline of the main events and characters in a story, making a time line for historical occurrences, classifying scientific phenomena, or separating foreign vocabulary into parts of speech are all organizational strategies. Some learning strategies involve analyzing or elaborating on what we are trying to learn to make it more meaningful and memorable. For example, using analogies to access relevant prior knowledge, comparing and contrasting the explanations offered by two competing scientific theories, and thinking about the implications of a policy proposal are examples of elaboration strategies.

We can have a tremendous impact on helping students to develop a useful repertoire of learning strategies. One of the most powerful ways for teaching these strategies is through modeling. By using different types of strategies in our teaching, we can expose students to a wide variety of strategies in different content areas. However, it is not enough to simply use strategies in our teaching. It is also necessary to teach students how to do this on their own when they are studying. For example, after paraphrasing a discussion in class, point out what you did and why. Briefly explain to the students what paraphrasing is and why it helps us to learn. You also could explain that it helps us to identify areas that we might not understand. If we have trouble paraphrasing something we are studying, it probably means that we have not yet really learned it. Finally, you should provide students with opportunities over time to use and perhaps describe their uses of different learning strategies. This is the second major method for teaching learning strategies—guided practice with feedback. Students need to have opportunities for practicing their new learning strategies. They also need feedback, at least initially, to help them polish their skills.

■ *Methods for Checking Understanding*

Strategic learners periodically check on the outcomes of their learning methods by monitoring their progress toward learning goals and subgoals (Brown, 1987). Without checking actively on their progress, many students may think that they understand, when, in fact, they do not. Often students do not realize there are holes in their understanding until they receive their grade on a test. This occurs because the test is the first occasion where they are asked to check on their new knowledge in a way that would identify gaps or misunderstandings. Strategic learners know that the time to check on their understanding is long before taking a test or other formal assessment measure. Checking on understanding and looking for gaps in knowledge integration should be an ongoing activity present in every studying and learning context.

Checking our understanding can be as simple as trying to paraphrase or apply what we have been trying to learn. In fact, many homework or project assignments are designed to help students identify gaps in their knowledge or areas of misunderstanding so that they can be corrected. Getting past these problems helps students to deepen their understanding of a topic. Many of the learning strategies we discussed earlier also can be used to test understanding. For example, trying to paraphrase in our own words what we are reading in a textbook is a good way to help build meaning, but it also helps us to identify gaps or errors in our understanding. If we try to apply our knowledge and have difficulty using it, or if we try to explain it to someone else and cannot do it, we would know that we have some comprehension problems. Monitoring our comprehension is an important part of strategic learning that fosters self-regulation. It is only if we know we have a problem in our understanding or a gap in our knowledge that we can do something about it.

A very useful method for checking on understanding and helping to teach a variety of learning strategies is the use of cooperative learning. Cooperative learning is a method that builds on peer tutoring. We have long known that in many traditional tutoring situations, it is the tutor, and not the student receiving the tutoring, who benefits the most. While processing the content for presentation, the tutor is consolidating and integrating his or her content knowledge. At the same time, the tutor is also learning a great deal about how to learn. The tutor needs to diagnose the tutee's learning problem, or knowledge gap, in order to help him or her overcome it. (Refer to Chapter 13, "Peer Learning, Collaborative Learning, Cooperative Learning," for a more complete discussion of the benefits of cooperative learning within learning cells.)

■■■■ *Knowing How to Learn Is Not Enough— Students Must Also Want to Learn*

Strategic learners know a lot about learning and the types of strategies that will help them meet their learning goals. However, knowing what to do is not enough; knowing how to do it is still not enough; students must *want* to learn if they are to use the knowledge, strategies, and skills we have addressed so far. It is the interaction of what Scott Paris and his colleagues have called "skill" and "will" that results in self-regulated learning (Paris, Lipson, and Wixson, 1983; Pintrich and De Groot, 1990). Many students know much more about effective study practices than they use. Just as the overweight person who is an expert in weight loss techniques, knowledge is not always sufficient for action. We all have many different potential goals and actions competing for our attention and resources at any point in time. Which goals we select and how much effort we put toward the goals we have selected is at least partially determined by our motivations. Strategic learners know how to learn, but they also want to be effective learners. It is the interaction of skill and will that gives direction to their actions and helps them to persist at tasks, even in the face of obstacles.

One way to enhance students' perceptions of their competence is by giving performance feedback that focuses on strategic effort and skill development. Simply telling students that they did well does not really focus on their role in the performance. Telling a student, "This is great! I can really see the effort you put into this," says a lot more. Talking directly about students' strategic efforts and the skills they are developing helps them to focus on their role in the learning process. Remember, a key component of strategic learning is believing that you can play an active role. If students do not believe they can make a difference, they will not use many of the effective strategies we have been discussing. Many students listen to strategy instruction and believe the strategies are very useful—but not for them! Our task as teachers is to help students understand that they can take more responsibility for their own learning.

Motivation results from a number of interacting factors (Pintrich and De Groot, 1990; McCombs and Marzano, 1990; Schunk, 1989). As we discussed with goal setting, establishing the potential usefulness of new learning helps to generate interest and direction for students' learning activities. (Chapter 31, "Motivating Students for Your Course and for Lifelong Learning," includes a more complete discussion of the effects of motivation on learning.)

▰▰▰ *Putting It all Together—Executive Control Processes in Strategic Learning*

We have discussed both skill and will as important components of strategic learning. A third essential component is executive control. Strategic learners use executive control processes to: 1) organize and manage their approach to reaching a learning goal; 2) keep them on target and warn them if they are not making sufficient progress toward meeting the goal in a timely and effective manner; and 3) build up a repertoire of effective strategies that they can call upon in the future to complete similar tasks, thereby increasing their learning efficiency and productivity (Weinstein, 1988). When students face new and unfamiliar tasks they must do a lot of planning to help identify potentially effective methods of achieving their goals for task performance. Unfortunately, many students simply adopt a trial and error approach to learning or try to adapt other familiar strategies they have used for different tasks to the current one. Students do not realize that this approach is often neither effective nor efficient. The time invested in generating, following, monitoring, and perhaps modifying a plan is a good investment for reaching learning goals now and in the future. As we develop expertise, we do not need to dwell on developing a plan for each task we face. Generating and evaluating plans for reaching learning goals help build up an effective repertoire that we can call upon fairly automatically in the future when similar learning needs arise.

College faculty can help facilitate self-regulated learning by encouraging students to share examples of successful approaches to learning with each other. Guided discussions about what is and is not working for others help students refine their own methods and get ideas for other potential approaches. These discussions also focus students' attention on the importance of not simply working hard but also working strategically to meet their goals.

▬ *Help! I Don't Have Time to Teach Strategic Learning*

Teaching strategic learning is more than an investment in your students' future learning; it is also an investment in the present. Strategic learners are better able to take advantage of your instruction and their studying activities. The time you invest will come back to you in enhanced student understanding and performance, as well as increased motivation. It is also important to remember that all of us have goals for what we hope the students in our classes will learn. In today's rapidly changing world, the ability to acquire or use knowledge and skills is more important than compiling a static knowledge base. There is an old Talmudic expression that loosely translates as, "If you feed a person a fish, you have fed them for a day, but if you teach them how to fish, you have fed them for a lifetime!" As college instructors our task is to provide edible fish (content knowledge), but our task is also to teach our students how to fish (learning how to become strategic learners in our field).

SUPPLEMENTARY READING

R. J. Menges and M. S. Svinicki (eds.), College Teaching: From Theory to Practice. *New Directions for Teaching and Learning No. 45* (San Francisco: Jossey-Bass, 1991).

B. J. Zimmerman (ed.), Self-regulated learning and academic achievement (special issue), *Educational Psychologist*, 1990, 25(1).

Teaching Thinking

*E*VERYONE AGREES that students learn in college, but whether they learn to think is more controversial.

Thinking is defined in so many ways that the boundary between "learning" and "thinking" is fuzzy and perhaps nonexistent. The two processes are inextricably entwined—even a simple learning task, such as reading a textbook assignment, requires thinking.

Thus the preceding chapter, "Teaching Students How to Learn," is actually about teaching students to think. Setting goals, thinking about what strategy to use in tackling an assignment, accessing relevant previous knowledge, and monitoring one's progress—these are all important components of critical thinking and problem solving.

When faculty members talk about teaching critical thinking, problem solving, or reasoning, they typically mean teaching students to use what they already know.

▅▅▅ *Can We Teach Thinking?*

Can we teach thinking? Some would argue that we can only give students the knowledge necessary for thinking—that the intellectual ability required for thinking is not teachable. There is increasing evidence, however, that measures of thinking, such as tests of general, verbal, and spatial/technical intelligence, improve with education (McKeachie, Pintrich, Lin, Smith, and Sharma, 1990).

▬▬ *How?*

So we do teach thinking skills, but how?

Almost every chapter of this book has dealt with methods of teaching thinking. Effective methods of learning discussions, lecturing, and testing are critical elements in a program for teaching students to think more effectively. Writing, laboratory work, field work, peer learning, project methods, case method, instructional games, journals, role playing, and computers can all contribute to teaching thinking. This chapter would be excessively long if we reviewed, or even summarized, all of the foregoing material on thinking. Therefore I shall simply highlight a few general points.

Knowledge is not enough. Our ever present pressure to "cover" the content may, in fact, militate against effectiveness in teaching thinking because we fail to allow time for thinking. Thinking, like other skills, requires practice, particularly practice that brings our thinking into the open where it can be challenged, corrected, or encouraged. Thus we teachers need to give students opportunities to talk, write, do laboratory or field projects, or carry out other activities that stimulate and reveal their thinking. One doesn't become a skillful musician or basketball player by listening to an expert three hours a week.

The bottleneck is time. I can only read one paper, or listen to one student, at a time. Fortunately the teacher does not have to be the only source of feedback. Other studies can help. (See Chapter 13 for peer learning.)

Even though knowledge is not sufficient, thinking requires knowledge. Our own research has shown that measures of thinking relate to how well students have achieved an organized structure of concepts.

Surprisingly, standard courses in logic do not seem to improve practical reasoning skills unless the abstract concepts are coupled with concrete examples. Training in statistics, however, can be generalized—even brief training (either by giving rules or examples) in the law of large numbers results in generalization, probably because students have intuitive ideas approximating statistical abstraction (Nisbett, Fong, Lehman, and Cheng, 1987). Typical laboratory courses in science have a poor track record in teaching thinking. Yet they, too, can have a positive effect when taught with specific emphasis upon thinking (Bainter, 1955).

If knowledge of subject matter, knowledge of logic, and knowledge of laboratory procedures fail to produce more effective thinkers, what can we do?

Learning to think usually begins by 1) bringing order out of chaos, 2) discovering uncovered ideas, and 3) developing strategies while avoiding jumping to conclusions. Teaching students to describe the elements of a problem or to create a schematic or graphic representation may help them bring order out of chaos. Verbalizing the reason for taking a step before the step is actually taken also can lead to improved thinking.

Bloom and Broder (1950) asked good students to think aloud while answering mock exam questions requiring problem solving. Other students were asked to compare their own thought processes with those used by the good students and to practice thinking procedures that were successful. Although this procedure was not effective for all students, thinking aloud has often been used since, both in research and training in thinking, and is an additional strategy for you to use in teaching thinking.

Alverno College has made measurable progress in teaching critical thinking by stressing explicitness, multiple opportunities to practice in differing contexts, and emphasis on developing student self-awareness and self-assessment (Loacker, Cromwell, Fey, and Rutherford, 1984).

Research on teaching problem solving in particular courses suggests explicitly focusing on the specific methods and strategies to be used in solving particular types of problems. Noting different approaches also helps.

Student participation, teacher encouragement, and student-to-student interaction positively relate to improved critical thinking. These three activities confirm other research and theory stressing the importance of active practice, motivation, and feedback in learning thinking skills as well as other skills. As we saw earlier, discussions are superior to lectures in improving thinking and problem solving.

Many studies point to the importance of developing understanding rather than simply teaching routine steps for problem solving. Increasing understanding and skill lead in turn to increased intrinsic motivation for thinking.

In conclusion, at least three elements of teaching seem to make a difference in student gains in thinking skills: 1) student writing and discussion, 2) explicit emphasis on problem-solving procedures and methods using varied examples, and 3) verbalization of methods and strategies to encourage development of metacognition.

SUPPLEMENTARY READING

There are a number of good books for courses in thinking. These books are also useful references for teachers who want to improve thinking in their own subject-matter courses. Here are a few:

J. D. Bransford and B. S. Stein, *The Ideal Problem Solver*, 2nd ed. (San Francisco: Freeman, 1993).

D. F. Halpern, *Thought and Knowledge*, 2nd ed. (Hillsdale, NJ: Erlbaum, 1989).

J. R. Hayes, *The Complete Problem Solver*, 2nd ed. (Hillsdale, NJ: Erlbaum, 1989).

CHAPTER 34

Teaching Values:
Should We? Can We?*

*A*S YOU MAY SUSPECT, this chapter would not be in the book if the answer to either question in its title were "No." So after answering "Yes," I will try to engage you in thinking with me about the more difficult questions, "What should we teach and how should we teach?"

Valuing is as natural as thinking or breathing. We automatically make value judgments about our experiences. "This was good, that was bad; this is beautiful, that's ugly." You have already made judgments about the value of this book. So our students are continually valuing. It would be strange if their college experiences had no impact on that valuing process. And, we as teachers are continually guided in our behavior by our values. I

---

* In thinking about our role in teaching values, I owe much to Brewster Smith, both for his writing about psychology and values and for my interactions with him through the years. We served together for many years on the Board of Directors of the American Psychological Association and I always admired the consistency with which he exemplified his own values in his behavior and comments on various controversial issues. We haven't always agreed but I think we both tried to represent our values when issues came before us. I have benefited from Brewster's comments on an earlier draft of this chapter as well as from thoughtful reactions by Larry Greenfield and George Lambrides, but none of the above should be held responsible for the final version which was influenced by some, but not all, of their ideas.

write on this topic because of my own basic values. They influence this choice of topic; they strongly influence what I'm going to write; and they influenced me in thinking that it was important to get teachers thinking with me about our role in teaching values. And because my major point is that we ought to be more open in our discussion of values, I should begin by giving you a brief statement of my own values—the perspective from which this chapter is written.

I'm a strongly religious person, a humanist active in my local American Baptist church. I believe strongly that love and respect for other human beings is not a *relative* value—simply a current norm taught in our society—but is rather a universal value that should guide the behavior of all human beings at all times. As a Baptist I have a passionate commitment to talking with people about theology, philosophy of religion, ethics, and values issues. I believe that no one has the ultimate answer to the question human beings have wrestled with since the beginning of human self-consciousness—"What is Good?" Each of us must make a commitment to the best we can conceive of, to give our insights to fellow human beings, and to welcome their thoughts in order that we may come closer to the unknowable, ultimate truth.

■ *Should We?*

That, of course, implies that I think we *should* teach values. In fact, I argue that we can't avoid teaching values. Our values inevitably influence our teaching. Value neutrality, so-called "value-free teaching," is simply advocacy by default. It's using our influence covertly, rather than openly. Our choice of content, our choice of teaching methods, our very manner of lecturing or conducting discussions reveal our values and influences our students' reactions. My own subject matter, psychology, is particularly value-laden. Concepts such as "mental health," "adjustment," "maturity," "personality integration," and "effective leadership" all involve value terms that we sometimes teach to our students as if they were scientific constructs developed in an empirical way on the basis of research without any value implications.

I was a mathematics major as an undergraduate, and even in this purest of disciplines there were values; some proofs were more beautiful than others; the examples and illustrations intended to maintain our interest carried certain implicit values. So, even though some disciplines probably face value questions less directly than others, we teachers cannot escape being influenced by our values. Thus the answer to the question "Should we teach values?" is, I suggest, that we can't avoid teaching values.

"But," you say, "isn't it a misuse of our position if we indoctrinate students with our values?" True. Probably our avoidance of explicit attention to values results from our concern about the evil of indoctrination. But there are two aspects to my answer.

> The *first* is that I would have no compunction about indoctrination with respect to such values as honesty and respect for other individuals as human beings. We cannot teach our students well if they plagiarize papers, fake laboratory results, or cheat on examinations. We cannot carry out effective classroom discussions without an atmosphere of respect for others' feelings or a sense of shared humanity. In a multicultural society such as ours there is a special need for thinking seriously about values—how we differ and what we share.

> The *second* is that we can help students to become more sensitive to values issues, to recognize value implications, to understand others' values, without indoctrination. Even with respect to fundamental values such as honesty, discussion, exploration, and debate about their implications are more useful than simple advocacy. Open consideration of value issues is probably less subversive than disregarding values altogether.

▬ *Can We?*

This leaves us with the second question: "Can we?" Do we have an impact? There is research evidence that we do. Or at least that somebody does. Students do change during their college years. There have been a number of studies of college graduates versus non-college graduates (with reasonable controls for socioeconomic status and other factors) that show differences. In general these are supported by longitudinal studies showing similar differences between student values at the beginning of their college years as compared with their values toward the end of their senior year (Pascarella and Terenzini, 1991).

Among the sometimes modest *average* changes, there are great *individual* changes, as well as changes of particular groups according to the curricula chosen, social groupings, or other elements of the college culture. So students change while they're in college; the issue for us is: Does our teaching make a difference?

Certainly teaching is one element of the culture that supports or opposes other elements of the culture, some of which may be pulling in different directions. The social culture, the fraternity/sorority culture, the athletic culture, the bar and tavern culture, the administrative, institutional culture—even the culture of religious groups—these and others are also influencing the students.

Here again we have some research evidence. Teaching can make a difference. A number of studies, in fact, have found changes in values and attitudes in individual courses in which different teaching methods were compared. In general, courses with more emphasis upon discussion or active learning methods have more influence than those in which students are passive (McKeachie et al., 1990). Thus we can answer the question "Can we?" affirmatively. The questions now become: "What should we be teaching? How should we teach values?"

▪ *What Values Should We Teach?*

Those who say we should be taking a neutral stance on values typically are restricting their definition of values to sociopolitical ones. Very few would dispute the fact that we are concerned about honesty, respect for others, and rationality. A major goal of education presumably is to increase students' skills in critical, rational thinking. We want students to value rational thought, but not at the exclusion of other ways of knowing and thinking. In considering problems in society or in their everyday lives our graduates will, I hope, look for evidence rather than react on the basis of unreasoning prejudice; they will be aware of the implications of their values, but not let their values close their minds.

Particularly in social science courses we ask our students to ask "What is the evidence?" before jumping to conclusions. Even those who point out that "rationality" has sometimes been defined in ways that confirm power and status relationships present rational arguments and evidence for their position. Our greater sensitivity to the issues raised by feminist and other critics is itself a tribute to rationality.

In psychology courses we expect our students to learn respect for individuality and freedom of choice, particularly as this involves treatment of human beings in research studies. We train our graduate students not to exploit their status or power over students or clients for participation in research or for sexual or other activities that are outside the bounds of the normal college course requirements.

Through the years my own thinking has changed. The first research project I coordinated was a study in which we compared three methods of teaching: discussion, tutorial, and recitation-drill. We worked very hard to be sure that the teachers in our sample conformed to these methods in their three classes. I now feel that it is not ethical for me to require a teacher, as part of an experiment, to teach in a way that the teacher thinks is not the best way that he or she can teach. So I no longer attempt to constrain my experiments in the same way. When I run an experiment in a real class, I try to add something beyond what the teacher would ordinarily do—something that both the teacher and I believe will enhance the students' educational experience, rather than constraining the teacher in ways that might be detrimental to the students.

The big question in teaching is what to do about controversial social and political values. Here it seems to me that we are not privileged to demand acceptance of our own values, as I think we are privileged to do with respect to requiring academic honesty. But this does not imply avoiding values issues. Too often we communicate by the way we handle touchy material—that you don't rock the boat by taking a position.

In avoiding controversial issues we communicate the notion that it may be all right to talk about these things in dormitories or in other places, but not in educational settings where rational arguments and the complexities of the issue are more likely to be salient.

The apple of temptation for us as teachers is that we may too easily accept affirmation of values that we share, letting students get away with simply stating a position that we agree with, without asking for rational support as we might for a position that conflicts with our own.

On the other side, however, is the problem of dealing with those with whom we disagree. There is the danger that we will yield to the temptation of demolishing the student with the force of our logic, but arguing can also be a way of showing respect. Remember that the power you have in your role as teacher may make it difficult for the student to muster a strong defense. Take it easy until students trust you enough to argue without fear of retribution. It is all too easy to intentionally, or unintentionally, coerce students into overt agreement.

Perry (1970, 1981) has described the development of Harvard students as progressing from the dualistic belief that things are either true or false, good or evil, through a stage of relativism in which they feel all beliefs are equally valid, to a stage of commitment to values and beliefs that are recognized to be incomplete and imperfect but are open to correction and further development. We may not all reach Perry's highest stage, or we may reach it in some areas but not in others, but Perry suggests that as teachers and members of the community of learners, we have the responsibility not only to model commitment and open-mindedness but also to share our own doubts and uncertainties. He says, ". . . we need to teach dialectically—that is, to introduce our students, as our greatest teachers have introduced us, not only to the orderly certainties of our subject matter, but to its unresolved dilemmas. This is an art that requires timing, learned only by paying close attention to students' ways of making meaning" (Perry, 1981, p. 109).

We need to teach students to begin to become aware of the complexities of their positions, of the fact that there are always costs and gains—trade-offs between competing values. Just as teachers in music are not satisfied when their students simply like a particular symphony or a particular kind of music, but insist that the students develop a disciplined appreciation of the complexity underlying their preferences, so too in other disciplines we need to help students value and understand the pros and cons, the arguments and evidence that are involved in critical judgments and decisions. In the social sciences we need to communicate that liking people or liking certain kinds of people or institutions and their values is not enough. Our ethical judgments in human affairs need to have at least as much complexity in their analysis and exposition as we would give to analyzing the strengths and weaknesses of our favorite baseball team or our judgments of restaurants.

My major concern is not that we teach values such as honesty that we agree are essential to the academic enterprise, but that we be open and explicit in helping our students to become *sensitive* to values issues. Whichever side they come out on, they should be aware that large numbers of things that we take for granted in this world involve serious moral and ethical values. Much of the evil that I see is not just the result of lack of values but rather a lack of sensitivity to value implications of actions or policies that are more or less taken for granted or are accepted as part of one's role in an institution—governmental, business, or academic.

In American political and foreign affairs it has often seemed to me that some of the members of our administration were ethically deficient. Their behavior was governed by immediate gains and what was expedient in the situation rather than by underlying basic values. But I also think there were some officials who had values, but simply were not sensitive to the values involved in their behavior in their political and institutional roles.

In college I hope that students will develop firm enough commitments and have enough practice in considering values issues that in most situations they automatically act in accordance with their values. But I also hope that they will be more likely and able to think about values implications in the many areas in which values are not salient or where values are in conflict.

The Dutch psychologist Elshout (1987) suggests that there are three levels of problems. I believe that his metaphor can be extended to values issues and decision making as well.

Elshout says that the first zone is one in which no thinking is needed. The problem solver can solve the problem automatically on the basis of previous knowledge and expertise. Similarly there are situations in which we don't have to think about values issues because we automatically do the right thing. (This is not to imply that such values are immune from examination!)

But there is a second, problematic zone where the solution is not obvious and the problem solver has to think about alternative ways of approaching the problem because there is no obvious solution. Nonetheless, the problem solver tackles the problem because he or she has skills and strategies that may lead to a solution. Similarly there are ethical issues that we recognize as ethical problems and can resolve with appropriate consideration of the pros and cons.

Elshout then suggests that there is a top zone where the situation is so complicated, so remote from our experience that we don't know what approach to use and our usual strategies of problem solving are no longer likely to be very effective. So too in ethics there are problems that we fail to recognize, or if recognized, simply avoid thinking about.

In the area of ethics and values we hope that as teachers we can expand the area in which humane values are carried out as the normal pattern of behavior; we hope to increase our students' ability to consider and weigh conflicting values in the middle zone, to consult others when in doubt, and we also hope to cut down the big area where our students avoid considering values because the whole area seems so complicated that they don't want to think.

■■■■ *How Can We Teach Values?*

We exemplify and communicate our values in the way we teach. The value of freedom of inquiry is exemplified in our reactions to challenges from students, as well as in the way we react to attacks on academic freedom at the level of the university as a whole.

Probably every teacher, whether in the arts, the sciences, or the professions, tries to teach students that it is not enough simply to respond to material or performance as good or bad, but rather to be able to back up one's judgment with evidence that is reasonable in terms of the standards of that discipline. We communicate that value by our comments on papers, our reactions to student comments or performance, and ultimately by our grades. So we have a group of values that we accept and either explicitly or implicitly communicate to our students through our behavior as teachers.

Our values also affect our course planning. We begin with the goals we take for the course. Who should determine those goals? Is this something to be determined by the university, by the department, by the instructor, or should students be involved? Personally, I have faith that in a situation in which students and faculty members participate jointly, our decisions will come out with reasonable values, reasonable content, and reasonable coverage—all the things that we worry about when we're thinking about how to set up a course. A cooperative approach exemplifies the value of respect for others.

Experiential Learning

Idealism isn't dead among students. The ACE surveys (Dey et al., 1991) show that goals such as helping other people and developing a philosophy of life have been dropping in relation to more materialistic goals, such as making lots of money. Nonetheless, half or more of our students see more altruistic values as major goals for their college years, and the more recent surveys show a slight upward trend for humanistic values.

Evaluations of our experiential courses, Project Outreach and Project Community, at the University of Michigan suggest that these courses have had some success in affecting student values. Such courses tend to confirm and reinforce altruistic values and probably help make students' altruistic impulses become more realistic as to the complexities of helping other people. Additional research supporting the value of experiential learning may be found in Quinn (1972) and D. Kiel (1972).

Confronting Alternative Views

One major values issue in teaching is whether to present a single view or multiple positions in areas where theories differ.

Certainly our students prefer that we tell them the "truth." They'd like to have the truth presented clearly and in a structured way. And I suppose that if you really believe strongly that a particular position is true, you should teach that position. But I don't think that relieves you of the obligation to let students know that there is a competing theory. One of the great barriers to learning is the students' belief that their teachers have the truth, that the teacher's job is to present the truth, and that the students' job is to learn the truth and be able to give it back on an examination.

As teachers and scholars we must hold to the faith that even though there is little, if any, unchanging absolute "truth," the positions we hold to be closer to truth than the alternatives can be supported by evidence and reason. Our task is to help students develop the habits of thinking that are used in our disciplines to determine what is more or less valid.

In the social sciences we can use cross-cultural research that indicates to our students that there are different ways of viewing the world and differing value positions on a number of things that we take for granted.

What kinds of teaching methods should we use? There is some relevant research evidence here. One of the classic studies was done by Stern and Cope (1956) (also Stern, 1962) at Syracuse some years ago. Using the scales developed by Stern, Stein, and Bloom (1956) to measure ethnocentrism, they selected students who had an authoritarian, conservative, rigid personality, with stereotyped conceptions of race, minorities, and others different from themselves. These students were assigned to a special discussion section. Their achievement in this homogeneous section proved to be superior to that of similar students in conventional sections of the course.

What did the teacher do with these students who were unusually difficult to teach? At the beginning of the term the instructor of the homogeneous section was distressed by the students' lack of responsiveness and negativism, but he adopted a strategy of frequently taking a devil's advocate position in which he would present strong positions that would arouse the students so much that they simply had to respond. The ensuing debate resulted in changes that didn't occur in the classes where similar students were able to sit back and not participate. The students in the experimental class not only performed better academically but also became less ethnocentric and authoritarian than similar students in the conventional classes. This finding fits with research comparing discussions versus lectures, suggesting that more attitude change occurs in discussion sections.

Cooperative peer learning often has a positive effect upon attitudes and values. Cooperation is itself an important value in our culture, and success in learning how to work cooperatively with other students in a project or other learning experience is likely to have a positive impact upon students' value for cooperation.

The results of the studies of discussion methods, cooperative learning, and experiential learning fit with our theories of change. If we want students to change, they have to have a chance to express their ideas and values in words or actions and see how they work. They need reactions not only from teachers but also from peers and others who share or oppose their positions.

We know that students remember the content of our courses better if they elaborate the content by relating it to other knowledge—if they question, explain, or summarize. Such elaboration is important in the values area as well. And, it's important that the discussion and experiences be in places where there is mutual respect and support. Values are not likely to be changed much simply by passively listening and observing a lecturer. Change is more likely in situations in which the teacher, as well as students, listen and learn from one another.

■■■ *The Teacher as a Person*

The teaching methods one uses may be less important than aspects of teaching that cut across methods. The degree to which students feel we know them as individuals and care about their learning, the extent to which they feel they know us as individuals (not simply as experts or authorities), the openness we have to questions and opposing points of view, our willingness to risk change in ourselves—these have much to do with the students' willingness to open their values to examination and change.

Teaching does not end at the classroom door. Wilson et al. (1975) found that professors who were perceived by students and colleagues as having significant impact on student development demanded high standards of performance and interacted a great deal with students both in and *out* of the classroom. When students see that you are willing to sacrifice time from your own endeavors in order to help them, you communicate your values.

◼◼◼ *Conclusion*

We develop values by observing and modeling ourselves after others and testing out our values in thought and words and action. Teachers are significant models, and teacher behavior is important, both as it models values and as teachers create situations in which the expression of values becomes salient.

The process of value development and value change is very much like the process of scientific theory development or of self-development in general. For example, we have experiences; we develop ways of trying to think about those experiences to make sense of them; we test our theories (in this case our values) by consciously thinking about them, by studying what others have said or done, by talking to other people, and by behaving and seeing what happens. My basic faith is that everyone has within himself or herself the capacity to discriminate good from evil and to act to achieve the good. William James said, "The significance of religious belief is not in affirmation, but in its consequences for behavior." And so it is with values in general.

St. Augustine wrote, "Hope has two lovely daughters, anger and courage. Anger at the way things are, and courage to see that they need not remain as they are." Let us have hope.

SUPPLEMENTARY READING

A thoughtful discussion of these as well as ethical issues in teaching may be found in:

W. L. Humphreys, Values in teaching and the teaching of values, *Teaching-Learning Issues No. 58* (Knoxville, TN: Learning Research Center, The University of Tennessee, 1986).

W. J. MCKEACHIE
*The University of Michigan**

Student Perceptions of Learning and Teaching

*T*HE ITEMS ON THIS QUESTIONNAIRE ask you to comment on various aspects of your course.

The questionnaire has eight brief parts. The first part is intended to assess your perception of your own learning; the second part is your perception of characteristics related to instructor effectiveness. Other parts are not evaluative, but are intended to assess aspects of teacher style. They ask for a description, not an evaluation. For example, either a high or low degree of structure may be effective.

Thank you for taking the time to fill this form out thoughtfully. Your answers and comments will help your teacher improve the course.

Date: _____   Your Class Standing (Circle):

Course: _____   FR   SOPH   JR   SR   GRAD

Instructor: _____

---

* Teachers are welcome to use this form or items from it without requesting permission from the author.

Your GPA in all courses at this college:

3.5–4.0 _____   2.0–2.4 _____   Sex: Male   Female

3.0–3.4 _____   0–1.9 _____

2.5–2.9 _____

Use the following scale:

1–almost never or almost nothing   4–often or much
2–seldom or little   5–very often
3–occasionally or moderate   6–almost always, a great deal
                                    If not applicable, leave blank

Impact on Students

1. My intellectual curiosity has been stimulated by this course.
   Comments:

2. I am learning how to think more clearly about the area of this course.
   Comments:

Student Information Processing

3. My mind wandered a good deal during class.
   Comments:

4. The instructor introduced new concepts so fast that I could not grasp them.
   Comments:

5. I tried to relate the course material to other things I know.
   Comments:

6. The course is increasing my interest in learning more about this area.
   Comments:

Instructor Effectiveness

7. The instructor is enthusiastic.
   Comments:

8. The instructor gives good examples of the concepts.
   Comments:

9. The instructor goes into too much detail.
   Comments:

10. The instructor is helpful when students are confused.
    Comments:

11. The instructor seems knowledgeable in many areas.
    Comments:

Rapport

12. The instructor knows students' names.
    Comments:

13. The instructor is friendly.
    Comments:

Group Interaction

14. Students volunteer their own opinions.
    Comments:

15. Students discuss one another's ideas.
    Comments:

16. Students feel free to disagree with the instructor.
    Comments:

Difficulty

17. The instructor makes difficult assignments.
    Comments:

18. The instructor asks for a great deal of work.
    Comments:

Structure

19. The instructor plans class activities in detail.
    Comments:

20. The instructor follows an outline closely.
    Comments:

Feedback

21. The instructor keeps students informed of their progress.
    Comments:

22. The instructor tells students when they have done a particularly good job.
    Comments:

23. Tests and papers are graded and returned promptly.
    Comments:

Notice!!! This Scale Is Different!!!

Student Responsibility

1–definitely false	4–more true than false
2–more false than true	5–definitely true
3–in between	If not applicable, leave blank

24. I had a strong desire to take this course.
    Comments:

25. I actively participate in class discussions.
    Comments:

26. I try to make a tie-in between what I am learning through the
    course and my own experience.
    Comments:

27. I attend class regularly.
    Comments:

28. I utilize all the learning opportunities provided in the course.
    Comments:

29. I have created learning experiences for myself in connection
    with the course.
    Comments:

30. I have helped classmates learn.
    Comments:

Overall Evaluation

Indicate your evaluation of characteristics below, using numbers based on the following scale:

1 Poor   2 Fair   3 Good   4 Very Good   5 Excellent

31. Rate the instructor's general teaching effectiveness for you.
    Comments:

32. Rate the value of the course as a whole to you.
    Comments:

Added Comments Below

Comments

References

Abbott, R. D., et al. Satisfaction with processes of collecting student opinions about instruction: a student perspective. *Journal of Educational Psychology* , 1990, *82*, 201–206.

Adams, J. C.; Carter, C. R.; and Smith, D. R., eds. *College teaching by television*. Washington, D. C.: American Council on Education, 1959.

Adams, M. Cultural inclusion in the American college classroom. In L. Border and N. Chism, eds. Teaching for diversity, *New Directions in Teaching and Learning, 49*, pp. 5–17. San Francisco: Jossey-Bass, 1992.

Ajzen, I., and Madden, T. J. Prediction of goal directed behavior: Attitudes, intentions, and perceived behavioral control. *Journal of Experimental Social Psychology*, 1986, *22*, 453–474.

Albright, M. J., and Graf, D. L., eds. Teaching in the information age: the role of electronic technology. *New directions for teaching and learning, no. 51*. San Francisco: Jossey-Bass, 1992.

Aleamoni, L. M. The usefulness of student evaluations in improving college teaching. *Instructional Science*, 1978, *7*, 95–105.

———. Student ratings of instruction. In J. Millman, ed. *Handbook of teacher evaluation*, pp. 110–145. Beverly Hills, CA: Sage, 1981.

Alexander, P. A., and Judy, J. E. The interaction of domain-specific and strategic knowledge in academic performance. *Review of Educational Research*, 1988, *58*(4), 375–404.

Allen, B. P., and Niss, J. F. A chill in the college classroom? *Phi Delta Kappan*, 1990, *71*, 607–609.

Allen, W. H. Audio-visual communication. In C. W. Harris, ed. *Encyclopedia of educational research*, 3rd. ed. New York: Macmillan, 1960.

American Association of University Professors. Statement on professional ethics. *Academe*, 1987, *73*(4), 49.

Anandam, K. Camelot is here and now. *TIES* (Technological Innovations in Educational Settings), 1984, No. 10, 1–2.

Anderson, C. A., and Jennings, D. L. When experiences of failure promote expectations of success: the impact of attributing failure to ineffective strategies. *Journal of Personality*, 1980, *48*, 393–407.

Anderson, J. A., and Adams, M. Acknowledging the learning styles of diverse populations: Implications for instructional design. In L. Border and N. Chism, eds. Teaching for diversity, *New directions in teaching and learning, 49*, pp. 19–33. San Francisco: Jossey-Bass, 1992.

Anderson, R. C. Learning in discussion: a resume of the authoritarian-democratic studies. *Harvard Educational Review*, 1959, *29*, 201–267.

Anderson, R. P., and Kelly, B. L. Student attitudes about participation in classroom groups. *Journal of Educational Research*, 1954, *48*, 255–267.

Andre, T. Questions and learning from reading. *Questioning Exchange*, 1987, *1*(1), 47–86.

Angelo, T. A., and Cross, K. P. *Classroom assessment techniques: a handbook for college faculty*, 2nd ed. San Francisco: Jossey-Bass, 1993.

Annis, L. F. Effect of preference for assigned lecture notes on student achievement. *Journal of Educational Research*, 1981, *74*, 179–181.

———. The processes and effects of peer tutoring. *Human Learning*, 1983, *2*, 39–47.

———. *Study techniques*. Dubuque: Wm. C. Brown, 1983.

Antioch College. Experiment in French language instruction. *Antioch College Reports*. Yellow Springs, OH: Office of Educational Research, Antioch College, October 1960.

Arbes, B., and Kitchener, K. G. Faculty consultation: a study in support of education through student interaction. *Journal of Counseling Psychology*, 1974, *21*, 121–126.

Argyris, C. Some limitations of the case method. *Academy of Management Review*, 1980, *5*, 291–298.

Arons, A. B. Computer-based instructional dialogs. *Science*, 1984, *224*, 1051–1056.

Asante, M. K. *The Afrocentric idea*. Philadelphia: Temple University Press, 1987.

———. *Afrocentricity*. Trenton, NJ: Africa World Press, 1988.

Asch, M. J. Non-directive teaching in psychology: an experimental study. *Psychological Monographs*, 1951, *65*, no. 4.

Ashmus, M., and Haigh, G. *Some factors which may be associated with student choice between directive and non-directive classes*. Springfield, MA: Springfield College, 1952.

Astin, A. *Preventing students from dropping out*. San Francisco: Jossey-Bass, 1975.

Atkinson, J. W., and Litwin, G. H. Achievement motive and test anxiety conceived as motive to approach success and motive to avoid failure. *Journal of Abnormal and Social Psychology*, 1960, *60*, 52–63.

Atkinson, J. W., and O'Connor, P. A. *Effects of ability grouping in schools related to individual differences in achievement-related motivation*. Final Report, Office of Education, Cooperative Research Project 1238, 1963.

Atkinson, R. C. Ingredients for a theory of instruction. *American Psychologist*, 1972, *27*, 921–931.

Attiyeh, R., and Lumsden, K. G. Some modern myths in teaching economics: the U. K. experience. *American Economics Review*, 1972, *62*, 429–433.

Axelrod, J. Group dynamics, nondirective therapy, and college teaching. *Journal of Higher Education*, 1955, *26*, 200–207.

Bainter, M. E. A study of the outcomes of two types of laboratory techniques used in a course in general college physics for students planning to be teachers in the elementary grades. *Dissertation Abstracts*, 1955, *15*, 2485–2486.

Balcziak, L. W. The role of the laboratory and demonstration in college physical science in achieving the objectives of general education. Ph.D. diss., University of Minnesota, *Dissertation Abstracts*, 1954, *14*, 502–503.

Banathy, B. H., and Jordan, B. A classroom laboratory instructional system (CLIS). *Foreign Language Annals*, 1969, *2*, 466–473.

Bandura, A. Self-efficacy: toward a unifying theory of behavioral change. *Psychological Review*, March 1977, *84*(2), 191–215.

Bane, C. L. The lecture vs. the class-discussion method of college teaching. *School and Society*, 1925, *21*, 300–302.

Banks, J. A. Approaches to multicultural curriculum reform. *Multicultural Leader*, Spring 1988, *3*.

Bargh, J. A., and Schul, Y. On the cognitive benefits of teaching. *Journal of Educational Psychology*, 1980, *72*(5), 593–604.

Barnard, J. D. The lecture demonstration vs. the problem-solving method of teaching a college science course. *Science Education*, 1942, 26, 121–132.

Barnard, W. H. Note on the comparative efficacy of lecture and social-ized recitation method vs. group study method. *Journal of Educational Psychology*, 1936, *27*, 388–390.

Barrow, H. S., Myers, A., Williams, and Moticka, E. J. Large group prob-lem-based learning: a possible solution for the '2 sigma problem.' *Medical Teaching* 1986, *8*(4), 325–331.

Bauer, R. The obstinate audience: the influence of process from the point of view of social communication. *American Psychologist*, 1964, *19*, 319–328.

Baxter Magolda, M. B. *Knowing and reasoning in college: Gender-related pat-terns in students' intellectual development*. San Francisco: Jossey-Bass, 1992.

Beach, L. R. Sociability and academic achievement in various types of learning situations. *Journal of Educational Psychology*, 1960, *51*, 208–212.

———. *Student interaction and learning in small self-directed college groups*. Final Report. Washington, D. C.: Department of Health, Education and Welfare, June 1968.

Beach, R., and Bridwell, L. Learning through writing: a rationale for writ-ing across the curriculum. In A. Pellegrini and T. Yawkey, eds. *The development of oral and written language in social contexts*. Norwood, NJ: Abbey, 1984.

Beard, R. M. *Teaching and learning in higher education*. Middlesex, England: Penguin Books, 1972.

Beardslee, D.; Birney, R.; and McKeachie, W. J. Summary of conference on research in classroom processes. Mimeo, Department of Psychology, University of Michigan, 1951.

Becker, S. K.; Murray, J. N.; and Bechtoldt, H. P. *Teaching by the discussion method*. Iowa City: State University of Iowa, 1958.

Belenky, M. F.; Clinchy, B. M.; Goldberger, N. R.; and Tarule, J. M. *Women's ways of knowing: the development of self, voice, and mind*. New York: Basic Books, 1986.

Bendig, A. W. Ability and personality characteristics of introductory psy-chology instructors rated competent and empathic by their students. *Journal of Educational Research*, 1955, *48*, 705–709.

Benjamin, L. Personalization and active learning in the large introductory psychology class. *Teaching of Psychology*, 1991, *18*(2), 68–74.

Berger, M. In defense of the case method. A reply to Argyris. *Academy of Management Review*, 1983, *8*, 329–333.

Berlyne, D. E. A theory of human curiosity. *British Journal of Psychology*, 1954a, *45*, 180–181.

———. An experimental study of human curiosity. *British Journal of Psychology*, 1954b, *45*, 256–265.

———. *Conflict, arousal, and curiosity*. New York: McGraw-Hill, 1960.

Berman, A. I. *Balanced learning*. New York: Harper & Row, 1973.

———. Media-activated seminar. *Educational Technology*, March 1974, 43–45.

Bills, R. E. Investigation of student centered teaching. *Journal of Educational Research*, 1952, *46*, 313–319.

Blackwell, J. E. Operationalizing faculty diversity. *AAHE Bulletin*, 1990, *42*(10), 8–9.

Bligh, D. A. A pilot experiment to test the relative effectiveness of three kinds of teaching methods. *Research in Librarianship*, 1970, *3*, 88–93.

Bligh, D. A.; Ebrahims, G. J.; Jacques, D.; and Piper, D. W. *Teaching students*. Devon, England: Exeter University Teaching Service, 1975.

Bligh, D., et al. *Methods and techniques of teaching in post-secondary education*. Paris: UNESCO, 1980.

Bloom, B. S. Thought processes in lectures and discussions. *Journal of General Education*, 1953, *7*, 160–169.

———, ed. *Taxonomy of educational objectives, handbook I: Cognitive domain*. New York: Longmans, Green, 1956.

Bloom, B. S., and Broder, L. J. *Problem solving processes of college students*. Chicago: University of Chicago Press, 1950.

Blumenfeld, P. C., et al. Motivating project-based learning: Sustaining the doing, supporting the learning. *Educational Psychologist*, 1991, *26*, 369–398.

Border, L., and Chism, N., eds. Teaching for diversity. *New directions in teaching and learning 49*. San Francisco: Jossey-Bass, 1992.

Borgida, E., and Nisbett, R. E. The differential impact of abstract vs. concrete information on decisions. *Journal of Applied Social Psychology*, 1977, *7*, 258–271.

Boris, E. Z. Classroom minutes: a valuable teaching device. *Improving College and University Teaching*, 1983, *31*(2), 70–73.

Bork, A. *The physics computer development project*. Irvine, CA: Department of Physics, University of California, 1975.

———. *Learning with computers*. Bedford, MA: Digital Press, 1981.

Bouton, C., and Garth, R. Learning in Groups. *New directions for teaching and learning, 14*. San Francisco: Jossey-Bass, 1983.

Bovard, E. W., Jr. Group structure and perception. *Journal of Abnormal and Social Psychology*, 1951a, *46*, 398–405.

———. The experimental production of interpersonal affect. *Journal of Abnormal Psychology*, 1951b, *46*, 521–528.

Bradley, R. L. Lecture demonstration vs. individual laboratory work in a natural science course at Michigan State University. *Dissertation Abstracts*, 1963, *23*, 4568.

Branch-Simpson, G. *Black student development: an Afrocentric perspective*. Paper presented at the Conference on the Decline of Black Enrollment in Higher Education, St. Louis, MO, February, 1988.

Bransford, J. D. *Human cognition: Learning, understanding, and remembering*. Belmont, CA: Wadsworth, 1979.

Bransford, J. D., and Stein, B. S. *The ideal problem solver*. 2nd edition. New York: W. H. Freeman, 1993.

Branson, R. K. The schoolyear 2000 concept. Address at Northwestern University, March 7, 1991.

Braskamp, L. A.; Brandenberg, D. C.; and Ory, J. C. *Evaluating teaching effectiveness: a practical guide*. Beverly Hills, CA: Sage, 1984.

Braunstein, D. N.; Klein, G. A.; and Pachla, M. Feedback, expectancy and shifts in student ratings of college faculty. *Journal of Applied Psychology*, 1973, *58*, 254–258.

Bronfenbrenner, U. A Cornell study relating to grading conditions. *Center for Improvement of Undergraduate Education Notes*, 1972, *3*, 2–4.

Brown, A. L. Metacognition, executive control, self-regulation, and other more mysterious mechanisms. In F. E. Weinert and R. H. Kluwe, eds. *Metacognition, motivation, and understanding*, pp. 65–116. Hillsdale, NJ: Erlbaum, 1987.

Brown, G. *Lecturing and explaining*. London: Methuen, 1980.

Brown, G., and Atkins, M. *Effective teaching in higher education*. London: Methuen, 1988.

Brown, R. D., and Krager, L. Ethical issues in graduate education: Faculty and student responsibilities. *Journal of Higher Education*, 1985, *56*, 403–418.

Burke, H. R. An experimental study of teaching methods in college freshman orientation course. Ph. D. diss., Boston University. *Dissertation Abstracts*, 1956, *16*, 77–78.

Butler, J. E. Transforming the curriculum: Teaching about women of color. In J. A. Banks and C. A. McGee Banks, eds. *Multicultural education: Issues and perspectives*, pp. 145–163. Boston: Allyn and Bacon, 1989.

Cahn, M. M. Teaching through student models. In P. Runkel et al., eds. *The changing college classroom*. San Francisco: Jossey-Bass, 1972.

Cahn, S. M. *Saints and scamps: Ethics in academia*. Totowa, NJ: Rowman & Littlefield, 1982.

Calvin, A. D.; Hoffman, F. K.; and Harden, E. L. The effect of intelligence and social atmosphere on group problem solving behavior. *Journal of Social Psychology*, 1957, *45*, 61–74.

Calvin, A. D.; McGuigan, F. J.; and Sullivan, M. W. A further investigation of the relationship between anxiety and classroom examination performance. *Journal of Educational Psychology*, 1957, *48*, 240–244.

Caron, M. D.; Whitbourne, S. K.; and Halgin, R. P. Fraudulent excuse making among college students. *Teaching of Psychology*, 1992, *19*(2), 90–93.

Carpenter, C. R. The Penn State pyramid plan: Interdependent student work study grouping for increasing motivation for academic development. Paper read at 14th National Conference on Higher Education, Chicago, March 1959.

Carpenter, C. R., and Greenhill, L. P. *An investigation of closed-circuit television for teaching university courses*. Instructional Television Research Project No. 1. University Park: Pennsylvania State University, 1955.

———. *An investigation of closed-circuit television for teaching university courses*. Instructional Television Research Project No. 2. University Park: Pennsylvania State University, 1958.

Carrier, N. A. The relationship of certain personality measures to examination performance under stress. *Journal of Educational Psychology*, 1957, *48*, 510–520.

Carroll, J. B. Research on teaching foreign languages. In N. L. Gage, ed. *Handbook of research on teaching*, pp. 1060–1100. Chicago: Rand McNally & Company, 1963.

Casey, J. E., and Weaver, B. F. An evaluation of lecture method and small-group method of teaching in terms of knowledge of content, teacher attitude, and social status. *Journal of Colorado-Wyoming Academy of Science*, 1956, *7*, 54.

Centra, J. A. The effectiveness of student feedback in modifying college instruction. *Journal of Educational Psychology*, 1973, *65*, 395–401.

———. The relationship between student and alumni ratings of teachers. *Educational and Psychological Measurement*, 1974, *34*(2), 321–326.

———. Colleagues as raters of classroom instruction. *Journal of Higher Education*, 1975, *46*, 327–337.

———. Student ratings of instruction and their relationship to student learning. *American Educational Research Journal*, 1977, *14*, 17–24.

———. *Determining faculty effectiveness*. San Francisco: Jossey-Bass, 1979.

Chance, C. W. Experimentation in the adaptation of the overhead projector utilizing 200 transparencies and 800 overlays in teaching engineering descriptive geometry curricula. *Audio-Visual Communications Review*, 1961, *9*, A17–A18.

Chang, T. M.; Crombag, H. F.; van der Drift, K. D. J. M.; and Moonen, J. M. *Distance learning: on the design of an open university*. Boston: Kluwer-Nijhoff, 1983.

Cheydleur, F. D. Criteria of effective teaching in basic French courses. *Bulletin of the University of Wisconsin*, August 1945.

Chi, M. T. H.; Glaser, R.; and Farr, M. J., eds. *The nature of expertise*. Hillsdale, NJ: Erlbaum, 1988.

Christensen, C. R., and Hansen, A. J. *Teaching and the case method*. Boston: Harvard Business School, 1987.

Churchill, L. R. The teaching of ethics and moral values in teaching. *Journal of Higher Education*, 1982, *53*(3), 296–306.

Churchill, R. *Preliminary report on reading course study*, (Mimeo). Yellow Springs, OH: Antioch College, 1957.

Churchill, R., and Baskin, S. *Experiment on independent study*, (Mimeo). Yellow Springs, OH: Antioch College, 1958.

Churchill, R., and John, P. Conservation of teaching time through the use of lecture classes and student assistants. *Journal of Educational Psychology*, 1958, *49*, 324–327.

Clark, R. E. Reconsidering research on learning from media. *Review of Educational Research*, 1983, *53*, 445–459.

Clarke, J. H. Designing discussions as group inquiry. *College Teaching*, 1988, *36*(4), 140–146.

Cohen, P.; Kulik, J.; and Kulik, C.-L. Educational outcomes of tutoring: a meta-analysis of findings. *American Educational Research Journal*, 1982, *19*(2), 237–248.

Cohen, P. A. Student ratings of instruction and student achievement: a meta-analysis of multisection validity studies. *Review of Educational Research*, 1981, *51*, 281–309.

Cole, M.; Cay, J.; Glick, J.; and Sharp, D. W. *The cultural context of learning and thinking*. New York: Basic Books, 1971.

Coleman, J., and McKeachie, W. Effects of instructor/course evaluations on student course selection. *Journal of Educational Psychology*, 1981, *73*, 224–226.

Coleman, W. Role-playing as an instructional aid. *Journal of Educational Psychology*, 1948, *39*, 427–435.

Collett, J., and Serrano, B. Stirring it up: the inclusive classroom. In L. Border and N. Chism, eds. Teaching for diversity, *New directions in teaching and learning, 49*, pp. 35–48. San Francisco: Jossey-Bass, 1992.

Collier, G. The arrangement of peer group learning: Syndicate methods in higher education. Guildford, England: Society for Research in Higher Education, 1983.

Collins, A. Processes in acquiring knowledge. In R. C. Anderson, R. J. Spiro, and W. E. Montague, eds. *Schooling and the acquisition of knowledge*. Hillsdale, NJ: Erlbaum, 1977.

———. Goals and strategies of inquiry teaching. In R. Glaser, ed. *Advances in instructional psychology*. Hillsdale, NJ: Erlbaum, 1982.

———. Different goals of inquiry teaching. *Questioning Exchange*, 1988, *2*(1), 39–45.

———. The role of computer technology in restructuring schools. *Phi Delta Kappan*. 1991, *73*(1), 28–36.

Collins, A. M., and Quillian, M. R. How to make a language user. In E. Tulving and W. Donaldson, eds. *Organization of memory*. New York: Academic Press, 1972.

Cones, J. H.; Noonan, J. F.; and Jahna, J., eds. Teaching minority students. *New directions in teaching and learning 16*. San Francisco: Jossey-Bass, 1983.

Coombs, P. H. *The world educational crisis: a systems analysis* (Swedish ed.). Stockholm, Sweden: Bonniers, 1971.

Costin, F. Three-choice versus four-choice items: Implications for reliability and validity of objective achievement tests. *Educational and Psychological Measurement*, 1972, *32*, 1035–1038.

Covington, M. V., and Omelich, C. L. Task-oriented versus competitive learning structures: Motivational and performance consequences. *Journal of Educational Psychology*, 1984, *76*(6), 1038–1050.

Craik, F. I. M., and Lockhart, R. S. Levels of processing: a framework for memory research. *Journal of Verbal Learning and Verbal Behavior*, 1972, *11*, 671–684.

Creager, J. G., and Murray, D. L., eds. *The use of modules in college biology teaching*. Washington, D. C.: Commission on Undergraduate Education in the Biological Sciences, 1971.

Cronbach, L. J., and Snow, R. E. *Aptitudes and instructional methods: a handbook for research on interaction*. New York: Irvington, 1977.

Crooks, T. The impact of classroom evaluation practices on students. *Review of Educational Research*, 1988, *85*(4), 438–481.

Cross, D. An investigation of the relationship between students' expressions of satisfaction with certain aspects of the college classroom situation and their achievement on final examinations. Honors thesis, University of Michigan, 1958.

Cutler, R. L.; McKeachie, W. J.; and McNeil, E. B. Teaching psychology by telephone. *American Psychologist*, 1958, *13*, 551–552.

Cytrynbaum, S., and Mann, R. D. Community as campus. In P. Runkel, R. Harrison, and M. Runkel, eds. *The changing college classroom*, pp. 266–289. San Francisco: Jossey-Bass, 1972.

Dahlgren, L. O., and Marton, F. Investigations into the learning and teaching of economics. *Reports from The Institute of Education, University of Göteborg*, September 1976, No. 54.

Davage, R. H. *The pyramid plan for the systematic involvement of university students in teaching-learning functions*. Division of Academic Research and Services, Pennsylvania State University, 1958.

———. *Recent data on the pyramid project in psychology*. Division of Academic Research and Services, Pennsylvania State University, 1959.

Davis, B. G.; Wood, L.; and Wilson, R. C. *ABCs of teaching with excellence*. Berkeley, CA: University of California, 1983.

Davis, J. R. *Teaching strategies for the college classroom*. Boulder, CO: Westview Press, 1976.

Davis, S. F. Students and faculty: a beneficial interface. *Psi Chi Newsletter*, Spring 1992, 3–4.

Davis, S. F.; Grover, C. A.; Becker, A. H.; and McGregor, L. N. Academic dishonesty: Prevalence, determinants, techniques, and punishments. *Teaching of Psychology*, 1992, *19*(1), 16–20.

Dawson, M. D. Lectures vs. problem-solving in teaching elementary soil section. *Science Education*, 1956, *40*, 395–404.

Day, R. S. Teaching from notes: Some cognitive consequences. In W. J. McKeachie, ed. Learning, cognition, and college teaching. *New directions for teaching and learning, 2.* San Francisco: Jossey-Bass, 1980.

Dearden, D. M. An evaluation of the laboratory in a college general biology course. *Journal of Experimental Education*, March 1960, *26*(3), 241–247.

De Cecco, J. P. Class size and coordinated instruction. *British Journal of Educational Psychology*, 1964, *34*, 65–74.

Deese, J., and Deese, E. K. *How to study*, 3rd ed. New York: McGraw-Hill, 1979.

Deignan, F. J. A comparison of the effectiveness of two group discussion methods. Ph.D. diss., Boston University. *Dissertation Abstracts*, 1956, *16*, 1110–1111.

Dekkers, J., and Donatti, S. The integration of research studies on the use of stimulation as an instructional strategy. *Journal of Educational Research*, 1981, *74*(6).

Della-Piana, G. M. Two experimental feedback procedures: a comparison of their effects on the learning of concepts. Ph.D. diss., University of Illinois. *Dissertation Abstracts*, 1956, *16*, 910–911.

de Sola Pool, I. *Technology without boundaries*. Cambridge, MA: Harvard University Press, 1990.

Deutsch, M. An experimental study of the effects of cooperation and competition upon group processes. *Human Relations*, 1949, *2*, 199–232.

Dey, E. L.; Astin, A. W.; and Korn, W. S. *The American freshman: Twenty-five year trends, 1966–1990*. Los Angeles: Los Angeles Higher Education Research Institute, Graduate School of Education, University of CA, 1991.

Diamond, M. J. Improving the undergraduate lecture class by use of student-led discussion groups. *American Psychologist*, 1972, *27*, 978–981.

Dill, D. D. Professional ethics. *Journal of Higher Education*, 1982, *53*(3), 255–267.

Dillon, J. T. The effect of questions in education and other enterprises. *Journal of Curriculum Studies*, 1982, *14*, 127–152.

———. Using questions to foil discussion. Address at School of Education, University of California, Riverside, 1983.

———. *Teaching and the art of questioning*. Bloomington, IN: Phi Delta Kappa Educational Foundation, 1983.

Di Vesta, F. J. Instructor-centered and student-centered approaches in teaching a human relations course. *Journal of Applied Psychology*, 1954, *38*, 329–335.

Domino, G. Differential prediction of academic achievement in conforming and independent sections. *Journal of Educational Psychology,* 1968, *59,* 256–260.

———. Interactive effects of achievement orientation and teaching style on academic achievement. *Journal of Educational Psychology,* 1971, *62,* 427–431.

———. Aptitude by treatment interaction effects in college instruction. Paper presented at the meeting of the American Psychological Association, New Orleans, 1974.

Donald, J., and Sullivan, A., eds. *Using research to improve university teaching.* San Francisco: Jossey-Bass, 1985.

Dowaliby, F. J., and Schumer, H. Teacher-centered vs. student-centered mode of college classroom instruction as related to manifest anxiety. *Journal of Educational Psychology,* 1973, *64,* 125–132.

Downing, R. E. Methods in science teaching. *Journal of Higher Education,* 1913, *2,* 316–320.

Doyle, J. L. Reviewing physics through student demonstrations. *The Physics Teacher,* 1987, *25*(4), 221–223.

Doyle, K. O., Jr. *Student evaluation of instruction.* Lexington, MA: Lexington Books, 1975.

———. *Evaluating teaching.* Lexington, MA: D. C. Heath, 1983.

Dressel, P. L., and Marcus, D. *On teaching and learning in college.* San Francisco: Jossey-Bass, 1982.

Drucker, A. J., and Remmers, H. H. Do alumni and students differ in their attitudes toward instructors? *Journal of Educational Psychology,* 1951, *42,* 129–143.

Duchastel, P. C., and Merrill, P. F. The effects of behavioral objectives on learning: a review of empirical studies. *Review of Educational Research,* 1973, *43,* 53–69.

Dunkin, M. J. Research on teaching in higher education. In M. C. Wittrock, ed. *Handbook of research on teaching,* 3rd ed., pp. 754–777. New York: Macmillan, 1986.

D'Ydewalle, G.; Swerts, A.; and de Corte, E. Study time and test performance as a function of test expectations. *Contemporary Educational Psychology,* 1983, *8*(1), 55–67.

Dzich, B. W., and Winer, L. *The lecherous professor.* Boston: Beacon Press, 1984.

Eble, K. E. *The aims of college teaching.* San Francisco: Jossey-Bass, 1983.

———. *The craft of teaching: a guide to mastering the professor's art,* 2nd ed. San Francisco: Jossey-Bass, 1988.

Edgerton, R.; Hutchings, P.; and Quinlan, K. *The teaching portfolio: capturing the scholarship in teaching*. Washington, D. C.: American Association for Higher Education, 1991.

Edmondson, J. B., and Mulder, F. J. Size of class as a factor in university instruction. *Journal of Educational Research*, 1924, *9*, 1–12.

Egan, D. E., and Greeno, J. G. Acquiring cognitive structure by discovery and rule learning. *Journal of Educational Psychology*, 1973, *64*(1), 85–97.

Elliot, D. N. Characteristics and relationships of various criteria of teaching. Ph. D. thesis, Purdue University, 1949.

Ellner, C. L., and Barnes, C. P. *Studies of college teaching*. Lexington, MA: D. C. Heath, 1983.

Elshout, J. J. Problem solving and education. In E. De Corte, H. Lodewijks, R. Parmentier, and P. Span, eds. *Learning and instruction: European research in an international context: Vol 1*. Oxford: Leuven University Press/Pergamon Press, 1987.

Entwistle, N. *Styles of learning and teaching*. London, Wiley: 1981.

Entwistle, N. J. Student learning and study strategies. In B. R. Clark and G. Neave, eds. *Encyclopedia of higher education*. Oxford: Pergamon, 1992.

Erickson, S. C. *Motivation for learning. a guide for the teacher of the young adult*. Ann Arbor: University of Michigan Press, 1974.

———. *The essence of good teaching*. San Francisco: Jossey-Bass, 1984.

Farmer, D. W., and Mech, T. F., eds. Information literacy: Developing students as independent learners. *New directions for higher education no. 78*. San Francisco: Jossey-Bass, 1992.

Faw, V. A. A psychotherapeutic method of teaching psychology. *American Psychologist*, 1949, *4*, 104–109.

Feldhusen, J. R. The effects of small- and large-group instruction on learning of subject matter, attitudes, and interests. *Journal of Psychology*, 1963, *55*, 357–362.

Feldman, K. A. The superior college teacher from the students' view. *Research in Higher Education*, 1976, *5*, 243–288.

Ferguson, M. The role of faculty in increasing student retention. *College and University*, 1989, *65*, 127–134.

Feurzeig, W.; Munter, P. K.; Swets, J. A.; and Breen, M. N. Computer-aided teaching in medical diagnosis. *Journal of Medical Education*, August 1964, *39*(8).

Flavell, J. H. Metacognition and cognitive mentoring: a new area of cognitive-developmental inquiry. *American Psychologist*, 1979, *34*, 906–911.

Foos, P. W., and Fisher, R. P. Using tests as learning opportunities. *Journal of Educational Psychology*, 1988, *88*(2), 179–183.

Frey, P. W.; Leonard, D. W.; and Beatty, W. W. Students' ratings of instruction: Validation research. *American Educational Research Journal*, 1975, *12*, 327–336.

Friedman, C. P.; Hirschi, S.; Parlett, M.; and Taylor, E. F. The rise and fall of PSI in physics at MIT. *American Journal of Physics*, 1976, *3*, 204–211.

Fuhrmann, B., and Grasha, A. *A practical handbook for college teachers*. Boston: Little, Brown, 1983.

Gamson, W. A. *SIMSOC: a manual for participants*. Ann Arbor, MI: Campus Publishers, 1966.

Gates, A. I. Recitation as a factor in memorizing. *Archives of Psychology*, 1917, *6*, No. 40.

Geis, G. L., and Hiscock, P. *How professors plan courses*. Paper delivered at AERA convention, Chicago, 1991.

Genova, W. J.; Madoff, M. K.; Chin, R.; and Thomas, G. B. *Mutual benefit evaluation of faculty and administrators in higher education*. Cambridge, MA: Ballinger, 1976.

Gerberich, J. R., and Warner, K. O. Relative instructional efficiencies of the lecture and discussion methods in a university course in American national government. *Journal of Educational Research*, 1936, *29*, 574–579.

Gerlach, V., and Ely, D. *Teaching and media: a systematic approach*, 2nd ed. Englewood Cliffs, NJ: Prentice-Hall, 1980.

Gibb, C. A. Classroom behavior of the college teacher. *Educational and Psychological Measurement*, 1955, *15*, 254–263.

Gibb, J. R. The effects of group size and of threat reduction upon creativity in a problem-solving situation. *American Psychologist*, 1951, *6*, 324 (Abstract).

Gibb, L. M., and Gibb, J. R. The effects of the use of "participative action" groups in a course in general psychology. *American Psychologist*, 1952, *7*, 247 (Abstract).

Gilbert, S. W., and Lyman, P. Intellectual property in the information age. *Change*, 1989, *21*, 23–28.

Glasnapp, D. R.; Poggio, J. P.; and Ory, J. C. End-of-course, and long term retention outcomes for mastery and nonmastery, learning paradigms. *Psychology in the Schools*, 1978, *15*(4), 595–603.

Glenberg, A. M.; Wilkinson, A. C.; and Epstein, W. Illusion of knowing: Failure in the self-assessment of comprehension. *Memory and Cognition*, 1982, *10*(6), 597–602.

Gmelch, W. H.; Lovrich, N.; and Wilkie, P. K. Sources of stress in academe: a national perspective. *Research in Higher Education*, 1984, *20*, 477–490.

Goldschmid, B., and Goldschmid, M. L. Peer teaching in higher education: a review, *Higher Education*, 1976, *5*, 9–33.

Goldschmid, C. A., and Wilson, E. K. *Passing on sociology: the teaching of a discipline*. Belmont, CA: Wadsworth, 1980.

Goldschmid, M. L. Instructional options: Adapting the large university course to individual differences. *Learning and Development*, 1970, *1*(5), 1–2.

———. The learning cell: an instructional innovation. *Learning and Development*, 1971, *2*(5), 1–6.

———. When students teach students. Paper presented at the International Conference on Improving University Teaching, Heidelberg, Germany, May 1975.

Goldschmid, M. L., and Shore, B. M. The learning cell: a field test of an educational innovation. In W. A. Verreck, ed. *Methodological problems in research and development in higher education*, pp. 218–236. Amsterdam: Swets and Zeitlinger, 1974.

Goldstein, A. A controlled comparison of the project method with standard laboratory teaching in pharmacology. *Journal of Medical Education*, 1956, *31*, 365–375.

Green, M. F., ed. *Minorities on campus: a handbook for enhancing diversity*. Washington, D. C.: American Council on Education, 1988.

Greene, E. B. Relative effectiveness of lecture and individual readings as methods of college teaching. *Genetic Psychology Monographs*, 1928, *4*, 457–563.

Greenhill, L. P. New direction for communication research. *Audio-Visual Communications Review*, 1959, *7*, 245–253.

Greeno, J. G. Process of understanding in studying from text. Paper prepared for the symposium, "Information Processing Analyses of Instruction," presented at AERA, San Francisco, April 1976.

Gregg, L. W., and Steinberg, E. R., eds. *Cognitive processes in writing*. Hillsdale, NJ: Erlbaum, 1980.

Gronlund, N. E. *Constructing achievement tests*, 3rd ed. Englewood Cliffs, NJ: Prentice-Hall, 1982.

Gronlund, N. E., and Linn, R. L. *Measurement and evaluation in teaching*. New York: Macmillan, 1990.

Gruber, H. E., and Weitman, M. Cognitive processes in higher education: Curiosity and critical thinking. Paper read at Western Psychological Association, San Jose, CA, April 1960.

————. *Self-directed study: Experiments in higher education*, Report No. 19. Boulder: University of Colorado, Behavior Research Laboratory, April 1962.

Guetzkow, H. S. *Simulation in social sciences: Readings*. Englewood Cliffs, NJ: Prentice-Hall, 1962.

Guetzkow, H. S.; Kelley, E. L.; and McKeachie, W. J. An experimental comparison of recitation, discussion, and tutorial methods in college teaching. *Journal of Educational Psychology*, 1954, *45*, 193–209.

Gullette, M. M., ed. *The art and craft of teaching*. Cambridge, MA: Harvard-Danforth Center for Teaching and Learning, 1982.

Haigh, G. V., and Schmidt, W. The learning of subject matter in teacher-centered and group-centered classes. *Journal of Educational Psychology*, 1956, *47*, 295–301.

Haines, D. B., and McKeachie, W. J. Cooperative vs. competitive discussion methods in teaching introductory psychology. *Journal of Educational Psychology*, 1967, *58*, 386–390.

Hall, R. H., et al. The role of individual differences in the cooperative learning of technical material. *Journal of Educational Psychology*, 1988, *80*, 172–178.

Hall, R. M., and Sandler, B. R. *The classroom climate: a chilly one for women?* Project on the Status and Education of Women. Washington, D. C.: Association of American Colleges, 1982.

Halonen, J. *Active learning during teacher absence*. Milwaukee, WI: Alverno College, 1990.

Halpern, D. F. *Thought and knowledge*, 2nd ed. Hillsdale, NJ: Erlbaum, 1989.

Hansen, W. L.; Kelley, A. C.; and Weisbrod, B. A. Economic efficiency and the distribution of benefits from college instruction. *American Economic Review*, May 1970, *60*(2), 364–369.

Harlow, H. F.; Harlow, M. K.; and Meyer, D. R. Learning motivated by a manipulation drive. *Journal of Experimental Psychology*, 1949, *40*, 228–234.

Hart, J., and Driver, J. Teacher evaluation as a function of student and instructor personality. *Teaching of Psychology*, 1978, *5*, 198–200.

Harter, S. Effective motivation reconsidered: Toward a developmental model. *Human Development*, 1978, *21*, 34–64.

Hartley, J., and Davies, I. K. Note-taking: a critical review. *Programmed Learning and Educational Technology*, 1978, *15*, 207–224.

Hartman, F. R. Recognition learning under multiple channel presentation and testing conditions. *Audio-Visual Communication Review*, 1961, *9*, 24–43.

Hartman, H. J. Factors affecting the tutoring process. *Journal of Developmental Education*, 1990, *14*(2), 2–6.

Hartman, N. Syndicate based peer group learning: an alternative process. *South African Journal of Higher Education*, 1989, *3*, 98–106.

Hayes, J. R. *The complete problem solver*, 2nd ed. Hillsdale, NJ: Erlbaum, 1989.

Haythorn, W., et al. The effects of varying combinations of authoritarian and equalitarian leaders and followers. *Journal of Abnormal Psychology*, 1956, *53*, 210–219.

Hechter, F. J.; Meneck, V. H.; and Weinberg, L. E. *Enhancing Achievement Motivation and Performance in College Students: Attitudinal Retraining Perspectives in Higher Education*. In press.

Heckhausen, H. How to improve poor motivation in students. Paper presented at the 18th International Congress of Applied Psychology, Montreal, August 1974.

Henderson, W. T., and Wen, S. Effects of immediate positive reinforcement on undergraduates' course achievement. *Psychological Reports*, 1976, *39*, 568–570.

Hettick, P. Journal writing: Old fare or nouvelle cuisine? *Teaching of Psychology*, *17*, 1990, 36–39.

Hill, R. J. *A comparative study of lecture and discussion methods*. New York: Fund for Adult Education, 1960.

Hill, W. F. *Learning through discussion*. Beverly Hills, CA: Sage, 1977.

Hillocks, G. The interaction of instruction, teacher comment, and revision in teaching the composing process. *Research in Teaching of English*, 1982, *16*, 261–278.

Hirsch, R. S., and Moncreiff, B. A simulated chemistry lab. Paper presented at the 56th national meeting of the American Institute of Chemical Engineers, San Francisco, CA, May 1965.

Hirschman, C. S. An investigation of the small groups discussion classroom method on criteria of understanding, pleasantness, and self-confidence induced. Master's thesis, University of Pittsburgh, 1952.

Hoban, C. F. The dilemma of adult ITV college courses. *Educational Broadcasting Review*, June 1968, 31–36.

Hockenberry-Boeding, C., and Vattano, F. J. Undergraduates as teaching assistants: a comparison of two discussion methods. Manuscript, 1975.

Hofstede, G. Cultural differences in teaching and learning. *International Journal of Intercultural Relations*, 1986, *10*, 301–320.

Hollingsworth, S. Prior beliefs and cognitive change in learning to teach. *American Educational Research Journal*, 1989, *26*, 160–189.

Horwitz, M. The verticality of liking and disliking. In R. Taguiri and L. Petrullo, eds. *Person perception and interpersonal behavior*. Stanford: Stanford University Press, 1958.

Houston, J. P. Alternate test forms as a means of reducing multiple-choice answer copying in the classroom. *Journal of Educational Psychology*, 1983, *75*(4), 572–575.

Hovland, C. I., ed. *The order of presentation in persuasion*. New Haven, CT: Yale University Press, 1957.

Hovland, C. I.; Lumsdaine, A. A.; and Sheffield, F. D. *Experiments in mass communication*. Princeton, NJ: Princeton University Press, 1949.

Hudelson, E. *Class size at the college level*. Minneapolis: University of Minnesota Press, 1928.

Humphreys, W. L. Values in teaching and the teaching of values. *Teaching-learning issues no. 58*. Knoxville, TN: Learning Research Center, The University of Tennessee, 1986.

Hunt, P. The case method of instruction. *Harvard Educational Review*, 1951, *3*, 1–19.

Hurd, A. W. *Problems of science teaching at the college level*. Minneapolis: University of Minnesota Press, 1929.

Husband, R. W. A statistical comparison of the efficacy of large lecture vs. smaller recitation sections upon achievement in general psychology, *Journal of Psychology*, 1951, *31*, 297–300.

Jackson, C. M. Experiment in methods of teaching gross human anatomy. In E. Hudelson, ed. *Problems of college education*, pp. 444–449. Minneapolis: University of Minnesota Press, 1929.

Janes, J., and Hauer, D. *Now what?* Readings on surviving (and even enjoying) your first experience at college teaching, 2nd ed. Acton, MA: Copley, 1988.

Jenkins, R. L. The relative effectiveness of two methods of teaching written and spoken English, Ph. D. diss., Michigan State University. *Dissertation Abstracts*, 1952, *12*, 258.

Johnson, D. M. Increasing originality on essay examinations in psychology. *Teaching of Psychology*, 1975, *2*, 99–102.

Johnson, D. M., and Smith, H. C. Democratic leadership in the college classroom. *Psychological Monographs*, 1953, *67*, no. 2 (Whole No. 361).

Johnson, D. W., and Johnson, R. T. *Learning together and alone: Cooperation, competition and individualization*. Englewood Cliffs, NJ: Prentice-Hall, 1975.

Johnson, D. W.; Maruyama, G.; Johnson, R.; Nelson, D.; and Skon, L. The effects of cooperative, competitive, and individualistic goal structures on achievement: a meta-analysis. *Psychological Bulletin*, 1981, *89*, 47–62.

Johnson, G. R., et al. *Teaching tips for users of the motivated strategies for learning questionnaire*. Ann Arbor, MI: National Center for Research to Improve Postsecondary Learning and Teaching, School of Education, University of Michigan, 1991.

Johnson, R. B., and Johnson, S. R. *Assuring learning with self-instructional packages or, up the up staircase, a how-to-do workbook*. Chapel Hill, NC: Self-instructional Packages, Inc., 1971.

Johnston, J. *Electronic learning: from audiotape to videodisc*. Hillsdale, NJ: Erlbaum, 1987.

Johnston, R. E., Jr. *Magnetic recordings and visual displays as aids in teaching introductory psychology to college students*. OE Grant No. 73056, Drexel Institute of Technology, Philadelphia, May 1969.

Jones, L. L., and Smith, S. G. Can multimedia instruction meet our expectations? *EDUCOM Bulletin*, 1992, *27*(1), 39–43.

Judd, W. A. Learner-controlled computer-assisted instruction. In K. Zinn, M. Refice, and A. Romano, eds. *Computers in the instructional process: Report of an instructional school*. Amsterdam: Elsevier, 1973.

Katona, G. *Organizing and memorizing*. New York: Columbia University Press, 1940.

Katz, D. *Gestalt psychology*. New York: Ronald Press, 1950.

Katz, J., and Henry, M. *Turning professors into teachers*. New York: Macmillan, 1988.

Keaton, M. T., et al. *Experiential learning: Rationale, characteristics, and assessment*. San Francisco: Jossey-Bass, 1976.

Keller, F. S. Goodbye teacher, . . . *Journal of Applied Behavior Analysis*, 1968, *10*, 165–167.

Keller, F. S., and Sherman, J. G., eds. *The Keller Plan handbook*. Menlo Park, CA: W. A. Benjamin, Inc., 1974.

Kelley, A. C. An experiment with TIPS: a computer-aided instructional system for undergraduate education. *American Economic Review*, May 1968, *2*, 446–457.

———. The economics of teaching: the role of TIPS. In K. G. Lumsden, ed. *Recent research in economics education*, pp. 44–66. Englewood Cliffs, NJ: Prentice-Hall, 1970.

Kemp, J. E. *Planning and producing audiovisual materials*, 4th ed. New York: Harper & Row, 1980.

Kiel, D. *Student learning through community involvement: a report of three studies of the service learning model*. Atlanta, GA: Southern Regional Education Board, 1972.

Kiewra, K. A. A review of notetaking: the encoding storage paradigm and beyond. *Educational Psychology Review*, 1989, *1*(2), 147–172.

King, A. Enhancing peer interaction and learning in the classroom. *American Educational Research Journal*, 1990, *27*, 664–687.

Kirk, T. G., ed. *Increasing the teaching role of academic libraries. New directions for teaching and learning, 18*. San Francisco: Jossey-Bass, 1984.

Kitchener, K. G., and Hurst, J. C. Education through student interaction manual. Manuscript, Colorado State University, 1972.

———. Faculty consultation: Changing role for the counseling psychologist. *Journal of Counseling Psychology*, 1974.

Klapper, H. L. *Closed-circuit television as a medium of instruction of NY University*. New York: NY University, 1958.

Koenig, K., and McKeachie, W. J. Personality and independent study. *Journal of Educational Psychology*, 1959, *50*, 132–134.

Kozma, R. B. The design of instruction in a chemistry laboratory course. *Journal for Research in Science Teaching*, 1982, *19*, 261–270.

———. Learning with media. *Review of Educational Research*, 1991, *61*, 179–211.

Kozma, R. B.; Belle, L. W.; and Williams, G. W. *Instructional techniques in higher education*. Englewood Cliffs, NJ: Educational Technology Publications, 1978.

Krathwohl, D.; Bloom, B. S.; and Masia, B., eds. *Taxonomy of educational objectives, handbook II*. Affective domain. New York: David McKay, 1964.

Krauskopf, C. J. The use of written responses in the stimulated recall method. Ph.D. diss., Ohio State University. *Dissertation Abstracts*, 1960, *21*, 1953.

Kruglak, H. Experimental outcomes of laboratory instruction in elementary college physics. *American Journal of Physics*, 1952, *20*, 136–141.

Krumboltz, J. D. The nature and importance of the required response in programmed instruction. *American Educational Research Journal*, 1964, *1*, 203–209.

Krumboltz, J. D., and Farquhar, W. W. The effect of three teaching methods on achievement and motivational outcomes in a how-to-study course. *Psychological Monographs*, 1957, *71*, no. 14 (Whole No. 443).

Kulik, J. A. Individualized systems of instruction. In H. E. Mitzel, ed. *The encyclopedia of educational research*, 5th ed. New York: Macmillan Co., 1982.

Kulik, J. A.; Cohen, P. A.; and Ebeling, B. J. Effectiveness of programmed instruction in higher education: a meta-analysis of findings. *Educational Evaluation and Policy Analysis*, 1980, *2*, 51–64.

Kulik, J. A., and Jaksa, P. *A review of research on PSI and other educational technologies in college teaching*. Report No. 10, Center for Research on Learning and Teaching, Ann Arbor, MI, May 1977.

Kulik, J. A., and Kulik, C. -L. C. Meta-analysis in education. *International Journal of Educational Research*, 1989, *13*, 221–340.

Kulik, J. A.; Kulik, C. -L. C.; and Bangert-Drowns, R. L. *Effectiveness of mastery learning programs: a meta-analysis*. Ann Arbor, MI: University of Michigan, Center for Research on Learning and Teaching, 1988.

Kulik, J. A.; Kulik, C.; and Cohen, P. Instructional technology and college teaching. *Teaching of Psychology*, 1980a, *7*, 199–205.

———. Effectiveness of computer-based college teaching: a meta-analysis of findings. *Review of Educational Research*, 1980b, *50*(4), 525–544.

Kulik, J. A.; Kulik, C.; and Smith, B. B. Research on the personalized system of instruction. *Programmed Learning and Educational Technology*, February 1976, *13*, 23–30.

Lahti, A. M. The inductive-deductive method and the physical science laboratory. *Journal of Experimental Education*, 1956, *24*, 149–163.

Lancaster, O. E., et al. The relative merits of lectures and recitation in teaching college physics. *Journal of Engineering Education*, 1961, *51*, 425–433.

Landsman, T. An experimental study of a student-centered learning method. Ph. D. diss., Syracuse University, 1950.

Lange, P. C. *Today's education*. National Education Association, 1972, *61*, 59.

LaPree, G. Establishing criteria for grading student papers: Moving beyond mysticism. *Teaching and Learning* (Indiana University), 1977, *3*(1).

Larkin, J. H.; Heller, J. I.; and Greeno, J. G. Instructional implications of research on problem solving. In W. J. McKeachie, ed. Learning, cognition, and college teaching. *New directions for teaching and learning, 2*. San Francisco: Jossey-Bass, 1980.

Larson, C. O., et al. Verbal ability and cooperative learning: Transfer of effects. *Journal of Reading Behavior*, 1984, *16*, 289–295.

Lederman, L. C., and Ruben, B. D. Systematic assessment of communication games and simulations: an applied framework. *Communication Education*, 1984, *33*, 152–159.

Lee, C. B. T., ed. *Improving college teaching*. Washington, D. C.: American Council on Education, 1967.

Leith, G. O. M. Conflict and interference: Studies of the facilitating effects of reviews in learning sequences. *Programmed Learning and Educational Technology*, 1971, *8*, 41–50.

———. Individual differences in learning: Interactions of personality and teaching methods. In Association of Educational Psychologists, *Personality and Academic Progress*, London, 1974a.

———. Goals, methods and materials for a small-group, modular-instruction approach to teaching social psychology. Paper presented for the Institute of Social Psychology, University of Utrecht, 1947b.

———. Implications of cognitive psychology for the improvement of teaching and learning in universities. In B. Massey, ed. *Proceedings of the Third International Conference, Improving University Teaching*, pp. 111–138. College Park, MD: University of Maryland, 1977.

———. The influence of personality on learning to teach: Effects and delayed effects of microteaching. *Educational Review*, 1982, *34*(3), 195–204.

Lempert, R. Law school grading: an experiment with pass-fail. *Journal of Legal Education*, 1972, *24*, 251–308.

Lenze, L. F., and Rando, W. D. *Sourcebook on early student feedback*. Evanston, IL: Northwestern University, National Center on Postsecondary Teaching, Learning, and Assessment, forthcoming.

Lepper, M. R., and Malone, T. W. Intrinsic motivation and instructional effectiveness in computer-based education. In R. E. Snow and M. J. Farr, eds. *Aptitude, learning and instruction: III. Conative and affective process analyses*. Hillsdale, NJ: Erlbaum, 1985.

Leventhal, L.; Abrami, P. C.; Perry, R. P.; and Breen, L. J. Section selection in multi-section courses: Implications for the validation and use of student rating forms. *Educational and Psychological Measurements*, 1975, *35*, 885–895.

Levine, A., ed. *Shaping higher education's future: Demographic realities and opportunities, 1990–2000*. San Francisco: Jossey-Bass, 1989.

Lewin, K. Group decision and social change. In G. E. Swanson, T. M. Newcomb, and E. L. Hartley, eds. *Readings in social psychology*, 2nd ed., pp. 330–344. New York: Holt, 1952.

Lewin, K.; Lippitt, R.; and White, R. K. Patterns of aggressive behavior in experimentally created social climates. *Journal of Social Psychology*, 1939, *10*, 271–299.

Lewis, D. R.; Dalgaard, B. R.; and Boyer, C. M. Is CAI economical in economics? Paper presented at AERA meeting, April 1984.

Lidren, D. M.; Meier, S. E.; and Brigham, T. A. The effects of minimal and maximal peer tutoring systems on the academic performance of college students. *Psychological Record*, 1991, *41*, 69–77.

Lifson, N.; Rempel, P.; and Johnson, J. A. A comparison between lecture and conference methods of teaching psychology. *Journal of Medical Education*, 1956, *31*, 376–382.

Light, R. J. *The Harvard assessment seminar, second report: Explorations with students and faculty about teaching, learning, and student life*. Cambridge, MA: Harvard Graduate School of Education, 1992.

Loacker, G.; Cromwell, L.; Fey, J.; and Rutherford, D. *Analysis and communication at Alverno: an approach to critical thinking*. Milwaukee, WI: Alverno Productions, 1984.

Locke, E. A., and Latham, G. P. *A theory of goal setting and task performance*. Englewood Cliffs, NJ: Prentice Hall, 1990.

Lowman, J. *Mastering the techniques of teaching*. San Francisco: Jossey-Bass, 1984.

Lowther, M. A.; Stark, J. S.; and Martens, G. G. *Preparing course syllabi for improved communication*. Ann Arbor, MI: NCRIPTAL, University of Michigan, 1989.

Lumsdaine, A. A. Instruments and media of instruction. In N. L. Gage, ed. *Handbook of research on teaching*, pp. 583–682. Chicago: Rand McNally, 1963.

Lumsden, E. A. Use of student feedback cards for diagnostic purposes during classroom lectures. *Improving college and university teaching yearbook 1976, 39*. Oregon State University Press, 1976.

Lyle, E. An exploration in the teaching of critical thinking in general psychology. *Journal of Educational Research*, 1958, *52*, 129–133.

Macomber, F. G., and Siegel, L. Experimental study in instructional procedures. *Progress Report No. 1*. Oxford, OH: Miami University, 1956.

———. A study of large-group teaching procedures. *Educational Research*, 1957a, *38*, 220–229.

———. Experimental study in instructional procedures. *Progress Report No. 2*. Oxford, OH: Miami University, 1957b.

———. Experimental study in instructional procedures. *Final Report*. Oxford, OH: Miami University, 1960.

Maier, N. R. F. *Principles of human relations*. New York: Wiley, 1952.

———. *Problem-solving discussions and conferences: Leadership methods and skills*. New York: McGraw-Hill, 1963.

———. Innovation in education. *American Psychologist*, 1971, *26*(8), 722–725.

Maier, N. R. F., and Maier, L. A. An experimental test of the effects of "developmental" vs. "free" discussion on the quality of group decisions. *Journal of Applied Psychology*, 1957, *41*, 320–323.

Maier, N. R. F., and Solem, A. R. The contribution of a discussion leader to the quality of group thinking. *Human Relations*, 1952, *5*, 277–288.

Maier, N. R. F., and Zerfoss, L. F. MRP: A technique for training large groups of supervisors and its potential use in social research. *Human Relations*, 1952, *5*, 177–186.

Maimon, E. P., et al. *Writing in the arts and sciences*. Cambridge, MA: Winthrop, 1981.

Malone, T. W., and Lepper, M. R. Making learning fun: a taxonomy of intrinsic motivations for learning. In R. E. Snow and M. J. Farr, eds. *Aptitude, learning, and instruction: III. Conative and affective process analysis*. Hillsdale, NJ: Erlbaum, 1985.

Maloney, R. M. Group learning through group discussion: a group discussion implementation analysis. *Journal of Social Psychology*, 1956, *43*, 3–9.

Mann, R. D., et al. *The college classroom: Conflict, change, and learning*. New York: Wiley, 1970.

Mann, W. R. Changes in the level of attitude sophistication of college students as a measure of teacher effectiveness. Ph. D. diss., University of Michigan, 1968.

Marsh, H. W. SEEQ: a reliable, valid, and useful instrument for collecting students' evaluations of university teaching. *British Journal of Educational Psychology*, 1982, *52*, 77–95.

———. Students' evaluations of university teaching: Dimensionality, reliability, potential biases, and utility. *Journal of Educational Psychology*, 1984, *76*, 707–754.

———. *Students' evaluations of university teaching: Research findings, methodological issues, and directions for future research*. Elmsford, NY: Pergamon, 1987.

Marsh, H. W., and Roche, L. The use of students' evaluations and an individually structured intervention to enhance university teaching effectiveness. *American Educational Research Journal*, 1992.

Marton, F.; Hounsell, D.; and Entwistle, N., eds. *The experience of learning*. Edinburgh: Scottish Academic Press, 1984.

Marton, F., and Säljö, R. On qualitative differences in learning: I—outcome and process. *British Journal of Educational Psychology*, 1976a, *46*, 4–11.

———. On qualitative differences in learning: II—outcome as a function of the learner's conception of the task. *British Journal of Educational Psychology*, 1976b, *46*, 115–127.

Mayer, R. E. *Thinking and problem solving: an introduction to human cognition and learning*. Glenview, IL: Scott Foresman, 1974.

Mayer, R. E.; Stiehl, C. C.; and Greeno, J. G. Acquisition of understanding and skill in relation to subjects' preparation and meaningfulness of instruction. *Journal of Educational Psychology*, 1975, *67*(3), 331–350.

Mazzuca, S. A., and Feldhusen, J. F. Effective college instruction: How students see it. Paper presented at the annual meeting of the American Psychological Association, San Francisco, August 29, 1977.

McClelland, D. C. *Human motivation*. Glenville, IL: Scott, Foresman, 1985.

McCluskey, H. Y. An experimental comparison of two methods of correcting the outcomes of examination. *School and Society*, 1934, *40*, 566–568.

McCollough, C., and Van Atta, E. L. Experimental evaluation of teaching programs utilizing a block of independent work. Paper read at the symposium, "Experimental Studies in Learning Independently," American Psychological Association, Washington, D. C., September 1958.

McCombs, B. L., and Marzano R. J. Putting the self in self-regulated learning: the self as agent in integrating will and skill. *Educational Psychologist*, 1990, *25*(1), 51–69.

McKeachie, W. J. Anxiety in the college classroom. *Journal of Educational Research*, 1951, *45*, 153–160.

———. Individual conformity to attitudes of classroom groups. *Journal of Abnormal and Social Psychology*, 1954, *49*, 282–289.

———. Improving your teaching. *Adult Leadership*, 1955, *3*, 14–16.

———. Students, groups, and teaching methods. *American Psychologist*, 1958, *13*, 580–584.

————. Appraising teaching effectiveness. In W. J. McKeachie, ed. *The appraisal of teaching in large universities*, pp. 32–36. Ann Arbor, MI: University of Michigan Extension Services, 1959a.

————. College grades: a rationale and mild defense. *AAUP Bulletin*, 1976, *62*, 320–322.

————. Student ratings of faculty: a reprise. *Academe*, 1979, *65*, 384–397.

————., ed. Learning, cognition, and college teaching. *New directions for teaching and learning, 2*. San Francisco: Jossey-Bass, 1980.

————. Faculty as a renewable resource. In R. G. Baldwin and R. T. Blackburn, eds. *College faculty: Versatile human resources in a period of restraint*, pp. 57–66. New Directions for Institutional Research. San Francisco: Jossey-Bass, 1983.

————. Learning, thinking, and Thorndike. *Educational Psychologist*, 1990, *25*(2), 127–141.

McKeachie, W. J., and Kulik, J. A. Effective college teaching. In F. N. Kerlinger, ed. *Review of research in education*, vol. 3. Itasca, IL: Peacock, 1975.

McKeachie, W. J., et al. Using student ratings and consultation to improve instruction. *British Journal of Educational Psychology*, 1980, *50*, 168–174.

McKeachie, W. J.; Lin, Y-G.; Forrin, B.; and Teevan, R. Individualized teaching in elementary psychology. *Journal of Educational Psychology*, 1960, *51*, 285–291.

McKeachie, W. J.; Lin, Y-G.; Milholland, J.; and Isaacson, R. Student affiliation motives, teacher warmth, and academic achievement. *Journal of Personality and Social Psychology*, 1966, *4*, 457–461.

McKeachie, W. J.; Lin, Y-G.; Moffett, M.; and Daugherty, M. Effective teaching and facilitative vs. directive style. *Teaching of Psychology*, 1978, *5*, 193–194.

McKeachie, W. J.; Pintrich, P. R.; and Lin, Y-G. Teaching learning strategies. *Educational Psychologist*, *20*(3), 1985, 153–160.

McKeachie, W. J.; Pintrich, P. R.; Lin, Y-G.; Smith, D. A. F.; and Sharma, R. *Teaching and learning in the college classroom: a review of the research literature*, 1990. 2nd ed. Ann Arbor, MI: NCRIPTAL, University of Michigan, 1990.

McKeachie, W. J.; Pollie, D.; and Speisman, J. Relieving anxiety in classroom examinations. *Journal of Abnormal and Social Psychology*, 1955, *50*, 93–98.

McKeachie, W. J., and Solomon, D. Student ratings of instructors: a validity study. *Journal of Educational Research*, 1958, *51*, 379–382.

McMichael, J. S., and Corey, J. R. Contingency management in an introductory psychology course produces better learning. *Journal of Applied Behavior Analysis*, 1969, *2*, 79–83.

McMillan, J. H., and Forsyth, D. F. What theories of motivation say about why learners learn. *New directions for teaching and learning, no. 45*, 1991, 39–52.

McNair, M., ed. *The case method at Harvard Business School*. New York: McGraw-Hill, 1954.

McTavish, C. L. *Effect of repetitive film showings on learning*. Instructional Film Research Report, SDC 269–7–12, Special Devices Center, Office of Naval Research, November 1949.

Means, G., and Means, R. Achievement as a function of the presence of prior information concerning aptitudes. *Journal of Educational Psychology*, 1971, *62*, 185–187.

Mehrens, W. A., and Lehmann, I. J. *Measurement and evaluation in education and psychology*. New York: Holt, Rinehart & Winston, 1973.

Meier, R. S., and Feldhusen, J. F. Another look at Dr. Fox: Effect of stated purpose for evaluation, lecturer expressiveness, and density of lecture content on student ratings. *Journal of Educational Psychology*, 1979, *71*(3), 339–345.

Melton, A. W.; Feldman, N. G.; and Mason, C. N. *Experimental studies of the education of children in a museum of schools*. Washington, D. C.: Publications of the American Association of Museums, 1936, *15*, 1–106.

Menges, R. J. Beliefs and behavior. *Teaching excellence*, 1990, *2*(6), 1–2.

Menges, R. J., and Mathis, B. C. *Key resources on teaching, learning, curriculum, and faculty development*. San Francisco: Jossey-Bass, 1988.

Menges, R. J., and Svinicki, M. D., eds. College teaching from theory to practice. *New Directions for teaching and learning, no. 45*. San Francisco: Jossey-Bass, 1991.

Menges, R. J., and Weimer, M. G., eds. *Better teaching and learning in college: Using scholarship to improve practice*. A publication of the National Center on Postsecondary Teaching, Learning, and Assessment. San Francisco: Jossey-Bass, 1994.

Messick, S., et al. *Individuality in learning*. San Francisco: Jossey-Bass, 1976.

Metzger, R. L.; Boschee, P. F.; Haugen, T.; and Schnobrich, B. L. The classroom as learning context: Changing rooms affects performance. *Journal of Educational Psychology*, 1979, *71*(4), 440–442.

Michael, D. N., and Maccoby, N. Factors influencing the effects of student participation on verbal learning from films: motivation vs. practice effects, feedback, and overt vs. covert responding. In A. A. Lumsdaine, ed. *Student response in programmed instruction: a symposium*. Washington, D. C.: NAS-NRC (National Academy of Sciences-National Research Council), 1953, *943*, 18.

Michaelsen, L. K. Team learning in large classes. *New directions for teaching and learning, 14.* San Francisco: Jossey-Bass, 1958.

Michaelsen, L. K.; Watson, W. E.; Cragin, J. P.; Fink, L. D. Team learning: a potential solution to the problems of large classes. *Exchange: The Organizational Behavior Teaching Journal*, 1982, *7*(1).

Miller, N. M. Scientific principles for maximum learning from motion pictures. *Audio-Visual Communication Review*, 1957, *5*, 61–113.

Miller, R. I. *Developing programs for faculty evaluation*. San Francisco: Jossey-Bass, 1974.

Milton, O. *Alternatives to the traditional*. San Francisco: Jossey-Bass, 1972.

Milton, O.; Pollio, H. R.; and Eison, J. *Making sense of college grades*. San Francisco: Jossey-Bass, 1986.

Monaco, G. E. *Inferences as a function of test-expectancy in the classroom*. Kansas State University Psychology Series, KSU-HIPI Report 73–3, 1977.

Moore, J. W.; Smith, W. I.; and Teevan, R. *Motivational variables in programmed learning: the role of need achievement, fear of failure, and student estimate of achievement*. Final Report U. S. O. E., Title 7, Grant No. 7–48–0070–149. Lewisburg, PA: Bucknell University Press, 1965.

Moore, M. R., and Popham, W. J. The role of extra-class student interviews in promoting student achievement. Paper read at a joint session of the American Association for the Advancement of Science and American Educational Research Association, Chicago, December 1959.

Morgan, C. H.; Lilley, J. D.; and Boreham, N. C. Learning from lectures: the effect of varying the detail in lecture handouts on notetaking and recall. *Applied Cognitive Psychology*, 1987, *2*, 115–122.

Morris, C. J., and Kimbrell, G. McA. Performance and attitudinal effects of the Keller method in an introductory psychology course. *Psychological Record*, 1972, *22*, 523–530.

Mueller, A. D. Class size as a factor in normal school instruction. *Education*, 1924, *45*, 203–227.

Mueller, D. J., and Wasser, V. Implications of changing answers on objective test items. *Journal of Educational Measurement*, 1977, *14*(1), 9–13.

Murray, H. G. *Evaluating university teaching: a review of research.* Toronto, Canada: Ontario Confederation of University Faculty Associations, 1980.

Murray, J. P. Better testing for better learning. *College Teaching*, 1990, *38*(4), 148–152.

Nachman, M., and Opochinsky, S. The effects of different teaching methods: a methodological study. *Journal of Educational Psychology*, 1958, *49*, 245–249.

Naftulin, D. H.; Ware, J. E.; and Donnelly, F. A. The Doctor Fox lecture: a paradigm of educational seduction. *Journal of Medical Education*, 1973, *48*, 630–635.

Nash, A. N.; Muczyk, J. P.; and Vettori, F. L. The relative practical effectiveness of programmed instruction. *Personnel Psychology*, 1971, *24*, 397–418.

Naveh-Benjamin, M., and Lin, Y-G. *Assessing students' organization of concepts: a manual of measuring course-specific knowledge structures.* Ann Arbor, MI: NCRIPTAL, University of Michigan, 1991.

Nelson, T. Teaching and learning at Kalamazoo College. Manuscript, Kalamazoo College, Kalamazoo, MI, 1970.

New Jersey Institute for Collegiate Teaching and Learning. *The challenges of the college classroom.* South Orange, NJ: Seton Hall University, 1990.

Nieves-Squires, S. *Hispanic women: Making their presence on campus less tenuous.* Washington, D.C.: American Association of Colleges, 1991.

Nisbett, R. E.; Fong, G. T.; Lehman, D.; and Cheng, P. W. Teaching reasoning. *Science*, 1987, *238*, 625–631.

Noll, V. H. The optimum laboratory emphasis in college chemistry. *School and Society*, 1930, *32*, 300–303.

Norman, D. *Teaching learning strategies.* Mimeo, University of California, San Diego, April 11, 1977.

Novak, J. D. An experimental comparison of a conventional and a project centered method of teaching a college general botany course. *Journal of Experimental Education*, 1958, *26*, 217–230.

Nuss, E. M. Academic integrity: Comparing faculty and student attitudes. *College Teaching*, 1984, *32*, 140–144.

Nyquist, J. D., Abbott, R. D., and Wulff, D. H., eds. Teaching assistant training in the 1990s. *New directions for teaching and learning, 39.* San Francisco: Jossey-Bass, 1989.

Nyquist, J. D.; Abbott, R. D.; Wulff, D. H.; and Sprague, J., eds. *Preparing the professoriate of tomorrow to teach.* Dubuque, IA: Kendall/Hunt, 1991.

Nyquist, J. D., and Wulff, D. H. Selected active learning strategies. In J. Daly, G. Freedrich, and A. Vangelisti, eds. *Teaching communication: methods research and theory*, pp. 350–354. Hillsdale, NJ: Erlbaum, 1990.

Olson, D. Toward a theory of instructional means. *Educational Psychologist*, 1976, *12*, 14–35.

Overall, J. U., and Marsh, H. W. Students' evaluations of instruction: a longitudinal study of their stability. *Journal of Educational Psychology*, 1980, *72*, 321–325.

———. Midterm feedback from students: its relationship to instructional improvement and students' cognitive and affective outcomes. *Journal of Educational Psychology*, 1979, *71*, 856–865.

Palmer, J.; Carliner, G.; and Romer, T. Leniency, learning and evaluations. *Journal of Educational Psychology*, 1978, *70*(5), 855–863.

Pambookian, H. S. The effect of feedback from students to college instructors on their teaching behavior, Ph. D. diss., University of Michigan, 1972.

Paris, S. G.; Lipson, M. Y.; and Wixson, K. K. Becoming a strategic reader. *Contemporary Educational Psychology*, 1983, *8*, 293–316.

Parman, Susan. The film essay as an educational device. *Innovation Abstracts*, 1984, *6*(26).

Parsons, T. S. A comparison of instruction by kinescope, correspondence study, and customary classroom procedures. *Journal of Educational Psychology*, 1957, *48*, 27–40.

Parsons, T. S.; Ketcham, W. A.; and Beach, L. R. Effects of varying degrees of student interaction and student-teacher contact in college courses. Paper read at American Sociological Society, Seattle, WA, August 1958.

Pascarella, E. T., and Terenzini, F. *How college affects students*. San Francisco: Jossey-Bass, 1991.

Pask, G. Conversational techniques in the study and practice of education. *British Journal of Educational Psychology*, 1976, *46*, 12–25.

Pask, G., and Scott, B. C. E. CASTE: a system for exhibiting learning strategies and regulating uncertainties. *International Journal of Man-Machine Studies*, 1973, *5*.

Patton, J. A. A study of the effects of student acceptance of responsibility and motivation on course behavior. Ph. D. diss., University of Michigan, 1955.

Paul, J. B. The length of class periods. *Educational Research*, 1932, *13*, 58–75.

Paul, J., and Ogilvie, J. C. Mass media and retention. *Explorations*, 1955, *4*, 120–123.

Pemberton, G. *On teaching the minority student: Problems and strategies.* Brunswick, ME: Bowdoin College, 1988.

Peper, R. J., and Mayer, R. E. Note taking as a generative activity. *Journal of Educational Psychology*, 1978, *70*(4), 514–522.

Perkins, H. V. The effects of climate and curriculum on group learning. *Journal of Educational Research*, 1950, *44*, 269–286.

Perry, R. P.; Abrami, P. C.; and Leventhal, L. Educational seduction: the effect of instructor expressiveness and lecture content on student ratings and achievement. *Journal of Educational Psychology*, 1979, *71*(1), 107–116.

Perry, W. G., Jr. *Forms of intellectual and ethical development in the college years: a scheme.* New York: Holt, Rinehart, and Winston, 1970.

———. Cognitive and ethical growth: the making of meaning. In A. W. Chickering, ed. *The modern American college*, pp. 76–116. San Francisco: Jossey-Bass, 1981.

Peterson, P. L. Interactive effects of student anxiety, achievement orientation, and teacher behavior on student achievement and attitude. Ph.D. diss., Stanford University, 1976.

Pintrich, P. R., and De Groot, E. V. Motivational and self-regulated learning components of classroom academic performance. *Journal of Educational Psychology*, 1990, *82*, 33–40.

Pintrich, P. R.; Smith, D. A. F.; Garcia, T.; and McKeachie, W. J. *A manual for the use of the Motivated Strategies for Learning Questionnaire (MSLQ).* Ann Arbor, MI: National Center for Research to Improve Postsecondary Teaching and Learning, University of Michigan, 1991.

Pollio, H. R.; Humphreys, W. L.; and Milton, O. Components of contemporary grade meanings. *Contemporary Educational Psychology*, 1989, *14*, 77–91.

Postlethwait, S. N.; Novak, J.; and Murray, H. T., Jr. *The audio-tutorial approach to learning: through independent study and integrated experiences*, 2nd ed. Minneapolis: Burgess, 1969.

Potter, S. *One-upmanship*. New York: Henry Holt, 1955.

Powers, S. M. Teaching the basic research paper: Use of a portfolio method. Paper presented at the 91st Annual Convention of the American Psychological Association, Anaheim, CA, August 1983.

Pressey, S. L. A simple apparatus which gives tests and scores—and teaches. *School and Society*, 1926, *23*, 373–376.

Pressley, M., et al. Encouraging mindful use of prior knowledge: Attempting to construct explanatory answers facilitates learning. *Educational Psychologist*, *27*(1), 91–109.

Quinn, J. *University professors read about teaching*. Evanston, IL: Northwestern University, National Center for Postsecondary Teaching, Learning, and Assessment, 1993.

Quinn, M. E. *An investigation of undergraduate field study at Michigan State University*. Unpublished Ph.D. dissertation, Michigan State University, 1972.

Raiford, N. G. Writing across the curriculum with an essay test on day two. *Innovation Abstracts*, 1991, *13*(3), 1–2.

Rando, W. C., and Menges, R. J. How practice is shaped by personal theories. *New directions for teaching and learning, no. 45*, 1991, 7–14.

Rasmussen, G. R. Evaluation of a student-centered and instructor-centered method of conducting a graduate course in education. *Journal of Educational Psychology*, 1956, *47*, 449–461.

Reder, L. M., and Anderson, J. R. Effects of spacing and embellishment on memory for the main points of a text. *Memory and Cognition*, 1982, *10*(2), 97–102.

Reed, S. K. *Cognition*, 3rd ed. Pacific Grove, CA: Brooks-Cole, 1992.

Remmers, H. H. Learning, effort, and attitudes as affected by three methods of instruction in elementary psychology. *Purdue University Studies in Higher Education*, 1933, *21*.

Riordan, R. J., and Wilson, L. S. Bibliotherapy: Does it work? *Journal of Counseling and Development*, 1989, *67*, 506–508.

Roberts, M. S., and Semb, G. B. Analysis of the number of student-set deadlines in a personalized psychology course. *Teaching of Psychology*, 1990, *17*, 170–173.

Robinson, P. TV can't educate. *New Republic*, August 5 and 12, 1978, 13–15.

Roman, T., and Mahler, S. A three-dimensional model for using case studies in the academic classroom. *Higher Education*, 1986, *15*, 677–696.

Romig, J. L. An evaluation of instruction by student-led discussion in the college classroom. *Dissertation Abstracts International*, 1972, *32*, 6816.

Rosen, E. F.; Frincke, G. L.; and Stolurow, L. M. Principles of programming: II, Champaign community unit school district number 4 high schools. *Comparative studies of principles for programming mathematics in automated instruction*, Technical Report No. 15. University of Illinois, September, 1964.

Ross, I. C. Role specialization in supervision. Ph. D. diss., Columbia University. *Dissertation Abstracts*, 1957, *17*, 2701–2702.

Roth, R. L. Learning about gender through writing: Student journals in the undergraduate classroom. *Teaching Sociology*, *12*(3), 325–338.

Rothkopf, E. Z. Variable adjunct question schedules, interpersonal interaction, and incidental learning from written material. *Journal of Educational Psychology*, 1972, *63*, 87–92.

Roueche, S. D., ed. Camelot: An individualized information system. *Innovation Abstracts*, 1984, *VI*(14).

———, ed. The film as an educational device. *Innovation Abstracts*, 1984, *VI*(26).

Royer, P. N. Effects of specificity and position of written instructional objectives on learning from a lecture. *Journal of Educational Psychology*, 1977, *69*, 40–45.

Ruja, H. Outcomes of lecture and discussion procedures in three college courses. *Journal of Experimental Education*, 1954, *22*, 385–394.

Runkel, P.; Harrison, R.; and Runkel, M., eds. *The changing college classroom*. San Francisco: Jossey-Bass, 1972.

Sadkar, M., and Sadkar, D. Ensuring equitable participation in college classes. In L. Border and N. Chism, eds. Teaching for diversity. *New directions in teaching and learning, 49*, pp. 49–56. San Francisco: Jossey-Bass, 1992.

Sadler, D. R. Specifying and promulgating achievement standards. *Oxford Review of Education*, 1987, *13*(2), 191–209.

Sax, G. *The Fields teaching tests*. Seattle: University of Washington, Department of Psychology, 1991.

Scheidemann, N. V. An experiment in teaching psychology. *Journal of Applied Psychology*, 1929, *13*, 188–191.

Schirmerhorn, S.; Goldschmid, M. L.; and Shore, B. S. Learning basic principles of probability in student dyads: a cross-age comparison. *Journal of Educational Psychology*, 1975, *67*(4), 551–557.

Schmidt, H. G. *Activatie van voorkennis, instrinsieke motivatie en de verwerking van tekst*. Apeldoorn, The Netherlands: Van Walraven bv, 1982.

Schomberg, S. F. Involving high ability students in learning groups. Paper presented at AERA in San Francisco, April 1986.

Schon, D. A. *The reflective practitioner*. New York: Basic Books, 1983.

Schramm, W. L. *The research on programmed instruction*. Washington, D.C.: U.S. Government Printing Office, 1964.

Schultz, P. A., and Weinstein, C. E. Using test feedback to facilitate the learning process. *Innovation Abstracts*, 1990, *12*(22).

Schunk, D. H. Social cognitive theory and self-regulated learning. In B. J. Zimmerman and D. H. Schunk, eds. *Self-regulated learning and academic achievement*, pp. 83–110. New York: Springer-Verlag, 1989.

Seashore, C. E. Elementary psychology: an outline of a course by the project method. *Aims and Progress Research*, No. 153. Iowa City: University of Iowa Studies, 1928.

Seashore, S. E. *Group cohesiveness in the industrial group.* Publication No. 14, University of Michigan Survey Research Center, 1954.

Sedlacek, W. E. Teaching minority students. In J. H. Cones, J. F. Noonan, and D. Jahna, eds. Teaching minority students. *New directions in teaching and learning, 16,* pp. 39–50. San Francisco: Jossey-Bass, 1983.

Seldin, P. *The teaching portfolio.* Bolton, MA: Anker, 1991.

Shaycroft, M. F. *Handbook of criterion-referenced testing.* New York: Garland, STPM Press, 1979.

Sherman, B. R., and Blackburn, R. T. Personal characteristics and teaching effectiveness of college faculty. *Journal of Educational Psychology*, 1975, *67*, 124–131.

Sherman, J. G. Reflections on PSI: Good news and bad. *Journal of Applied Behavior Analysis*, 1992, *25*, 59–64.

Shipton, J., and Steltenpohl, E. In A. W. Chickering, ed. *The new American college.* San Francisco: Jossey-Bass, 1988.

Shore, B. M., et al. *The teaching dossier: a guide to its preparation and use.* Montreal: Canadian Association of University Teachers, 1986.

Shulman, L. S., and Tamir, P. Research on teaching in the natural sciences. In R. N. W. Travers, eds. *Second Handbook of Research on Teaching,* pp. 1098–1148. Chicago: Rand McNally, 1973.

Siegel, L.; Adams, J. F.; and Macomber, F. G. Retention of subject matter as a function of large-group instructional procedures. *Journal of Educational Psychology*, 1960, *51*, 9–13.

Siegel, L., and Siegel, L. C. The instructional gestalt: a conceptual framework and design for educational research. *Audio-Visual Communication Review,* 1964, *12*, 16–45.

Simpson, B. Heading for the ha-ha. *British Journal of Educational Technology*, 1983, *14*, 19–26.

Singhal, A., and Johnson, P. How to halt student dishonesty. *College Student Journal*, Spring 1983, 13–19.

Sleeter, C. E. *Empowerment through multicultural education.* Albany, NY: State University of New York Press, 1991.

Slomowitz, M. A comparison of personality changes and content achievement gains occurring in two modes of instruction. Ph.D. diss., New York University. *Dissertation Abstracts*, 1955, *15*, 1970.

Smith, D. E. P. Application transfer and inhibition. *Journal of Educational Psychology*, 1954, *45*, 169–174.

Smith, D. E. P., et al. Reading improvement as a function of student personality and teaching methods. *Journal of Educational Psychology*, 1956, *47*, 47–58.

Smith, H. C. Team work in the college class. *Journal of Educational Psychology*, 1955, *46*, 274–286.

Smith, N. H. The teaching of elementary statistics by the conventional classroom method vs. the method of programmed instruction. *Journal of Educational Research*, 1962, *55*, 417–420.

Smith, W. F., and Rockett, F. C. Test performance as a function of anxiety, instructor and instructions. *Journal of Educational Research*, 1958, *52*, 138–141.

Snow, R. E. *Research on aptitudes: a progress report.* Technical Report No. 1, Aptitude Research Project, School of Education, Stanford University, September 1976.

Snow, R. E., and Peterson, P. L. Recognizing differences in student attitudes. In W. J. McKeachie, ed. Learning, cognition, and college teaching. *New directions for teaching and learning, 2.* San Francisco: Jossey-Bass, 1980.

Solomon, D.; Rosenberg, L.; and Bezdek, W. E. Teacher behavior and student learning. *Journal of Educational Psychology*, 1964, *55*, 23–30.

Spence, R. B. Lecture and class discussion in teaching educational psychology. *Journal of Educational Psychology*, 1928, *19*, 454–462.

Spinrad, R. J. The electronic university. *EDUCOM Bulletin*, 1983, *18*(5), 4–8.

Stanton, H. *The University Teacher*, 1992, *13*(1).

Stark, J. S., et al. *Planning introductory courses: Influences on faculty.* Ann Arbor, MI: National Center to Improve Postsecondary Teaching and Learning, University of Michigan, 1990.

———. *Student goals exploration user's manual, classroom research guide.* Ann Arbor, MI: National Center to Improve Postsecondary Teaching and Learning, University of Michigan, 1991.

Stasheff, E., et al. *The television program: its direction and production,* 5th ed. New York: Hill and Wang, 1976.

Steele, C. M. Race and the schooling of black Americans. *The Atlantic Monthly*, 1992, *269*(4), 68–78.

Stern, G. G. Environments for learning. In N. Sanford, ed. *The American college.* New York: Wiley, 1962.

Stern, G. G., and Cope, A. H. *Differences in educability between steropaths, non-steropaths and rationals.* Paper presented at the American Psychological Association meeting in Chicago, September 1956.

Stern, G. G.; Stein, M. I.; and Bloom, B. S. *Methods in personality assessment.* Glencoe, IL: Free Press, 1956.

Stinard, T. A., and Dolphin, W. D. Which students benefit from self-mastery instruction and why. *Journal of Educational Psychology*, 1981, *73*(5), 754–763.

Stolurow, L. M., et al. Pilot studies of principles of programming. *Comparative studies of principles for programming mathematics in automated instruction,* Technical Report No. 9. University of Illinois, July 1964.

Stuit, D. B., and Wilson, J. T. The effect of an increasingly well-defined criterion on the prediction of success at Naval Training School (Tactical Radar). *Journal of Applied Psychology*, 1946, *30*, 614–623.

Sturgis, H. W. The relationship of the teacher's knowledge of the student's background to the effectiveness of teaching: a study of the extent to which the effectiveness of teaching is related to the teacher's knowledge of the student's background. Ph.D. diss., New York University. *Dissertation Abstracts*, 1959, *19*, No. 11.

Sullivan, A. M.; Andrews, E. A.; Hollinghurst, F.; Maddigan, R.; and Noseworthy, C. M. The relative effectiveness of instructional television. *Interchange*, 1976, *7*(1), 46–51.

Sullivan, A. M., and Skanes, G. R. Validity of student evaluation of teaching and the characteristics of successful instructors. *Journal of Educational Psychology*, 1974, *66*, 584–590.

Svensson, L. *Study skill and learning.* Göteborg, Sweden: Acta Universitates Gothoburgensis, 1976.

Tabachnick, B.; Keith-Spiegel, P.; and Pope, K. Ethics of teaching: Beliefs and behaviors of psychologists as educators. *American Psychologist*, 1991, *46*(5), 506–515.

Thistlethwaite, D. L. College environments and the development of talent. *Science*, 1959, *130*, 71–76.

———. *College press and changes in study plans of talented students.* Evanston, IL: National Merit Scholarship Corporation, 1960.

Thomas, E. J., and Fink, C. F. The effects of group size. *Psychological Bulletin*, 1963, *60*, 371–385.

Toombs, W., and Tierney, W. Meeting the mandate: Renewing the college and department curriculum. ASHE-ERIC Higher Education Report No. 91–6. Washington, D.C.: Association for the Study of Higher Education, 1992.

Travers, R. M. W. Appraisal of the teaching of the college faculty. *Journal of Higher Education*, 1950, *21*, 41–42.

———. *How to make achievement tests:* New York: Odyssey Press, 1950.

Trotter, V. Y. A comparison of the laboratory and the lecture demonstration methods of teaching survey of food preparation for freshman home economics at the University of Vermont. Unpublished paper, Ohio State University, 1960.

Trowbridge, N. An approach to teaching a large undergraduate class. Manuscript, Drake University, Des Moines, IA, 1969.

Trujillo, C. M. A comparative examination of classroom interactions between professors and minority and non-minority college students. *American Educational Research Journal*, 1986, *23*, 629–642.

Vandermeer, A. W. *Relative effectiveness of instruction by films exclusively, films plus study guides, and standard lecture methods.* Instructional Film Research Report SDC 269–7–12. Special Devices Center, Office of Naval Research, July 1950.

Van Overwalle, F.; Segebarth, K.; and Goldchstein, M. Improving performance of freshmen through attributional testimonies from fellow students. *British Journal of Educational Psychology*, 1989, *59*, 75-85.

Vattano, E. J.; Hockenberry, C.; Grider, W.; Jacobson, L.; and Hamilton, S. Employing undergraduate students in the teaching of psychology. *Teaching of Psychology Newsletter*, March 1973, 9–12.

Wakely, J. H.; Marr, J. N.; Plath, D. W.; and Wilkins, D. M. Lecturing and test performance in introductory psychology. Paper read at Michigan Academy, Ann Arbor, MI, March 1960.

Wales, C. E., and Nardi, A. *Teaching decisionmaking with guided design.* Idea paper no. 9. Kansas State University, Center for Faculty Evaluation and Development, November 1982.

Wales, C. E., and Stager, R. A. *Guided design.* Morgantown, WV: Center for Guided Design, West Virginia University, 1977.

Walter, T., and Seibert, A. *Student success*, 3rd ed. New York: Holt, Rinehart & Winston, 1984.

Walton, J. M. Self-reinforcing behavior change. *Personnel Journal*, 1989, *68*(10), 64–68.

Ward, J. Group-study vs. lecture-demonstration method in physical science instruction for general education college students. *Journal of Experimental Education*, 1956, *24*, 197–210.

Warren, R. A comparison of two plans of study in engineering physics. Ph. D. diss., Purdue University. *Dissertation Abstracts*, 1954, *14*, 1648–1649.

Waterhouse, I. L., and Child, I. L. Frustration and the quality of performance. *Journal of Personality*, 1953, *21*, 298–311.

Watson, C. E. The case-study method and learning effectiveness. *College Student Journal*, 1975, *9*(2), 109–116.

Weaver, R. L., II, and Cotrell, H. W. Mental aerobics: the half-sheet response. *Innovative Higher Education*, 1985, *10*, 23–31.

Webb, N. J. Student preparation and tape recording of course lectures as a method of instruction. *Psychological Reports*, 1965, *16*, 67–72.

Webb, N. J., and Grib, T. F. *Teaching process as a learning experience: the experimental use of student-led groups.* Final Report, HE–000–882. Washington, D.C.: Department of Health, Education and Welfare, October 1967.

Weiland, A., and Kingsbury, S. J. Immediate and delayed recall of lecture material as a function of note taking. *Journal of Educational Research*, 1979, *72*(4), 228–230.

Weimer, M. G., ed. *Teaching large classes well.* San Francisco: Jossey-Bass, 1987.

———. Reading your way to better teaching. *College Teaching*, 1988, *36*(2), 48–53.

Weinstein, C. E. Executive control processes in learning: Why knowing about how to learn is not enough. *Journal of College Reading and Learning*, 1988, *21*, 48–56.

Weinstein, C. E., and Mayer, R. E. The teaching of learning strategies. In M. Wittrock, ed. *Handbook of research on teaching*, pp. 315–327. New York: Macmillan, 1986.

Weinstein, C. E.; Palmer, D. R.; and Schutte, A. C. *Learning and study strategies inventory.* Clearwater, FL: H&H Publishing, 1987.

Weinstein, C. E.; Schutz, P. A.; Ridley, D. S.; and Glanz, R. S. Goal setting and goal-using: Developing personal meaning to enhance the use of learning strategies. *Innovation Abstracts*, 1989, *11*(11), 1–2.

White, J. R. A comparison of the group-laboratory and the lecture demonstration methods in engineering instruction. *Journal of Engineering Education*, 1945, *36*, 50–54.

Wieder, G. S. Group procedures modifying attitudes of prejudice in the college classroom. *Journal of Educational Psychology*, 1954, *45*, 332–334.

Wilhite, S. C. Prepassage questions: the influence of structural importance. *Journal of Educational Psychology*, 1983, *75*(2), 234–244.

Wilson, R. C. Improving faculty teaching: Effective use of student evaluations and consultation. J*ournal of Higher Education*, 1986, *57*, 196–211.

Wilson, R. C., et al. *College professors and their impact on students.* New York: Wiley, 1975.

Wilson, T. D., and Linville, P. W. Improving the academic performance of college freshmen: Attribution therapy revisited. *Journal of Personality and Social Psychology*, 1982, *42*, 367–376.

———. Improving the performance of college freshmen with attributional techniques. *Journal of Personality and Social Psychology, 49,* 1985, 287–293.

Wine, J. Test anxiety and direction of attention. *Psychological Bulletin*, 1971, *76*(2), 92–104.

Wispe, L. G. Evaluate section teaching methods in the introductory course. *Journal of Educational Research*, 1951, *45*, 161–168.

Witkin, H. A., and Moore, C. A. *Field-dependent and field-independent cognitive styles and their educational implications.* Princeton, NJ: Educational Testing Service, 1975.

Witters, D. R., and Kent, G. W. Teaching without lecturing: Evidence in the case for individualized instruction. *Psychological Record*, 1972, *22*, 169–175.

Wittich, W. A., and Schuller, C. F. *Instructional technology: its nature and use*, 6th ed. New York: Harper & Row, 1979.

Wolfle, D. The relative efficacy of constant and varied stimulation during learning. *Journal of Comparative Psychology*, 1935, *19*, 5–27.

Wood, L. E. An "intelligent" program to teach logical thinking skills. *Behavior Research Methods and Instrumentation*, 1980, *12*(2), 256–258.

Wortman, C. B., and Hillis, J. W. Undergraduate-taught "minicourses" in conjunction with an introductory lecture course. *Teaching of Psychology*, 1976, *3*(2), 69–72.

Wrigley, C. Undergraduate students as teachers: Apprenticeship in the university classroom. *Teaching of Psychology Newsletter*, March 1973, 5–7.

Wulff, D. H., and Nyquist, J. D. Using field methods as an instructional tool. In J. Kurfiss, L. Hilsen, S. Kahn, M. Sorcinelli, and R. Tiberius, eds. *To improve the academy*, pp. 87–98. Stillwater, OK: POD/New Forums Press, 1988.

Wulff, D. H.; Nyquist, J. D.; and Abbott, R. D. Students' perceptions of large classes. In M. G. Weimer, ed. Teaching large classes well. *New directions for teaching and learning, 32,* pp. 17–30. San Francisco: Jossey-Bass, 1987.

Yelon, S. L., and Cooper, C. R. Discussion: a naturalistic study of a teaching method. *Instructional Science*, 1984, *13*, 213–224.

Zeleny, L. D. Experimental appraisal of a group learning plan. *Journal of Educational Research*, 1940, *34*, 37–42.

Zimbardo, P. G., and Newton, J. W. *Instructor's resource book to accompany psychology and life.* Glenview, IL: Scott, Foresman, 1975.

Zimmerman, B. J., ed. Self-regulated learning and academic achievement (special issue). *Educational Psychologist*, 1990, *25*(1).

Index